Instructional Models
for Physical Education

Instructional Models for Physical Education

Michael W. Metzler

Georgia State University

Allyn and Bacon

Boston • London • Toronto • Sydney • Tokyo • Singapore

Editor-in-Chief: *Paul A. Smith*
Series Editor: *Joseph Burns*
Series Editorial Assistant: *Tanja Eise*
Marketing Manager: *Rick Muhr*
Composition and Prepress Buyer: *Linda Cox*
Manufacturing Buyer: *Dave Repetto*
Cover Administrator: *Jenny Hart*
Editorial-Production Service: *Shepherd, Inc.*

Copyright © 2000 by Allyn & Bacon
A Pearson Education Company
Needham Heights, Massachusetts 02194

Internet: www.abacon.com

Library of Congress Cataloging–in–Publication Data

Metzler, Michael W., 1952–
    Instructional models for physical education   /   Michael W. Metzler.
        p.   cm.
    Includes bibliographical references and index.
    ISBN 0–205–26418–2
    1. Physical education and training—Study and teaching—United
States.   2. Physical education teachers—Training of—United States.
I. Title.
GV363.M425   1999
613.7'071'073—dc21   99–36589
                                               CIP

Printed in the United States of America

10 9 8 7 6 5 4 3 2 1   03 02 01 00 99

Don Sebolt died from injuries suffered in an auto accident in the spring of 1998, while this book was being written. Don was a colleague and close friend of mine at Virginia Tech. He also co-authored the Personalized Sport Instructional System series with me, and played a significant role in my own understanding of that model. In his truly unique way, he was a great teacher.

This book is dedicated to the fond memory of The 'Bolt.

CONTENTS

FOREWORD

Do not be deceived. There is more here than will meet the eye of the casual textbook browser—and not all of it is named in the table of contents!

In many respects this book delivers precisely what the author claims. It is a compendium of models for teaching physical education—systematically organized, each carefully dissected into component parts, and all thoughtfully analyzed in terms of teaching decisions and actions. Further, the seven core models have been situated in what is best described as a pedagogical pharmacopeia, a system designed to help the reader determine which model is most effective for producing particular educational outcomes.

That sounds like a great deal to pack into a single volume, and indeed it is. If you look closely, however, the obvious content is not all you will find between these covers—far from it. This also is a book with an attitude!

Attitudes, those deeper dispositions and beliefs of an author, are like the devil—they reside in the silent spaces between the details. Because he writes with a crisp, decisive voice and avoids lengthy rhetorical excursions into exhortation and academic theory, the author has given the book a no-nonsense, businesslike tone. Added to that is a completely transparent organization. Once past the front material, it truly is easy to move around and find things in this book. Clearly, Professor Metzler intended to create a usable resource, one that would be more at home amid the clutter of a working desk than on a bookshelf—a characteristic that is very practical, seemly, and laudable. It will not take long, however, for most readers to detect the fact that the author is working from some assumptions about the nature of physical education, teaching, teachers, teacher training and development, and the strategies of curriculum reform that are anything but conventional. Those assumptions give the book its attitude, and it is there that some readers will find its highest commendation, and others will find themselves most discomforted.

From cover to cover, the central presumption here is that the reason students study physical education is to learn—to be permanently changed in what they feel, know, and can do. There are no suggestions that life in the gym is about recreation (relief from the stressful rigors of "real" academic endeavors) or any form of social or psychological therapy (socialization into compliant behavior). There is subject matter to be taught, practiced, and acquired. That is the core vision of purpose behind these seven models of teaching. If it is a limited definition of educational intentions, and one to which there is not universal subscription, it is clear, unwavering, and intentional.

Likewise, the content of physical education as a subject matter is defined in consistent and unapologetic terms as sports, games, dance, exercise, and all forms of vigorous and physically active play. Although cognitive and affective outcomes have status as major goals for achievement, there never is the slightest doubt about which knowledge, attitudes, and values students are to acquire—everything is attached to the subject matter. At a time when there are many people who regard physical education as the applied extension of an academic discipline (kinesiology, exercise science, motor learning, sport sociology, etc.), situating the definition of the subject matter in the engagements of physically active play forms—rather than knowledge about those forms—is a sharp departure from the status quo.

In this book the predominant model for improving the delivery of physical education in K–12 schools simply is ignored. The ubiquitous proposition that teacher effectiveness (and curricular quality) can be developed by incremental means is replaced by the notion that rethinking and restructuring the whole is the only viable strategy. If attending conference workshops and scanning professional journals for new ideas with which to grow the stock of tricks in your pedagogical tool box is your definition of sound professional development, this is not the book for you. Metzler expects readers to go back to basics and build anew from there.

It will come as no surprise, then, that the author spends no time exhorting readers about the many wonderful virtues of physical education as part of the school curriculum, as preparation for the good life, and as an agency for transmission of culturally sanctioned values. Metzler assumes that the reader already holds the subject matter in high regard, and that ink and paper are better used to improve the ways in which it is taught in schools. This is in sharp contrast to the posture of many professional organizations, which expend large portions of their fiscal and political capital on public relations and "selling" the field. It also is contrary to the latest style of writing in textbooks designed for use in teacher preparation. If you already are persuaded about the importance of physical education, you will be very much at home with the focus of this text.

Another subversive theme is infused into all of the models presented here. Contrary to one of the tenets held most dear in the culture of teachers, Metzler asserts that fidelity to the model is not an option—it is a requirement. Full credence is given to the obvious facts concerning differences in style and repertoires of skill among teachers, but concrete benchmarks are established for correct performance within each model. If you do not comply with those essential demands, says the author, do not expect the model to work in the gym or classroom. This is not a book for free spirits who cherish the idea that good teaching is achieved by tinkering without discipline.

Finally, although this is a book about teachers and teaching, one gradually realizes that something else occupies the author's deepest concern. The ultimate tests of success do not focus on what the teacher did within the confines of a model, but on what the students did in response. That is a subtle distinction, and a reflection of a profoundly important idea. Teachers do not produce learning—students do. Attending, engaging, practicing, persisting, processing, connecting, and refining—these are the architects of learning, and they are all things done by students. Teachers envision purposes, structure environments, and manipulate consequences, but students do the learning. Professors, novice trainees, and veteran practitioners who are comfortable with that understanding will find valuable resources in this book, and perhaps inspiration as well.

Lest there be any misunderstanding, as you might guess, I do share many (though not all) of Professor Metzler's attitudes about physical education. I have, nonetheless, noted the limitations of his book. It seems possible, for example, that not all viable models for teaching have been included. The limits of text space alone made that inevitable. He has only partially attended to the messy task of sorting out the differences between models for teaching and for curriculum—though I doubt that a more complete analysis will be greatly missed by many readers. Finally, he has not taken on here the enormous and daunting task of imagining a teacher education that would provide the needed clinical internships to immerse preservice students in K–12 programs exemplifying even one or two of the models presented here. That, I suspect, is a topic he has reserved for a future literary effort.

Larry Locke

Emeritus Professor, School of Physical Education
University of Massachusetts/Amherst
March 1999

PREFACE

From Method to Models

Physical education has long been a teaching profession. Our earliest roots were established by people trained in medicine but who used therapeutic and instructive techniques to help people learn and participate regularly in physical activity. And, while it is true that many contemporary professionals have interests far removed from the teaching of physical activity, it still remains that the largest group of physical educators today carry out activity instruction as their primary function. Most of that group teaches physical education in P–12 schools, and a number of them teach in college-level basic instruction programs. This book is written for those teachers of physical activity so that they can approach their instruction from a new model-based perspective, increasing their students' knowledge, skills, appreciation, and participation in the many forms of movement available today.

The earliest teachers of physical activity defined "how they taught" as *the physical education method,* a direct and formal approach that called for teachers to closely follow accepted procedures and which gave students a limited role in the operation of classes. Essentially, the teacher gave directions and the students followed them. Most activities, regardless of context and grade level, were instructed by this singular approach. In the 1960s physical educators expanded the concept of method to include some innovative *teaching strategies* and *teaching styles,* the latter set forth in Musska Mosston's (1966) Spectrum of Teaching Styles. Both of these developments served to open the possibilities for how teachers could plan and implement instruction in our field. A third movement began in the 1980s that viewed *effective teaching* as a constellation of decisions and actions that led students to increased levels of learning. Teachers developed a repertoire of effective teaching skills that they applied within strategies and styles. So, after promoting the use of the physical education method for over a half century, suddenly there were many innovative ways to instruct students in the growing content in P–12 programs.

The notions of method, strategies, styles, and skills are very helpful in promoting limited, short-term outcomes in physical education. In that sense they are decidedly temporary as each one might be used for just a few moments in a class and then give way to another—perhaps as many as three or four in a lesson. Because of that, they lack a larger, more unified perspective from which to view the process of planning, implementing, and assessing instruction in physical education.

Over the past thirty years there has been a fourth movement in the search for ways to teach physical education and other subjects. While that movement has taken longer to grow, I would argue that its time has come as the best way to conceptualize how we teach physical activity to all students. Bruce Joyce and Marsha Weil published their first edition of *Models of Teaching* in 1972. In it, they made a case that instruction should be comprised of "structured, logically consistent, cohesive, and lucidly described *patterns* of teaching" (p. 1). Each distinctive set of these patterns is called a *teaching model* that ties together theory, planning, classroom management, teaching learning processes, and assessment. The scope of its perspective on instruction is much larger and more holistic than our current notions of method, strategies, styles, and skill. A models approach is meant to address long-term learning outcomes—those intended for entire units and even programs.

We now have many well-articulated and effective instructional models. Most of them have been developed in other subject areas and adapted for physical education, such as Cooperative Learning, Personalized Systems for Instruction (PSI), and Direct Instruction. A few have been developed exclusively for teaching students physical activity and related concepts. The Sport Education and Tactical Games models presented in this book were developed by physical educators for use in elementary, secondary, and college/adult instruction. What we now have is a group of models that have been developed separately, and which appear in isolated books and journals. What we need is a model-based *perspective* for instructing physical education that will help teachers to learn about, select, and practice these comprehensive patterns of teaching. It is my hope that this book can serve to develop such a perspective.

Instructional Models for Physical Education has two primary goals for its readers. The first is to familiarize you with the notion of model-based instruction for physical education, including what it is, what you need to know to use it, the components and dimensions that determine a model's *pattern* of teaching, and how to select the "right model for the right job." The second goal is to describe each of seven instructional models you can choose from for your teaching. These descriptions will give you enough information to get "up and running" with any model you select, so that you can begin to use it with confidence and results.

I also have a third goal for this book—one that is more ambitious than familiarizing you with a model-based approach. If you are a preservice teacher, I want you to learn your craft from a model-based perspective so that it becomes "how you teach." If you are a practicing teacher, I want to change how you teach physical education! I don't want to simply adjust a bit here and there; I want to give you a totally new perspective on the important educational mission you carry out every school day. In short, I want readers of this book to go from *method to models* in their approach to teaching physical activity to students of all ages. I made that shift myself several years ago and now teach physical activity courses with PSI, Cooperative Learning, Direct Instruction, and Sport Education. I work with many practicing teachers who have also made that shift. Some of the examples used in Part 2 of this book were developed by those teachers and represent field-tested models that really work in physical education at all grade levels. It is my hope that readers of this book will become curious and innovative enough to take a model-based perspective, so that as a profession we can more often achieve the varied and diverse goals of contemporary physical education programs.

M. W. M.
March, 1999

ACKNOWLEDGMENTS

There are many people who directly or indirectly contributed to the completion of this book, and to whom I would like to express my sincere thanks—even if they were not fully aware of their contribution. In many ways, this book reflects my own development as a teacher, which could not have occurred without the help of many colleagues, mentors, students, friends, and advisors. Some of the people to be mentioned are all of those things in my life.

I would like to acknowledge two GSU colleagues who lent me open ears about ideas for this book and who generously shared their expertise when I needed to know more about certain models and content. Theresa Walker gave me first-hand experience in inquiry teaching during the many times we have team-taught. Bonnie Tjeerdsma was always willing to hear my ideas, even when I wasn't quite sure how to communicate them clearly. Most of all, I would like to thank them for their patience and understanding during the busiest times of writing this book, and for accepting "huh?" as a regular response from me when I was preoccupied with this project.

I am also indebted to a wonderful group of Atlanta-area physical education teachers who were willing to develop and implement model-based instruction in their programs, and allow me to observe, take notes, videotape, talk to their students, ask all sorts of questions of them, and in some cases gave me permission to use their materials in this book: Lorie Furr, JoBeth Weaver, Donna Wright, Karla Rosenthal, Randy Watts, David Ovrick, Guy Petrone, and Kathy Williams.

There is a particular debt owed to physical education professionals who were instrumental in the development of some of the models presented in this book. It is no exaggeration to say that without their vision, creativity, and perseverance to carry their ideas into action this book would not have been possible: Linda Griffin, Steve Mitchell, and Judith Oslin (Tactical Games); the late Don Sebolt (PSI); and Daryl Siedentop (Sport Education).

Special thanks go out to Suzy Spivy, my original editor at Allyn and Bacon. It was she who fortuitously knocked on my office door out of the blue almost four years ago, asked me if I had any ideas for a textbook—and then listened while I presented my thoughts for this book off the top of my head. Her advocacy led to the development of this book, and her patience allowed me the extra time I needed to finish it through some unexpected delays. I am also appreciative of the work and patience of Joe Burns, who subsequently became my editor when Suzy left that role. Marybeth Finch and Susan Walther-Jones at Allyn and Bacon were very helpful in the editing and production of the book. Meadow Overstreet is to be thanked for her photography work in the book. Thanks also go out to the physical education teachers and their students who volunteered as models in the book's photographs: Karen Lynch at Riverwood High School, Cindy Meme at Trickum Middle School, and Larry Satchwell at Shiloh Elementary School.

One unexpected (but wonderful) delay occurred as I met, began a relationship with, and then started a marriage with my wife Cindy in the early stages of writing this book. Not wanting her to be an "author's widow," I purposely delayed my writing for several months after we were married. Once I did start to write regularly, Cindy was enthusiastically supportive, understanding, and gracious all of the times I bunkered down in my home office to work on something she knew meant a lot to me. Undoubtedly, this book was possible because of her support, and I love her even more for that. Thanks, Lady.

PART ONE

Foundations for Model-Based Instruction in Physical Education

This book is based on two primary assumptions about teaching physical education. First, instruction is most effective when it occurs within a coherent framework held by the teacher and communicated to students. Such frameworks will be called *instructional models* in this book, with seven such models for physical education presented in Part 2. Part 2 will provide you with detailed plans for designing and implementing each model, along with examples of lesson plans for various grades and content units. The second assumption is that teachers must understand the foundations for model-based instruction in order to select the best model to meet stated goals, match student developmental readiness, and manage the learning environment. That is the purpose of Part 1 of this book.

It will be tempting for some readers to bypass Part 1 and search through Part 2 for one or two "favorite" models from personal experience as a student or teacher. While the descriptions of each model would give you enough information to begin to use a model, eventually you will be left with questions like, "Why am I teaching this way?", "How do I know my students are really learning according to the model's design?", and "How do I make modifications for my situation?" Part 1 is intended to help you answer these and other questions so you can make informed decisions about model-based instruction over a sustained period of time.

At their essence, instructional models are tools for physical education teachers to use in helping students achieve stated goals. Part 1 will help you understand where these tools came from, how they can help you build an instructional plan, how to select the right tool for the right activity, and how to know when a tool has given you the results you want. With that knowledge, you will be much better informed, and ready to implement model-based instruction as a physical education teacher.

CHAPTER

1

Contemporary Physical Education Programs and Instruction

Physical education programs can be viewed as the sum of their personnel, goals, the content and activities taught, and the ways in which teachers instruct. Throughout their history in the United States, P–12 physical education programs have reflected larger patterns in American culture, people's needs and choices regarding physical activity, and trends in our educational system. As you will see, the goals, content, and instruction in physical education have evolved and will continue to evolve in ways that call for new approaches in how school programs are designed and how the teaching-learning process is carried out.

The Evolution of Goals for U.S. Physical Education

In the early and mid-1800s, there were few formal physical education programs as we would recognize them today. Most of the existing programs took place in small, private boarding schools and were typically labeled *physical training* to reflect their primary purposes of teaching military-type discipline and providing the school with needed manual labor. Little emphasis was placed on the educational value of physical activity.

With the establishment of the U.S. public school system and the emergence of many new forms of sport, the last half of the 1800s brought about many visions of what physical education could be, leading to an expansion of its goals and purposes. In 1879 Dudley Sargent, a Harvard physical education professor, listed four major aims of what was still called physical training: it should be hygienic, educative, recreative, and remedial (Van Dalen & Bennett, 1971). Sargent also recognized the capability of such activity to improve self-discipline and character. These goals for physical education are still prominent today (Siedentop, 1998).

Many gymnastics "systems" were introduced in the late 1800s. Two of them reached the greatest prominence, although each had its own distinct purpose. The German system, led by Friedrich Jahn, intended to develop in young persons a sense of civic duty and a desire to make the body healthy, agile, and strong. Jahn's system was also used to promote military and political outcomes. The other major system was based on the Swedish gymnastics tradition, led in the United States by Nils Posse. Posse expressed the goals of this system in terms of proper physical development and the discipline to learn precise, simple, and beautiful movement. The differing aims, objectives, and programs of the German and Swedish systems met head-on in the 1895 Boston Conference, which was convened to decide which system, among some others, would be the most prominent in U.S. public school physical education curriculums. No one system emerged the victor, as many large school districts opted to keep their own right to choose—not only between the gymnastics-based programs, but also between the emerging sports-based programs.

After the turn of the century, the goals and aims of U.S. physical education continued to expand. They were clearly linked to new philosophies, such as educational developmentalism, and legislation that influenced our fledgling system of public schooling. Championed by such educational leaders as G. Stanley Hall, Charles Eliot, and John Dewey, developmentalism broadened the concept of schooling to include extracurricular and work-based experiential learning. No longer was the schoolhouse the only place of learning in U.S. education, and no longer were the three R's the only subjects learned by school children and youth. That broadening of goals and scope provided a legitimate place in public education for the relatively new field of physical education. It also signaled a change from the physical training philosophies of the previous half-century to the *physical education* movement. In 1910, Clark Hetherington outlined four main purposes for the "New Physical Education," drawn directly from educational developmentalism. It should include:

1. Organic education—the development of muscular and skeletal vigor
2. Psychomotor education—the development of skill in neuromuscular activities
3. Character education—the development of moral, social, and personal characteristics
4. Intellectual education—the development of cognitive, expressive knowledge (Van Dalen & Bennett, 1971)

Physical education's formal acceptance in U.S. schools occurred just a few years after Hetherington's aims were published. The Smith-Hughes Act of 1917 set forth the major goals and purposes for all of U.S. public schooling, which became known as the Seven Cardinal Principles of Education. The physical education profession, perhaps based on Hetherington's four aims, adopted three of the principles within its rationale to secure more widespread recognition and a place in the school curriculum: health and safety, worthy use of leisure, and ethical character. Under this broad set of objectives, schools were able to justify the inclusion of many new and diverse forms of activity in elementary and secondary programs.

Hetherington's four main objectives and the three adopted principles continued to guide the aims and purposes of physical education into the middle of this century and are still present in some form today (Siedentop, 1998). Twenty years after the publication of Hetherington's landmark paper, Jesse Ferring Williams at Columbia University identified this as the beginning of a shift from education *of the physical* (physical training) to education *through the physical* (physical education). It was now clear that physical activity in schools would be considered less of an end in itself and more as a means to reach a variety of accepted educational outcomes. While it might appear to be just a semantic difference, this shift is significant because it greatly broadened the scope of school programs; the boundaries of physical education expanded to address its growing vision for public school students. As you will see later in this chapter, this led to an explosion of different types of curriculums and content.

Between 1950 and 1990 physical education continued to state aims for school programs that were strongly based on the combination of Hetherington's goals and the Seven Cardinal Principles. But in that same period we witnessed a gradual, and now unmistakable, change in the balance among those purposes. Sports-based activity was the predominant content area in physical education as that period began, and placed a strong emphasis on development in the psychomotor component of programs. Character development, from participation in rigorous individual and team sports, was also highly valued as a goal in physical education. As the period moved along, organic education development began to have a stronger position among those goals. That emergence came from several research reports which noted alarmingly low cardiovascular and muscular fitness levels in U.S. children and youth (Kraus & Hirschland, 1954; Ross & Gilbert, 1985). Similarly low fitness levels had been noted at earlier times of war among service-age men and women, but new data on school-aged children in the 1970s and 1980s, along with research that correlated low fitness levels with increased later risks for degenerative diseases and conditions, prompted a quick elevation of the organic education goal in school programs. The fitness movement was gaining momentum.

The latter part of that same period also saw an increased emphasis on Hetherington's goal of intellectual development in physical education. That goal was advanced in two ways. First, the scientific disciplines of physical education generated an enormous amount of new knowledge that could be applied by teachers and learners. Simply, there was just more to think about! Second, educational philosophy had begun to promote the idea of higher-order thinking and interactive learning for students of all ages and in all subjects. Rote learning of facts, dates, and cursive writing had been replaced by discovery learning, "learning how to learn," and word processors in many schools. In physical education, that meant the development of students' creative, expressive, and intellectual abilities would receive greater attention.

As physical education entered the 1990s, it was a profession that appeared to be seeking a real balance among Hetherington's four main purposes, repackaged in a contemporary version for schools. In reality there were many contemporary versions, all vying to be a prominent voice that could lead our profession and our school programs into the approaching millennium. It seemed that nearly every individual professional and every professional group had a notion of what physical education programs should strive to be in schools. In a less formalized way, it was similar to the "Battle of the Systems" that prompted the Boston Conference almost a century earlier. While we are not near unanimity yet, there does appear to be a growing consensus to support one professional group's goals and outcomes for today's school programs. In 1992 the National Association for Sport and Physical Education (NASPE) released *Outcomes of Quality Physical Education Programs* (NASPE, 1992a). The work of the Blue Ribbon committee that developed this report was based on the position that P–12 physical activity instructional programs must strive to meet a variety of needs in order for students to become "Physically educated persons." According to the NASPE outcomes document, a physically educated person is one who:

Has *Learned Skills Necessary to Perform a Variety of Physical Skills*

1. Moves using concepts of body awareness, space awareness, effort, and relationships
2. Demonstrates competence in a variety of manipulative, locomotor, and non-locomotor skills
3. Demonstrates competence in combinations of manipulative, locomotor, and non-locomotor skills performed individually and with others
4. Demonstrates competence in many different forms of physical activity
5. Demonstrates proficiency in a few forms of physical activity
6. Has learned how to learn new skills

Does *Participate Regularly in Physical Activity*

7. Participates in health-enhancing physical activity at least three times a week
8. Selects and regularly participates in lifetime physical activities

Is *Physically Fit*

9. Assesses, achieves, and maintains physical fitness
10. Designs safe personal fitness programs in accordance with principles of training and conditioning

Knows *the Implications of and the Benefits from Involvement in Physical Activity*

11. Identifies the benefits, costs, and obligations associated with regular participation in physical activity
12. Recognizes the risk and safety factors associated with regular participation in physical activity

13. Applies concepts and principles to the development of motor skills
14. Understands that wellness involves more than being physically fit
15. Knows the rules, strategies, and appropriate behaviors for selected physical activities
16. Recognizes that participation in physical activity can lead to multicultural and international understanding
17. Understands that physical activity provides the opportunity for enjoyment, self-expression, and communication

Values *Physical Activity and Its Contributions to a Healthful Life-style*
18. Appreciates the relationships with others that result from participation in physical activity
19. Respects the role that regular physical activity plays in the pursuit of lifelong health and well-being
20. Cherishes the feelings that result from regular participation in physical activity (adapted from NASPE, 1992a)

The NASPE outcomes clearly emphasize a balance across diverse goals and multiple purposes. If this document is to lead physical education programs into the millennium, it is clear we must get past the notion of promoting one goal at the expense of others and agree that a *physically educated person,* more than anything else, is someone who demonstrates well-rounded knowledge, skill, regular participation, health-related fitness, and values physical activity enough to make it an integral part of her* life, now and across the life span. That appears to be a formidable task for a profession that has not held anything close to a unified vision. But there are signs of growing acceptance of the NASPE goals nationally and within many states' own objectives for school programs.

The Evolution of Program Content in U.S. Physical Education

The predominant aims and purposes of physical education during each era, combined with social forces and trends at any given time, have played a large role in determining the content of school physical education programs throughout our history. Content refers to the activities and subject matter that are taught so that students can achieve the program's aims. Content is what teachers know about movement forms and movement concepts, and what they try to teach children and youth. Remember that the earliest programs in this country were called physical training, which reflected a limited set of aims and objectives. Accordingly, those programs consisted mainly of manual labor and

---

*Rather than use the sometimes cumbersome convention of he/she and his/hers, this book will alternate male and female pronouns in the text.

military-style drills. Students chopped wood, learned to march in formation, cultivated the school's vegetable garden, took long hikes, and practiced field maneuvers. The program at Round Hill School was the first to expand the content by including several sports units and outdoor education, in addition to the physical training focus (Van Dalen & Bennett, 1971).

The well-defined but restricted goals of the German and Swedish gymnastics systems in the mid- and late 1800s also led to predictably limited content in the curriculum—still called physical training. The German program included group drills, large-group games, individual movements, stunts with and without large apparatus, and free exercises. Until the very end of the century, many programs took place at turnvereins, which resemble today's YMCA and YWCA facilities in some ways. The Swedish gymnastics system emphasized free exercise much more than movements that required the use of an apparatus, although some small apparatuses were used. Even though both systems expanded their content over time, programs never ventured too far away from their foundation in gymnastics. In the mid-1800s that single-content focus was the systems' greatest strength, as it provided a clear purpose and unmistakable identity. As the century came to an end, the limited content of the gymnastics systems proved to be their greatest weakness. Expanded goals and aims for physical education would leave them unable to provide the breadth and scope of content needed to meet new learning goals for students.

The gymnastics-based curriculums gave way to programs that held a broader vision for school physical education within the emerging developmental philosophies. The diverse and growing number of competitive sports developed in the United States or brought here from other countries in the second wave of immigration in the late 1800s provided the content to meet those new goals. From 1850 to 1900, many of today's most popular sports began to be played by large numbers of Americans, including basketball (separate men's and women's versions), volleyball, tennis, baseball, football, badminton, and golf.

The period from 1900 to 1950 saw the predominance of sports-based curricular content in school programs. This can be attributed to Hetherington's stated aims and our profession's adoption of three of the Seven Cardinal Principles in 1918. Sports were viewed as an effective vehicle for the promotion of outcomes related to health, worthy use of leisure time, and character development. Two significant interruptions occurred during World War I and World War II, when secondary schools and colleges used combatives, calisthenics, swimming, and other activities to foster military-type training for soldiers-to-be. Some physical education programs emphasized rehabilitative exercises for returning wounded and injured soldiers. The content of school physical education programs remained stable and predictable through most of the 1950s and 1960s. Even though the list of activities offered in school programs grew gradually, it tended to grow in the same general area of competitive sport.

The period since 1960 has seen rapid growth in both the types and numbers of activity- and conceptually-based offerings in physical education. That diversity and expansion has been the result of several factors:

1. Opposition to competitive and sports-based content
2. State and national standards for physical education
3. Designation of separate developmentally appropriate activities for elementary, middle/junior, and high school levels, resulting in three distinct curriculum contents
4. The promotion of different and competing theories for designing program content
5. Results from research, particularly regarding children's and youth's fitness needs
6. The development of new movement forms (e.g., New Games, "extreme" sports)
7. Title IX, which mandated equal opportunities for girls and young women
8. P.L. 94-142 and other legislation and policies for inclusion of students with special needs in nearly all classes

In the past forty years, and particularly in the past two decades, we have witnessed an explosion of nonsport and alternative-sport movement forms in our society. It is clear that people still want to move in meaningful ways; they just want to participate in activities besides the traditional and more popular sport forms. Activities like New Games, adventure programming, rock and indoor wall climbing, ultimate Frisbee, skateboarding, off-road cycling, in-line skating, surfing, power walking, and many others have shown increased levels of participation in this decade. While all of these activities have been around for some time, it is only in this decade that they have reached mainstream levels of participation.

Just think about it. If you are an American today and want to be active, you have literally hundreds of ways to participate, ranging from the established forms of sport, dance, and exercise to cutting-edge, alternative, "extreme" forms of movement. Each year brings new forms, any one of which could reach a high level of mainstream participation and one day be viewed as traditional!

Along with the explosion in the number and variety of movement forms has come a more broad-based participation by people of all ages and abilities. Many of the barriers of sexism and agism have been reduced or eliminated, so that men, women, boys, and girls of all ages are now finding their own interests in one or more forms of dance, exercise, sport, and games. Besides an interest in moving, they all share a common need—to learn how to become better skilled and more knowledgeable at whatever form of movement they have chosen. Where there is a need for people to learn, there is a matching need for someone to teach them. Instruction plays a key role in opening doors for people of all types and ages who wish to learn how to move.

The predictable result of promoting a balanced "physically educated person" in a time of almost limitless choices for activity is a broadening of the content choices offered to P–12 students. While no single program can offer more than a small portion of the possible choices at each grade level, teachers (especially new teachers) will need to have an ever-expanding content knowledge base to keep in step with the times. A partial listing of contemporary program content for the two major grade level groupings is shown in Figure 1.1. The important thing to keep in mind is that a physical education teacher at each grade level grouping is expected to know not only the content itself, but safe, effective, and developmentally appropriate ways to teach each content area to students.

FIGURE 1.1   **Scope of Physical Education Curriculum Content**

Elementary Programs

Content Strand	Examples
Fitness	Aerobics, circuit training, fitness concepts, jogging, stretching, walking
Developmental gymnastics	Low balance beam, tumbling, rolling
Dance and rhythmical activity	Hand clapping, line dance, marching, square dance
Low organization games	Relays, tag games, partner games
Lead-up games	Newcomb, tee ball, tetherball, three-on-three soccer
Modified games	Reduced field/court games, games with rule changes
Manipulative games	Catching, dribbling, juggling, kicking, striking
Nonlocomotor skills	Balancing, stretching, twisting
Locomotor skills	Crawling, dodging, galloping, jumping, hopping, leaping, running, skipping, sliding, walking
Movement concepts	Body awareness, distance, duration, force, level, skill themes, speed

Secondary Programs (Middle/Junior High and High School)

Content Strand	Examples
Adventure activities	Backpacking, hiking, rappelling, rock climbing, ropes courses
Aquatics	Canoeing, SCUBA diving, snorkeling, swimming
Fitness	Aerobics (dance, step, water), cycling, fitness concepts, jogging, weight training, personal fitness program design
Team sports	Baseball, basketball, flag football, flickerball, floor hockey, lacrosse, soccer, softball, speedball, team handball, ultimate Frisbee, volleyball
Individual/dual sports	Archery, badminton, bowling, fencing, golf, pickleball, racquetball, tennis, track and field, wrestling
Cooperative games and group initiatives	Group initiatives, New Games, trust games
Recreational activities	Fly casting, Frisbee golf, hackey-sack, horseshoes, in-line skating, table tennis
Dance and rhythmical activity	Ballroom dance, break dancing, contemporary dances, international and ethnic dances, line dance, modern dance, square dance
International and ethnic games	Australian rules football, cricket, goal ball, rounders
Gymnastics	Floor exercises, apparatus, tumbling
Martial and Eastern arts	Aikido, self-defense, tai chi

The Evolution of Instruction in Physical Education: From Method to Models

The determination of programmatic goals and the selection of program content lead directly to the types of instruction that teachers will use in physical education classes. Just as the aims of physical education and the kinds of activities students engage in have evolved in the past 150 years, so too have the ways in which teachers instruct. The very earliest programs of physical training in this country used instructional methods that were very direct and formal, especially for the military-style training portion of the program (Van Dalen & Bennett, 1971). *Direct* means that the teacher made all of the decisions in class, and students simply followed instructions. *Formal* means that the teacher's actions were based on a prescribed series of procedures and steps that were to be carried out as the lesson progressed. This type of instruction would have been highly effective in teaching students the precision of military drill and proper field conduct.

Jahn's German gymnastics system was based on instruction by imitation, in which the teacher and advanced students modeled exercises for groups of novice students to follow. Because much of the program required apparatus, the German system included many small-group exercises, although massed group practice was used for free exercise. Jahn was among the first teachers to separate classes into ability groups and provide differentiated instruction (Van Dalen & Bennett, 1971). The competing Swedish system also used advanced students as models for novices to imitate, but the leaders were typically dispersed throughout the massed group as all students simultaneously imitated the lead instructor and squad leaders. The Swedes introduced the notion of planned progression as class activities were completed in a predetermined order of increasing complexity and difficulty. As you will recall, the goals and content of the gymnastics systems were quite narrow, so the accompanying teaching methods would also be limited. While not as strongly militaristic as their predecessors, the two major gymnastics systems did rely heavily on direct and formal instructional methods.

Even when the content changed from gymnastics to sports-based physical education after the turn of the century, teaching methods remained strongly direct and formal well into the 1960s. There was an emphasis on the drills, repetition, and adherence to technique needed to develop proficiency in sports and athletics. While the content had changed dramatically over the previous fifty years, teaching methods remained mostly rigid and strongly teacher-directed. In 1962, Oberteuffer and Ulrich wrote

> The formal method means "Do as I say, when I say it, and how I say it," and in strict discipline and order. The atmosphere of formalism has been particularly distasteful to young Americans so the method has largely been discredited. It has however, not disappeared . . . It is one of the plagues of modern physical education and its presence means a lessening of educational value. The muscular work is done by the students, but nine-tenths of the thinking by the drill master (p. 300).

Oberteuffer and Ulrich were correct, but in the 1960s the formal teaching methods of physical education, and education in general, were already giving way to new ideas about how to engage students in their subject matter and for teachers to carry out instruction. Since that time we have developed many new methods for teaching physical education, now called teaching *strategies:*

1. Task/station teaching
2. Reflective teaching
3. Partner teaching
4. Team teaching
5. Inquiry-based teaching

These strategies represent ways to organize instruction for physical education, and delineate certain functions that teachers and students complete in class. Many of these strategies are less direct, allowing students to have more interaction with the teacher, other students, and the content itself. They are also considerably less formal, calling on teachers to demonstrate more flexibility and to make more "real time" decisions in class. Most of them are designed to be used temporarily for short-term outcomes, and can be highly effective for that purpose when selected properly.

These new approaches to teaching were developed separately, and lacked a unifying relationship that could help teachers see a bigger picture for ways to teach physical education. That changed in 1966 when Musska Mosston introduced his Spectrum of Teaching Styles in *Teaching Physical Education,* which would become one of the most influential books ever written on teaching in physical education. That text, and in subsequent editions (Mosston & Ashworth, 1994), conceptualized a unified series of teaching *styles* that progressed from strongly teacher-centered (formal and direct) to strongly student-centered (informal and indirect), based on the control of decision making before, during, and after class. The anatomy or structure of each teaching style was determined by decisions made in the preimpact (before), impact (during), and postimpact (after) stages of instruction. Quite simply, when the teacher retains most or all of the decisions, the resulting style is more formal and direct. Conversely, as students are given more decisions to make, a style becomes more informal and indirect. While one style could be maintained over several lessons or an entire unit, styles typically change to meet short-term instructional needs, so it is possible for two or more styles to be used in a given lesson, and several styles can be used in a content unit.

The 1980s saw the introduction of other approaches for teaching physical education. Some were based on Mosston's seminal work, while others originated from research on teaching effectiveness in physical education and other subject areas. The notion of effective teaching started in research that correlated teacher and student in-class behaviors with increased achievement—particularly student engagement patterns. The important message was that student behavior was more predictive of learning than teacher behavior, so the focus shifted from "What should the teacher be doing?" to "What should the teacher be getting the students to do in class?" Therefore, an effective teaching method was any decision or action that increased the possibility of student learning in class, and not necessarily a recognizable teaching style in the Mosston tradition.

During the development of teaching styles for physical education in the last three decades, there emerged a broader conceptualization of method, or "ways to instruct." The notion of an *instructional model* was based on a view of instruction that included simultaneous consideration of learning theory, long-term learning goals, context, content, classroom management, related teaching strategies, verification of process, and the assessment of student learning. Joyce and Weil (1980) define an [instructional] model as "a plan or pattern that can be used to shape curriculums (long-term courses of studies), to design instructional materials, and to guide instruction in the classroom and other settings" (p. 1). Methods, strategies, styles, and models differ mainly in scope. A method, strategy, or style is typically used for one or a few short-term learning activities and outcomes, and then gives way to another method, strategy, or style. A model is designed to be used for an entire unit of instruction and includes all of the planning, design, implementation, and assessment functions for that unit. In fact, it could include multiple teaching methods, strategies, or styles within the unit, again highlighting the difference in scope.

Teaching models have strong theoretical foundations, and most have been the object of much research in their development and implementation. They are usually field-tested in schools and other settings to ensure that they are capable of being used efficiently and effectively for their intended purposes. Most teaching models have been initially developed for use in classrooms, for outcomes primarily in the cognitive and affective domains. Several models, like the ones presented in this book, showed great promise for the outcomes and content of physical education programs, and have been adapted for use in our subject area.

The rest of the chapters in Part 1 will explain instructional models in more detail. The key point here is that such comprehensive and unified plans for instructing physical education go far beyond the limitations of methods, strategies and styles, as part of an ongoing evolution of "ways to teach" our subject matter to students of all ages. I would argue that models for planning, implementing, and assessing instruction will provide us with the most effective ways to reach our balanced aims for learning within the great diversity of content now in school physical education programs.

The planning stage of the NASPE Outcomes project led to the publication of *Moving into the Future: National Standards for Physical Education* (NASPE, 1995), which outlined programmatic goals for all grades and described some general instructional strategies for achieving them (see Figure 1.2).

It is important to note that NASPE recognized the need for varied and diverse ways to teach children and youth in order to achieve these standards. If contemporary physical education programs are going to strive for a variety of learning outcomes, teachers will need to instruct in more than one way. They will also require physical education teachers to progress past teaching methods, strategies, and styles to a new conceptualization of "ways to teach" based on instructional models like those presented in this book.

It is significant that NASPE's definition of a physically educated person encompasses all three of the major domains of learning: psychomotor, cognitive, and affective. The psychomotor domain refers to the ability to move part or all of the body in skillful ways. The cognitive domain refers to one's intellectual ability to think, recall, conceptualize, and solve problems. The affective domain refers to inner feelings, attitudes, and socially acceptable

FIGURE 1.2   NASPE's Program Standards for Physical Education

Content Standards in Physical Education

A physically educated person:
1. Demonstrates competency in many movement forms and proficiency in a few movement forms
2. Applies movement concepts and principles to the learning and development of motor skills
3. Exhibits a physically active lifestyle
4. Achieves and maintains a health-enhancing level of physical fitness
5. Demonstrates responsible personal and social behavior in physical activity settings
6. Demonstrates understanding and respect for differences among people in physical activity settings
7. Understands that physical activity provides opportunities for enjoyment, challenge, self-expression, and social interaction

behavior in a given setting. Learning domains will be discussed more in Chapter 2. For now it is important to know that they represent different types of knowledge that students acquire from instruction. Unlike most other school subjects that emphasize learning in just one or two domains (e.g., mathematics and science), professional physical educators have long recognized the need to help students in all three domains, further supporting the need for teachers to know how to instruct in a variety of ways.

No "One Best Way" to Teach

If physical education programs and the teachers in them strive to meet NASPE's (1995) standards to help students become truly physically educated persons, it is apparent that teachers cannot instruct in the same manner all the time, or be limited to methods, strategies, and styles. If programs are to work toward multiple learning outcomes, across all three learning domains, teach students with differing abilities, and include a wide variety of program content in the curriculum, there can be no "one best way" to teach physical education. Each time a teacher instructs a different content, for different learning outcomes, to a different group of students, that teacher must change his way of instructing in order to help those students learn more effectively and enjoyably. Sometimes those differences will call for only minor changes—small variations in a few teaching and learning behaviors. At other times those differences will require major changes in how a teacher instructs, calling for the use of a completely different approach—or, what we will call in this book, an instructional model.

Instructional Models: Tools for Teaching and Learning

To effectively teach to a variety of outcomes in all three domains and address the ranges of students' abilities, physical education teachers will need to know and use a number of different instructional models. An *instructional model* refers to a comprehensive and coherent plan for teaching that includes: a theoretical foundation, statements of intended learning outcomes, teacher's content knowledge expertise, developmentally appropriate and sequenced learning activities, expectations for teacher and student behaviors, unique task structures, assessment of learning outcomes, and ways to verify the faithful implementation of the model itself. The best instructional models link theories of teaching and learning to specific processes that a teacher should promote in the gymnasium. Each model is a sort of "blueprint" a teacher should follow to help students learn in physical education. Each model calls for its own set of decisions, plans, and actions by the teacher and students. The most effective teachers will be familiar with a number of instructional models and know which model to use at a given time (depending on outcomes, domains, students' learning styles, and content).

Each instructional model can also be considered a tool a teacher can select and use at the appropriate time with a given content to help students learn in the most effective way. The best teachers are not necessarily the ones with the largest "toolbox" of instructional models at their command; the best teachers are the ones who know and can use the "right tool for the right job" to promote learning outcomes identified in their school's physical education program. It is more likely that a teacher's needed set of tools will be determined mostly by the range of students' developmental stages at her school and the specific content units to be offered. As you can now see, there is a strong link between content, student ability/stage, stated learning outcomes, and the instructional model to be used by the teacher in a content unit.

One of the major purposes of this book is to provide you with an introduction to instructional models for teaching physical education. Once you are familiar with the idea of instructional models and know how to use them, you will be able to implement each one at the most appropriate time, and then be ready to learn even more models—making your "toolbox" larger and more diverse. If you are using this book as part of a teaching methods course, it is likely that you will have a limited amount of time to learn and practice each model, so you will be a beginner, of sorts, on each one. That's OK. You will get more opportunities to improve during field experiences, student teaching, and then as a full-time teacher in schools. Just like anything else you have learned well in your life, it will take time, planning, practice, hard work, and patience to improve your effectiveness with each instructional model you use.

If you are an experienced teacher, it is my hope that you learn those models that fit your students' needs and match your program's content. Then, you can select the best model for each content unit and begin to understand how to plan for it, implement it, and assess its effectiveness in your program. In that process you will also learn how to modify each model for maximum effectiveness in your setting.

Model-Based Instruction for Physical Education

It is argued here that physical education instruction is typically based on content, the activity being taught to students. That is, the *organizing center* for instruction is most often determined by the content (e.g., basketball, floor hockey, tennis, aerobic dance), and not goals or instructional models. If you mention the content, a teacher will likely tell you how he teaches it to his students: "I teach archery this way . . .", "I teach games this way . . .", "I teach line dancing this way . . .", and so on. And, as a profession, we tend to teach the same content in the same way to students of varying grade levels. If the unit is volleyball, the content, task structure, and the sequencing of learning activities remain quite similar, whether it is being taught to sixth graders or twelfth graders. The bump is learned first, then the set, then the spike, then the serve, followed by some rules and full game play. The drills and other learning activities used to teach each component are remarkably similar as well: the "triangle" bump drill, the wall set drill, and other easily recognizable tasks and organizational structures. All of this sameness stems from the assumption that there are tried-and-true ways to teach volleyball, and that those ways will be equally effective for students at all grade levels. Again, the content becomes the most influential factor (the organizing center) in determining how to teach a physical education unit. When this happens, it will be referred to as *activity-based instruction,* and represents the most common way for teachers to design instruction in physical education today.

The unit content is important, but it should not be the only consideration in how to teach. It is likely that instruction will be more effective, safe, and enjoyable if content is considered equally with other factors, such as:

- Intended learning outcomes
- Context and teaching environment
- Student developmental stage and readiness
- Student learning preferences
- Domain priorities
- Task structure and organizational patterns
- Sequencing of learning tasks
- Assessment of learning outcomes
- Assessment of instructional practices

Good instructional models require the teacher to consider all of those factors (along with content) before making the key decision of *how to instruct students* in a unit. When a teacher analyzes all of these factors, which then leads her to teach that unit with a unified, coherent, and comprehensive plan, we will refer to that as *model-based instruction*. The *organizing center* for the unit becomes the selected instructional model, chosen after considering all of the factors listed.

Under a model-based approach, when one or more major factors change, it will likely result in the selection of a different instructional model. That will be true even when the content is the same. For instance, if two middle school physical educators are about to begin their own units of soccer, and they have different learning outcomes for each class, it would stand to reason that the teachers would instruct in different ways with two different instructional models. If Mr. Hart wishes to promote higher levels of skill development with independent student progressions, he could design his unit with a Personalized System of Instruction (Chapter 8). If Mrs. Blue wishes to develop students' strategic knowledge, she could design her unit to be instructed with the Tactical Games model (Chapter 13). Both are soccer units in the same middle school physical education context, but the decision about "how to teach" is not based on the unit content; it is based on preferred learning outcomes and other factors, which should lead teachers to select a different instructional model for their respective units.

There are several good reasons for using a model-based approach in physical education:

1. It allows a teacher to consider and weigh several factors before deciding which model to use in a unit. This consideration recognizes the relationship between all of those factors and helps the teacher to make a deductive decision about instruction.
2. By using a deductive process, it is much more likely that the selected model will match the context, content, and goals for each unit. Therefore, the effectiveness of instruction will be consistently high.
3. Most instructional models have strong research to support the theory behind them and their effectiveness in promoting certain kinds of learning outcomes.
4. Each instructional model can be viewed as a sort of blueprint for a teacher to follow in designing and implementing instruction. This blueprint helps the teacher to make congruent decisions when using a model.

5. A good instructional model will include ways for a teacher to know if he is using the model correctly and to know if the model is working to help students achieve the stated learning outcomes. This provides the teacher with essential feedback about his instruction.
6. Each instructional model provides the teacher and students with descriptions of expected behaviors, roles, decisions, and responsibilities—increasing clarity for everyone in the class.
7. The best instructional models are flexible and allow each teacher to adapt the model to the unique needs of learners and the context. This recognizes the ability of teachers to make professional judgments and decisions based on their expertise, experience, and teaching situation.

The Need for Multiple Models in Physical Education

You have already recognized that physical education, more than any other school subject, offers the most complex challenges for teachers. No other subject requires its teachers to address learning outcomes in all three major domains, to be knowledgeable in so many content areas, and to work in ever-changing learning environments. Most other teachers use the same classroom all the time, but physical education teachers can have many classrooms: the gymnasium, auxiliary gyms, outside fields, multiple-purpose rooms, the ropes course, paved areas, the school stage, and others. In addition, they must often share the teaching area with other teachers and classes.

That is not to say classroom teachers instruct the same way all of the time. Many new, exciting, and effective instructional models have been developed for use by classroom teachers. Some of the models included in this book were initially developed for classroom teaching in many subject areas and grade levels. However, with intended student outcomes in more learning domains, more content to cover, and the greater dynamics of the typical gymnasium, physical education teachers likely need to know how to use more instructional models than classroom teachers.

Overview of This Book

As previously mentioned, the purpose of this book is to provide you with knowledge about instructional models—tools that can be used to achieve a variety of learning outcomes in your physical education classes. Once you know how to use each tool, you will be able to choose and implement the most effective way to instruct every content unit, allowing your students the best opportunity to learn what you intend for them to learn. In order to help you select, plan, implement, and assess your use of instructional models, this book will follow a series of steps as you progress though the chapters.

Chapter 2 will outline the most essential types of knowledge needed by teachers for effective instruction in a model-based approach. As you will see, a physical education teacher will have to draw from several knowledge bases simultaneously in order to effectively arrange and carry out instruction.

Chapter 3 identifies instructional strategies used to teach physical education from a model-based approach. Strategies are preplanned procedures for events that take place in physical education lessons to promote short-term learning outcomes. Strategies can be designed for grouping students in class, organizing learning tasks, getting and maintaining student attention, increasing safety, presenting information, assessing student learning, and other key operations.

Chapter 4 will describe the necessary effective teaching skills for physical education that serve as the next level of building blocks for model-based instruction. These are things that effective teachers do (and get students to do) before, during, and after class to maximize the potential for student learning. The teaching skills in this chapter were derived from research on teaching in classrooms and in physical education over the past three decades.

Chapter 5 provides a comprehensive description of unit and lesson planning for physical education. It explains the difference between just planning and *being prepared* for teaching physical education. In this book, planning is viewed as a series of questions that a teacher should ask before the unit and each lesson in it begins. Once the questions have been asked and answered, the teacher will have a better chance to implement smooth, coherent, and effective instructional episodes for all models. A generic planning template is presented so that you can have a place to start in this important function of teaching.

Chapter 6 is perhaps the most important chapter in this book. It is where Chapters 2 through 5 converge, setting the stage for you to learn each of the models presented in Part 2. An instructional model is a unique plan of action, designed to facilitate certain learning outcomes for students. Each model establishes its own pattern of decision making, classroom operations, and responsibilities for both the teacher and students. This chapter provides a framework for describing the components and dimensions that make up each model and set it apart from other models. That knowledge is essential in helping the teacher to select and implement the best model for every learning setting and content unit.

Each of the chapters in Part 2 will provide a complete description of one instructional model for physical education, based on the components and dimensions presented in Chapter 6. Those models (and their chapters in this book) are:

7. Direct Instruction
8. Personalized Systems for Instruction
9. Cooperative Learning
10. Sport Education
11. Peer Teaching
12. Inquiry Model
13. Tactical Games

These chapters will provide examples of lesson plans and suggestions for adapting each model to various teaching contexts. The Learning Activities at the end of each chapter in Part 1 and practice teaching experiences will assist you in the initial stages of learning how to implement model-based instruction for physical education.

LEARNING ACTIVITIES

1. Make a list of your participation in physical activity at each stage of your life: preschool, elementary school, secondary school, college, and the present. At each stage describe: (a) your motivation for participating, (b) your goals, and (c) who taught you each of the activities.

2. Go back to part (c) from the previous Learning Activity. Describe in your own words the methods used by your teacher(s) at each stage. Be sure to include the degree of directness and formalness in those methods.

3. If you presently teach physical education, coach, or instruct learners in physical activity of any kind, describe your own teaching methods.

4. In your own words, write a definition for *a physically educated person* in the form of a list. For each item on the list, explain how you would go about instructing to help students learn that part of your definition. By the way, "no fair" using the NASPE definition given in this chapter!

5. The content of P–12 U.S. physical education programs has shown a clear evolution in the past century. What do you think those programs will look like in the year 2020? What will learners need to know to participate in these programs?

SUGGESTED READINGS

Mosston, M., & Ashworth, S. (1994). *Teaching physical education* (4th ed.). New York: Macmillan.

National Association for Sport and Physical Education. (1992). *Outcomes of quality physical education programs.* Reston, VA: Author.

National Association for Sport and Physical Education. (1995). *Moving into the future: National standards for physical education.* St. Louis: Mosby.

Siedentop, D. (1998). *Introduction to physical education, fitness, and sport* (3rd ed.) Mountain View, CA: Mayfield.

Van Dalen, D., & Bennett, B. (1971). *A world history of physical education: Cultural, philosophical, comparative* (2nd ed.). Englewood Cliffs, NJ: Prentice Hall.

2 Knowledge Areas for Model-Based Instruction in Physical Education

Physical education teachers must have expertise in many areas that directly or indirectly determine how they instruct and how well students will learn in each content unit and lesson. It is an oversimplification to suggest that teachers need to know about their students, physical education content, and instructional models. Effective teachers do need to know these things, but in much more sophisticated and interactive ways. The sophistication comes from having extensive knowledge in many areas of teaching; superficial knowledge is not adequate to attend to the complexities of most physical education teaching settings. The interaction comes when a teacher must apply several types of knowledge at the same time—and often with little time to consider the options or to consult with others.

Shulman's Knowledge Base for Teaching

Over the years there have been many attempts to define a knowledge base for teaching—all of the things a person needs to know in order to teach their subject effectively in P–12 schools. Since research has not determined a definitive knowledge base at this time, any list of what knowledge teachers need will depend greatly on who is writing the list. Recognizing that many such lists exist in the literature, and in the opinions of teacher educators, there has been some consensus in the past decade on the knowledge base proposed by Lee Shulman (1987). Christensen (1996) reports that Shulman's knowledge base was the one cited as most often used by teacher education programs undergoing accreditation review by the National Council on Accreditation for Teacher Education (NCATE). Shulman's knowledge base for teaching includes seven categories:

1. Content knowledge — Knowledge about the subject matter to be taught

2. General pedagogical knowledge — Knowledge about teaching methods that pertain to all subjects and situations

3. Pedagogical content knowledge — Knowledge about how to teach a subject or topic to specific groups of students in a specific context

4. Curriculum knowledge — Knowledge about developmentally appropriate content and programs at each grade level

5. Knowledge of educational contexts — Knowledge about the impact of context on instruction

6. Knowledge of learners and their characteristics — Knowledge about human learning as it applies to teaching

7. Knowledge of educational goals — Knowledge about the goals, purposes, and structure of our educational system

Teachers need to have knowledge at three different levels within each category: declarative, procedural, and conditional. *Declarative knowledge* is that which a teacher can express verbally or in writing. It is what one "knows about" the many things that make for effective instruction in physical education. *Procedural knowledge* is that which a teacher can actually apply before, during, and after instruction. It is the ability to carry out declarative knowledge in ways that facilitate class management and student learning. *Conditional knowledge* informs a teacher when and why to make decisions that fit the specific context of the moment. All three types of knowledge are strongly related to each other. Declarative knowledge is prerequisite to procedural knowledge—one must first have basic knowledge about teaching and learning and then how to operationalize that knowledge. Once a teacher can operationalize knowledge one time or in one setting, conditional knowledge allows the teacher to generalize those operations to many other times and settings and "know why" before acting to "make it happen." Following are some examples of declarative, procedural, and conditional knowledge for physical education teachers.

Declarative	Knowing the concept of developmentally appropriate curriculum and instruction
Procedural	Knowing how to write lesson plans that use developmentally appropriate teaching strategies
Conditional	Knowing how to modify activities in class when they are not developmentally appropriate for students
Declarative	Knowing the rules of team and individual sports
Procedural	Being able to model correct rules as part of a task presentation
Conditional	Using different words and terms for fourth graders and tenth graders to explain rules
Declarative	Knowing three interesting rhythmic activities for fifth graders
Procedural	Being able to monitor and provide accurate feedback while students practice those activities
Conditional	Knowing how to motivate reluctant students to participate
Declarative	Knowing why a certain movement pattern improves performance
Procedural	Being able to plan and implement lead-up games that provide students with increased repetitions of that movement pattern
Conditional	Knowing when it's time for students to progress from lead-up games to full games

All three types of knowledge are needed for effective instruction. The important thing to learn is that each kind of knowledge will be used at different times in the process of planning and carrying out instruction. Effective teachers will have strong declarative and procedural knowledge *and* will know how to make that knowledge work in many different settings.

A Proposed Knowledge Base for Physical Education Instructional Models

While it is helpful to identify a knowledge base on teaching, Shulman's categories are quite general in nature, and do not address specific knowledge needed for teaching physical education from a model-based perspective. I am proposing eleven areas of knowledge that will be needed by physical educators who choose to plan and implement instructional models.

Figure 2.1 shows the eleven areas of teacher knowledge for model-based instruction in physical education. This knowledge forms the basic foundation upon which instructional models are built and implemented for effective instruction in physical education. Subsequent chapters will include other types of knowledge that rely on those presented in Figure 2.1.

FIGURE 2.1   **Knowledge Areas for Model-Based Instruction**

1. Learning contexts
2. Learners
3. Learning theories
4. Developmental appropriateness
5. Learning domains and objectives
6. Physical education content

7. Task analysis and content progression
8. Assessment
9. Social/emotional climate
10. Equity in the gym
11. Curriculum models for PE

This knowledge base for using instructional models in physical education does not have specific research support for that purpose. However, each part of the knowledge base does have strong support in the general literature on teaching; I am attempting here to transfer that support into the planning and implementation of instructional models in physical education so that you can become aware of the declarative, procedural, and conditional knowledge you will need when using such models. Therefore, this knowledge base will be referred to here as *proposed areas* of expertise needed for our purposes in this book.

At this level, much of the knowledge will be declarative—being aware of the major concepts included in each area and how they relate to model-based instruction in physical education. Procedural and conditional knowledge will be developed later when a teacher selects, plans for, and implements each teaching model in a specific context.

Learning Contexts

All physical education programs occur in some context that facilitates or inhibits the planning and implementation of instruction. Context refers to the total of all factors that can influence what and how content is taught and learned in a program. One key thing to keep in mind is that most contextual factors are stable, out of the teacher's control. Most teachers have little power to change their context. The best that can be done is to become familiar with a given context and maximize the potential for teaching and learning in that place. That does not automatically imply that all contexts are limiting for teachers; many physical education programs occur in contexts that allow teachers a wide variety of positive options for instruction.

Every school has unique characteristics that offer opportunities and challenges for physical education teachers. It is important that all teachers in a school know that context well, and how each part of the context can affect the physical education program. Rink (1997) emphasizes this point: "The context of the teaching situation affects how teachers develop, what skills they acquire, how they think about those skills, and what they think the goals are for their [physical education] programs" (p. 18). There are many ways to categorize and describe a school's context. For our purposes, I am including five major factors: location, student demographics, administration, physical education faculty, and instructional resources (see Figure 2.2).

FIGURE 2.2   Major Contextual Factors for Physical Education Programs

Major Contextual Factor	Subfactors	Possible Impact on Physical Education Program
School location	1. Urban, rural, suburban	1. Class size Outdoor facilities School security Travel to off-campus activities
	2. School district	2. Policies Personnel hiring
	3. Regional climate	3. Weather for outdoor activity Local natural resources for activity (lakes, mountains, parks)
Student demographics	1. Size of school	1. Class size Scheduling options
	2. Student SES profile	2. Ability to afford PE uniforms Ability to take optional for-charge activities Students' range of experience with movement forms
	3. Community values	3. Student experience and preference for movement forms Preference for traditional or alternative movement forms
	4. Academic ability	4. Ability to comprehend instructional information Ability to read task cards, keep score, or work independently
	5. Absentee rate	5. High rates require more teaching reviews High rates can lead to starts/stops in student learning
	6. Transitory student rate	6. High rates can lead to loss of continuity High rates lead to constantly teaching class rules to new students
	7. Non-English speaking students	7. Teacher inability to communicate Student inability to communicate Student waiting/isolation until teacher can "catch him up" Excessively slow class progress due to ESOL students' needs

FIGURE 2.2 Continued

Major Contextual Factor	Subfactors	Possible Impact on Physical Education Program
Administration	1. District level	1. Program policies for all subjects Program policies for PE General budget allocations Hiring of new staff Approval for major renovations/ repairs Curriculum guidelines
	2. School level	2. Departmental budget allocations Hiring of new staff Evaluation of teachers Support for PE policies Scheduling Permission for off-campus classes Space allocations Approval of equipment requests Familiarity with PE program goals and content
Physical education staff	1. Number of teachers and support personnel	1. Teacher/aide to student ratio Number of concurrent classes offered Ability to team teach
	2. Gender, racial, ethnic composition	2. Ability to provide role models for students Ability to relate to diverse student population
	3. Age	3. Ability to relate to younger generations
	4. PE teaching experience	4. Need for mentoring (new) Ability to provide mentoring (veteran) Ability to assimilate new content and ideas
	5. Content expertise	5. Determines what can and cannot be taught Determines match/mismatch with students' preferences and needs
Instructional resources	1. Teaching spaces	1. Class size Number of classes sharing space Available teaching stations
	2. Equipment	2. Student safety Student participation rate Ability to vary task difficulty
	3. Time and scheduling	3. Instructional minutes for each lesson Frequency of PE lessons

Teachers should conduct a complete contextual analysis of their school regularly to determine if changes have occurred, and if so, how they will affect the content and conduct of the program. This analysis will influence every part of the physical education program, including the selection and implementation of instructional models.

Learners

Some of what teachers need to know about students refers to contextual characteristics that describe how many students are in each class, their background, and their previous experience and knowledge of the unit content. Other important areas of knowledge center on the teacher's familiarity with the general growth and developmental stages of school-age learners. This knowledge is critical to the planning and implementation of developmentally appropriate instruction for children and youth, giving teachers good starting and reference points for identifying student needs and abilities. Young children and adolescents develop as whole persons, with the cognitive, psychomotor, and affective domains in constant interaction. Discussions of learners' development can be simplified by presenting each domain separately; as the teacher applies this knowledge, however, she must be aware that a person's development is fully interactive across all three domains.

Cognitive Development.   Jean Piaget (Phillips & Soltis, 1991) describes four phases of cognitive development in humans: (1) sensorimotor, (2) preoperational, (3) concrete operations, and (4) formal operations (see Figure 2.3).

Many contemporary physical education curriculums are based on Piaget's stages of learning, with carefully planned activities, modified equipment, teaching strategies, and assessment techniques that strongly adhere to the appropriate cognitive stage for each grade level. At times, cognitive development is the primary focus of instruction; at other times, it facilitates development in the psychomotor domain.

Motor Development.   Motor development refers to the way each person acquires (learns) patterns of movement through the life span. Some movement patterns are more generic, used in everyday activities (e.g., walking, climbing steps, sitting, standing, reaching, grasping, etc.). These and many other motor patterns are learned for the purpose of applying them in sport, dance, and exercise situations. The purpose of most physical education instruction is the development of these motor patterns. The remainder of this discussion will focus on this development.

Gallahue (1996) presents a scheme for describing motor development in children and youth. It is comprised of: (1) phases, which delineate major progressions from birth to adulthood; (2) stages, which differentiate learned motor patterns within phases; and (3) levels, which describe learners' proficiency (advances) within each stage. See Figure 2.4 for the phases and stages of his model.

Skill levels describe a learner's proficiency within each stage. As a learner enters each new stage, he is at the *beginner/novice level,* characterized by uncoordinated, hesitant, conscious, and inefficient movement. The learner typically pays attention to all stimuli in the environment because he has not yet learned what is important and what can be ignored. At the *intermediate/practice level* the learner is able to practice with more efficiency and begins

FIGURE 2.3 Piaget's Four Stages of Cognitive Development

Cognitive Stage and Approximate Age Range	Learner Characteristics	Implications for Learning Movement Concepts
Sensorimotor (birth–2 yrs.)	Makes initial relationship (operations) between movement and cognition Develops instinctual patterns (grasping, lifting, handling) through personal exploration	Learners at this stage are not ready for learning movement from others
Preoperational (2–7 yrs.)	Still learns in the "concrete" Cannot yet form or learn from abstractions	Learners need tactile experiences (holding, feeling, moving the body in space) with simple, explicit verbal directions
Concrete operations (7–11 yrs.)	Begins to be able to learn with abstract experiences, but still relies on "concrete"	Can begin to problem solve Can explore relationships between thought and movement Can learn with logic Needs fewer and less explicit directions
Formal operations (11–14 yrs.)	Mastery of conceptual learning Able to transform previous knowledge and experience into new structures	Can solve complex problems Can develop new knowledge for self Can learn from few or implied directions

to approach the final desired pattern or skill. He begins to formulate learning strategies, or little "tips" that facilitate practice and performance. Task focus increases by having sorted out necessary information. The learner at the *advanced/fine-tuning level* has a complete understanding of both task and process, and acquires automaticity that makes it appear that he is "not even thinking" about how to perform—he "just does it" (Gallahue, 1996).

Gallahue's (1996) model has many implications for the design and conduct of instruction in physical education, at all grades and developmental phases. Once a teacher can identify a student's current phase, stage, and level, it can be used as the starting point for planning developmentally appropriate learning tasks and measuring progress (learning) over time. This scheme can also provide teachers with a general starting point for entire classes and grade levels in the school by matching the age of most students with each phase and stage. For instance, most second graders are six or seven years old, which places most of them at the mature stage in the fundamental movement phase. Instructional planning and task progressions can start at that point, and then be adjusted once the content unit begins.

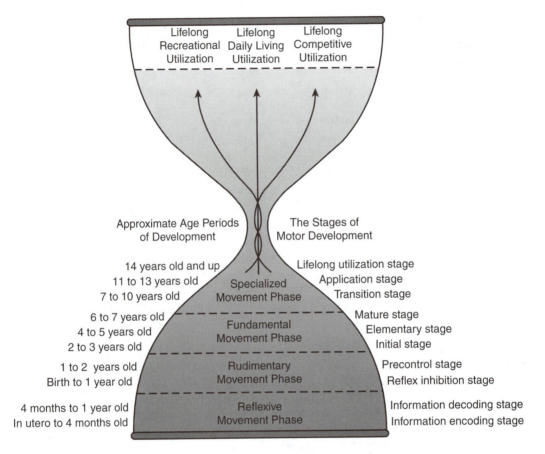

FIGURE 2.4   A Descriptive View of the Phases and Stages of Motor Development

From Gallahue, D. J. (1996). *Developmental physical education for today's children* (3rd ed.). Madison, WI: Brown & Benchmark. Reproduced with permission of The McGraw-Hill Companies.

Affective Development.   While teachers pay lots of attention to the affective domain, we are much less knowledgeable about how children and youth actually learn and develop in this domain (Snow, Corno, & Jackson, 1996). Therefore, teachers have fewer "starting points" for designing and implementing learning experiences that can lead to somewhat predictable outcomes in affective development. This can be attributed to at least two major factors: (1) affective learning is very private and individual—teachers have very few indicators they can rely on to know students' needs and when affective learning has actually occurred; (2) there is a complicated and often poorly understood interaction between affect and learning in the other two domains. Theorists are sure that the other two domains contribute to affective learning, but beyond that the relationship is vague and strongly debated.

Student Motivation.   One of the most essential factors in the learning process is the motivation to be engaged in the learning activity of the moment—whether that activity is listening, watching, thinking, or doing. Student learning is directly affected by their willingness to learn. Effective teachers not only plan for developmentally appropriate content and effective teaching strategies—they always consider a critical question: Why should students want to learn (this content) in the first place? Keller (1983) reviewed many of the theories about student motivation and reduced them to four nearly universal concepts: (1) interest—the degree to which the learner's curiosity is aroused and maintained; (2) relevance—the degree to which the content and instruction addresses the learner's personal goals and needs; (3) expectancy—the learner's perceived success in the task; and (4) satisfaction—the learner's intrinsic motivations and/or extrinsic rewards for engagement.

Building on Keller's (1983) principles, Brophy (1987) developed a framework for classifying motivational strategies that teachers can use to get and keep students motivated to learn. The framework is built upon four essential preconditions: (1) a supportive environment, (2) an appropriate level of challenge/difficulty, (3) meaningful learning objectives, and (4) moderation/optimal use of strategies. According to Brophy, no motivational strategy will be effective if all of these preconditions are not met for students.

The second level of his framework includes three principles: (1) motivate by maintaining students' success expectations, (2) motivate by suppling extrinsic incentives, and (3) motivate by capitalizing on students' existing intrinsic motivation. The third level of the framework mentions specific strategies for stimulating student motivation to learn. Refer to Figure 2.5 for a complete illustration of Brophy's framework.

It is essential that a teacher can motivate students to be engaged, stay engaged, and learn the intended content and goals of instruction. There are many ways to do that, but in the long run the most effective strategies will be those that are inviting, positive, and rewarding for students rather than alienating, negative, or punitive. Physical education teachers need to develop a large repertoire of motivational strategies that adhere to Keller's and Brophy's principles.

Learning Styles and Preferences.   Much attention in education has been given to learning styles. Jonassen and Grabowski (1993) define *learning style* as "learner preferences for different types of learning and instructional activities" (p. 5). According to learning style theory, each of us has our own most effective way of learning, determined by a complex interaction between personal abilities, past learning experiences, and the instructional environment. Psychologists and learning theorists have developed many ways to define, describe, determine, and measure individuals' learning styles. Unfortunately, this has led to much confusion for those teachers who wish to understand learning styles better and consider them in their instructional practices. The various conceptualizations can be divided into two large groups: (1) those based on descriptions of the learner's perceptual and information-processing abilities (e.g., Gregorc, 1982; Kolb, 1981); and (2) those based on the learner's preferred contextual factors while attempting to learn (e.g., Dunn, Dunn, & Price, 1989; Reichmann & Grasha, 1974). The main difference is that the first type places learners in categories (styles) and tends to describe them with one descriptor, such as diverger, assimilator, converger, or accommodater (Kolb, 1981), or they attempt to identify each learner's preferred perceptual mode, such as visual, kinesthetic, thinking, or listening (Coker, 1996). The second type tends to describe multifaceted conditions (preferences) under which a learner is likely to learn most effectively, such as the learning environment,

FIGURE 2.5   Brophy's Framework for Classifying Motivational Strategies

A. Essential Preconditions
   1. Supportive environment
   2. Appropriate level of challenge/difficulty
   3. Meaningful learning objectives
   4. Moderation/optimal use of strategies

B. Motivating by Maintaining Success Expectations
   5. Program for success
   6. Teach goal setting, performance appraisal, and self-reinforcement
   7. Provide remedial socialization for discouraged students
      a. Portray effort as investment rather than risk
      b. Portray skill development as incremental and domain specific
      c. Focus on mastery
      d. Provide attribution retraining
      e. Minimize test anxiety

C. Motivating by Supplying Extrinsic Incentives
   8. Offer rewards as incentives for good (or improved) performance
   9. Structure appropriate competition
   10. Call attention to the instrumental value of academic activities

D. Motivating by Capitalizing on Students' Existing Intrinsic Motivation
   11. Adapt tasks to students' interests
      a. Incorporate content that students find interesting or activities that they find enjoyable
      b. Offer choices of alternative tasks or opportunities to exercise autonomy in selecting among alternative ways to meet requirements
      c. Encourage student comments and questions
      d. Include divergent questions and opportunities for students to express opinions or make other responses to the content

   12. Plan for novelty and variety
   13. Provide opportunities to respond actively
   14. Provide immediate feedback to student responses
   15. Allow students to create finished products
   16. Incorporate "fun features" into academic activities
      a. Fantasy or imagination elements
      b. Simulation exercises
      c. Gamelike features
      d. Peer interaction opportunities

E. Strategies for Stimulating Student Motivation to Learn
   17. Model interest in learning and motivation to learn
   18. Communicate desirable expectations and attributions about students' motivation to learn
   19. Minimize students' performance anxiety during learning activities
   20. Project intensity
   21. Project enthusiasm
   22. Induce task interest or appreciation
   23. Induce curiosity or suspense
   24. Induce dissonance or cognitive conflict
   25. Make abstract content more personal, concrete, or familiar
   26. Induce students to generate their own motivation to learn
   27. State learning objectives and provide advance organizers
   28. Model task-related thinking and problem solving

the social structure, the emotional climate, and the physical stimuli received by learners (Dunn, Dunn, & Price, 1989; Reichmann & Grasha, 1974).

The relatively simple scheme developed by Reichmann and Grasha (1974) is quite useful in helping to match student learning preference with a given instructional model. It is based on three dimensions that describe a student's (1) attitudes toward learning; (2) view of teachers and/or peers; and (3) reactions to classroom procedures. The model describes how these key features of the learning environment establish student approach tendencies and motivation in that type of instructional arrangement. That perspective goes well with the notion of instructional models, since each model is essentially a unique and different way to structure the learning environment.

Learning Theories

The most fundamental design component for all instructional models is the learning theory upon which it is based. The best way to define learning theory is to define each word separately and then combine them. Shuell (1986) defines *learning* as an enduring change in behavior, or in the capacity to behave in a given fashion, which results from practice or other forms of experience. Schunk (1996) defines *theory* as "a scientifically acceptable set of principles offered to explain a phenomenon" (p. 3). So, a *learning theory* is a way to explain or describe how learning occurs. The next step in this logic is important for instructional models. If psychologists and instructional designers hold different theories and assumptions about how people learn (and they do), each theory will lead to a somewhat different instructional model. Since we have many theories of learning, we also have many and often contrasting instructional models.

All teachers have their own personal theories for how people learn best and how to teach physical education to them. When personal theories differ from the theory upon which a particular model is based, there is a tendency to avoid using that model and to even criticize it. It is important that a teacher has a personal theory, but even more important that she be open to other theories about teaching and learning so that she can choose the "right tool (model) for the right job" to pursue her intended learning outcomes for students. Holding on to one theory means that a teacher will teach the same way all of the time.

There are many learning theories, but not all of them apply to educational settings, or ultimately contribute to the design of instructional models. Those which do apply for our uses in this book are shown in Figure 2.6, along with a brief description of how each theory views the learning process.

Each theory will be explained further in Part 2 as it applies to the foundation of the appropriate instructional model. At this time it is important that you know the contribution of learning theories to the design and development of instructional models.

FIGURE 2.6   Major Learning Theories and Their Assumptions (Adapted from Schunk, 1996)

Learning Theory	Basic Assumptions about How People Learn
Operant conditioning	Learning occurs through the consequences of human behavior. Behavior that is reinforced will be more likely to recur; behavior that is punished will be less likely to occur in the future. The three-term contingency $$S^D \rightarrow R \rightarrow S^R$$ is the basic building block of learning. The discriminative stimulus (S^D) sets the occasion for a response (R) to be emitted, which is then followed by a reinforcing stimulus (S^R) that increases the probability that the behavior will occur again when the discriminative stimulus is present.
Social cognitive learning, including self-efficacy	Learning occurs as people observe others in their environment and imitate that behavior. Socially learned behavior is reinforced in much the same way as operant conditioning. It is strongly determined by reciprocal interactions between the learner, the environment, and behavior. Learning can occur either by actually doing or vicariously through observational experience.
Information processing	The learning act is conducted through internal (mental) processes. Learners select and attend to certain features in the environment, transform and rehearse information, relate new information to previously acquired knowledge, and then organize knowledge to make it meaningful. The use of the memory function is critical to learning.
Cognitive learning and processes, including constructivist learning	Learning occurs as a process of cognitive growth and development through the expansion of one's ability to make meaning of previously learned facts, symbols, concepts, and principles. In the constructiveness approach, students learn by *self-building* on existing knowledge. People hold implicit beliefs about learning that play a key role in this process.
Problem solving	A cognitive theory that refers to people's efforts to achieve a goal for which they do not have an automatic solution. It relies on three main operations: trial and error, insight, and heuristics (self-developed strategies).
Motivation	The learning process originates with an innate need held by the learner. That need fuels the drive (or motivation) to emit a behavior that will reduce or eliminate the need. A need can be physiological, psychological, or some combination.
Humanistic theory	Related to motivational theory, in which a person attempts to fulfill five levels of needs: physiological, safety, belongingness, esteem, and self-actualization (Maslow, 1970). Learning occurs as a result of meeting subordinate needs, freeing the person to begin the learning process at the next highest level.

Developmentally Appropriate Practice in Physical Education

In 1987 the National Association for the Education of Young Children (NAEYC) published an important monograph that outlined preferred teaching practices based on the concept of developmental appropriateness (Bredekamp, 1987). Developmentally appropriate practice in all subjects, including physical education, is based on the recognition that the content of learning, the learning environment, and the instruction must match students' current developmental stages and readiness for learning. The second edition of the NAEYC monograph states that developmentally appropriate practice is based on twelve principles of child development and learning (Bredekamp & Copple, 1996–97). Keep in mind that while the NAEYC is referring to the young children, these principles will apply to all learners as the developmental process continues throughout the life span.

1. Domains of development—physical, social, emotional, and cognitive—are closely related. Development in one domain influences and is influenced by development in the other domains.
2. Development occurs in a relatively orderly sequence, with later abilities, skills, and knowledge building on those already acquired.
3. Development proceeds at varying rates from learner to learner as well as unevenly within different areas of each person's functioning.
4. Early experiences have both cumulative and delayed effects on an individual's development; optimal periods exist for certain types of development and learning.
5. Development proceeds in predictable directions toward greater complexity, organization, and internalization.
6. Development and learning occur in and are influenced by multiple social and cultural contexts.
7. Humans are active learners, drawing on direct physical and social experience as well as culturally transmitted knowledge to construct their own understandings of the world around them.
8. Development and learning result from interaction of biological maturation and the environment, which includes both the physical and social worlds in which we live.
9. Play is an important vehicle for children's social, emotional, and cognitive development, as well as a reflection of their development.
10. Development advances when learners have opportunities to practice newly acquired skills and when they experience a challenge just beyond the level of their present mastery.
11. Individuals demonstrate different modes of knowing and learning and different ways of representing what they know.
12. People develop and learn best in the context of a community where they are safe and valued, their physical needs are met, and they feel psychologically secure (adapted from Bredekamp & Copple, 1996–97, pp. 9–15).

These statements about developmentally appropriate instruction go hand in hand with Gallahue's stages of development for motor skills discussed earlier in this chapter (see Figure 2.4). Gallahue's model addresses only the content portion of this concept, while the NAEYC guidelines are concerned with the entire instructional environment.

The Council on Physical Education for Children (COPEC) and NASPE's Motor Development Task Force followed the NAEYC's guidelines with their own position statements, carrying this concept into the teaching of physical education. These statements include descriptions of instruction, curriculum, program philosophy, and learning progressions that adhere to the principles of developmentally appropriate practice applied in physical education. The position paper from the Motor Development Task Force (NASPE) provides an overall definition of a developmental perspective for physical education programs:

1. Developmental change is qualitative
2. Developmental change is sequential
3. Developmental change is cumulative
4. Developmental change is directional
5. Developmental change is multifactorial
6. Developmental change is individual

Their statement highlights one of the most important concepts about developmentally focused instruction: Development is age-related but not age-determined. Teachers must realize that they cannot teach all eight-year-olds, all twelve-year-olds, or all sixteen-year-olds the same way. While students at each of those ages will share many developmental characteristics, some important differences will exist between individuals which should deter decisions to instruct all students the same way all the time.

The position statement from COPEC (NASPE, 1992b) addresses specific program components for designing and implementing developmentally appropriate programs and instruction for elementary physical education. Some of these components are shown in Figure 2.7.

While the concept of developmental appropriateness eventually leads to some specific curriculum, planning, and instructional actions, the concept serves to define a broad set of values and practices that should guide physical education teaching at all times so that students can pursue learning in environments that are physically, emotionally, and educationally beneficial to them. It is the teacher's responsibility to establish and maintain that appropriateness at all times.

Learning Domains and Objectives

Learning theorists recognize three major types of human learning that can be used to categorize the primary outcomes of instruction. Each one is referred to as a domain, or a "territory," and includes specific kinds of learning that students will acquire within it. The three traditional domains are cognitive, psychomotor, and affective.

Program Component	Appropriate Practice	Inappropriate Practice
Curriculum	The physical education curriculum has an obvious scope and sequence based on goals and objectives that are appropriate for all children. It includes a balance of skills, concepts, games, education, and gymnastics.	The physical education curriculum lacks developed goals and objectives and is based primarily on the teacher's interests, preferences, and background rather than those of the children. For example, the curriculum consists primarily of large-group games.
Development of movement concepts and motor skills	Children are provided with frequent and meaningful age-appropriate practice opportunities that enable individuals to develop a functional understanding of movement concepts (body awareness, space awareness, effort, and relationships) and build competence and confidence in their ability to perform a variety of motor skills (locomotor, nonlocomotor, and manipulative).	Children participate in a limited number of games and activities where the opportunity for individuals to develop basic concepts and motor skills is restricted.
Concepts of fitness	Children participate in activities that are designed to help them understand and value the important concepts of physical fitness and the contribution they make to a healthy lifestyle.	Children are required to participate in fitness activities, but are not helped to understand the reasons why.
Assessment	Teacher decisions are based primarily on ongoing individual assessments of children as they participate in physical education class activities (formative evaluation), and not on the basis of a single test score (summative evaluation). Assessment of children's physical progress and achievement is used to individualize instruction, plan yearly curriculum and weekly lessons, identify children with special needs, communicate with parents, and evaluate the program's effectiveness.	Children are evaluated on the basis of fitness test scores or on a single physical skill test. For example, children receive a grade in physical education based on their scores on a standardized fitness test or on the number of times they can continuously jump rope.
Regular involvement for every child	Children participate in their regularly scheduled physical education class because it is recognized as an important part of their overall education.	Children are removed from physical education to participate in classroom activities and/or as a punishment for not completing assignments or for misbehavior in the classroom.

(continued)

FIGURE 2.7 Continued

Program Component	Appropriate Practice	Inappropriate Practice
Active participation for every child	All children are involved in activities that allow them to remain continuously active. Classes are designed to meet a child's need for active participation in all learning experiences.	Activity time is limited because children are waiting in lines for a turn in relay races, to be chosen for a team, or because of limited equipment. Children are organized into large groups where getting a turn is based on individual competitiveness or aggressive behavior. Children are eliminated with no chance to return to the activity, or they must sit out for long periods of time.
Games	Games are selected, designed, sequenced, and modified by teachers and/or children to maximize the learning and enjoyment of children.	Games are taught with no obvious purpose or goal other than to keep children "busy, happy, and good."
Gender-directed activities	Girls and boys have equal access to individual, partner, small group, and team activities. Both girls and boys are equally encouraged, supported, and socialized toward successful achievement in all realms of physical activity.	Girls are encouraged to participate in activities that stress traditional feminine roles, whereas boys are encouraged to participate in more aggressive activities. Boys are more often provided with leadership roles in physical education classes. Statements by physical education teachers reinforce traditional socialization patterns that provide for greater and more aggressive participation by boys and lesser and more passive participation by girls.
Success rate	Children are given the opportunity to practice skills at high rates of success adjusted for their individual skill levels.	Children are asked to perform activities that are too easy or too hard, causing frustration, boredom, and/or misbehavior. All children are expected to perform to the same standards with no allowance for individual abilities and interests.
Equipment	Enough equipment is available so that each child benefits from maximum participation. For example, every child in a class would have a ball. Equipment is matched to the size, confidence, and skill level of the children so that they are motivated to actively participate in physical education class.	An insufficient amount of equipment is available for the number of children in a class. Regulation or "adult size" equipment is used, which may inhibit skill development, or injure and/or intimidate the children.

Cognitive Domain.   The cognitive domain focuses on learning that includes logic, concepts, facts, and recall from memory. It is intellectual learning. Bloom et al.'s (1956) *Taxonomy of Educational Objectives* includes a hierarchy of cognitive processes, from simple to complex:

1. Knowledge

   The ability to recall previously learned information
   Examples:
   Student can identify the parts of a tennis racquet.
   Student can recall five parts of the golf swing.

2. Comprehension

   The ability to grasp the meaning of information
   Examples:
   Student can explain the importance of proper footwork.
   Student can explain how leverage is used in weight training.

3. Application

   The ability to use information in new and concrete applications; to use information in some way
   Examples:
   Student can adapt game rules to make competition more fair.
   Student can create two dances from the same musical piece.

4. Analysis

   The ability to break down material into its component parts and to understand the relationship between those parts
   Examples:
   Student can observe a peer's performance and identify errors made.
   Student can identify proper strategy for a game situation.

5. Synthesis

   The ability to put elements into a whole; can involve abstract relationships
   Examples:
   Student can recognize similarities and differences between the tennis swing and the swing used in racquetball.
   Student can plan offensive plays for flag football.

6. Evaluation

   The ability to judge the value of material with defensible opinions
   Examples:
   Student can judge a gymnastics competition.
   Student can compare two dance performances.

Psychomotor Domain.   The psychomotor domain focuses on the development of physical skills and abilities, learning that is primarily acquired and demonstrated through movement. Skills can be simple or complex and involve fine (small) or gross (large) movements. This domain also has a taxonomy to classify this type of learning

(Harlow, 1972). Some examples from each level of learning in the psychomotor domain are:

1. **Reflexive**

   Involuntary actions that occur in response to a stimulus
   Examples:
   Student can recognize and move to avoid a potentially dangerous situation.
   Student can hold himself in the proper posture.

2. **Basic fundamental**

   Innate movement patterns formed by combining reflex movements
   Examples:
   Student can run, walk, jump, hop, skip, leap, etc.

3. **Perceptual abilities**

   Actions that require the translation of stimuli through the senses and into appropriate movements
   Examples:
   Student can track a thrown ball through the air.
   Student can strike a ball with two different implements.

4. **Physical abilities**

   Combine basic movement and perceptual abilities into simple skilled movements
   Examples:
   Student can perform calisthenics.
   Student can hear and follow square dance calls to the music.

5. **Complex skills**

   Higher-order skills that require efficiency, stamina, and the combination of more than one physical ability at the same time
   Examples:
   Student can learn the skills needed to play sports.
   Student can complete a fitness "obstacle course."

6. **Nondiscursive**

   The ability to communicate through body movement; to express feelings, thoughts, and meaning through actions
   Examples:
   Student can "act like a flower in bloom on a sunny day."
   Student can create a dance that expresses happiness to the audience.

Affective Domain.   The affective domain includes the learning of feelings, attitudes, and values as they relate to movement. In a sense, it is learning about one's self as it pertains to physical activity. Learning in the affective domain is sometimes difficult to observe and measure since the outcomes of such learning are internal states known only to the individual. These states can be expressed to others, but can often be miscommunicated or misinterpreted. One way to monitor affective learning is to observe the behaviors associated with a certain affect, such as watching for instances of good sport behavior during and after a competition, or watching students pursue an activity outside of class (as an indicator that they value the activity). Krathwohl and his colleagues (1964) developed a taxonomy that can help teachers plan learning progressions in the affective domain:

1. Receiving

The ability to pay attention, to watch, and to listen so that information can be received
Examples:
Student reads a history of women in sport in the United States.
Student listens to another student's description of her favorite dance.

2. Responding

The ability to discuss, debate, or agree/disagree to things that are heard or seen by the learner
Examples:
Student can list five reasons why he likes physical education.
Student can discuss the pros and cons of competition in sports.

3. Valuing

The ability to determine the importance of an action or event
Examples:
Student understands why people should exercise regularly.
Student expresses the need to follow rules of fair play.

4. Organizing

The ability to place values in relation to other values, and to organize in order to make judgments and choices
Examples:
Student can state a preference for health-related fitness activities.
Student can set goals and work toward improvement on skills or performance.

5. Characterizing

The ability to internalize values and carry those values out in the student's life
Examples:
Student can follow game rules and etiquette outside of class time.
Student makes proper choices for healthy eating when less-healthy selections are available.

Domain Priorities and Domain Interactions. Learning occurs in physical education through students' direct engagement in planned instructional activities. All learning activities will emphasize outcomes in one domain over the others, determining its intended *domain priority.* That means each activity will place the highest emphasis on outcomes in one domain, and less emphasis on outcomes in one or both of the other domains. It is important to remember that a domain priority is temporary, and the emphasis can change any time the students begin a different activity or the teacher decides to change the main learning focus of the present activity.

FIGURE 2.8   Domain Priorities and Potential Domain Interactions

Learning Activity	Teacher's Domain Priorities	Domain Interactions ("→" can be interpreted as "while at or near the same time")
Learning basic dance steps	1. Cognitive 2. Psychomotor 3. Affective	(1) Thinking about the order and timing → (2) rehearsing → (3) enjoying successful practice and liking dance
Tag games	1. Psychomotor 2. Cognitive 3. Affective	(1) Running and dodging → (2) acquiring strategy and tactics to avoid being tagged → (3) learning what it feels like to be "it"
Cooperative games	1. Affective 2. Cognitive 3. Psychomotor	(1) Being part of a group; meeting the objective → (2) learning trial and error for strategies → (3) performing the physical movements needed to carry out strategy
Skill themes	1. Cognitive 2. Psychomotor 3. Affective	(1) Recognizing movement concepts and examples/nonexamples → (2) moving to demonstrate the concept → (3) discovering new ways to move and be creative
Practicing sport skills	1. Psychomotor 2. Affective 3. Cognitive	(1) Learning necessary motor performance patterns → (2) learning positive sport behaviors and attitudes → (3) understanding applications for skills in game situations

Rarely in physical education will student engagement result in learning solely in one domain. Even when an activity focuses strongly in one domain, student learning will take place in the other domains, although not as directly. Therefore, a *domain interaction* typically occurs when one domain is given the direct intent of the activity, and learning occurs in one or both of the other domains at the same time. Physical education teachers need to know how to determine domain priorities for all planned learning activities, and understand the potential for interactions as students pursue learning in the primary domain of the moment. With that knowledge, teachers can be more confident that students are learning just what is intended in each lesson segment.

Figure 2.8 shows how domain priorities set by the teacher lead to domain interactions as students are engaged in some common physical education learning activities.

Learning Objectives.   Knowing about learning domains, priorities, and interactions represents primarily declarative knowledge needed in this area of teaching. The procedural part of this knowledge is the ability to write clear learning objectives that students will pursue during instruction. Teachers who can write good objectives have an understanding of the domain priority, domain interaction, how student learning will be organized, and how long it will likely take that learning to happen. Instructional objectives should have three components: the conditions under which the learning will occur, the behavior/knowledge/affect to be learned, and the degree of mastery needed to demonstrate that learning has occurred (Mager, 1984). The specific form and content of the objective will depend on the domain and level of the intended learning outcome. The following are some examples of learning objectives written for various taxonomic levels in the cognitive, psychomotor, and affective domains.

Cognitive Domain (Application Level)
Given an explanation of a 2-3 zone defense in basketball and locating the ball at the top of the key (condition), the student will diagram (knowledge) all five players in their correct position (mastery).

Cognitive Domain (Evaluation Level)
Being shown two performances of a three-meter dive (condition), the student will determine a score for each dive (knowledge) and correctly identify (mastery) the best dive between the two.

Psychomotor Domain (Perceptual Level)
Using a single jump rope and self-turning it (condition), the student will be able to make ten repetitions (performance) without stopping (mastery).

Psychomotor Domain (Skilled Level)
Playing quarterback in a flag-football game situation (condition), the student will be able to complete downfield forward passes (performance) on 40 percent of her attempts (mastery).

Affective Domain (Valuing)
In a multimedia collage (condition), the student will express his five favorite (affect and mastery) activities in physical education class this year.

Affective Domain (Characterizing)
After eating at a local restaurant (condition), the student will make a list of foods she chose (affect) and determine how healthy (mastery) her choices were at that meal.

As you can see, objectives in the affective domain are not as straightforward and can be a bit more subjective than those in the other domains—again due to the difficulty in actually observing and monitoring the internal learning that occurs in this domain. That is not to say teachers should stay away from objectives in this domain, but it does mean teachers will have to understand those differences and the unique phrasing needed to write and assess objectives in this domain.

Physical Education Content

Physical education teachers need strong knowledge of the content they will teach in their program. Content refers to the sports, games, dances, skill themes, fitness, and concepts students will learn in physical education. It is the subject matter—what will be taught and learned. There has been some debate over just what content knowledge means for physical education. Is it the teacher's knowledge about a movement or skill—the ability to observe it and evaluate it against some expected standard? Or is it the teacher's own ability to perform a movement or skill with proficiency? Or is it some combination of both? Regardless of how it is defined, no one will disagree that a teacher can never have too much of it! This essential knowledge can be acquired in several ways: through one's own performance experiences, by observing others perform, by reading books or viewing other resource materials, by attending clinics, through conversations with teachers and other experts, and by actually teaching the content to learners.

Good knowledge of content allows a teacher to be more organized for instruction, to better articulate learning objectives, provide safer environments, develop better learning progressions, and have increased discrimination when observing and analyzing learners' movement patterns and skills in class. In short, it promotes more effective instruction and higher levels of teacher confidence when planning and implementing instruction for physical education. When combined with knowledge about context and learners, it is then called *pedagogical content knowledge* (PCK) and indicates that the teacher "knows his stuff" and also how to teach it to students in his own school program (Shulman, 1987). According to Grossman (Griffin, Dodds, & Rovegno, 1996), teachers develop PCK by combining four related types of knowledge and abilities:

1. They keep both broad and narrow goals clearly in mind
2. They understand readily what various students already know and can do
3. They are highly knowledgeable about curriculum content
4. They vary instructional strategies (p. 58)

Movement Skill Classifications.   Physical education teachers can plan for a variety of movement skills in their lessons. Each type of skill calls for different task presentations, learning cues, student engagement patterns, and observation during practice. The expert teacher will know how to classify movement skills in order to better prepare learning activities under each one.

> *Nonlocomotor skills* are those that do not involve traveling through space or the use of an object or implement. They are executed in a standing, sitting, or other stationary position. Some examples include static balancing, bending, stretching, twisting, and turning.

> *Locomotor skills* involve bodily movement through space, without using an object or implement. Walking, jogging, hopping, skipping, and dodging are common types of locomotor skills.

> *Object manipulation skills* are those used to control a piece of equipment that is not held in the hand or somehow fastened to the body. Common objects in physical education are balls, hoola hoops, batons, Frisbees, and shuttlecocks. The object is typically controlled (thrown, tossed, kicked, caught, or dribbled) with the hands or feet.

> *Implement manipulation skills* are those that involve a piece of equipment usually held in one or both hands, most of the time for the purpose of controlling an object. The implement is used as a "tool" in this sense. Common implements in physical education are bats, rackets, gloves, and clubs. They can be used to control an object in many ways, such as striking, batting, bouncing, dribbling, and catching/stopping. Because many implement manipulation skills call for the ability to control both the

implement and an object at the same time, they require well developed hand-eye coordination and visual tracking abilities.

Strategic movement and skills can be any of the previous movement types as they are applied in dynamic situations—typically games. It is a combination of movement skill and situational decision making to produce a certain outcome such as playing defense in team handball, stealing a base in baseball, running pass patterns in football, or being creative to solve a group initiative.

Skill themes combine basic motor skills with movement concepts to develop progressively more complex patterns of movement (Gallahue, 1996; Graham, Holt/Hale, & Parker, 1998). A basic motor skill could be any nonlocomotor, locomotor, object manipulation, and implement manipulation skill in the previous four categories. The movement concept delineates requirements for space awareness (where the body moves), effort (how the body moves), and relationships (between body parts, other people, implements, and objects). This conceptualization of learning forms the basis of an entire curriculum and approach to teaching typically intended for elementary physical education (Graham, Holt/Hale, & Parker, 1998).

Expressive and interpretive movements are not viewed as skills to be executed with proficiency or used to produce an outcome. Sometimes a movement is made to express feelings, concepts, ideas, and themes. Many styles of dance are based on expressive movements such as ballet, modern, and jazz. They are often done with musical accompaniment. The teaching of expressive movement requires specific expertise by the teacher, and the knowledge of the "language of the body" that translates movements into meaning for the mover and the audience.

Movement Patterns and Skills Analysis.   Regardless of which type of movement is being taught, it is essential that the teacher has the ability to critically observe and analyze the movement patterns and skills performed by students in class. That ability is based on knowledge of the movement (what it should look like), the teacher's own performance experience, knowledge of students' developmental level, and observational skills to recognize key elements in the performance. *Key elements* are those parts of the movement or skill needed for proficiency. Knowing the key elements for a movement skill allows the teacher to focus on specific parts of the performance rather than the entire performance. The key elements can then be used as the basis of congruent, specific feedback provided to the learner.

Coker (1998) suggests five strategies for improving a physical education teacher's skill analysis effectiveness:

1. Determine the focus of observation (What is being watched for?)
2. Determine the best viewing perspective
3. Watch several skill performances to determine a pattern
4. Avoid being distracted
5. Use a video camera if it is practical

Part of the teacher's expertise in the observation and analysis in physical education is based on the knowledge of students' developmental stages relative to the movement or skill being learned. Young learners should not be expected to execute movements and skills with the same level of maturity as older and adult learners. There are acceptable versions of performance at each stage of development, from which the teacher should base his analysis of the key elements. Gallahue (1996) describes four phases of motor development that contain ten differentiated stages within them. Refer to Figure 2.4 on page 28. Teachers need to know the key performance elements for any skill or movement at each stage so they can analyze the observed performance within this developmental scheme. This helps the teacher to make better analyses of performance and provide usable feedback to learners.

Task Analysis and Content Progression

A task analysis is conducted to identify the components of a skill to be learned and to determine the order in which students will learn each component. The ability to do a good task analysis is strongly based on one's content knowledge and organizational skills. It is accomplished in several steps. Let's use tennis as an illustration of this process (see Figure 2.9). The first step is to identify the final learning outcome in the learning sequence. This is referred to as the Level 1 task or Terminal Objective (TO) (Mager, 1984). For tennis that might be stated generally as "the ability to play a singles' match at a beginner's skill level."

The next step involves listing all of the skills and knowledge needed to perform the Level 1 task. In this case, the list will be serving, forehand drive, backhand drive, returning serves, and singles' strategy and rules (including scoring). These are the Level 2 tasks and are placed on the flow chart under the Level 1 task. There is usually a hierarchy in the order which students learn Level 2 tasks because some tasks are prerequisite to others at that same level. In this chart, students will progress through the tasks in a sequence going from left to right in Level 2.

Level 3 consists of the component skills and knowledge needed to perform each of the Level 2 tasks, placed in ascending order of progression (the ones lower on each list are learned first by students). Students begin by learning the tasks lowest on each list, progressing to higher tasks once those are mastered.

The task analysis begins the process of deciding what content will be included in the unit because it reveals just how much content can be learned with the amount of instructional time and other resources available to the teacher. It is very common for the task analysis to result in the teacher deciding to cover less content in the unit than originally thought.

Content Progression.   A task analysis will provide a clear plan for the learning that must occur in the unit and the order in which students will learn content. However, it does not explain which types of learning activities students will engage in and how students will progress from one activity to the next in each lesson. That process is called *content development,* which includes the planned progression of learning activities that allows students to acquire the content listed in the task analysis. Rink (1998) uses a scheme for content development in physical education with five types of learning tasks: informing, refining, extending, applying, and repeating. The following list

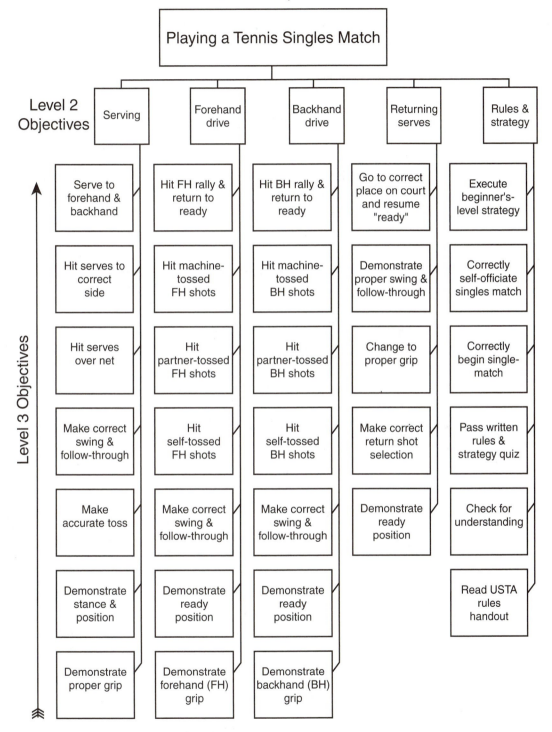

Level 1 Objective

Playing a Tennis Singles Match

Level 2 Objectives

| Serving | Forehand drive | Backhand drive | Returning serves | Rules & strategy |

Level 3 Objectives

Serve to forehand & backhand	Hit FH rally & return to ready	Hit BH rally & return to ready	Go to correct place on court and resume "ready"	Execute beginner's-level strategy
Hit serves to correct side	Hit machine-tossed FH shots	Hit machine-tossed BH shots	Demonstrate proper swing & follow-through	Correctly self-officiate singles match
Hit serves over net	Hit partner-tossed FH shots	Hit partner-tossed BH shots	Change to proper grip	Correctly begin single-match
Make correct swing & follow-through	Hit self-tossed FH shots	Hit self-tossed BH shots	Make correct return shot selection	Pass written rules & strategy quiz
Make accurate toss	Make correct swing & follow-through	Make correct swing & follow-through	Demonstrate ready position	Check for understanding
Demonstrate stance & position	Demonstrate ready position	Demonstrate ready position		Read USTA rules handout
Demonstrate proper grip	Demonstrate forehand (FH) grip	Demonstrate backhand (BH) grip		

FIGURE 2.9   **Three Levels of Task Analysis for Learning Tennis Singles**

includes an explanation of each category and a sample content development progression for dribbling in a sixth-grade soccer lesson.

1. Informing   The initial task in a new skill progression
Example:
Students are presented with a demonstration, then dribble a ball in general space for five minutes.

2. Refining   A task that promotes improved quality of performance
Example:
The teacher shows students three key elements for better control of the ball and students practice in general space for ten minutes to perform those elements.

3. Extending   A task that is slightly more complex or difficult than the preceding (similar) task
Example:
Students do a slalom dribbling drill for five minutes. The drill calls for them to dribble their ball through a course of eight cones placed on the floor.

4. Application   A task to be performed to a stated performance criterion, or performed against an opponent or standard
Example:
Students are timed as they dribble through the same slalom course. They are prompted to try to beat their "personal best" on each subsequent trial.

5. Repeating   Any previous task that is repeated for review or increased proficiency
Example:
Students' control has been reduced as they increase speed in the application task, so the teacher directs them to go back and practice the extension task for five more minutes.

Some of the models in this book will have specific content development plans designed within them. When that is not the case, the teacher will need to prepare a content development progression as part of the unit plan. Teacher knowledge in content development is needed for two important reasons. First, it helps the teacher to plan good sequences of learning tasks that allow students to progress at a more even rate while building on previous performances. Second, it can help the teacher make well-timed decisions about when to move from one task to the next in class.

Time-Based or Mastery-Based Task Progression.   Content progression decisions can be made in two ways. They can occur according to a time allocation "budget," or when students have demonstrated mastery on the current learning task. In a *time-based progression* the teacher estimates how much time it should take the majority of students to learn each task, and then goes to the next task after that amount of practice time has elapsed. Task allocations can change when estimates are not accurate (students need less or more time to practice), but the teacher's schedule generally guides the progression. In *mastery-based progressions,* the teacher determines a performance criterion for the current task, a group acceptance rate, and then moves to the next task when both have been satisfied. For example:

> When 75 percent (acceptance rate) of my fifth graders can make ten jumps in a row (performance criterion), we will move to the next task.
>
> When every student (acceptance rate) can pass (performance criterion) the written rules test, we can begin the tournament.

Time-based progressions allow the teacher to make long-range plans in a unit, but at the risk of knowing that some students will not be ready for a new task when it begins. And, those same students are very likely to fall further behind as more progressions occur. Mastery-based progression ensures that most or all of the students can perform the current task before they move to the next one, but using even simple performance criteria and a relatively low acceptance rate can cause some learning tasks to take a long time to complete. The teacher needs to give careful thought as to how his students will progress through learning tasks, while keeping the advantages and disadvantages of each way in mind.

Assessment

One of the most important functions of teaching is to determine how much student learning occurred relative to the intended outcomes of the instruction. This process is called assessment and can be conducted for three primary purposes:

1. To describe how much learning has taken place over a given amount of instructional time
2. To judge or evaluate the quality of that learning (usually for grading)
3. To make decisions about how to improve learning based on that gathered information

Formative assessments are conducted during the unit of instruction. They provide the teacher with "mid-stream" feedback on student learning so that needed modifications can be made while the unit is ongoing. *Summative* assessments are conducted at the end of the unit and allow the teacher to determine how much learning occurred across the entire time of instruction. Formative and summative assessments provide a teacher with important information, so it is advantageous to plan for both in a unit. Following are a few examples of each.

Formative	Summative
Short weekly quizzes	Written final exam
Self-check performance tasks each day	Skills test at the end of the unit
Checking for understanding after task presentation	Final written or skills test
Weekly log of fitness activity	Once-a-year fitness testing

Assessment techniques can be either norm-based or criterion-based. *Norm-based assessments* require the collection of a large number of scores on standardized tests, such as fitness tests. Scores are then compiled into subgroups according to some common factors of those who have taken the test, usually age and gender (e.g., ten-year-old boys, fourteen-year-old girls). The large number of scores for each group will generate a *normal distribution* of scores that allows any one student's score to be compared to other students of the same age and gender. Raw scores can be determined and reported, but normed test scores are usually reported as a percentage of students who scored above and below each individual student. For example, being in the 85th percentile of ten-year-old boys means that 84 percent of all other similar test-takers scored lower and 15 percent of all other similar test takers scored higher.

Criterion-based assessments are those in which the performance standards are determined by the person who uses the assessment technique, and reflect one's professional judgment about the quality of each score. A teacher who sets the passing grade for a written test on volleyball rules at 75 percent or determines that students must score 45 out of 50 possible points to get an A on a tennis skills test is using criterion-based assessment.

Traditional Assessments in Physical Education.   There are many techniques for assessing learning in physical education, regardless of whether they are designed to be formative or summative, norm-based or criterion-based. They can be divided into two broad categories: traditional and alternative. Traditional assessments have been in our field for many years, as their label indicates. Alternative assessments have been recently developed to provide information about learning that is quite different from traditional techniques. It is important to keep in mind that neither type of assessment is inherently better than the other—they simply produce different kinds of information about learning. It is up to the teacher to decide the best type of assessment to use in each situation.

Traditional assessments in physical education follow three primary principles derived from the subdiscipline of measurement and evaluation (Wood, 1996).

1. Establish (and formally state) appropriate instructional objectives
2. Use appropriate (validated and reliable) tests to measure characteristics related to the instructional objectives
3. Develop an evaluation (grading) scheme that reflects attainment of instructional objectives (pp. 202–203)

This process is characterized by a decidedly formal approach that looks much like the way data are collected and analyzed for research purposes. It typically involves rigorous standards in all parts of the process to ensure that the data are valid and reliable. As the following will discuss, that rigor can make for a double-edged sword for teachers who wish to use these traditional assessments. Some of the most common forms of traditional assessment used in physical education are:

1. *Informal teacher observation.* The most commonly used type of assessment in physical education is probably the teacher's observation of students as they practice skills, play games, and answer questions in class. This is not truly assessment, but it does provide the teacher with some level of confidence that learning has occurred.

2. *Standardized skills tests.* Many sports in the physical education curriculum have standardized skills tests that assess student performance abilities (Strand & Wilson, 1993). Most of these involve static tests that measure a limited range of skills needed to play each sport. A static test is one that uses a mostly artificial display of skills that test the student's ability to perform in nongame situations. The front wall volley tests in racquetball (Hensley, East, & Stillwell, 1979) and any test that calls for the student to hit a ball into a fixed target (such as tennis serving accuracy tests) are static.

3. *Fitness tests.* Our field has a long history of testing children and youth on several parameters of physical fitness. Over the years, we have developed many valid and reliable standardized test batteries used in school programs. The most prominent tests used today are the Prudential Fitnessgram protocol developed at The Cooper Institute for Aerobic Research (1994) and the President's Council on Physical Fitness and Sports (1985). With proper administration, these tests can provide students with results that help them determine their level of fitness relative to other students of the same gender and age (Safrit, 1995).

4. *Written tests.* Many teachers use written tests to assess students' cognitive knowledge in physical education. Nearly all of these tests are developed by individual teachers who use them in their own program; we do not have standardized written tests in physical education like those developed nationally for subjects like math, science, and reading. Written tests can use questions and problems in several formats: multiple choice, short answer, fill-in-the-blank, matching, diagraming, and open-ended.

5. *Psychometric scales and inventories.* While not valid for grading purposes, psychometric scales and inventories can be used to measure student learning in the affective domain. A scale or inventory is a paper-and-pencil measure of student personality, values, preferences, and other characteristics that can be used to detect changes over time.

Within certain limits, skills tests, fitness tests, written tests, and psychometric instruments can provide valid and reliable information on which to base assessment. They measure learning in ways that are sufficiently objective, use valid measuring techniques and instruments, and can be carried out with strong consistency. Standardized skill and fitness tests have met rigorous standards in their development and have been field tested on many subjects who are similar in age, gender, and ability to those for whom the test is designed.

Skills tests, fitness tests, and most psychometric instruments are normative, meaning that they have been used to measure many people in different age, gender, and ability groups—providing a large data base on each test from those who have taken it. Having that data base allows a teacher to compare her students' results with those from similar test takers in other schools, states, and regions.

Traditional assessments also have the advantage of including content, procedures, and scoring developed by trained experts so the teacher does not have to take the time to design, validate, field test, and determine how to score the assessment. Many such tests today include software and data-entry procedures that simplify the tasks of scoring and reporting results to students. In addition, these types of assessments usually produce large amounts of numeric data that can undergo statistical treatment to generate many kinds of informative analyses, ranging from simple measures of central tendency to sophisticated tests of learning effects.

On the other hand, traditional assessments have some distinct disadvantages, which has resulted in their limited use in P–12 physical education programs. Some of the issues focus on the true validity of test design relative to typical outcomes in physical education. For instance, does the serving accuracy test for tennis (AAHPERD, 1989) measure one's ability to play the game (a typical program outcome) or one's proficiency in a limited, controlled, and static aspect of tennis skill performance? Are health-related fitness tests good predictors of one's risks in later years, or one-time "snapshots" of a child's present condition with little relationship to the future? Most likely, the second answer is correct in both examples.

For a large number of teachers, the disadvantages of traditional assessments center around problems of practicality when they are used in large classes and with limited class time (Wood, 1996). The rigor with which most standardized tests generate data comes with a price; many of them must be administered by the teacher to individual students, taking an inordinate amount of time away from learning itself. That forces the teacher into a real trade-off: taking the extra time needed to conduct the assessment away from instructional time might result in lower performance scores on the assessment. Because of the time and effort needed to complete them, traditional assessments are often limited in the types of information they provide for the teacher and students; they tend to focus on a small portion of the intended learning outcomes, leaving many unanswered questions about student achievement.

The final disadvantage with traditional assessments is that they tend to focus on identifying discrepancies between what was learned and what should have been learned, with little consideration given to informing teachers and students how to improve knowledge, performance, or fitness levels. A written test results in a score, or a percentage of items answered correctly. It does not help students improve their knowledge. Fitness tests and skills tests give students normative results, letting them know how they compare to others of the same age and gender, but there is nothing inherent in those tests that allows a student to learn how to improve personal fitness levels for the next time the test is taken or how to increase activity levels in daily life.

Alternative Assessments in Physical Education.   There has been much reform in educational assessment in recent years. Some of that reform has been driven by people who outweigh the disadvantages of traditional assessment over the advantages. A second factor has been the expansion in the scope and variety of new learning outcomes in physical education that cannot be assessed with traditional techniques (Wood, 1996). This growing movement is called *alternative assessment,* to indicate that it was developed, in large part, as a direct contrast to traditional assessment in education and physical education. In the most simplistic sense, it means "something other" than the traditional assessments just discussed. However, it really is much more than just an opposition movement. Proponents of alternative assessment techniques are quick to point out that these techniques have a sound theoretical foundation and sufficiently rigorous procedures. They represent logical ways to assess students on the diverse types of learning pursued in many contemporary physical education programs such as those included in the NASPE (1995) physical education standards discussed in Chapter 1.

Alternative assessments are based on four principles:

1. Knowledge can be demonstrated in a variety of ways, all of which are valid indicators of student learning.
2. The process of learning can be as important to assess as the outcomes.
3. Diverse types of learning goals require diverse types of assessment.
4. Higher-order learning, particularly in the cognitive domain, requires inventive assessment that is not possible with traditional techniques.

Many kinds of alternative assessments have been developed for physical education. Because these assessments are designed by teachers, and not test-making experts, they are "home made" and customized to allow each teacher/designer to assess learning outcomes specific to their own instruction. Some common types of alternative assessment used in physical education are:

1. Group projects
2. Multimedia presentations
3. Activity logs
4. Personal journals
5. Role playing
6. Oral examinations
7. "Show-and-tell" collages
8. Interviews (of students and by students)
9. Teacher, peer, and self-observations with performance checklists
10. Portfolios

The last type, portfolios, are used to allow a student to collect and organize various artifacts (photographs, videotapes, drawings, newspaper articles, etc.) that demonstrate the student's knowledge of a certain topic or concept. The process of learning to identify an organizing theme for the portfolio and gathering artifacts is just as important as the final contents of the portfolio itself.

The cornerstone of alternative assessments are scoring *rubrics,* used to determine the quality of the learning demonstrated by students. Rubrics are used to inform students of the performance criteria on the assessment which become the basis of the teacher's review of the completed work. The rubric translates the quality of the demonstrated learning into a descriptor (e.g., novice, intermediate, advanced, or incomplete, almost complete, complete) or a numeric/value rating (e.g., 1/poor, 2/fair, 3/good, 4/excellent) based on criteria stated in advance.

Goodrich (1996–97) includes seven steps in the process of creating good rubrics:

1. **Look at models.** Show students examples of good and not-so-good work from previous assessments.
2. **List and discuss criteria.** Use the models to help students make a list of what counts as quality work.
3. **Articulate gradations of quality.** Present and discuss what separates each level of quality from the others.
4. **Practice on models.** Have the students use the rubric on the models.
5. **Use self- and peer-assessments.** Allow for periodic assessments as the task is being completed. Provide students with formative feedback.
6. **Revise.** Allow students time to make revisions based on the feedback given in step 5.
7. **Use teacher assessment.** Apply the rubric in the same way students have learned it.

Here are three examples of alternative assessment tasks in physical education and the scoring rubric for each.

Grade level:	3–4 (At the end of a four-week newcomb unit)
Knowledge assessed:	Newcomb rules
Assessment task:	Three teams are made at each court. Two teams will play, while the third team on the sideline will watch the action and record the results and score after each volley. Teams rotate after every ten volleys, regardless of the score. *The teacher also keeps a score sheet for assessing students' answers when the teams change (this constitutes the rubric for assessing students' accuracy).*

	Side out by team A or B?	Type of side out?	What is the score now?	Does anyone rotate?
Volley #1				
Volley #2				
Volley #3				
Volley #4				
Volley #5				
Volley #6				
Volley #7				
Volley #8				
Volley #9				
Volley #10				

Type of side out
1. Foot fault
2. Net serve
3. Out of bounds
4. Ball touched too many players' hands
5. Did not return the ball back over the net

Does anyone rotate?
Y = YES
N = NO

Developed by Donna Wright, Physical Education Teacher at Hickory Flat Elementary School, McDonough, GA. Used with permission.

Grade level: Middle school
Knowledge assessed: The Olympic Spirit
Assessment task: Following a unit on summer Olympic sports, make a collage that shows ath-
                          letes competing and displaying the "Olympic spirit."
Time allowed: Out of class, due in one week

Scoring rubric:

Medal level	Assessment criteria
Gold medal	1. Your collage uses three or more types of media 2. Your collage shows at least five different sports 3. Your collage shows many types of sports, athletes, and many countries 4. Your collage shows athletes displaying the Olympic spirit in many ways
Silver medal	1. Your collage uses two types of media 2. Your collage shows three or four different sports 3. Your collage shows a few types of sports, athletes, and countries 4. Your collage shows just a few examples of the Olympic spirit
Bronze medal	1. One type of media is used 2. One or two sports are displayed 3. Only competition is shown
Future Olympian	1. Collage includes non-Olympic examples 2. Collage does not fill up the poster you selected 3. Incorrect examples of the Olympic spirit are included

Grade level: High school
Knowledge assessed: Ability to analyze key elements of the golf swing
Assessment task: Choose a partner. One partner will take ten swings with a driver while the
                                other partner observes each trial. The observer will evaluate each key ele-
                                ment on the checklist to reflect how well his/her partner performed that
                                component each time. The observer's checks will be compared to those
                                made by the teacher, who will also watch the practicing student. Switch roles
                                after every ten tries.

Key element	1	2	3	4	5	6	7	8	9	10
1. Stance and alignment										
2. Grip										
3. Backswing										
4. Point of contact										
5. Follow-through										

After each shot, score: 1 if element was fully correct
                                2 if element was almost fully correct
                                3 if element was incorrect

Scoring rubric for the observer (1 point for each analysis that matches the teacher's—
possible 50 points)

          45–50   Teaching professional
          40–44   "Scratch" player
          35–39   Low handicapper
          25–34   High handicapper
          24 or lower   Novice

As with traditional techniques, alternative assessments have advantages and disadvantages that teachers need to know. Perhaps the greatest advantage of alternative assessments is their ability to be designed to monitor the specific learning outcomes planned by
the teacher. The teacher can be confident that the assessment targets what he really wants
his students to learn. Alternative assessments also allow students to demonstrate their
learning in a variety of ways—not just the recall of information or skill performance on
standardized tests. Because we know that students have different styles of learning and
engage in diverse kinds of learning activities, it makes sense that they should be able to
demonstrate their knowledge in a way that matches how they actually learned it.

By using a scoring rubric, students know the performance standards of the assessment task ahead of time. They are then able to make choices and devise strategies for the

process of completing the assessment as well as the final demonstration of their knowledge. In other words, it fosters the ability to *learn how to learn.*

A rubric provides another advantage for this kind of assessment. It is a common set of standards used by the teacher for making evaluations of students' work. It lends a suffi-cient degree of objectivity to the review process and makes for more consistent evaluations within and across classes. Finally, alternative assessment, particularly through the rubric, provides students with feedback about their learning and identifies ways for them to improve performance.

While providing unique, creative, and diverse ways to assess student learning in phys-ical education, alternative assessments are not without their disadvantages. Because they are customized, it takes time for a teacher to design each one used in her class. The resources mentioned earlier can give a teacher some ideas for assessment, but unless those examples are perfect matches, they will need to be adapted or completely redesigned for use by other teachers. This design effort can also include some trial-and-error time needed to get the assessment "just right" for its intended use.

Alternative assessments typically take longer for students to prepare and the teacher to review. Many of these assessment tasks require extended time for students to make process plans, conceptualize answers, organize materials, and develop the final product. While all of these are part of the learning process itself, they do take time to accomplish. Similarly, it will take the teacher some time to review each completed assessment—usually more time than needed to score written tests and skills tests.

Authentic Assessment for Physical Education. Authentic assessment, sometimes called performance assessment, refers to the practice of making assessments in ways that involve, or simulate, the real-life settings in which student knowledge learned in school will be applied (McTighe, 1996–97). Some examples follow for clarification. Health-related fit-ness tests (e.g., Fitnessgram, President's Council) measure student abilities on several parameters that are *indicators* of present fitness levels. They do not assess health-related *behaviors and choices* made in other parts of the school day, after school, and at home that more accurately determine patterns of healthy living. If a stated goal of the physical educa-tion program is to promote active and healthy lifestyles, then an authentic assessment of that learning would be made at those times and places students make health-related choices and practice health-related behaviors. Student journals that include the foods they eat and the moderate-to-vigorous activity they engage in would be an appropriate authen-tic assessment.

If the goal is to have students learn how to play the game of softball, then an authen-tic assessment would take place during an actual game, not with a standardized skills test in a nongame context. In this case an authentic assessment could be based on students' game statistics, or a performance checklist completed as the game is played. The Game Per-formance Assessment Instrument (GPAI) developed by Griffin, Mitchell, and Oslin (1997) does this by analyzing players' performance in several categories of involvement, skill, strat-egy, and decision making during game play.

It should be emphasized that authenticity is determined by the *degree* to which the assessment calls for students to demonstrate learning in a way that approaches real-life applications of the knowledge. Rarely is any assessment technique totally nonauthentic or entirely authentic.

Physical education teachers need to know that all assessments, traditional or alternative, and at whatever degree of authenticity, are essentially tools used to understand what students have learned through instruction in a content unit or program. The key is to know what each assessment tool can do and when it is appropriate to use it. Teachers should not start by saying, "I am going to use an alternative, authentic assessment in this upcoming dance unit." Rather, it should be a deductive process that starts with "What and how will students learn in this unit?", which leads to "How do I want them to demonstrate that new knowledge for me?", and then, "Which assessment technique will provide the best demonstration (of learning)?" From this, the teacher will select the "right (assessment) tool for the right (assessment) job."

The Social/Emotional Climate

Every physical education class is a small community with its own social and emotional climate that determines *what it feels like* to students when they are with the teacher and their classmates. A positive climate is one in which every student feels like a valuable part of the larger group and can pursue learning in a comfortable, supportive, and nurturing environment. A negative climate is just the opposite. Students feel isolated and ignored, and their efforts to learn are hindered by unsafe and harmful conditions caused by the teacher and/or other students. Even when the climate in physical education is more negative than positive, teachers are quite able to change the climate so that it is positive for all students all of the time. There can be many ways to promote a positive climate in physical education. The following are some suggestions.

1. Establish firm and consistent expectations for student behaviors, and communicate those expectations often
2. Do not pay attention only to inappropriate behavior; be sure to acknowledge and reward appropriate behavior when it occurs
3. Include students in decisions about class management
4. Acknowledge students' effort, not just performance
5. Avoid being overly emotional
6. Do not use derogatory, stereotyping language
7. Avoid sarcasm
8. Design learning tasks that are developmentally appropriate in all domains
9. Make all learning tasks inclusive for all students
10. Do not use physical activity as punishment (e.g., running laps for being tardy)
11. Interact with students often to let them know you are paying attention to their efforts to learn

An overly negative climate can lead to student dislike and avoidance of physical education and eventually of physical activity itself. It can also lead to a dysfunctional cycle of events that makes the teacher's day stressful and emotionally draining. Students' reaction to a negative climate can lead directly to misbehavior and confrontations with the teacher, who then feels that he must respond with harsh words and strong actions, which then deepens the negative climate, stimulating even more misbehavior and confrontation. As you might expect, students leave class with negative feelings toward physical education and the teacher, while the teacher has negative affect toward students and little personal enjoyment to take from his day in school.

Teachers need to be aware of the concept of classroom climate and to know how to monitor it in their classes. They also need to be aware of when changes occur in the climate and whether that change is positive or negative. They need to know how to establish a positive climate with some of the previous suggestions, and how to turn a negative climate into a positive one. The nice thing about classroom climate, unlike the climate outside, is that a teacher can establish the kind of atmosphere she wishes to have in her gymnasium and change it when it is not beneficial for student learning and enjoyment of physical education.

Equity in the Gym

In recent years there has been much attention given to issues of student equity in education, and in physical education. *Equity* refers to fair and equal access to social, developmental, and educational opportunities in schools and individual classes—regardless of a student's gender, race, ethnicity, abilities, socio-economic status, and family/home background. That is not to say that all students will always get the same instruction or that they can all achieve to the same level; it refers to the identification and elimination of factors that inhibit students' access to opportunities to learn to their fullest potential for no other reason than who they are. Inequity in the classroom can promote bias, prejudice, and stereotyping by making false assumptions about certain students and then basing instructional practice on those assumptions.

Critical pedagogy is the study of fairness and justice in educational settings. It is based on the principle that schools and classrooms represent micropolitical contexts with definite and disproportionate distributions of power, status, and opportunity to learn. Sometimes that unfairness comes from a teacher's ignorance of inequitable practice, a lack of intent, submission to social norms and stereotyping, or a lack of experience. In the extreme, it comes from intentional bias and prejudice toward certain types of students. Whether intended or not, it leads to the establishment of curriculums, instruction, language, and interactions that favor some students while depriving other students of an equal opportunity to gain from the educational experience.

Our government and the educational system have tried, in part, to legislate equitable practice in schools and in physical education. Title IX of the Educational Amendments of 1972 specifically prohibits the segregation of boys and girls in sports and physical education. By implication, it also prohibits many covert practices that made for "separate but unequal" school physical education programs and instruction. The Education for All Handicapped Children Act of 1975 (Public Law 94-142) stipulated that students with disabilities receive a free and appropriate education in the least restrictive environment (LRE). In other words, whenever it suits the educational needs of a student, he should pursue learning in the regular classroom and gymnasium. Many students who were previously scheduled into segregated special education classes now take physical education with nondisabled students, with the full expectation that their individual needs will be addressed in that setting. That practice was originally called mainstreaming: thus, P.L. 94-142 was often referred to as the "Mainstreaming Law." Today it is called *inclusion* to indicate that students with many different educational needs are now included in the same class on a regular basis. Students with severe disabilities are scheduled into adaptive physical education classes, but most students with special needs are included in physical education classes with their peers. The current legislation in this area is the 1997 Individuals with Disabilities Education Act (IDEA).

Title IX, P.L. 94-142, and IDEA have led to major strides in the establishment of equitable learning environments, but they have not come close to eliminating inequities in the gymnasium. Other sources of inequity exist along with those stemming from students' disabilities and gender, such as students' race, ethnicity, religion, culture, sexual preference, and motor ability. Napper-Owen (1994) mentions six ways in which inequities can occur in physical education:

1. Organizational patterns that favor higher-skilled students (e.g., picking teams with "captains")
2. Gender-separated grouping for instruction (e.g., "The boys can play a game. The girls can stay on the side and practice, or whatever.")
3. Using teaching methods that don't address a variety of student learning styles
4. Using teacher-student interaction patterns that favor certain groups of students
5. Using stereotyped (e.g., "girls pushups") or biased (e.g., "You throw like a girl") language
6. Inappropriate role modeling by teachers

Teachers can become aware of their own practices and patterns in class that may lead to student perceptions that "things are not fair here" and result in imbalanced educational opportunities and reduced comfort levels for certain types of students. Once aware of these patterns, a teacher can usually make immediate changes to promote equity in the gymnasium.

Curriculum Models for Physical Education

Contemporary physical education includes many options for program design and movement activities, and a growing number of programs are now based on well-articulated themes following a particular curriculum model to promote student learning within those themes. Like the instructional models in this book, curriculum models are comprehensive and coherent plans for designing and implementing entire physical education programs in a school or district. They originate with program-level goals and objectives that lead to the selection of content units, instruction, and polices that allow students to achieve the goals of the program. Most models promote a limited number of student learning outcomes, all of which are strongly related to the model's stated purpose or theme. This reduced focus gives the program a better identity and makes planning decisions much easier.

Several good curriculum models have been developed for physical education programs at all grade levels. The models have been implemented in many school settings, giving them strong support as effective ways to conceptualize, design, and implement entire programs. The following are examples of models for elementary physical education:

1. *Movement education.* Promotes the learning of basic movement skills and movement concepts that can be used later in specialized and sport-specific situations (e.g., games, dance, fitness) (Kruger & Kruger, 1982).

2. *Skill themes.* A variation of movement education in which content is organized around basic motor skills (e.g., running, jumping, hopping) and developed through accompanying fitness, motor, cognitive, and affective strands, called skill themes (Gallahue, 1996; Graham, Holt/Hale, & Parker, 1998).

3. *Fitness concepts and education.* These models are based on the learning of developmentally appropriate content related to fitness. They typically emphasize the learning of basic fitness knowledge and concepts as the precursor to actual fitness development activities in later grades.

4. *Games-based.* This model uses games as the basic organizing structure from which to teach children the necessary components of skill, cognitive knowledge, and strategy. Games can be competitive but are usually cooperative in nature. The complexity and structure of each game will match the students' developmental abilities; low organizational, group-based, and modified games are usually planned (Werner & Almond, 1990).

The following are examples of models for secondary (middle, junior high, high school) physical education.

1. *Multiactivity.* Promotes a wide range of goals through a variety of activity content units organized in identifiable strands in the program. This is not to imply that such a program would be eclectic or lack coherency. Rather, the program would strive for a balance of outcomes across all three major learning domains and offer content units drawn from several strands, such as fitness, individual/dual sports, team sports, cooperative games, dance, and adventure activities (Siedentop, 1998).

2. *Sport education.* Structures the program into seasons, not units. Within each unit students assume and learn various roles and responsibilities associated with organized sport (e.g., coaching, playing, officiating, administration) (Siedentop, 1994).

3. *Outdoor and adventure programming.* Activities that feature safe challenge and risk are used to foster goals that promote cooperation among students, individual achievement, self-confidence, and resourcefulness. Many of the learning activities take place away from the school, in natural settings.

4. *Social responsibility.* Originally developed for inner-city, at-risk youth, this model is now used in many kinds of schools to develop positive personal and social outcomes through physical activity (Hellison, 1995). It features five levels of student goal setting and development. Each level is defined by a set of behaviors that indicate student progress and learning.

5. *Academic discipline-based.* First promoted by AAHPERD (Kneer, 1981) in its *Basic Stuff* series then updated (Carr, 1987), this model is based on the need for students to understand concepts related to human movement. The concepts are derived from the several recognized subdisciplines in our allied fields: kinesiology, biomechanics, exercise science, sport psychology, sport sociology, and the sport humanities. Many of the learning activities in this model are classroom- and laboratory-based, and do not necessarily involve student movement.

6. *Personal fitness.* Based on Florida's lead, many states and school districts are now including large components in personal fitness. This model contains a foundation of basic knowledge and concepts related to fitness, but extends that into the design and conduct of personal fitness plans for each student (Harageones, 1993).

Physical education teachers need to know the theoretical foundation and major learning goals of each model that is suited for the grade levels they teach. It is also important to understand what each model *does not* attempt to do, so that teachers and students are not misled into false expectations. Once the goals have been clearly identified, it will be easier to select content units that are most effective in fostering those goals. It will also be easier to assess those outcomes at a later time.

Developing Expert Physical Education Teachers

There is much debate over just what a physical education teacher needs to be able to know and do in order to be considered an expert professional. Even though Shulman's (1987) seven categories of the teacher knowledge base have been extremely helpful in recent discussions about what teachers need to know, it cannot be used to help us identify expert and nonexpert teachers in schools. Some of its limitations come from the realization that good teaching (and expertise) is strongly based in context and involves a complex interaction between declarative knowledge, procedural knowledge, where the teacher instructs, and who the teacher instructs. So, a teacher not only needs to have all of the types of knowledge just discussed, he also needs to know how to adapt and apply that knowledge in his specific school, program, and classes. As you will recall, that is referred to as conditional knowledge.

An interesting area of research on teaching has focused on the expertise needed to instruct effectively in physical education and other subjects (Schempp, 1997). Manross and Templeton (1997) mention six characteristics of expert physical education teachers: (1) they plan thoroughly and completely, (2) they focus on individual student performance, (3) they develop automaticity of behavior, (4) they give creative feedback, (5) they attain command of their subject matter, and (6) they use reflective practices. All parts of the knowledge base outlined in this chapter are represented in one or more of those elements and require a precise, situationally-specific combination of declarative and procedural knowledge.

Summary

This chapter outlined a proposed knowledge base for teachers who will instruct physical education from a model-based approach. It represents categories of knowledge that provide the foundation for all of the instructional models presented in this book. As you have surely noticed, this knowledge base is quite general, and most of it describes declarative knowledge for teaching. At this point, some of its components are rather abstract and without specific examples to further your understanding. But that will soon change. The next level for building instructional models is comprised of instructional strategies and other teaching practices that originate from within this knowledge base and lead directly to the development of pedagogical knowledge (Shulman, 1987). While Chapter 3 will be more specific, it too will remain somewhat general because the selection and use of each strategy will depend on which model is being used by the teacher in an instructional unit.

LEARNING ACTIVITIES

1. Reflect for a moment on how you presently teach physical education. Make a list of the ways you learned how to teach (e.g., from past teachers, from colleagues, at conferences, in your teacher education program). Cite how each source of knowledge influences the ways you now teach.

2. Cite your personal knowledge in each of the eleven areas presented in this chapter. What do you know in each area? What do you still need to learn?

3. Select a unit or lesson for any grade level and content and design an alternative assessment for one stated learning objective. Be sure to include a description of the assessment task and your scoring rubric.

4. If you will have the chance to actually teach the unit or lesson in Activity 3, implement your alternative assessment and write a brief report that explains what your students learned.

SUGGESTED READINGS

Bredekamp, S., & Copple, C. (1996–97). *Developmentally appropriate practice in early childhood programs* (rev. ed.). Washington, DC: National Association for the Education of Young Children.

Hopple, C. (1995). *Teaching for outcomes in elementary physical education: A guide for curriculum and assessment.* Champaign, IL: Human Kinetics.

National Association for Sport and Physical Education. (1992). *Developmentally appropriate physical education practices for children.* Reston, VA: NASPE Council on Physical Education for Children.

National Association for Sport and Physical Education. (1995). *Moving into the future: National standards for physical education.* St. Louis: Mosby.

National Association for Sport and Physical Education. *Looking at physical education from a developmental perspective: A guide to teaching.* Reston, VA: NASPE Motor Development Task Force.

Safrit, M. J. (1995). *Complete guide to youth fitness testing.* Champaign, IL: Human Kinetics.

Strand, B. N., & Wilson, R. (1993). *Assessing sport skills.* Champaign, IL: Human Kinetics.

3 Model-Based Strategies for Teaching Physical Education

If the types of knowledge presented in Chapter 2 are the foundations of instructional models, then teaching strategies can be thought of as the bricks and mortar that hold each model together, giving it a unique look and allowing it to work toward its designed purpose. A teaching strategy is a set of preplanned actions intended to bring about a specific, short-term goal within the lesson or content unit. Unlike most effective teaching skills which happen quickly and interactively during a lesson, a strategy is always determined ahead of time as part of the teacher's lesson plan. Essentially, it is the way the teacher intends for each segment of the lesson to be operationalized—how it will get carried out by the teacher and/or students.

By design, a predetermined set of teaching strategies makes each model look and operate according to the designer's plan, leading students to preferred types of engagement and learning outcomes. Some models will rely on many teaching strategies; others will use relatively few. However, as you will see in Part 2, each model will use only those strategies

FIGURE 3.1 **Strategies for Teaching Physical Education**

Strategies for Teaching Physical Education

Managerial	*Instructional*	
1. Preventive	1. Task presentation	5. Student safety
2. Interactive	2. Task structure	6. Task progression
3. Grouping	3. Task engagement	7. Use of questions
	4. Learning activities	8. Review and closure

Knowledge Areas for Model-Based Instruction

1. Learning contexts	6. Physical education content
2. Learners	7. Task analysis and Content progression
3. Learning theories	8. Assessment
4. Developmental appropriateness	9. Social/emotional climate
5. Learning domains and objectives	10. Equity in the gym
	11. Curriculum models for PE

that are congruent with its foundational learning theory, its purpose, and its plan for implementation. Teaching strategies can be divided into two main groups of operations: managerial and instructional. Each group contains specific actions that teachers and students complete according to the design of a particular model to promote learning outcomes within it. As you can see in Figure 3.1, teaching strategies are built upon the teacher's knowledge base and rely strongly on procedural and conditional expertise in physical education.

Managerial Strategies

All of the instructional models in this book depend on the teacher's plan for class management. This allows available resources to be used to their fullest potential in ways that foster each model's unique set of domain priorities and student learning outcomes. Each managerial plan should be consistent with the model for which it is used. The most essential managerial plan is the one devised for *preventive management* to increase appropriate student behavior and engagement in class. All physical education lessons and units require some amount of management time, planned for in identified lesson segments: the start of class, transitions, and the end of class. There are many effective strategies to prevent or reduce instances of managerial problems in complex physical education instructional settings.

Preventive Management Plans

While it is not possible to completely eliminate student misbehavior in class, a teacher can prepare a preventive management plan to greatly reduce the likelihood of behavior problems in class in order to increase time on task and student learning. Such problems can result in minutes taken away from the opportunity to learn, teacher stress, and a negative climate in the gymnasium.

Management Strategies at the Start of Class.   It is important that a physical education lesson begin with a quick and stimulating start that can carry through the entire lesson. Siedentop (1991) calls this *getting momentum.* The use of good management strategies as class starts also sets the teacher's tone and expectations for the lesson with a clear message to students that "this is learning time."

Posting the Lesson Plan for Students.   Too often students come to physical education class with no idea of what is planned for their lesson. They arrive to the gym and must wait for the teacher to give a vague or incomplete preview, such as "Today we are going to work on tennis serves. . . ." Too often the students reply with, "When are we going to get to play?" In secondary schools, it would be simple to post a more complete overview of the lesson plan in the locker room so that students can know what to expect in the lesson. For elementary classes it would be a matter of making a more complete preview of the lesson as it begins.

Posting or Announcing Special Instructions of the Day.   Physical education classes can take place in many areas in and around the school and can be subject to the weather outside. This sometimes requires changes in the regular class plans, as students need special information for getting dressed or finding the location of class. Typically, the teacher must "pass the word around" through a few students or wait until all students have arrived in class to move to the new location. For secondary schools a more time-efficient plan would involve the use of a written notice to students as they enter the locker room, before they begin to change clothing. In elementary schools the physical education teacher could ask that a brief statement be made to classroom teachers about any changes as part of the daily announcements. Therefore, classes would be able to come to physical education ready to make the needed changes in location, scheduling, or procedures.

Instant Activity.   Some managerial problems occur because students find themselves at the start of class with little to do other than wait for the teacher to begin the lesson. As the number of students in the gymnasium increases before the class begins, there is an opportunity for misbehavior while the students are less directly supervised by the teacher. As will be suggested in Chapter 4, it is possible for a teacher to post an "instant activity" that students can engage in as soon as they enter the gym, reducing the opportunity for misbehavior to occur while the rest of the students arrive for class.

Contingency Management.   Contingency management for classrooms is based on behavior modification techniques that have been shown to be highly effective (Alberto & Troutman, 1999). In such a plan there is an explicit statement of the relationship between student behavior and the consequences for it. If a student is observed or heard to say a predefined appropriate behavior in class, that student is rewarded, or reinforced, as a consequence. This increases the likelihood that the student will repeat or maintain that behavior. If a student is observed or heard to say a predefined inappropriate behavior, that student receives no reward, or can be punished, thereby reducing the likelihood that the inappropriate behavior will occur again. There are many contingency-based strategies for preventive management in physical education.

Good Behavior Game.   In this strategy students are assigned to a team, with individual members receiving a one-point deduction for inappropriate behavior observed by the teacher. Each team is competing against the other team/s to win the good behavior game for that class period. The teacher or an assistant keeps a tally sheet for each team during class, with the winning team earning a small reward at the end of the period.

Behavior Contracting.   The essence of the behavior contract is that the teacher and individual students negotiate an agreement for student conduct during a predetermined length of time (e.g., one week, three classes in a row) and the reward that the student will earn if she meets her part of the contract. A simple (but binding) written contract is made and signed by the teacher and student. The key part of this plan is that the student participates in the process and agrees beforehand to how well she will behave and what the consequences will be for not following class rules.

Token Economies.   Token economies are effective ways to get appropriate behavior to occur and be maintained without taking away class time on a regular basis. In a token economy students receive a point, sticker, or some other nonvaluable coupon for each instance of appropriate behavior observed by the teacher. Once a student accumulates a predetermined number of "tokens" they can be exchanged for small material rewards (e.g., healthy snacks, a badge, a coloring book) or class privileges (e.g., free time at the end of class, being "Class Leader of the Day," or extra time in the locker room after class).

Time Out.   One of the most often used behavior management techniques is time out, in which a student who has been observed or heard in an inappropriate behavior is taken out of the class activity for a set amount of time. The designated time-out area is usually on the perimeter of the gymnasium, but within sight of the teacher. The student may observe the class activities but is not allowed to do anything else. The length of the time out for each infraction is known to students as part of the posted class rules so that they are aware of the contingency in effect and in some way "make their own choice" to be in time out. Once the time-out period has elapsed, the student is allowed to join the class activity in progress.

Assertive Discipline.   Started in the 1970s, this is really a philosophy for how teachers can arrange a preventive discipline plan in their classrooms (Canter & Canter, 1976). It is based on the teacher expressing clearly to students the *needs* of the classroom environment so that learning can take place, and then getting students to accommodate those needs through appropriate behavior. For instance, the teacher might say to the class, "We need to make absolutely sure that the equipment is placed back were you found it, so that the next person can use it without having to search for it." Once that need has been stated and all students understand it, the teacher then expects this to happen and becomes assertive with students to ensure that it does happen, settling for nothing less. If an expectation is not being met, it becomes the immediate focus of the lesson and the rest of the lesson does not proceed until the teacher is satisfied with student behavior.

School Rule Plans.   Many schools today are choosing to implement their own school-wide discipline plan. The unique part of these plans is that the rules apply everywhere in the school and the consequences for infractions carry over across teachers/subjects and time. A typical plan for infractions might be:

First infraction:	Verbal warning from a teacher
Second infraction:	"Warning" written on the board or recorded by a teacher
Third infraction:	Ten-minute time out
Fourth infraction:	Twenty-minute time out
Fifth infraction:	Note or call to parents
Sixth infraction:	In-school suspension
Seventh infraction:	Out-of-school suspension

Since the infractions carry over across all subjects, these plans send a message to students that they cannot misbehave in one class and "start all over" in the next class. And, since a student's record of infractions is kept over time, the consequences for the next infraction remain no matter how long until it occurs. These plans make all of the teachers and administrators in the school a part of a common plan for promoting appropriate student behavior.

Student Choice Plans.   Most preventative management plans are designed by teachers and imposed on students who have no choice or ownership in the plan. As students mature and develop they have an increasing capacity to make choices and hold themselves responsible for those choices. They can assume a more active part in the process of making a discipline plan in physical education. Such a plan can be negotiated between the teacher and students by allowing the students to suggest a list of class rules and consequences for infractions. While there will be some student-choice rules that the teacher cannot accept for reasons of safety and liability, it is possible for the teacher to state the boundaries of student choice and let students decide within those boundaries.

For instance, a high school physical education teacher might ask a tenth-grade class, "What is a fair amount of time needed to change out for class and be in the gym, ready to start?" Through some negotiation with the class, it is decided that five minutes allows students sufficient time without being too hurried or cutting into too much class time. With that agreed upon, the teacher then asks, "What should happen to students who do not get dressed and to the gym in five minutes from the previous bell?" Some suggestions from students might be, "Run ten laps," "five minutes of time out once we start to play," or "They must stay at the end of class to help take up equipment." The teacher explains that he is against having students punished with exercise, so would like the class to vote on the other two choices. The majority vote becomes the new class rule.

Peer and Group Conflict Resolution Plans.   Many behavior problems are not between the teacher and one or more students; they can be situations that involve a student-to-student conflict. Therefore, it is not necessary for the teacher to be the only person responsible for classroom management in physical education. Students at all grade levels can learn strategies for managing the behavior of themselves, other individuals, and groups in class. This does not mean that "class cops" or "tattletales" are used to report infractions to the teacher. Instead, it means that students learn negotiation and problem-resolution skills that allow them to prevent and reduce problems without the need for the teacher's interventions or arbitrations.

Interactive Management Strategies

Most class-management episodes occur once the class is out of the opening routine and into the planned lesson segments. Some of this management can be planned for ahead of time, but most of the decisions are made when the teacher directs students to end a current lesson segment and transition into the next one. This is called interactive management because it involves consideration of many things going on at the moment, leading to some immediate verbal interaction with students. The success of many lessons will hinge on the teacher's effectiveness during interactive managerial times. They can lead to major disruptions and loss of momentum if not resolved quickly.

Have Students Assist with Equipment Dispersal and Return. When it is not possible to set up equipment before students arrive to class, the teacher can ask students to assist in getting it out for use and returning it when they are finished. This reduces management time considerably and keeps students involved in the flow of the lesson. The teacher needs to give students clear directions at both times to make this kind of transition quick and orderly.

Prepare for the Next Activity While the Current One Is Going On. Once the teacher decides that the class will change to another activity that needs different equipment or a new space configuration, it is possible to get the upcoming activity ready while the first one winds down. When possible, a "change of scenery" can be made quickly and safely so that all that is needed is to stop the current activity and immediately redirect students to the new one.

Prepare for some Class Emergencies Ahead of Time. Emergencies can include injuries or sudden illnesses, intruders, or sudden environmental hazards (bees in the area, water leaks, etc.). In these emergencies the teacher must stay with the class but arrange for help to be notified. If students must be sent to get assistance, the teacher must consider: Who should be sent? Do they know where to go? Exactly what should they say to the person being notified? A few potential messengers can be trained as part of an overall plan to cover emergencies. The idea is to be prepared for any emergency situations.

Have a Backup Plan. What happens if it rains while the class is outdoors and must finish the lesson indoors? What will the teacher do if a key piece of equipment breaks or fails during class? How will the class be restarted after a fire drill? What will be done if the principal schedules your gym with no notice and you must relocate your classes? These situations can be less disruptive if the teacher gives some prior thought to their occurrence and prepares a back-up plan.

Have a Plan for Student Injury Situations.   Other emergencies will require unanticipated decisions and action, such as what to do when a student gets injured or becomes ill during class. This is similar to your emergency plan but does require more on-the-spot decisions and actions. What will the rest of the class do while you are attending to that student? Who will be sent to get more assistance, if needed? How do you explain the injury to other students to reduce their fear of the same thing happening to them?

Use Behavioral Extinction for Students Who Just Want Attention.   Some students just want to be noticed by the teacher and may initiate minor disruptions to get attention. When the teacher suspects this to be the case, a good strategy is to extinguish the behavior by simply ignoring it. Many times it will stop because the student fails to get the attention that reinforces the behavior to begin with. This strategy is far more effective than attending to every instance of attention-seeking or constantly punishing small misbehaviors. Both of these responses give the student just what she wants—the teacher's attention, whether it is positive or negative.

Learn to Overlap Classroom Events.   Overlapping refers to a teacher's ability to attend to more than one thing at a time during class. This ability is especially important in physical education, with big classes, large spaces, and lots of activity. For instance, if a child needs individual attention, the teacher should be able to provide that and keep track of time so as not to miss the next class transition. Other examples include the ability to get class going while tardy students arrive one at a time or the ability to keep track of a song on the CD player that is cuing a learning station rotation while interacting with students as they practice.

Strategies for Getting Students into Groups

Many of the models in this book require that the teacher groups students during class to promote more effective use of time and to implement more developmentally appropriate learning tasks. When it is not planned to teach the whole class at once, there are several grouping strategies that are sensitive to students' feelings, save time, and facilitate the immediate goals in the lesson.

Selecting Groups Randomly.   Random group selection saves time by placing the grouping process in the control of the teacher. It can save minutes and reduces the tendency for some students to want to be grouped for social reasons. Almost invariably, asking students to make their own groups results in increased transition time, elevated noise levels, some hurt feelings, and uneven or unfair groups. Physical education teachers can use any number of quick, random-based strategies for forming groups when student abilities or characteristics are not a factor.

Cut and Go.   The teacher wishes to form five groups and have each group stand in a different location in the gym. The teacher points to individual students while counting aloud, "1, 2, 3, 4, and 5—you students stand up and go to the far corner of the gym," and then repeats the process until all five groups are formed and in place.

Birth-Month Groups.   The teacher says, "Everyone born from January 1st to the end of April are in Group 1. Everyone born from May 1st to the end of August are in Group 2. Everyone born from September 1st to the end of the year are in Group 3." The students get into their respective groups and the teacher balances out the group numbers as needed.

Clothes Color Groups (if Students Are Not in Uniforms).   The teachers says, "Everyone who has on something that's red, get in a group. Everyone who has on something that's green, get in a group. Everyone who has on something that's yellow, get in a group. If you don't have on one of those colors you can make up your own group." The students get into their respective groups and the teacher balances out the group numbers as needed.

Selecting Practice Groups by Ability Levels.   It is appropriate to make groups based on actual or student-selected ability levels. It is discriminatory to make such groups based on assumed, subjective, stereotyped, or arbitrary determinations of student abilities. When the instructional situation calls for placing students into ability groups for practice or competition, the teacher needs to make it clear that the students are grouped on ability alone and not with discriminatory decisions.

Nondiscriminatory
Students who scored 65 percent or higher on the unit skills test are in the game on field 3.

Students who scored less than 65 percent on the unit skills test are in the game on field 1.

Anyone who feels like they know the rules of table tennis can go to the far end and start playing.

Anyone who is not sure of the rules come with me and we will do a review. Then you can play.

Discriminatory
The boys are on court 1.
The girls are on court 2.

The boys can practice at the "tall" basket.
The girls can practice at the lower basket.

The varsity players in class can practice here.
Everyone else can practice at the other end.

Choosing Teams for Games.   We are all familiar with stories about hurt feelings and lopsided teams that result from "captains" (usually higher-skilled boys) being selected to pick teams for class games in physical education. This strategy can be miseducative for several reasons and the source of many students' avoidance tendencies toward competition and physical education. In addition, it usually takes many minutes to accomplish—minutes that could be spent playing the game. Teachers can use a few simple strategies to eliminate all of the negative issues related to this process and ensure that class competition is fair and educational.

1. Teacher determines balanced teams before class. Teams are balanced by skill ability and student demographics.
2. Teams are made randomly by counting off or by using one of the random grouping strategies.
3. Game rules and scoring can be modified to foster more equitable participation patterns.
4. Losing teams and players are not punished or denigrated after the game, reducing students' concerns about unfair teams or playing with lower-skilled teammates.

Instructional Strategies

Instructional strategies refer to a wide range of operations that are intended to directly promote the intended learning outcomes in a lesson. While managerial strategies set the stage for learning to occur, instructional strategies serve to give students active engagement with the content of the lesson, which then leads to learning. Learning strategies can be placed into eight operations: task presentation, task structure, task engagement, learning activities, student safety, task progression, using questions, and review/closure.

Strategies for Task Presentation

Students must get information about an upcoming learning task before they can begin to pursue the task. Rink (1998) calls the collected strategies for providing students with necessary learning task information *task presentation,* which includes five operations: (1) getting the attention of the learner, (2) sequencing the content and organizational aspects of tasks, (3) improving the clarity of communication, (4) choosing a way to communicate, and (5) selecting and organizing learning cues (p. 88). Chapter 4 will outline the specific teaching skills needed for effective task presentation. Physical education teachers can use many types of communication strategies (modes) to provide such information to students. The best mode in any given situation is the one that provides the clearest task presentation information in the briefest amount of time.

1. *Teacher verbal lecture.* The teacher verbally communicates while students listen.
2. *Teacher-modeled demonstration.* The teacher provides his own model of the information.
3. *Combined lecture/demo.* The teacher models each piece of information as she tells it to students.
4. *Active demonstration.* The students follow along as the teacher talks and demonstrates.
5. *Slow motion.* Similar to the active demonstration, but the students follow in slow motion.

6. *Peer-directed, verbal.* A student makes the verbal communication to another student, a group of students, or the whole class.
7. *Peer-directed, modeled.* A student provides a model for another student, a group of students, or the whole class.
8. *Task sheets.* Learning-task information is provided on sheets given to each student and students read them individually.
9. *Station signs/sheets.* Each learning station has its own information sign or sheet that students read when they first arrive at the station.

Physical education teachers do not have to rely only on themselves or other students to provide task information. Several types of media can be used for that purpose:

1. Videotapes (commercial or produced by the teacher)
2. Films
3. Audiotapes, records, CDs
4. Photographs and drawings
5. CD ROMS
6. PETV

The first task presentation of each class should include a brief *set induction* which is used to: (1) preview the lesson content for students, (2) state the learning goals, (3) relate the content to other areas of learning, and (4) increase student interest and motivation. For instance, a teacher who has planned a fourth-grade lesson on balance could use the following set induction:

> "In today's lesson we are going to work on our dynamic balance—that's the ability to stay balanced while you are moving around. Can anyone tell me some sports that use a lot of static balance?" Students mention soccer, football, tennis, and ice skating. The teacher picks up on the ice skating example and asks the class if they have been watching the Winter Olympics figure skating on TV the past week. Several students nod their heads and the teacher continues. "If you want to be like those Olympic skaters, you need to have good dynamic balance so you can go fast, turn quickly, and land safely when you jump. Even though you will not be skating, those same skills are important as you move around in general space. First, we are going to work on static balance in self-space, then move to some more-difficult tasks using dynamic balance in three or four ways. While you are practicing, imagine that you are on ice skates and getting ready for the next Winter Olympic Games. OK, let's have some fun, you future Olympians!"

A good strategy to use after each task presentation is *checking for understanding*. This is a brief series of questions to determine how much of the presentation students retained or understood. Questions should not be rhetorical, such as "Did everyone understand?" or "Any questions?" The teacher should use purposeful questions that ask students to recall the most important information that was given to them, such as "Who can tell me the three main things to keep in mind when you try to strike a ball?", "Why do we not want to 'high stick' when we are practicing around others?", or "If you are not having success from a long distance, what should you do?" It is sometimes a good idea to spot-check certain students who do not always pay attention so that they know to listen during task presentations.

Strategies for Task Structure and Engagement

Task structure refers to the way a learning task or activity is designed for student engagement. Task structure as it will be used in this book includes three components of what Jones (1992) called a task system (task presentation and task structure combined): (1) a set of operations or procedures used to pursue the learning task, (2) resources and conditions that are available to accomplish the task, and (3) a means of accountability that indicates the importance or significance of the task (p. 412). Operations include the location and organization of the learning environment and directions for safe participation. Resources and conditions include equipment and the number of minutes allocated for the task. Accountability includes expectations for student behavior, a proficiency goal, or an explanation of how the task relates to subsequent learning activities in the lesson or unit. Teachers can use several strategies to ensure that the task structure facilitates the learning goals of the moment and provides students with the maximum amount of successful engagement.

Varying the Task Difficulty.   Effective teachers will design learning tasks to accommodate several levels of student abilities at the same time, allowing all students to be appropriately challenged and to experience a high rate of success. This can be accomplished by planning varying levels of difficulty for each learning task and requiring students to demonstrate proficiency at a lower level before moving on to the next one. This will result in practice groups based on actual ability and will allow students to work with others at their same ability level. The level of difficulty can be changed by progressively modifying one or more aspects of the practice task:

1. Distance to the target
2. Time required to complete (speed)
3. Implement size and weight
4. Object size, weight, and texture
5. Number of needed repetitions
6. Size or height of the target

Teaching by Invitation.   In this strategy, students are encouraged (invited) to pick their own level of difficulty and challenge among those offered (Graham, 1992). A teacher could set up three tossing stations for a first-grade class, each with a different type of ball (larger, smaller, bouncier, etc.) and target size (small, medium, large) and invite students to choose their own practice station. The teacher could add another variation of difficulty at each station by having three tossing distances marked by cones. Again, students would be invited to practice at the distance they think provides the best challenge for their ability.

Developmental Appropriateness.   Are the students able to meet the managerial and performance requirements of the task? Managerial requirements refer to the students' ability to comprehend and follow directions, assume responsibility, abide by safety rules, and to stay engaged without the teacher's direct supervision. Performance requirements refer to the match between the difficulty of the task and students' cognitive and psychomotor abilities. Tasks should be designed so that students can comprehend the purpose and form of the task and have at least a moderate level of success when they attempt the task. Tasks that are too simple or easy can cause students to become bored; tasks that are too complex or difficult can cause students to become frustrated. In either circumstance, it is likely that students will quickly choose to disengage from the task, alter it, or turn to off-task behavior.

Breaking Down Task Segments for Practice.   Some skills are best learned by being broken down into subskills that can be practiced one at a time in a planned sequence. When *partial skill* practice tasks are designed, the teacher should provide a task structure that isolates the desired part of the skill to be learned with maximum repetitions. Some examples of partial practice task structure are shown in Figure 3.2.

At some point it will be necessary to sequence all of the partial tasks into the *whole-skill* performance. Sometimes whole-skill practice will occur as the result of several partial skills sequenced together. Other skills can be practiced only in their entirety, such as the bowling delivery, basketball dribbling, golf swing, and swimming. When the whole skill is to be practiced, the teacher can use several kinds of *lead-up* task structures to maximize quality learning trials and to assist students as they attempt skills with many performance components in them. Figure 3.3 shows some examples of lead-up task structures for physical education.

Each of these task structures will provide students with more successful practice trials as they learn the movement or skill. Eventually the task structure can progress to where students practice the complete task at full speed with no assistance from the teacher. These lead-up task structures help students to acquire the desired pattern quickly and safely until they are ready to practice unaided.

Closed and Open Tasks.   A closed skill is one that has few or no changing variables as the skill is being performed. The performer controls the pacing of the attempt, no one is playing defense, the playing area is constant, and the target does not move or change while

FIGURE 3.2   Examples of Partial Practice Task Structure

Movement/Skill	Parts to Be Practiced in Isolation
Tennis serve	1. Toss 2. Swing 3. Follow-through
Punting	1. Grip 2. Step with kicking foot 3. Step with other foot 4. Drop ball 5. Kick 6. Follow-through
Tumbling routine	1. Tripod 2. Handstand 3. Backward roll 4. Finish

FIGURE 3.3   Lead-Up Task Structures

Task Structure	Examples
Slow motion	1. Tennis forehand and backhand drives 2. Dance steps 3. Football plays
Reverse chaining	1. Golf putting (start at hole and progress to longer putts)
Follow the leader	1. Aerobic dance routines 2. Basketball defensive "slide" drill 3. Obstacle course
Verbal guides	1. Calling out steps in a dance along with the music
No-object	1. Golf swing with no ball 2. Tennis swing with no ball
Modified object or implement	1. Choking up on a tennis racquet 2. Using a "light" volleyball

the skill is being attempted. Indoor archery and bowling are classic examples of closed skills. The distance to the target is always the same, the target does not move, the performer can control when a shot is made, and the climatic conditions do not change. Task structure for these skills should be designed to create and maintain these unchanging conditions and to give learners opportunities to repeat the precise movements needed for these tasks. Closed-skill proficiency requires good concentration and strong performance routines so the task structure should allow students time to develop both under familiar conditions.

Few motor skills are completely closed. Many skills have some stable environmental characteristics, like the closed skills just discussed, but they also have a few changing variables as well. In golf putting the target (hole) is always the same size and does not move, and the player controls when and how the putt is attempted. However, the distance, the undulations in the putting surface, and weather conditions can make every putt different, causing the player to make small changes in how the skill is executed each time. For the lack of a better term, we will call these *relatively closed skills* because they have more variables that are constant than changing. Performers must recognize when conditions have changed and learn how to adjust accordingly. The task structure must allow a combination of (1) consistency to acquire the basic movement patterns and routines and (2) changing conditions to learn how to apply those skills situationally.

An *open skill* is one in which many or all of the variables that impact performance can, and do, change as the skill is being executed. Many open skills also involve teammates and/or opponents that increase both the number and complexity of variables that must be considered as the skill is performed.

Task progression for open skills requires several stages of development. The first stage looks much like that for closed skills, in which the learner practices the skill in isolation from interfering variables, often with partial task trials and at a slower speed. The number of task components are gradually increased, as is the speed of the performance. The second stage introduces a limited number of open-task variables, typically through drills that

Closed Skills	Relatively Closed Skills	Open Skills
Bowling	Golf	Tag games
Archery (fixed target)	Badminton serves	Field hockey
Darts	Tee-ball striking	Ultimate Frisbee
Basketball free throws	Juggling	Catching ground balls
Gymnastics routines	Line dance	Football pass defense

involve an opponent, obstacle, or specific performance criteria. The third stage features lead-up games that begin to approach the full number and complexity of performance variables. These might be scrimmages, half-court games, or reduced-numbers games (i.e., six vs. six in soccer). The final stage of task structure would be practicing and learning these skills as they are performed in the unpredictable situations of full game or competitive play. The last two stages would feature learning tasks that allow students to continue their development from "teaching moments" recognized by the teacher as opportune times to highlight tactical decisions and skill execution that characterize open-skill proficiency.

Grouping for Task Practice. Part of the task structure will be defined by how students are grouped for practicing the learning activity. A grouping strategy should be based on the following considerations:

1. Safety
2. Maximum engagement opportunity
3. The objectives for the task
4. Students' level of responsibility
5. The instructional model being used
6. The need for students to assist each other
7. Available space and equipment

Once all of these factors are considered the teacher has many options for grouping students in learning tasks:

Individual practice. Every student has a personal practice space, needed equipment, and is allowed to decide when to begin each trial. All students may or may not be doing the same task.

Partner practice. Students are grouped in pairs for practice. Both students can be practicing the same task together, or one student can be practicing while the other student assists.

Small-group practice. Students are placed in groups of three to six for practice. This is a common grouping strategy for many learning tasks in physical education.

Large-group practice. Students are placed in groups of seven to fifteen, with all of them practicing the same task or playing in the same game.

Whole-class practice. A few learning tasks in physical education call for whole-class practice structure. This means that all students are practicing the same task together. This is typically a game structure, but can be whole-class problem-solving or initiatives.

As with all other parts of the lesson plan, student grouping should be carefully considered because the need to change grouping plans can lead to a loss of momentum in the lesson and excessive amounts of management time. However, it is possible to make a *progressive* grouping plan by starting students out in individual practice, then having them move into pairs, then small groups, then large groups, and so on with each new task.

Types of Learning Activities for Physical Education

There are many ways to organize learning activities in physical education, determining how students will be engaged as they attempt to learn the skills, knowledge, and attitudes intended by the teacher. The kind of engagement leads directly to the kinds of learning that can occur from the activity, so teachers must carefully consider the learning goals of the moment, domain priorities, domain interactions, student readiness, and the specific task structure to be used.

Learning Activities When the Psychomotor Domain Is Primary.
Learning Centers.   In this type of organization (also called *learning stations*), students are placed in small groups and rotated through several designated "centers" arranged around the gym or practice area. Each center is designed to focus on a different skill (e.g., one for kicking, one for throwing, one for batting, etc.) or represent a different level of difficulty for the same skill (e.g., beginning, intermediate, or advanced basketball ball handling). Intratask variation (Graham, 1992) can be used to allow students several ways to practice the same skill, all with about the same level of difficulty. To practice the overhand throw, for example, centers could be set up to: (1) throw for accuracy, (2) throw for distance, (3) throw to a low target, (4) throw to a high target, (5) throw to a slowly moving target, and (6) throw to a partner.

Drills.   Many times it is helpful to practice skills in a simple, controlled setting to provide numerous repetitions on one or two performance components. This can be accomplished with the use of drills in which students practice individually, in pairs, or in small groups. There are dozens of drills for each kind of activity in physical education, and they are typically practiced for short periods of time due to their simplicity and the number of repetitions students get. It is possible to set up several drills as learning centers that students rotate through in class.

Lead-Up Games.   A lead-up game contains some of the features of drills and some of the features of a full game. A lead-up game is a simpler version of the full game and focuses on a few performance aspects with many repetitions. Some common lead-up games are new-comb (for volleyball), pickleball (tennis, racquetball), Frisbee golf (ultimate Frisbee), and floor hockey (field hockey).

Modified Games.   Games can be modified in many ways to provide students with increased action, more opportunities to use strategy and tactics, and better competition. Modifications can be made in the size of the field/court, the size of the goal/target, the number of players on a side, playing rules, and scoring rules.

Scrimmage. A scrimmage is a full version of a game with many anticipated stoppages in play at "teaching moments" that occur within the flow of the game. A scrimmage does not include keeping score or the enforcement of certain rules (e.g., eliminations due to fouls, proper player substitutions). It also allows students to replay certain events that occur so they can have a second look at some situations.

Games. Full games are common task organizations for many sport content units in physical education. To keep games as positive learning experiences, teachers need to make the competition as fair as possible and eliminate any negative consequences for the losing player or team.

Role Playing. Many sport activities involve participants other than the players, such as officials, referees, judges, score keepers, coaches, and trainers. Students can learn much about a sport by assuming the roles of these positions. The Sport Education Model (Chapter 10) is largely based on student role playing in organized sport "seasons," during which they learn the knowledge, skills, and responsibilities associated with playing and nonplaying positions such as coach, referee/official, and statistician.

Videotape Self-Analysis for Key Elements. Students can make short video clips of themselves performing learning tasks in class and then use a checklist of key performance elements to analyze their skills. This allows them visual feedback on their skills and also promotes the development of movement observation and analysis knowledge.

Cooperative Tasks. A growing trend in task organization for physical education involves the use of small student groups in cooperative learning activities. Typically the teacher gives each group a problem to solve or a task to complete and then directs the group to work together toward that goal, with little direction or intervention. The group must work at two levels: how to use each member's abilities to the fullest and how to achieve their given objective. As the name indicates, the cooperative learning model (Chapter 9) is based entirely on this kind of task organization.

"Play-Teach-Play" (Graham, 1992). Sometimes students can be engaged right away, even before they receive any key elements or formal task structure. Once engaged, it will become apparent to them and the teacher what students' needs are for more and better information about doing the task well. In "play-teach-play" the students are given little or no task information and then asked to practice. As they practice, the teacher notes common mistakes and then stops the class with an attention signal. The teacher comments on those common mistakes and then provides a short task presentation to help students improve. A second "play" segment follows, with more monitoring, and then another "teach" segment. This task structure has two important benefits: (1) students become active right away and (2) the task information is highly relevant, since it is directed to already observed mistakes.

Learning Activities when the Affective Domain Is Primary.
Reflection Tasks. At times a teacher will want students to be introspective about their participation in physical education to explore some of the personal meaning learned from

those experiences. This type of learning can be fostered through tasks which direct students to reflect (think back) upon recent events in class. Reflection can be developed from written and oral activities in physical education. Some good reflection tasks include journal writing and "show and tells" to share something of personal meaning with the class.

Values Clarification Tasks.   Similar to some reflection tasks are those which focus on helping students to determine their personal values in relationship to physical activity, classmates, and themselves. Values clarification does not mean that students learn the teacher's or some other person's values—it means that the teacher uses probing and clarifying questions to allow students to articulate and examine values in a public way. Some examples of the kinds of learning tasks associated with this process are shown in Figure 3.4.

Learning Activities When the Cognitive Domain Is Primary.
Critical Thinking Tasks.   Critical thinking for physical education has been defined by McBride (1992) as "reflective thinking used to make reasonable and defensible decisions about movement tasks or challenges" (p. 115). Tishman and Perkins (1995) include four areas in the critical thinking process: (1) broad and adventurous thinking, (2) causal and evaluative reasoning, (3) planning and strategies thinking, and (4) metacognition. Each of these areas call for different kinds of learning strategies. Because one's critical thinking ability is related to developmental stages, learning strategies that promote critical thinking

FIGURE 3.4   Values Clarification Tasks and Questions

Value to Be Examined	Associated Learning Task or Activity	Reflective Questions
Sharing	Floor hockey (after game)	1. How did it feel not to have the puck passed to you? 2. Boys, why did you not pass the puck to the girls? 3. What happened when your team did pass the puck to everyone?
Trust	Trust games (questions during and after games)	1. Why won't you volunteer for the "trust fall"? 2. Why won't you let Sharon belay you on the climbing wall? 3. How does it feel to rely on your classmates for your safety?
Persistence	Individual games	1. What did you do to make that great comeback to beat Mickey? 2. Have you been practicing outside of class? Why?

must be appropriately considered. Figure 3.5 shows some examples of learning strategies for the development of critical thinking in physical education.

Check for Understanding.   Once a teacher has provided a task presentation or a learning cue it is necessary to ascertain if the student/s has understood what was just said or shown. Checking for understanding (CFU) can be accomplished by asking students key questions based on the information they just saw or heard. The best way to check for understanding is to ask questions that do not lead students to simple "yes" or "no" answers. Some good CFU questions might be:

Can you tell me two important cues to remember in hitting tennis serves?
What is the main safety rule in floor hockey?
What are two ways you can improve static balance?
When (in the music) do you begin this dance step?

FIGURE 3.5   Critical Thinking Strategies for Physical Education

Grades	Movement Skill or Concept	Learning Strategies for Critical Thinking
Elementary*	1. Throwing	1. Students experiment with different components of the skill and describe how each one impacts performance.
	2. Spatial awareness and locomotor movement	2. Students make a "movement map" on paper with several locomotor movements, explain why each movement is on the map, then travel along the map with those movements.
Middle school[†]	1. Creative dance	1. Students choreograph a dance using the music and lyrics from a popular dance of their choice. Their dance must include four distinct "phases."
	2. Gymnastics	2. With partners, students link together two or more discrete movements into one graceful sequence.
High school	1. Volleyball[‡]	1. Using a study sheet to learn positioning and strategy.
	2. Fitness/wellness[§]	2a. Students interview each other about current fitness activity patterns.
		2b. Students complete a family health history, personal health history, and a physical activity inventory.

*(Cleland & Pearse, 1995)

[†](Woods & Brook, 1995)

[‡](Blitzer, 1995)

[§](Greenockle & Purvis, 1995)

If students know that the teacher will check for their understanding regularly, students will be more likely to pay attention during task presentations and try to retain information in anticipation of being asked for it.

Written In-Class Assignments.   It is possible to design brief, written assignments for students to complete as they go through a physical education class. These assignments should serve to compliment the movement components of class and not become the major learning activity in physical education. Some examples of in-class assignments for different grade levels are:

Elementary:	Students circle a smiley face on a task sheet after completing each station.
Middle/junior high:	"List the things (key elements) you did to be successful today."
High school:	Students exercise for three minutes and determine if they are in or out of their target heart-rate zone.

Homework Assignments.   Physical education does not have a strong tradition of assigning homework. While we might think of "PE homework" as out-of-class activity, there are some kinds of assignments that can be given to help students learn in the cognitive domain.

Keep an activity log or journal.

Watch a ballet on TV and list all the locomotor skills used by the dancers.

Ask one of your parents what PE was like for them in school. How is your class different?

Watch a game on TV and write an "article" about it for the morning paper.

Make a list of PE-related sites on the World Wide Web.

Videotape Self-Analysis for Key Elements.   Students can make short video clips of themselves performing learning tasks in class and then use a checklist of key elements to analyze their skills. This provides visual feedback on their skills and promotes the development of movement observation and analysis knowledge.

Visual Analysis of Peers.   Students can develop movement observation and analysis knowledge by observing the performance of their peers in class. Using a checklist of key performance elements they can observe other students practicing "live" or review video clips, as in the previous self-analysis strategy.

Individual and Group Projects.   Students can learn physical education content by completing outside projects, either individually or in an assigned group. The project develops skills in locating resources, organizing thoughts, selecting materials, and making a presentation (oral, written, multimedia, etc.).

Student-Designed Activities and Games. Most often it is the teacher who determines which learning activities will be practiced, which games will be played, and what game rules will be followed. Student creativity and cooperation can be developed by allowing them to design their own learning tasks, games, and game rules. This is done by offering them the opportunity to explore variations on familiar activities and games and allowing the needed time to experiment with their ideas until a new form of activity or game is created.

Curriculum Integration. In recent years there has been a noticeable attempt to combine physical education with other content areas in the school curriculum. When both areas are being developed with equal emphasis and learning occurs by using knowledge from both areas, it is called *curriculum integration.* When designing and implementing integrated learning activities, teachers must be careful that real integration is occurring, not just *coincidental* learning in two areas. Some examples of coincidental and actual curriculum integration are shown in Figure 3.6.

FIGURE 3.6 "Coincidental" and Actual Curriculum Integration with Physical Education

Integrated Areas	Learning Content or Activity	"Coincidental" Integration	Actual Integration
Physical education and social studies	International dance	"This dance is from Spain."	1. Inform students of the dance's origin. 2. Explain the meaning of the dance to the Spanish people. 3. Explain when and why it is danced (significance). 4. Use authentic music (with Spanish words). 5. Have students translate words/calls from Spanish (from Spanish/English dictionary or by a Spanish-speaking student). 6. Have students look up the dance on the World Wide Web.
Physical education and math	Finding target heat rate (THR)	Using software to determine one's THR zone	1. Explain the major components of THR. 2. Have students enter their own values and perform the math operations to get THR. 3. Have them exercise and calculate HR every ten minutes.

Strategies for Maximizing Student Safety in Physical Education

One of the main functions of teaching in physical education is that of planning and maintaining a safe learning environment for students. The most obvious reason for this is to prevent students from injury. In addition, if students are aware of any existing safety problems, they will likely choose not to participate fully, or refuse to participate at all. So, students must not only have a safe environment, they must *feel safe* as well. A few preventive strategies can be used to improve and maintain safety in physical education.

Develop and Post Gym Rules on Safety.   Students need to know that the gymnasium is no different than any other classroom in the school and that some basic safety rules apply in that setting. Most gym rules will involve how to move relative to others in that space, proper use of equipment, and the identification of potentially unsafe areas or situations. Teachers need to communicate all safety rules to students early in the school year (Fink & Siedentop, 1989) and post those rules in a visible part of the gym.

Review Rules.   As the school year progresses, it is likely that some students will forget safety rules, especially if a rule has not been violated for a long time. It is often helpful to remind students of safety rules from time to time, even when no infractions have occurred. This keeps safety as a regular part of routines and can reduce some types of accidents that happen when students simply forget.

Contingency Management.   Behavior modification techniques can be put in place that systematically reward students for safe behavior in the gym, or punish them for being unsafe regarding posted rules. This is called *contingency management,* since there is a known relationship between student behavior and its consequences; students are either rewarded or punished, *contingent* on how they follow the teacher's safety rules.

Student "Buddy System."   Accidents in physical education can sometimes occur when a student gets caught up in the excitement of the moment and does not pay attention to potential hazards in the gym—even those the teacher has pointed out and reviewed. If students are in pairs or small groups, the teacher could ask members of the group to watch out for their "buddies" as they practice and warn them of any safety problems (e.g., balls rolling into the practice space or other students inadvertently coming into the area).

Monitor as Students Start Engagement.   One of the easiest and best strategies is for the teacher to simply monitor students when a new practice task or game begins. The teacher should pay attention to proper spacing among students, check for the correct use of equipment, and examine the potential for groups to interfere with each other. If a practice task gets off to a safe start it will be more likely to stay that way.

Strategies for Task Progression

All physical education content units include a series of learning tasks for students to practice or otherwise be engaged in. The teacher will need to make decisions about when to move from one task to the next. Task progression decisions can be made in two ways: mastery-based and time-based.

Mastery-Based. Mastery-based task progression occurs when students must complete the current learning task to a stated criterion before moving on to the next task in the series. Performance criteria are given to students, along with an open-ended time to demonstrate proficiency or "mastery" of each task.

Time-Based. Most task-progression decisions in physical education are made on a teacher's planned time allocation for each learning task. The teacher estimates how much time it will take for the majority of students to learn a task and then moves to the next task when that time elapses. Some adjustments can be made, but the majority of task progressions are determined by the teacher's planned schedule.

Both types of task progression schemes have strengths and weaknesses. Mastery-based progressions ensure that students have demonstrated a readiness before moving to more difficult and complex tasks in a series, but it is not always possible for all students to master a task in a reasonable time, if at all. Time-based progressions are efficient and orderly due to their predictability, but if a group of students falls behind the rest of the class on early tasks, those same students will likely get farther behind as the unit moves along.

Strategies for Using Questions for Learning

Many teaching models in Part 2 will call for the use of teacher questions to promote student learning. Questions can be used to help students learn in all three domains, depending on what type of question is given and how students are expected to make their response. The Inquiry Model (Chapter 12) uses questions as the key pedagogical operation to promote student learning.

Ask, Don't Tell. Typically when a teacher wishes to give students some information or review a previous point, she will use a direct kind of communication—she will simply tell the students. While it is a quick way to impart information, it puts the students in a passive mode and fosters little thinking on their part. Metzler (1990) proposes a strategy called "ask, don't tell," in which the teacher provides very little direct information and uses questions instead.

Use Divergent Questions Whenever Possible. Convergent questions lead students to one, or a few, possible answers. When they have that one answered, they stop considering more possible answers. Divergent questions require students to consider many possibilities, and keep the intellectual process going.

Use Wait Time. Wait time refers to a deliberate pause made by the teacher right after asking a question. This pause should be between three and fifteen seconds, depending on the difficulty of the question. Research (Tobin, 1987) has shown that wait time allows more students to think of their own answer, instead of just getting the answer from the first student who responds to the teacher.

Ask for Clarification and Reasons.   There is a tendency for teachers to stop asking questions when the students have provided an answer. Getting the initial answer is only a part of the learning process. Teachers can probe students to find out how they arrived at an answer or give their reason/s for their answer. Questions like, "How did you figure that out?", "Where did you learn that?", or "What made you think of that?" allow students an opportunity to reflect on an answer, providing a deeper level of learning and good information for other students.

Call for Group Answers.   Much of the time, students think about questions privately and individually. They do not get the benefit of other students' views and knowledge. Sometimes a teacher can ask a question to a group of students and direct them to formulate an answer "by committee." This strategy will work only with higher-order questions.

Verbal Question with a Movement Response.   Answers to teacher questions are not limited to the cognitive domain and verbal responses. Some teaching models are based on teacher questions that students must think about and then show their answer with a movement response. While cognition is used initially to formulate an answer, students must then transfer that knowledge to the psychomotor domain to show their knowledge to the teacher.

Strategies for Lesson Review and Closure

It is a good idea to end lessons with a review and closure segment. This part of the lesson should be planned for like all other segments and have an intended learning purpose for students. It is not just a quick review of what was done in class that day; it should allow students to reflect back on completed learning tasks, be reminded of key performance cues, and make the connection between those concepts covered in class. The brief closure in the review should bring the lesson to a logical and complete ending to ensure that the intended learning goals were reached and that students have no unanswered questions. The closure then leads directly to the final management directions (lining up, going to the locker rooms, etc.) and dismissal of the class.

Transitioning to the Review.   Because time is usually short near the end of class, teachers must use quick and simple ways to get students organized for the review segment. It is best to get students to one location with no equipment in their hands, so the teacher should stop the final activity, direct students to quickly put away their equipment, and meet in a place near the equipment collection area. If the teaching area is small, the teacher can use an attention signal to get students to stop the activity and conduct the review while students are standing in place, and then have students put the equipment away.

Getting Attention.   Like any other time when the teacher will talk to the entire class, it is important to get students in a close formation and pay quiet attention. Since this is "listening and thinking" time, the teacher should not proceed with the review until students are quiet and attentive. This is a good time to use an attention signal.

Use Interactive Communications.   The best reviews will require students to reflect back on the lesson—to think, not just listen. Teachers can do this by checking for understanding or with an "ask, don't tell" strategy that prompts students to provide answers to review questions. This will make the review interactive, not just a passive listening time for students.

Interactive (Ask)	*Passive (Tell)*
"Who can tell me three things we learned in class today?"	"Today in class we learned how to balance on one foot, on two body parts, and with a partner."
"Why did we need to have a no-high-stick rule today?"	"We had a no-high-stick rule today because I saw several of you with your hockey sticks in a dangerous position in our drills."
"How do you think you could apply the skills we learned today?"	"Once you know how to strike objects with short-handled implements, you could use that in sports like racquetball and table tennis"

Summary

Teaching strategies work as a bridge between a teacher's declarative and procedural knowledge. The general declarative knowledge becomes a bit more focused when it is applied to planning managerial and instructional strategies in physical education. Each instructional model will call for a unique set of strategies that gives it a large part of its identity by determining "how things will look" for the teacher and students in that unit. Across all of the content areas and student developmental levels, the number of needed teaching strategies is very large for physical education. However, in a model-based approach each model will call for a specific set of strategies, so a teacher will need to have far fewer strategies at hand for use in any given model. The actual implementation of teaching strategies, the conditional knowledge link in this chain, will be demonstrated through the use of effective teaching skills presented in the next chapter.

LEARNING ACTIVITIES

1. If you are not now teaching, select a content area and grade level that you are likely to teach in the future. Make a list of the preventive and interactive managerial strategies that you would use in that unit.

2. If you are presently teaching, make a list of the preventive and interactive managerial strategies you use in your teaching. Mention why you use each one and explain how effective it is for your intended purpose.

3. Make a list of every way you can think of to get students into random groups for physical education. (No fair using the examples given in this chapter!)

4. Make a task presentation to a group of students—either actual students or your peers/colleagues. Ask them to rate you on each element of the task presentation shown on pages 70–71.

5. Make the same task presentation you made in Activity 4 and use a model other than yourself.

6. Select a content area and a grade level. Now identify your primary learning domain. List and explain at least five learning activities that could be used to promote student achievement in that domain. Finally, select another primary domain and make another list of five activities for that domain.

CHAPTER

4

Effective Teaching Skill Areas for Model-Based Instruction

Discrete teaching skills are individual, situation-specific teacher and/or student behaviors carried out before and during class. Discrete teaching skills form the third tier of building blocks for instructional models by determining the moment-to-moment decisions and actions that teachers and students carry out within instructional strategies. Many discrete teaching skills are applied generally within all strategies and models. However, each strategy and model will call for certain skills to be used more often than others. Every teacher possesses a *repertoire* of such skills, which is then applied at key times within instructional strategies to facilitate the functioning of each model. Teaching skills can be decisions and actions carried out by the teacher or they can be decisions or actions that teachers do to promote desired student behaviors in class. These skills represent conditional knowledge that is applied in specific situations within the teaching strategies presented in Chapter 3.

While teachers and students do many things in a physical education class, not all of them fall under the definition of a teaching skill, which is characterized by intentional decisions and actions carried out before and during class. These decisions and actions become *effective teaching skills* when they contribute to the achievement of stated learning goals in a lesson or unit of instruction. Research on teaching in the past twenty-five years has begun to identify teacher and student behaviors that correlate strongly with increased levels of student achievement. While most of that research has been completed in subjects like math, science, and reading, there is a similar body of evidence from the study of physical education instruction (Silverman & Ennis, 1996).

A correlation means that there is a relationship between two variables, so that when one of those variables changes, we can make predictions about what will happen to the other variable. That is not to say that there is a causal relationship—changes to the first variable will not automatically lead to changes in the other variable. A correlation simply means that once we have measured the first variable we can have a good idea of what the second variable will look like. Effective teaching skills are those teacher decisions and actions that correlate with increased levels of student learning. By teachers doing certain things, and by getting students to do certain things, the possibility of student learning is increased. Those "certain things" are called *effective teaching skills.*

Effective teaching skills begin with declarative knowledge, when teachers become aware of things they can do before and during class to increase the likelihood of students achieving the lesson or unit goals. Procedural knowledge helps the teacher to know how to successfully carry out an effective teaching skill when it is called for. Perhaps the most important type of knowledge for effective teaching skills is conditional knowledge—knowing exactly when and why each decision and/or action is needed. It is essential that teachers know how to do "the right thing, in the right way, at the right time, and for the right reason(s)." The last two parts reflect a teacher's conditional knowledge.

There are many discrete, effective teaching skills used by physical education teachers before and during class. They can be grouped into seven areas of related decisions and actions: (1) planning for instruction, (2) time and class management, (3) task presentation and task structure, (4) communication, (5) instructional information, (6) use of questions, and (7) lesson review and closure. Figure 4.1 shows how effective teaching skills for model-based instruction in physical education are built upon the proposed knowledge base presented in Chapter 2 and the instructional strategies presented in Chapter 3.

FIGURE 4.1   **Effective Teaching Skills for Model-Based Instruction in Physical Education**

Effective Teaching Skill Areas for Model-Based Instruction

1. Planning
2. Time and class management
3. Task presentation and structure

4. Communication
5. Instructional information
6. Use of questions
7. Review and closure

Strategies for Teaching Physical Education

Managerial	*Instructional*	
1. Preventive	**1.** Task presentation	**5.** Student safety
2. Interactive	**2.** Task structure	**6.** Task progression
3. Grouping	**3.** Task engagement	**7.** Use of questions
	4. Learning activities	**8.** Review and closure

Knowledge Areas for Model-Based Instruction

1. Learning Contexts
2. Learners
3. Learning theories
4. Developmental appropriateness
5. Learning domains and objectives

6. Physical education content
7. Task analysis and content progression
8. Assessment
9. Social/emotional climate
10. Equity in the gym
11. Curriculum models for PE

Area 1: Planning for Instruction

It might be said that the effectiveness of any lesson is determined before it begins by how well the teacher has planned for it. Good planning facilitates the flow of the lesson and leads to a more efficient use of time and other instructional resources. This, in turn, leads to higher levels of student learning in the lesson and content unit.

Effective teaching does not happen by accident. Teachers who are better prepared before class will use class time and other resources more efficiently, increase appropriate student engagement, and promote higher levels of student learning (Clark, 1983; Stroot & Morton, 1989). Novice and expert teachers will differ on the amounts of written planning they will need to be ready for a lesson (Housner & Griffey, 1985; Graham et al., 1993), but that is not really the most critical factor. It is more important that the teacher is *sufficiently prepared* when the lesson begins, regardless of whether the lesson plan is written in detail on paper, condensed on note cards, or "in one's head" from past experience. Specific components of a lesson plan for physical education will be discussed in Chapter 5. Once the instructional model has been selected, unit and lesson planning should contain:

1. Learning goals for the unit and each lesson
2. An overall managerial plan
3. Task presentation and learning cues
4. Needed equipment and facilities
5. A list of learning activities and content development plan
6. A floor/space plan for activities
7. An estimated "time budget" and transitions between class segments
8. Safety plans
9. Learning assessment procedures
10. Lesson review and closure plans

Area 2: Time and Classroom Management

Perhaps the most consistent findings from research on teaching is that there is a strong relationship between how students spend time in physical education and how much they achieve (Metzler, 1989). Early descriptive research indicated that students in physical education classes were more likely to be listening or waiting than actively engaged in learning tasks. Process-product research then established a positive relationship between student engagement and learning, meaning that the more time students spend in appropriate tasks, the more likely they are to achieve (Rink, 1996).

Time Management

Time management refers to the teacher's ability to maximize one of the most important learning resources available to her—the number of minutes allocated for each lesson. A lesson will consist of several segments or blocks of time, each one given to certain operations: management/organization, transition (moving students between segments), task presentation, learning activities, and closure/review. Since it is not possible to extend class longer than its scheduled length, extra minutes used in one segment must be taken away from other segments, including active learning time. Some amount of management, organization, and transition time is necessary in physical education, but it is the more effective teacher who keeps that time to the lowest possible amount, thereby maintaining optimal amounts of time in those segments that lead directly to learning. There are many actions that a teacher can take to maximize the use of available class time. Some of these decisions are made in the planning stage, others are made during the course of the lesson.

Set Out Equipment before Class.   Instructional time can be lost when the teacher must arrange equipment and materials during a class. Increased management time comes not only from having to do the arranging, but in lost momentum as students wait for the next activity to be organized (Siedentop, 1991). When safe and possible, the teaching area should be arranged before students arrive to class. If that is not possible, the teacher can then have equipment and materials in close proximity to where they will be set up and have students assist when it is time to arrange equipment for use.

Use an Alternative Role-Call Method. Using the traditional method of taking class roll by calling out each student's name to note attendance is time consuming and gets class off to a "sitting start," neither of which are good ways to begin physical education classes. If roll must be taken before class can begin, it should be taken as quickly as possible, such as having squad captains identify absent students or by using a sign-in sheet posted in the gym. If attendance can wait for a few minutes, it can be taken while students are warming up or are in their "instant activity" before the main part of the lesson begins.

Use Attention and Start Signals. Physical education teachers often hold class in large open spaces and noisy gymnasiums with many students. It can sometimes be difficult to get students' attention and to let them know it is OK to proceed. An attention signal is used to get students to stop what they are doing at that moment, put down their equipment, be silent, and pay attention to the teacher. These signals help the teacher to maintain a safe and orderly class and to bring activity to a quick stop. Signals can be verbal ("3 . . . 2 . . . 1 . . . Stop", a whistle, a shout), non-verbal (a raised hand, a finger over the mouth, waved arms), or a combination of both.

Start signals ensure that activity starts correctly and safely for all students at the same time. These signals indicate that the teacher is satisfied that "all is ready" and provides students with a cue that activity can begin. The teacher can tell students, "When I say 'go', you may begin to practice." After seeing that all is quiet and ready, the teacher then says "Go" to start the segment. It is also possible to use nonverbal start signals such as a hand clap or "starter's motion."

Practice and Review Classroom Management Routines. At times it will be useful to have students practice and review classroom management routines such as getting in lines, finding self-space, and putting equipment away properly. While this practice does take some time in the beginning, those minutes will be made up when the routines are completed quickly and correctly in the future.

It is helpful at times to review a managerial routine when it has not been used for a while. This can be done by reminding students or asking them to recall the correct procedure before the start signal is given. Once again, although this will take a few minutes, that time will be made up as students complete the routine quickly and correctly after being reminded.

Post Class Rules in Public. A good way to teach students class rules and to have the rules to review at all times is to post them in a public place, such as the locker room or entry into the gymnasium. Rather than reading or presenting rules to the class, the teacher can save time by having students read the rules on their own.

Post and Use an "Instant Activity" to Start Class. Too many physical education classes begin by students being inactive while the teacher takes roll or waits for the entire class to get to the gym. That early inactivity can set the tone for the rest of the lesson and lead to excessive management time as the teacher tries to overcome that initial inertia. In most cases the students are inactive because they simply do not have anything to do when they enter the gym. Instead, an *instant activity* can be planned to get the lesson off to an energetic, movement-based start. The activity should last only about three to five minutes, or until all students are present. It can be a general warm-up activity or one that will lead into the main part of the lesson content. The instant activity can be posted in the locker room or near the entry to the gym so that students can read it as they arrive and begin to participate immediately. Rauschenbach and Vanoer (1998) mention eight characteristics of instant activities (p. 7):

1. Require little set up
2. Take less than five minutes to complete
3. Are easy to learn
4. Can begin with little help from the teacher
5. Get students moving quickly
6. Are large muscle activities
7. Are designed for maximum success
8. Are modifiable for different ability levels

Some examples of instant activities are:

- Throwing and catching a ball
- Jogging or walking laps to music
- Stretching
- Nonelimination tag games
- Minigames (one-on-one, two-on-two, etc.)
- Cooperative games
- "Messing around" with equipment to be used later in class

Class Management

Class management is broader than time management, and its contribution to effective teaching is just as important. It refers to a number of decisions and teaching skills that provide an underlying structure to facilitate student learning and to establish a positive environment for the teacher and students. A good classroom manager can be likened to an orchestra conductor who must coordinate many musicians with the written music simultaneously in order to achieve the desired harmony. Although in the teacher's case, some of the contributing factors cannot be predicted before the class begins! Regardless, there are many discrete teaching skills that contribute to classroom management and good harmony.

Establishing the Learning Environment.   Students need to understand that class time in physical education is *learning time,* and that the gymnasium or other physical education settings are *places for learning*—just like all other classrooms in the school. It is the teacher's responsibility to establish his learning environment by making students aware of particular expectations, rules, conduct, and routines that apply in physical education. Effective teachers take extra time and effort to establish the learning environment in the first two weeks of school and to maintain that environment throughout the school year (Fink & Siedentop, 1989). Since the learning environment is typically complex, the teacher will have to establish it in several ways:

1. Have and enforce class rules about student safety, conduct, and responsibility
2. Use a set induction to set the stage for each lesson
3. Establish physical boundaries within which students must practice
4. Use and enforce attention and start/stop signals
5. Have students practice listening skills
6. Set rules for the care and use of equipment
7. Have and use a plan for student discipline
8. Be sure not to talk until all students are quiet and ready to listen

Manage Facilities and Equipment.   The teaching of most physical education content requires the use of much equipment and large instructional spaces. Effective teachers must plan ahead and during classes to maximize the distribution of equipment and the allocation of space to increase student engagement time and safety. Several considerations must be made for these managerial concerns.

Facilities
- Allocate activity space for safe participation
- Check the teaching area for safety hazards
- Remind students of out-of-bounds areas
- Make students aware of temporary hazards (wet grass, water on floor)
- Determine the number and location of learning centers and how many students can use each center at one time

Equipment
- Check condition, repair, and safety of equipment
- Check that equipment is sized correctly for students' safety and developmental readiness
- Check for the needed number of objects and implements for planning learning tasks
- Color code and match equipment when possible
- Teach and remind students of safety rules
- Use modified/adapted equipment when called for
- Use enough equipment to reduce or avoid student waiting

Monitor during Learning Activities.   Once the task presentation is complete and students are actively participating, it is important for the teacher to observe, or monitor, students. It is recommended that the teacher give the students a few minutes to organize themselves in the activity and get going on it. Once all of the students are active, the teacher should monitor to make sure that they are participating safely and according to the intended task structure.

Even the best-made plans do not guarantee classes will run smoothly and that students will always behave appropriately during managerial and learning tasks. Teachers must constantly monitor students to make sure they are doing what is expected of them in class. Some discrete teaching skills can be used for effective monitoring during class.

Circulate While Monitoring. Physical education teachers usually have many students spread out in large activity areas. It is not convenient to interact with students across the gym or field, so the teacher should be prepared to monitor by circulating around the area while students are practicing. This allows the teacher to more easily observe student practice and to quietly interact with one or a few students when needed.

"Back to the Wall." If a teacher monitors only from the middle of the gym or field (even while circulating), it is likely that many students are out of sight, behind the teacher's back. When the situation allows, it is a good idea for the teacher to circulate and monitor with her "back to the wall" as she moves around the activity area, thereby keeping all students in front and in eyesight (Graham, 1992).

Proximity Control. Given the number of students in a physical education class and the typically large activity area, some students will choose to take advantage of the distance between themselves and the teacher at any one moment and become off-task. Many times it is possible to get a student back on task simply by moving closer to him to let him know the teacher is paying attention. At other times it might be necessary to move the student to where the teacher is standing so he will be under direct supervision. Both ways of doing this are called proximity control which can be a very effective way of getting a student back on task without having to single him out or to stop class to discipline him.

Withitness. Kounin (1970) developed a description of a teacher monitoring skill that can be quite useful for physical education teachers. The idea of *withitness* means that a teacher can discern class events that she did not actually see happen through a keen ear for listening. We have all heard of the teacher who has eyes "behind his head" and seems to be aware of everything that goes on in his classroom or gym—even when students think he is not paying attention. That teacher is said to have good withitness and is able to monitor class events while doing other things at the same time. Withitness comes from knowing the typical patterns and sounds of events in the gym so as to be aware when something is not right at the moment.

Area 3: Task Presentation and Task Structure

One of the main functions of teaching is to provide students with information about learning activities they will be engaged in during class. For many types of learning in physical education it is critical that students become familiar with the skill or learning task, what the desired performance standard looks like (how well to do it), and how they will participate in the learning activity. The first two functions are provided in the *task presentation,* in which students see and/or hear what the next skill or task will be and how to perform it correctly. Information about how the learning task will be organized determines the *task structure* for the upcoming activity. The functions of task presentation and task structure will be separated here to increase clarity, but often a teacher will include both in a single episode. That is, the teacher's demonstration of the skill and its key performance elements occur within a simulation of the task structure for the upcoming activity. Task presentation and task structure represent both strategy and teaching skills in physical education. The strategic part is determined by how each one is designed and organized. The skilled part is determined by how the teacher communicates and interacts with students to facilitate each selected presentation and structure.

Task Presentation

Teachers plan for a variety of learning tasks in physical education. A learning task is the specific activity that students will engage in to acquire a motor skill, cognitive knowledge or concept, or affective outcome. Most learning tasks in physical education are activity-based, so students must have an understanding of what the task entails and how it should be performed before they can attempt the task. The process of providing that information to students is called *task presentation* (Rink, 1998). In a task presentation the teacher will provide students with learning cues—specific pieces of information about how to perform key elements of the task correctly. A full and complete task presentation requires the use of many effective teaching skills.

Getting and Keeping Student Attention. Even the best-planned task presentation will not be effective if students are not paying attention when the information is being given by the teacher. It should be conducted in a location that is comfortable for students and where the fewest possible distractions will be present. Attention signals are particularly helpful in getting students ready to listen and watch. Students should be organized around the teacher so that all of them can see and hear easily. The teacher can do some things to keep student attention once he has it:

- Ask questions often
- Check for understanding during and after each task presentation
- Make frequent eye contact with students
- Avoid repeating information too often
- Use proximity control by moving nearer to students who are not paying attention
- Make the task presentation interesting and "snappy"

Presenting Information Clearly to Students. Most task presentation information is given to students verbally and visually. Effective communications will include a well-paced and orderly flow of information to students, so it is important that the teacher carefully plans this part of class. When speaking, the teacher should check that all students are paying attention and are able to hear all that is said without having to raise her voice to strenuous levels. When presenting visual information, most often modeled examples of how to perform skills, the teacher should check that the model is presented from the best viewing angle and that all students have a good line of sight.

Providing a Full and Correct Model.   When demonstrating tasks that involve implements and/or objects, the teacher should provide students with a full example of the skill
or task using the correct form and desired result. It is not a good idea to model the skill/task
with an imaginary implement or object and by saying something like, "You get the picture,
even though I did not have a bat in my hand when I showed you."

Providing Verbal and Visual Information Together.   It is always more helpful to students if they get information in two modalities, typically verbal and visual. There is a powerful connection made when a student can see and hear information at the same time. In
addition, the teacher should accurately give both kinds of information and alert students
that what is being said goes with what is being modeled. Therefore, it is more effective to
overlay the modeled information with the verbal information (i.e., deliver both at once)
and not separate them (e.g., tell them, then show them).

Using an Active Task Presentation Whenever Possible.   An active task presentation
occurs when the students are hearing and seeing the key elements of the task and performing those elements at the same time. This allows students to see, hear, and move in
"real time" so that all three sensory modalities are being employed at once.
     It is not always possible to use an active task presentation. Sometimes it is not safe,
or the performance of the skills needs too much room. However, when possible to use, this
is an effective way to give students task presentation information and it allows the teacher
to directly check for students' comprehension before they are dispersed for practice. It is
also helpful to give a visual demonstration in slow motion the first few times as the verbal
cues are being matched with the physical movements. This allows students to comprehend
better by pairing each verbal cue with its movement counterpart. As students' comprehension increases, so too can the speed of the demonstration.

Using a Vocabulary That Students Can Understand.   The physical education teacher
will have a greater understanding of the skill/task and a more advanced technical vocabulary
than students, especially younger or novice students. It is not sufficient that the teacher can
understand what he is telling students; the task presentation must be communicated with
words and terms at the students' comprehension level. Sometimes it is necessary to translate
complex terms and concepts into words that are simpler and more familiar to students.

Determining the Best Model for the Presentation.   The teacher is most often the one
to show or model skill performances in task presentations. The teacher has the skill and
experience to provide an accurate and time-efficient demonstration. However, it should be
kept in mind that the teacher will typically demonstrate a more mature version of the performance than most students are capable of understanding, much less duplicating. When
feasible, the teacher can ask one student in the class to serve as the model to demonstrate
a more age-appropriate example for the other students to follow.
     There are other ways to provide students with models during task presentations.
Videotapes, CD ROMs, books, drawings, and photographs can also be used to give students the needed information about the skill and how to perform it. Perhaps the greatest advantage of these media is that students can use them independently from the

teacher when they are ready to get that information. There is less reliance on the teacher as the only source of skill information, allowing for more options in the delivery of task presentations.

Providing Appropriate and Accurate Models. Regardless of how the task presentation is delivered, it is critical that the students get appropriate and accurate information about the upcoming task. The *appropriateness* of task information is determined in several ways. It can refer to the *amount* of information given to students at one time. If students are given too little information they cannot achieve to their fullest potential. If students are given too much information or too many cues at once they will likely be confused and overwhelmed. Appropriateness can also refer to *how much of the task/skill* students get in one presentation. Some skills can be learned better by learning component parts one at a time; other skills are learned best by practicing the entire sequence of movements in one series. Whether to use part- or whole-task learning will depend on the specific task, students' readiness, and the teacher's expertise with that task.

The *accuracy* of task presentation information refers to how *correct* it is relative to some standard for performance. Proper technique is essential for many skills in physical education. Teachers must know the proper technique for the skill being explained and be able to communicate that information correctly to students. Teachers should remember that most students they instruct are novices and will follow any cues given to them— correct or incorrect. Therefore, it is important that teachers provide accurate cues at all times so that the "worst-case scenario" of teaching does not occur—students practice and learn the wrong techniques well!

Task Structure

Task presentation refers to what will be learned or practiced, while *task structure* describes for students how the practice segment will be organized. The way it will be used in this book, task structure includes three components from what Jones (1992) called a *task system* (task presentation and task structure combined): (1) a set of operations or procedures used to pursue the learning task, (2) resources and conditions that are available to accomplish the task, and (3) a means of accountability that indicates the importance or significance of the task (p. 412). Operations include the location and organization of the learning environment and directions for safe participation. Resources and conditions include equipment and the number of minutes allocated for the task. Accountability includes expectations for student behavior, a proficiency goal, or an explanation of how the task relates to subsequent learning activities in the lesson or unit. According to Jones (1992), once students become engaged in a learning task they can respond in any one of five ways (p. 418):

1. Pursue the stated task with success
2. Pursue the stated task with little or no success
3. Self-modify the task to make it more difficult and challenging
4. Self-modify the task to make it easier
5. Become off-task

You will note that only the first of these five ways of engaging contributes to student achievement on the learning task. This underscores the importance of the teacher planning and supervising to get students actively engaged in interesting tasks at a moderate to high success rate. Otherwise, students might choose to engage in ways that reduce their opportunity to learn while increasing inappropriate behavior in class. Teachers should be sure to include some of the following important elements in each task structure.

An Explanation of How Long the Task Will Last.   If students do not know how long each task will last, they cannot properly pace themselves to complete it within the allocated time. Some students might hurry to finish the task and then have to wait several minutes for the next task to begin. This leads to boredom. Other students might be too deliberate at the start of the segment and then run out of time at the end. This leads to anxiety and frustration. Students should know that a task has been allocated a set number of minutes ("Practice your shooting for fifteen minutes"), or be given at least an estimate ("Practice for about ten minutes and I will give you a two-minute warning before we stop").

Explanation of the Performance Criteria.   Performance criteria provide students with information about how well they should perform a given task, and help them make performance evaluations while they are practicing the task. Performance criteria can also be used to help students know when they have completed a task to a desired standard ("Do this until you can make seven out of ten") or to signal the end of one task and student readiness for the next task ("When you can complete five sets in a row, raise your hand, and we'll move on to something else"). Criteria can be established from several metrics: time, distance, accuracy, height, weight, form, consistency, percent correct or completed, by average score, or by beating one's previous "personal best" performance (see Figure 4.2). Whatever metric is used, it is important for the teacher to state the metric and the standard for performance as part of the task structure.

Designation of Task Space Configuration.   Every learning task will take place in a designated location in the gym, on a field, etc. Sometimes the entire class will be using one location (as in a game situation), a few locations (grouped practice), or multiple locations (station teaching). Students will need to be informed of the exact space plan for the upcoming task and how each area has been set up for that task. Advanced learners will need little of such information, but novices and young children will need to get explicit directions and even be shown how each learning area is set up. It is sometimes a good idea to draw up a floor/field space "map" as part of the lesson plan to provide a picture that can allow the space to be organized more efficiently and safely.

Expectations for Student Conduct and Responsibility.   Students are rarely passive participants in learning tasks. Except in the most direct teaching strategies, they will be given some degree of choice and responsibility for their behavior. Sometimes their responsibility is to other students as spotters, partners, team members, or assistants (e.g., tossing and retrieving balls, playing defense in an offensive drill). The task structure should communicate to students what is expected of them during each task regarding proper engagement, safety, waiting time, team/group participation, or assisting other students.

FIGURE 4.2   Metrics for Determining Task Performance Criteria

Performance Criterion Metric	Examples
Time	1. Complete an obstacle course in under 3 minutes. 2. Juggle three balls for at least 15 seconds. 3. Dribble a soccer ball through eight cones in less than 30 seconds.
Distance	1. Throw a softball 50 feet. 2. Run three laps around the track. 3. Hit the ball to the outfield.
Accuracy	1. Hit the smallest target. 2. Kick the soccer ball into the left side of the goal. 3. Throw to your partner so she does not have to move to catch the ball. 4. Make legal serves (tennis, badminton, pickleball).
Height	1. Jump over the lowest bar. 2. Toss the ball 3 feet over your head and catch it. 3. Walk at a low level.
Weight	1. Lift 25 pounds with a bench press. 2. Use the heaviest ball.
Form	1. Use the correct technique. 2. Balance on two body parts. 3. "Do it just the way I showed you."
Consistency	1. Complete twenty-five rope jumps in a row. 2. Get five serves in the target in a row before you move back.
Percent completed	1. Score higher than 75% on the test. 2. Get 60% of your first serves in play.
Average score	1. Try it four times. Your average score should be 8 or better. 2. A good bowling average is around 75 for middle-schoolers.
Personal best	1. Try [it] once, then try [it] again. Try to beat your first score the second time. 2. Look in your fitness log for your best time. Try to beat that today.

Explanation of Intratask Variations.   Many times a teacher will plan for several versions of a learning task, typically set up as different centers. This is called intratask variation (Graham, 1992), designed to give students different ways to practice the same or related skill. For instance, five centers could be set up for kicking practice with each one using a different kind of ball to be kicked or using a slightly different kicking technique—all at about the same level of difficulty. The teacher will need to inform students of the different organization, criteria, and safety points for each center as part of the task structure.

It is not correct to assume that students, especially young ones or novices, will be able to detect the differences as they move from center to center.

Explanation of Student Options to Change Task or Its Difficulty.   Graham et al. (1998) use a technique called teaching by invitation, in which multiple centers or tasks are set up to practice the same skill with varying degrees of difficulty. The teacher explains the key elements for each center/task in the task presentation and then permits ("invites") each student to pick which level of difficulty he/she wishes to attempt. Task structure information is used to help students determine the requirements for each center/task, to help them select where they will begin, and how to know if the level of difficulty is inappropriate for them. Some restrictions might need to be made on the number of students who can work at one center or task, again communicated as part of the task structure.

Using Attention, Start, and Stop Signals.   An important part of the task structure is to inform students when they can begin and what signal will indicate when to stop and pay attention. Any familiar signal will work, but it is a good idea to remind students of it during the task structure briefing.

Checking for Understanding of Task Structure.   Just as a teacher should check for understanding of the task presentation content, she should check for understanding of the task structure before students are dispersed for practice. Some simple questions can be used, such as "When I say 'go' where will Squad 1 line up?", "How long will we be practicing this task?", "What should you do when I give the 'stop' signal?", "How can you tell when you are in a safe area of the gym?", or "What should you do when you have finished?"

Monitoring Task Structure Early and Regularly.   Once students are dispersed for practice the teacher should take a moment to monitor the class to check that students are engaged according to the directions that were just given. Immediate and appropriate engagement are indicators of good task structure information. Delayed or incorrect task engagement can mean that some students did not understand the task structure and should alert the teacher to stop the class and make things clear to students before more time is lost. The teacher should also monitor for appropriate task engagement periodically during the activity segment, making adjustments as needed.

Area 4: Communication

Effective teachers communicate in ways that allow students to understand instructional information and questions well, and which use the least amount of class time possible. There are many aspects to effective class communications.

Get students' attention.   Communication will not be effective if the listeners are not ready to receive it. In physical education that means using an attention signal, getting students in close proximity, getting them quiet, and eliminating distractions—all before the teacher begins to speak.

Be clear. Information must be presented in a manner that allows for all students to comprehend. The teacher should face the students directly, be articulate, and speak at a rate that students can follow.

Use an appropriate vocabulary level. The words and terms used should be at the appropriate vocabulary level for students. This means that the teacher will need to use different words across grade levels, even for the same task or content. There is one precaution to keep in mind—just because the teacher understands what was said does not mean that students understand it!

Use voice inflections. Students will pay less attention to verbal information given with a monotone delivery. Teachers should use voice inflections to keep students alert and to help students discern the more important pieces of information they receive.

Check for understanding. Mentioned previously, it is important that the teacher knows students have heard and understood verbal information before letting them follow the directions or engage in the learning task. If the teacher's initial monitoring indicates that students did not understand, additional time must be taken to stop class, get the students' attention again, and repeat the directions. This wastes time and breaks the flow of the lesson—and it can be annoying to the teacher. Teachers should develop the habit of checking for understanding every time students receive information.

Area 5: Instructional Information

Most of the information that teachers provide to students is given for the purpose of enhancing learning. Such information can be provided before, during, and after skill attempts or learning activities. *Cues* are pieces of information given before practice and intended to facilitate the upcoming learning trials. *Guides* are given to students during a practice trial. Performance *feedback* is provided to students after the trial is completed and pertains directly back to the attempt.

Cues

Teachers provide students with "bits" of learning information during task presentations—called *cues*. Cues alert students to key performance elements in the upcoming task as tips about how to perform with greater proficiency. Although most cues are given during the task presentation, they can occur at any time in a lesson and can be directed to one student, a group, or the entire class. Cues can be delivered in a variety of ways:

1. Verbal: Spoken information about how to perform better
2. Nonverbal: Gestures and modeled examples of correct or incorrect movements
3. Combination: Simultaneous verbal and nonverbal information

| 4. Manipulative: | "Hands-on" cues in which the teacher moves parts of the student's body to make the communication (e.g., moving the student's hand into the correct tennis grip, turning the student's shoulders into the proper alignment in the golf set-up, moving a dancer's foot into the proper position) |
| 5. Mediated: | Cues that are provided through audio-visual media, such as videotapes, CD ROMs, drawings, and photographs |

Guides

Students often need performance information while they are still attempting a skill or are involved in a dynamic task, such as a lead-up or full game setting. This type of instructional information is called a *guide*. It is typically delivered verbally, but could come from non-verbal and manipulated information. Some examples of guides are:

1. Students are in a full-court basketball game and a fast break develops. The teacher yells, "Get the ball to the middle, and fill the passing lanes . . . defense, get back, get back!"
2. Students are practicing a square dance. As the music plays, the teacher says, "OK, now get ready for the next call, keep with the music . . . keep your head up and find your partner."
3. Students are stretching. The teacher moves one student's leg into the correct position for the quad stretch.

Feedback

One of the teacher's most essential instructional functions is to provide students with information about the adequacy of completed task performances. This information is called *feedback* and is critical to the learning process. Interestingly, while we have known for many years about the importance of performance feedback in physical education, recent research has raised some questions about the exact role it plays in this process (Silverman, Tyson, & Krampitz, 1993). Researchers are confident that learners need performance feedback; they are less confident about describing when and how feedback becomes most effective (Rink, 1996).

There are many dimensions to describe what type of performance feedback a student is receiving at any given moment in class (see Figure 4.3):

1. Origin or agent
2. Congruency
3. Content
4. Accuracy
5. Timing
6. Modality
7. Evaluation
8. Corrective attributes
9. Direction

FIGURE 4.3 Dimensions of Performance Feedback

Dimension	Types	Examples
Origin or feedback agent Refers to the source of feedback information.	**1.** Task intrinsic Feedback information that a student can ascertain for herself by observing the result of a skill attempt. That general information provides the student with some degree of feedback about performance, typically on its success or nonsuccess. **2.** Task extrinsic (or augmented) Performance information provided by another person or agent that is not part of the task itself. That person is usually the teacher, but it could also be another student. Task extrinsic feedback can refer to any part of the completed still attempt, including the performance result, form, technique, effort, or quality.	**1.** Student sees a ball hits its intended target. Student hears and feels solid contact on a swing. **2.** Teacher says, "I liked your follow-through that time." A classmate tells another student, "Way to go!"
Congruency of feedback Refers to how well the feedback matches the key elements being practiced at the moment.	**1.** Congruent Includes a reference to the specific learning cue/s emphasized during the task presentation. **2.** Incongruent Does not include a reference to the specific learning cue/s of the moment.	**1.** If the teacher told students in his task presentation to "really concentrate on making a nice, long follow-through on your (tennis backhand) swing," then any feedback that pertains to the follow-through is considered congruent. **2.** If after that same task presentation the teacher directs feedback toward a student's service form, forehand shot, or *some other part* of the backhand shot, that feedback is considered incongruent at the moment.
Feedback content Refers to the reference point of the feedback information.	**1.** General Contains no mention of which part of the completed skill attempt is being referred to by the teacher. It makes only a general indication that the attempt was satisfactory or not. **2.** Specific Includes a reference to which part of the completed skill attempt is being described by the teacher. Specific feedback provides the learner with more useful information and is preferred over general feedback in nearly all situations.	**1.** "That was good." "Way to go." "That wasn't right." "Nice." **2.** "You really followed through that time." "Your wrist was not in the right position." "You were not quick enough to cover the base." "You really had good balance that time."

(continued)

FIGURE 4.3 Continued

Dimension	Types	Examples
Accuracy of feedback Refers to the correctness of the feedback. Does the information communicated to the student really describe the performance?	1. Accurate The performance information is a correct description of the skill attempt. 2. Inaccurate The performance information is not a correct description of the skill attempt.	Self-explanatory
Timing Refers to the span between the end of the skill attempt and the delivery of the feedback information to the learner.	1. Immediate Feedback is provided to the learner right after the skill attempt is completed or at least before the next skill attempt occurs. 2. Delayed Feedback is not provided immediately or soon after the skill attempt, or not until more skill attempts have been completed.	1. Student finishes a high jump and the teacher tells her right away, "You really had good form on that jump." 2. Twenty minutes later, as the class is ending, the teacher says to the same student, "It looked like you were not extending your kick leg fully enough in your jumps today."
Modality Refers to how augmented feedback is provided to students.	1. Verbal Provided to students in the form of spoken words or phrases. It is what the teacher says to students about the completed skill attempt. 2. Nonverbal Provided in the form of gestures made to students. 3. Combination Verbal and nonverbal information given at the same time.	1. "You really did a nice job that time." "I liked your effort." "You did not run fast enough." 2. Giving the "OK" signal Hand clapping A pat on the back A reenactment of part or all of the skill attempt 3. Saying, "Way to go" while the teacher pats a student on the back. Saying, "You gave a really nice fake on the defender" while modeling the faking move for the student at the same time.

Evaluation
Indicates whether or not the teacher is expressing approval/agreement or disapproval/disagreement to the student about the adequacy of the completed performance.

1. Positive
   Approval or agreement with the completed performance.
2. Negative
   Disapproval or disagreement with the completed performance.
3. Neutral
   It is not clear if the teacher is stating a positive or negative indication.

1. "I really liked that."
   "I think you made the right decision on that play."
   "Nice try."
2. "That was the wrong play by the goal keeper."
   "Team 2 is not trying very hard."
   "You gave up that time."
   "Your balance was way off on that last swing."
3. "Not bad."
   "You had some of it correct that time."

Corrective attributes
Is the feedback coupled with information about how to correct mistakes?

1. Noncorrective
   Contains only information that the performance was incorrect or not approved of by the teacher.
2. Corrective
   Provides feedback plus information (cues) about how to improve the next performance.

1. "Your feet were in the wrong place."
   "You missed the ball."
   "You will never succeed that way."
2. "That was better, but next time keep your head up."
   "Your elbow was extended too far. Keep it tucked right next to your body."

Direction
Refers to whom the feedback information is directed.

1. Individual feedback is directed to a single student.
2. Group feedback is directed to a recognized group of students in class.
3. Class feedback is directed to all students in the class.

1. "Donna was really trying hard in class today."
2. "Squad 2. . . ."
   "Jerry's team. . . ."
   "Everyone at this end of the gym . . ."
3. "Everyone was really well-behaved today."
   "This class showed great teamwork."

We know that feedback is an important part of the learning process, but we do not yet know the best way to use it in every situation (Rink, 1996). However, research from motor learning and pedagogy provides some "rules of thumb" that teachers can keep in mind for this important teaching skill:

1. More feedback is usually better than less feedback
2. Specific feedback is more effective than general feedback
3. Immediate feedback is more effective than delayed feedback
4. Corrective feedback helps the learner more than negative feedback
5. Combination feedback is more helpful than verbal or nonverbal alone
6. Advanced learners can get by with less feedback, but it should be more specific
7. Novice learners need all the feedback they can get, including feedback that motivates and acknowledges effort

Area 6: Use of Questions

Teachers' use of questions has been emphasized in classroom subjects for many years. Only recently has it become an integral part of the effective physical education teachers' repertoire. The increased need for effective questioning skills in physical education has come with the expanded use of interactive teaching strategies for content areas such as movement education, skill themes, concept learning, and affective outcomes. Questions can be categorized according to their focus and type.

Question Focus

The focus of a question is determined by that aspect of the class to which it pertains. *Managerial questions* focus on noninstructional parts of the lesson such as class organization, preparation of the learning environment, class procedures, and routines. Typical managerial questions are "Where does the equipment go when you are finished with it?", "What time is class supposed to begin?", or "Can I have three volunteers to help me set up the nets?" *Behavior questions* focus on student in-class conduct such as class rules or safety. Some examples are "Who can tell me two things to keep in mind about safety in this next drill?", "What is our rule about improper language?", "Marie, do you know it's not OK to get a drink of water without my permission?", or "What do you do when I give the attention signal?" *Content questions* are used to develop student learning of the subject matter. They can promote learning in all three domains depending on the type of response given by students to the question.

Types of Content Questions

Benjamin Bloom and his colleagues (Bloom, Englehart, Furst, Hill, & Krathwohl, 1956) developed a classification system for content questions based on their classic taxonomy of the cognitive domain. Because of the strong link between the cognitive and psychomotor domains, it is possible for physical educators to use each type of question to promote learning in both domains. From the same or similar question, a student can develop two kinds of responses: a verbal response in the cognitive domain and/or a movement response in the psychomotor domain. Examples of questions for each domain, based on the levels of Bloom's taxonomy, are shown in Figure 4.4.

Knowledge, comprehension, and application questions in Bloom's taxonomy are referred to as *lower-order questions* because they appear on the bottom half of the original taxonomic scheme. Typically they require less knowledge and ability for making responses. Analysis, synthesis, and evaluation questions are referred to as *higher-order questions* because they are positioned on the top half of the taxonomic scheme. Because they build

FIGURE 4.4   Levels of Questions for Physical Education

Content Question Type	Purpose	For Cognitive Response	For Movement Response
A. Knowledge	Asks students to recall previously learned facts, simple ideas, or concepts.	"Can you tell me three key elements for the batter's stance we discussed last time?"	"Can you show me the correct batting stance we learned yesterday?"
B. Comprehension	Requires students to translate, interpret, or compare facts or ideas.	"What is a hop? What is a jump? How are they different?"	"Who can show me a hop, then a jump, then another hop?"
C. Application	Asks students to solve problems that are based on previously learned facts or ideas.	"What is the best formation for receiving a 'floater' volleyball serve?"	"Team 1, can you get yourselves into correct position and receive the 'floater' serve I am sending to you?"
D. Analysis	Asks students to break down the elements of complex concepts, to examine relationships, and to detect organizational patterns and principles.	"When do you run a fast break and when do you go into your half-court offense?"	In a drill the teacher directs point guards to either make a fast break or "slow it up" when they get an outlet pass.
E. Synthesis	Ask students to generate new knowledge by putting together two or more facts, ideas, or concepts.	"How do you know when you have reached your optimal heart rate zone for exercise?"	"Can you practice an exercise that will place you in your target zone within 5 minutes of starting it?"
F. Evaluation	Ask students to make judgments based on personal knowledge and feelings, or knowledge generated by other people.	"What makes the difference between a 6.7 and 7.0 on a floor exercise routine?"	"Can you perform two floor exercise routines with one that would be judged higher than the other?"

on knowledge from the lower order and involve the creation of new knowledge, they are more complex and difficult to answer in both the cognitive and motor dimensions. The best question at any given moment depends on the teacher's purpose for asking it and student readiness to make a successful response.

Convergent questions most often lead to one correct answer, whether the response is made in the cognitive or psychomotor domains. They are sometimes called *close-ended questions* because the teacher will have one correct answer in mind and ask a convergent question to prompt that single response. Examples are "How many positions are there in soccer?", "Can you show me the sideline boundary for tennis singles?", or "Who can use their compass to find and point to due north from here?" *Divergent,* or *open-ended questions* allow multiple correct or feasible answers to a single question—usually a higher-order question. Again, responses can be made primarily in either the cognitive or psychomotor domains. Some examples are "Can you show me how many ways you can hold a static balance with your partner?", "When would you use the high deep serve in badminton?", or "Under what conditions might a compound bow not be the best kind for you to use?" Again, the choice of a convergent or divergent question will depend on what the teacher is trying to have students learn, their level of ability/knowledge, and the students' experience with the content.

Effective Teaching Skills for the Use of Questions

It is not enough for a teacher to know the focus and types of questions to use in class. There are some skills that teachers should use to make questioning a more effective part of the instructional process.

Use Wait Time.   *Wait time* refers to the amount of time that passes from the end of the teacher's question to calling on an answer from students (Rowe, 1986). It is generally best for the teacher to have about three seconds of wait time, which allows more students to develop an answer and keeps the students with the faster answers from getting called on more often than others (Tobin, 1987). Adequate wait time allows every student to come up with their own answer and to then privately compare their answer to the student who was called on by the teacher.

Have Rules for Responding to Questions.   Effective teachers develop rules for students to follow when responding to questions. These rules make the process more orderly and provide students with the best opportunity to learn from questions asked in class. Some rules are:

- Students must raise a hand to be called on.
- Students cannot say the answer out loud until called on.
- Students cannot use inappropriate gestures to get the teacher's attention.
- Teacher and students should not criticize answers given by other students (especially for divergent and personal responses).
- Teacher and students should allow complete answers. Do not cut off students who answer slowly.

Responding to Incorrect Answers.   Students who get called on to say or show their answer to a teacher's question can give an incorrect answer at times. Since that moment is very public for the student, the teacher must be sensitive and careful when providing comments and feedback. Some guidelines can be followed when this happens:

- Do not ignore the answer and quickly call on another student.
- Give the student a chance to clarify by asking a "redirect" question.
- Be sensitive in your reply. Say, "That was not the answer I was looking for," not, "That was wrong. Sit down. Next."
- Give the student more time if you think she is close to the correct answer.

Area 7: Lesson Review and Closure

In nearly all instructional models a well-planned physical education class will end with a brief review of the lesson and a defined closure. The purpose of this segment is to bring the lesson to "full cycle" by tying together set induction, task presentation, instructional activities, and observed student learning. It can also be used to preview the next lesson in the unit. Good lesson review and closure includes several elements:

1. *A quick transition to closure.* Since time is short it is essential that the teacher get students out of the last learning activity and into closure quickly. This allows adequate time for that purpose and avoids doing it hurriedly or "on the run" to the exit door or locker room. A key decision at this junction is whether the teacher should bring the students back to one group or to conduct the review/closure with students dispersed around the gym. That decision can be based on the amount of time left and the need to put equipment away. If there is enough time, bring the students into one group in a convenient place. If time is short, and equipment must be put up, conduct the review with students "in place" and have them put up the equipment after the closure is made.

2. *Review the organization and structure of class.* The teacher should ask students general questions like "Who can tell me what kinds of things we did in class today?", "Was there anything special about the way we did those things today?", or "From now on, that's the way we will enter the gym and line up. Can you remember that until next class?" This allows students to realize that the class had a definite organization and plan and that they should remember that plan for next time.

3. *Review learning cues.* During the course of the lesson, students can often forget the learning cues and key elements covered in the task presentation segment. This is a good time to get them to review those cues or to ask them analysis questions like "Which of the cues were the most important ones to remember while you practiced?" It is important to make this review interactive by asking students questions rather than just telling them the cues once again.

4. *Review student conduct, rules, and safety procedures.* Be sure to compliment students when they were well behaved and followed the rules.

5. *Make an informal assessment of learning.* One of the best uses of this segment is to informally assess what students learned in the lesson. This can be accomplished with a few brief questions, like "How many of you were able to . . .", "How many completed their goal at every station?", or "If you know all three cues we learned today, please raise your hand."

6. *Preview of next lesson.* The last part of the closure should give students a preview of their next lesson to spark their interest and let them know what they can expect next time in physical education.

7. *Have a dismissal.* The class should end just as it began, in an orderly fashion. The teacher can give a verbal signal to students that class is over and that they should walk to the locker room or to the exit door.

That is a lot to do within a lesson segment that should last no more than three minutes! However, most parts of the review/closure last only a few seconds. The largest amount of time should be given to the review of actual lesson content so that students leave the gym with an understanding of what and how they learned in physical education.

Summary

The lists of effective teaching skills and their component parts in this chapter can be intimidating to read, especially for novice teachers. Do effective teachers really do all of those things in class? Yes and no. Effective physical education teachers will have the complete repertoire of those skills, along with good procedural and conditional knowledge for each one. However, the instructional model in place and its accompanying instructional strategies will call upon a smaller number of teaching skills to be used in any given lesson. As has been emphasized many times in this book, the teacher who can successfully apply situation-specific decisions and actions will be effective more often. That use of effective teaching skills comes from good planning, experience, and regular updating of one's instructional abilities.

LEARNING ACTIVITIES

1. Select one of the seven application areas for effective teaching skills in physical education presented in this chapter. Conduct a brief literature review on the research findings for that area in physical education. Make a list of "What we know" and "What we still need to learn" about that area. You might need to ask your instructor for a list of sources for your review.

2. Using the same sources from Activity 1, explain what an effective physical education teacher would do, or not do, in that area of instruction. How does research inform practice in that area?

3. The next time you teach a lesson provide a self-assessment of your own skills in each of the seven areas of effective teaching presented in this chapter. What evidence did you use to make your assessment?

4. Assume you are a mentor teacher trying to help a novice physical educator improve on each of the seven areas of effective teaching. What advice would you give that novice teacher for learning how to be effective in each area? Be sure to write out your answers as if you were talking to this teacher in person.

SUGGESTED READINGS

Rink, J. (1998). *Teaching physical education for learning* (3rd ed.). Boston: WCB McGraw-Hill.

Siedentop, D. (1991). *Developing teaching skills in physical education* (3rd ed.). Mountain View, CA: Mayfield.

Silverman, S., & Ennis, C. (1996). *Student learning in physical education: Applying research to enhance instruction.* Champaign, IL: Human Kinetics.

5 Planning for Effective Instruction in Physical Education

One of the most important contributions to effective instruction in physical education is planning. Research on teaching has demonstrated that effective instruction is intentional and purposeful. Well-organized units and lessons have a greater chance of leading to student achievement of the intended learning goals (Clark, 1983). Planning needs to take place before the unit begins and regularly during the length of the unit. You will notice that I did not say "daily" because some instructional models use *modular planning* that covers two or three consecutive lessons, or *unified planning* that covers the entire unit, eliminating the need for daily lesson planning. That does not mean the teacher does no planning—only

FIGURE 5.1   **The Role of Planning in a Teacher's Knowledge Base**

Planning for Model-Based Instruction

Unit Planning		*Lesson Planning*	
Context analysis	Selecting learning	Context description	Learning activities
Content analysis	activities	Lesson objectives	Task presentation and structure
Learning objectives	Assessment	Time and space	Assessment
Selecting a model	Teacher functions	allocations plan	Review/closure
Management scheme	Student functions		

Effective Teaching Skill Areas for Model-Based Instruction

1. Planning
2. Time and class management
3. Task presentation and structure
4. Communication
5. Instructional information
6. Use of questions
7. Review and closure

Strategies for Teaching Physical Education

Managerial	*Instructional*	
1. Preventive	1. Task presentation	5. Student safety
2. Interactive	2. Task structure	6. Task progression
3. Grouping	3. Task engagement	7. Use of questions
	4. Learning activities	8. Review and closure

Knowledge Areas for Model-Based Instruction

1. Learning Contexts
2. Learners
3. Learning theories
4. Developmental appropriateness
5. Learning domains and objectives
6. Physical education content
7. Task analysis and content progression
8. Assessment
9. Social/emotional climate
10. Equity in the gym
11. Curriculum models for PE

that the majority of planning is completed before the unit begins so the model operates from a "flowing" plan that carries over from lesson to lesson.

Figure 5.1 shows the relationship between planning and other aspects of a teacher's knowledge for teaching physical education. Planning serves to facilitate the transfer of content knowledge and general pedagogical knowledge into content pedagogical knowledge—the ability to effectively teach a specified content to a certain group of learners (Shulman, 1987).

Why Plan?

Instructional planning ties together the context, the learning goals, the learning activities, classroom management, and assessment within the model being used for each unit. It requires the teacher to consider many complex factors that will interact in a dynamic setting and take place in a predetermined (and usually restricted) span of time. Planning and anticipation are essential skills that allow a teacher to efficiently organize herself, students, facilities, and available resources to lead students toward stated instructional goals in the shortest amount of time. Teachers may plan so they will feel more comfortable in front of class because the planning process lets them review the content ahead of time or because it allows others to see how well they are organized. In my opinion, the single most important reason for planning is to improve the likelihood that students will learn the intended instructional outcomes with the most efficient expenditure of time, effort, and resources. In other words, planning should be done for no other reason than to increase the teacher's effectiveness within each unit and lesson. This clearly puts the *function* of planning well ahead of the *form* of planning.

Novice teachers soon discover the difference between planning and being prepared. *Planning* is the process of making decisions and producing a written document for each unit and lesson to be taught. However, having planned does not always mean a teacher is actually prepared and properly organized for effective instruction. The catch is that you can plan but not be prepared; but if you are prepared you have planned well enough. That also answers the question: How much planning should a teacher do? Enough to be prepared! Sometimes planning time will be quite short, particularly when a teacher has instructed the same content to the same grade level in the same context several times in the past. When the teacher is not familiar with the students, the content, or the context, much longer planning time should be expected in order to be prepared.

Guidelines for Planning

It is easy for a novice teacher to underestimate or overestimate the planning process in physical education. To underestimate the planning process means that the teacher will not be prepared and the instruction will not be as effective as it could have been. There is also a tendency for underprepared teachers to become anxious and confused in the midst of poorly planned lessons, with that anxiety and confusion being apparent to students. To overestimate the planning process means that the teacher will spend more time and energy than necessary to get ready—time that could be given to other aspects of one's professional and personal life.

Planning for effective instruction in physical education is done on two levels: the unit and the lesson. Unit planning includes all of the decisions and readiness actions that take place before the unit begins. It provides the "big picture" on learning goals, content to be taught, learning activities, needed resources, and class management—all within the instructional model selected for the unit. Lesson planning includes many of the same types of decisions and readiness actions made right before and during each lesson in the unit. It should be emphasized that both levels of planning are critical to effective teaching and learning. In order to approach the planning process realistically at both levels, the following guidelines should be helpful:

Make "firm but flexible" plans.   *Firm* plans give the teacher a good idea of how the instruction will proceed before it begins. This allows the teacher to anticipate many of the key factors and events that will affect the conduct, management, and outcomes of instruction. *Flexible* plans give the teacher a few reasonable options when unforeseen conditions or events force changes in the original plan.

Write the plan primarily for your own use.   It is the teacher who must use the plan to promote effective classroom management and learning. Therefore, the plan should be written in a way that the teacher can understand and implement. The specific form of the plan should be chosen by the teacher to match the needs of his situation. Some teachers have a "personal shorthand" for making notes to themselves; this is a good practice, especially for lesson plans. Plans should be as detailed and as functional as the *teacher* needs them to be.

When in doubt, overplan a bit.   It is sometimes difficult to project how long it will take the majority of students to progress through content. Therefore, it is recommended that teachers prepare a bit more in each unit and lesson than is anticipated in case students move along faster than expected.

Have a related alternate plan.   Physical education units and lessons often depend on factors that are out of the teacher's control: prolonged bad weather during outdoor units, equipment breakage or failure, changes in the school's schedule, availability of facilities, and excessive student absences. When these and other situations arise it is important that the teacher is able to provide students with learning activities that are directly related to the present content and are not from a makeshift plan. A teacher can plan ahead for a "fail-safe" lesson on unit content that can be implemented under nearly any circumstance to maintain continuity in the instruction. Good fail-safe lessons are: coverage of rules and strategy, officiating, how to select and purchase equipment, history and background of the content, group projects, modified games, internet searches, media presentations, or group discussions.

Keep all written planning records.   Most content units have a short useful life within a school year. They last anywhere from a few days to several weeks and are not taught again until the next year. Lesson plans have a much shorter useful life. Most are used just once, then not again until the next time the unit is offered. Some plans are not needed for another whole year. Diligent teachers will increase the "shelf life" of planning records by filing them away after each use and then referring to them in the planning stage the next time the unit is offered.

Reflect on completed units and lessons.   Because units and each lesson in them are usually taught only once each year, it is important for teachers to take time to reflect on, evaluate, and make notes for modifying plans that have just been used. These notes can then be filed with the plan and will be there as reminders the next time the plan is used.

Planning as a Blueprint for Action

Whether for a single lesson or an entire unit, the written plan serves as a blueprint for the teacher and students. Like drawing a blueprint for a building, the planning process allows the teacher to think about, decide, and visualize a series of steps that will promote more effective and efficient instruction. This becomes a tangible picture of how events will happen and a source for making well-informed modifications as the unit progresses. And, just like the builder who has a blueprint in hand when the construction starts, a written plan gives the teacher several advantages:

1. Predetermined starting and ending points are made for the unit and each lesson
2. The plan can be referred to along the way to check for progress
3. The plan provides reference points for making long- and short-term decisions
4. The plan can be used as the basis for making modifications along the way
5. The plan allows for better evaluations of teaching effectiveness by comparing what was planned with what actually happened
6. The teacher can use the plan to verify that she is teaching according to the design of the instructional model

Unit Planning

Physical education instructional units can last from a few days to several weeks. Regardless of the length of the unit, the instruction is more likely to be effective when the teacher has made a clear and coherent plan before the unit begins. Once the unit plan is in place, the planning for daily lessons becomes much easier as the unit progresses. A complete unit plan should contain nine components: (1) a contextual analysis, (2) a content analysis and listing, (3) learning objectives, (4) selection of the instructional model to be used, (5) a managerial scheme, (6) learning activities, (7) assessment and/or grading, (8) a description of the teacher's functions in the unit, and (9) a description of the students' functions in the unit.

Contextual Analysis

The role of context in teaching is extremely important. Context refers to the sum of all temporal, human, and material factors that influence what is taught, how it is taught, and what students will learn in the unit. Some contextual factors will facilitate instruction and learning by providing the teacher with many ways to be effective. Other contextual factors will inhibit the teacher's effectiveness by reducing options for providing effective instruction. Most contextual factors are given; that is, they simply "are there" and cannot be controlled by the teacher to any significant extent in the unit. The four main determinants of context are the teacher, the students, the content, and available resources. Figure 5.2 shows these determinants and some key questions that must be asked within the context analysis for any unit of instruction.

FIGURE 5.2 **Major Contextual Determinants for Unit Planning**

Determinant	Key Questions for Context Analysis
The teacher	1. What do I know about this content?
	2. What experience do I have teaching this content to this grade level?
	3. Where can I go to gain content knowledge? (e.g., books, colleagues, clinics)
The students	1. How many will be in this class each time?
	2. How many and which students have special learning needs?
	3. What are those needs and what do I know about teaching those students?
	4. What is the typical developmental stage in this class?
	5. What is the students' motivation to learn this content?
The content	1. What is the expected range of student ability and knowledge of this content?
	2. What do students at this age/stage need to know about this content?
	3. What specific content should be covered in this unit?
	4. In what order should the content be learned? Does it matter?
	5. Will I need to modify the content to meet students' abilities?
	6. How long should it take most students to learn each part of the unit?
	7. What learning goals should students pursue?
	8. How can I assess that learning?
Available resources	1. How many lessons will the unit include?
	2. How many actual minutes are available for instruction in each class?
	3. How much content can students reasonably learn in that amount of time?
	4. What is my teaching area for the unit?
	5. How many stations, courts, fields, etc. can the area accommodate?
	6. What equipment do I have for this unit?
	7. What is the ratio of equipment/implements/objects to students?
	8. Do I have to modify equipment for safe and effective usage?
	9. Will I have any assistance (team teacher, teacher's aide)?

Content Analysis and Listing

A content analysis determines what will be included in the unit and the order in which students will learn the content. It is important to know that the results of the content analysis will have a strong bearing on what can be taught and learned in the unit, so it must be the first step after the contextual analysis. The content analysis begins by listing the developmentally appropriate psychomotor skills, cognitive knowledge areas, and affective dispositions essential to the activity, sport, dance, or skill themes. The teacher then considers the students' current abilities, knowledge, and attitudes, using those considerations as the starting point for the unit content. The ending point is determined by estimating how long it will take most students to learn each part of the content while considering the number of lessons in the unit. That will help the teacher decide how much progress (and content) is reasonable for that unit, determining the *amount* of content to be taught and learned. The content areas to be taught are then placed in a logical order of progression (if it matters), completing the content analysis and listing. Some examples of content lists are shown in Figure 5.3.

Learning Objectives

A key part of the planning process is the determination of student learning objectives in the unit. The stated objectives must reflect the results of the contextual analysis and the content selected for the unit. Objectives can be stated at two levels: general and behavioral. General objectives are just what the term implies: global areas of intended student learning within each domain. Behavioral objectives describe specific performance criteria that stu-

FIGURE 5.3   Content Listings for Some Physical Education Units

Grade Level	Content Unit	Lessons	Content Listing
First	Movement concepts	First eight of the year	1. PE class rules 2. Safety in PE class 3. Self space, general space, scatter space 4. Pathways 5. Levels 6. Balancing 7. Twisting 8. Leaping 9. Hopping 10. Dodging 11. Low-organization movement games
Fifth	Soccer	Ten	1. Dribbling 2. Trapping 3. Passing 4. Shooting on goal 5. Goal-keeping 6. Basic rules and strategies 7. Offensive positions 8. Basic offensive plays 9. Modified games (4 vs. 4, smaller field)
Eleventh	Personal fitness	Twenty	1. Concepts of personal fitness 2. Planning a safe fitness program 3. Safe stretching 4. Introduction to workout options 5. Guided instruction on workout machines 6. Preassessment 7. Design and complete a personal fitness program 8. Postassessment

dents will demonstrate within each general objective area. Figure 5.4 provides some examples of how general objectives lead to behavioral objectives in physical education.

Note that the behavioral objectives have three main parts: (1) the setting or conditions for performance; (2) the behavior, skill, or knowledge to be demonstrated; and (3) established performance criteria. These kinds of objectives are called Mager objectives, after the person who first developed them (Mager, 1984). The setting or condition describes the context or situation under which the learning will be demonstrated. Some of the conditions can occur before the performance, like "Given ten minutes of practice time . . .", or be in place during the performance, like " . . . in a badminton match." The behavior/skill/knowledge states exactly what will be demonstrated, such as "tennis etiquette" or "moving in pathways and levels." The performance criterion states in objective terms how proficient, correct, consistent, accurate, etc. the performance must be to indicate that learning has occurred, such as "score at least 80 percent correct" or "no (zero) arguing." It should be noted that the three parts of a Mager objective will not always appear in the same order, but they must always be present to be considered good objectives for most types of learning.

Selecting the Instructional Model for the Unit

Once the teacher has analyzed the context, determined the content listing, and stated the intended learning objectives for the unit, he can then make a well-informed decision about which instructional model (or models) will be the most effective to help students learn. Chapter 6 will explain the process of selecting a model in more detail, but a brief mention will be made here as it pertains to unit planning. Two things must be kept in mind when selecting a model for a unit. First, selection is a *deductive* process: the decision is made after

FIGURE 5.4 General and Behavioral Objectives for Physical Education

Domain	General Objective	Behavioral Objective
Cognitive	1. Students will learn rules and strategies for soccer	1. Student will score at least 80% on a soccer game-rules and strategy test
	2. Students will know common square dance calls	2. Student will correctly recite the five most commonly used square dance calls
Affective	1. Students will learn the proper etiquette for tennis	1. During a three-set match, student will display no more than two violations of tennis etiquette
	2. Students will be good team members in a cooperative game	2. Student will participate in a cooperative game without arguing with teammates
Psychomotor	1. Students will learn the basic skills for golf	1. Student will make 3 of 5 putts on the green from a distance of 6 feet
	2. Students will learn pathways and levels	2. Student will correctly demonstrate how to move in three different pathways at two different levels in scatter space

consideration of context, content, and objectives. The stated learning objectives will indicate the domain priorities and domain interactions that directly influence the selection. Second, student learning will be maximized if one model is used throughout the entire unit. It is not advisable to change models after the unit has started or to freely combine the components of two or more models. Because each model has unique characteristics and patterns for teacher and student behavior, it is important that consistency is maintained from start to finish.

Management Scheme

The management scheme serves to identify important rules, routines, and procedures that will make the learning environment safe and efficient. The plan will also inform the teacher and students of each others' responsibilities in class. A typical management plan should include:

1. Determination and communication of rules
2. Procedures for entering and leaving the gym or teaching area
3. Procedures for the distribution, care, and collection of equipment
4. Safety rules to follow
5. Procedures for taking class roll
6. Designation of a signal for attention and start/stop

Student Learning Activities

All instructional units include a series of planned learning activities that allow students to interact with the content and learn the stated objectives. Chapter 3 describes learning activities that can be used in physical education for each of the three major domains: cognitive, psychomotor, and affective. Before the unit begins the teacher should make a list of the activities for the unit and the order in which they will be presented to students. Plans can then be made for the task presentation, task structure, and assessment of each activity. This allows the teacher to plan ahead for equipment and other resources needed for each activity.

Assessment and/or Grading

Before the unit begins, the teacher must plan for assessing student learning. That plan will also include policies, procedures, and criteria for determining grades given at the end of a unit. Assessment and grading decisions must be made regarding:

1. Which goals and outcomes are to be assessed or graded
2. What kind of assessment(s) will be used (traditional, alternative, authentic)
3. When assessment will take place (formative, summative, both)
4. How assessments will be planned and conducted

It is not necessary to prepare specific assessment materials before the unit begins, but it is important to have a general assessment plan in place at that time so the teacher can be looking ahead and preparing. Chapter 2 includes more detailed information about assessment types and procedures for physical education.

The Teacher's Role and Functions in the Unit

Each instructional model will designate a unique pattern of decision making and behaviors for the teacher. That will transfer into certain roles the teacher will assume and certain operations the teacher will carry out in the unit. It is important that the teacher recognizes her role expectations and functions within each unit and makes plans to carry them out accordingly. Much of this can be done by reviewing the characteristics of each model before it is implemented as a preview or reminder of how to teach during the upcoming unit.

Students' Roles and Functions in the Unit

Just like the teacher, students will have patterns of decisions, behavior, and responsibility within the model selected for each unit. Direct models will call on them to be more passive, while interactive and indirect models will require them to have an active role in the unit. Some models will demand very little responsibility on their part, and others will place students in control of many class decisions and operations. When the teacher begins a unit with a new model, he will need to help the students learn "how things will work" during that unit and give students some time to acclimate to a new pattern of class participation. It is the teacher's responsibility to make plans for initially *teaching the model* as well as the content until students accept and take on new roles and responsibilities in class.

Lesson Planning

Good planning at the unit level greatly facilitates the planning for each lesson in the unit. The unit and lesson plans should be strongly congruent. If the unit plan is viewed as the outline for the action blueprint, then the lesson plan provides the specific instructions and details to guide the teacher in each class meeting. The main task is to then "fill in" that part of the unit plan to be implemented in each lesson. There are many ways to format and write a lesson plan for physical education, but most plans will include seven common components: (1) a brief contextual description; (2) lesson objectives; (3) time and space allocations; (4) a list of learning activities; (5) task presentation and structure; (6) assessment of learning; and (7) review and closure.

Brief Contextual Description

The contextual description includes a summary of the major factors that need to be considered for the lesson: students (grade level/s, the number of them, and which ones have special needs), the time or class period, and where this lesson fits in the unit sequence (e.g., first class, fourth of ten classes, last class). Obviously the teacher will be aware of all of these factors—the description is there to help the teacher recall the lesson when it is used the next time.

Lesson Objectives

The teacher should write down the specific objectives for the upcoming lesson. The objectives can be taken directly from the unit plan. Usually one to three objectives will be sufficient for each lesson.

Time and Space Allocations

It is helpful for the teacher to think ahead about how much time will be given to each class segment, how the learning environment will be set up, and how management episodes will proceed. A time allocation plan can be made for the lesson:

Lesson: Fitness Obstacle Course for Seventh Graders

9:15–9:20	Students in locker room, take roll
9:20–9:24	Warm up and stretch
9:24–9:25	Set induction
9:25–9:30	Task presentation and station descriptions
9:30–9:40	Rotate through first three stations
9:40–9:43	Review first three stations
9:43–9:53	Rotate through last three stations
9:53–9:55	Review last three stations
9:55–10:00	Walk to cool down
10:00–10:05	Lesson review, closure, and dismissal

The time allocation plan is mostly an estimate and does not have to be followed to the minute. It serves as a series of starting and ending points that can be altered as the lesson progresses. After class the teacher can make notes about how long each segment actually took for use the next time the lesson is taught. Over a few repetitions, a teacher can become very accurate in making these allocations.

The space allocation plan can be a simple diagram that allows the teacher to see how the learning environment will be set up for each activity. This helps visualize where learning stations will be, if they are too close together, too far apart, unsafe, or might result in a "bottleneck" that causes excessive waiting in class.

Learning Activities List

Once objectives have been chosen, the teacher can refer to the unit plan to find the learning tasks planned to achieve each objective. Again, if good unit planning has taken place, this is a simple matter of selecting the appropriate learning tasks from the unit plan for each lesson. The list of lesson activities should be made in the order students will be given the tasks.

Task Presentation and Task Structure

Plans will need to be made to prepare for each learning task included in the lesson. That preparation will have two parts: task presentation and task structure. Chapter 3 provides a complete description of both components. The lesson plan should show the following considerations for this part of class:

1. Set induction to gain the students' interest
2. Models and cues to be used for task presentation
3. Description of task structure, including directions for students
4. A check for understanding
5. The sequence and progression for multiple tasks in one lesson

Assessment

The lesson plan should indicate how each stated objective will be assessed. Most often assessments are informal—checking for understanding, question-and-answer periods, teacher observation, or just asking students how many completed each task to a certain standard. In those cases the lesson plan should indicate when and how the assessments will be made as a reminder to the teacher.

If the assessment is more formal, the plan will need to show it as a defined lesson segment and be given its own management and procedural considerations. That means allocating sufficient time to complete the assessment, planning how it will be set up, and organizing the necessary equipment and materials.

Review and Closure

A well-planned lesson will end with a review segment and an orderly closure, giving students one more time to be engaged with the content. The lesson plan should include a brief segment at the end that allows for teacher and student interaction and any last comments or observations. The best review segment will find the teacher bringing the students' attention back to where the lesson started by recalling performance cues and asking what they learned and why it was important. If the closure is planned and completed in an orderly way, it will allow students to be dismissed quietly, giving the entire lesson a sense of purpose and accomplishment for the teacher and students alike.

The Unwritten Parts of a Lesson Plan—
Being Completely Prepared

Physical education classes can be very complex and dynamic. Several things can be going on at any moment, and any one of them can change instantly to prompt the teacher into making a new decision or action. A *pedagogical move* occurs any time the teacher makes and carries out an instructional decision in class. Research on teaching suggests that physical education teachers make about fifteen pedagogical moves **each minute** of class (Anderson, 1980). That means in a thirty-minute class the teacher will make and act upon approximately 450 decisions; in a forty-five-minute lesson that means nearly 700 pedagogical moves could happen! The number of decisions and different actions underscores the importance of good planning, *being prepared,* and for the teacher to anticipate what must be done within each class segment—the "jobs" of teaching, so to speak. Most of these jobs are not in the written plan but must be on the teacher's mind as class progresses. The well-prepared teacher will not only know what is on the written plan but will anticipate what she and her students will be doing at all times in class. Some common anticipation questions are:

Before the Class Begins

1. What is my students' motivation?
2. What in my lesson is interesting, educational, and fun?
3. What if this "bombs"?
4. Reminder—Make sure to tell the class how well they did last time.

As Students Enter the Gym

1. Where do I want them to stand or sit while I take roll?
2. Is all of my equipment out and ready? If not, how will students get it?
3. Do I have any special announcements to make before class begins?
4. Reminder—Be sure to check for proper footwear on all students.

As Students Move to the First Task Presentation

1. Where will they go to get the task presentation?
2. Reminder—Be sure to speak clearly and slowly. This is new content for them.
3. What are the cues I will tell them, and what is the best way to explain them to students?
4. How do I get and keep every student's attention?
5. How will I check for understanding?
6. How will I get them into groups and moved to the first activity?

While Students Are Practicing

1. Are they on task? If not, what is the problem?
2. Are they doing the task as I requested?
3. Are too many students waiting?
4. Are they practicing safely?
5. Are most students successful at the task? If not, how do I modify it for them?
6. How will I know when it's time to go to the next task?

As the Lesson Comes to a Close

1. How do I get them to stop and pay attention?
2. Can I do the closure while students are spread out, or do I need to bring them together?
3. Reminder—Make the closure interactive. Do not just review what we did in class.
4. Reminder—Be sure to give them "wait time" after each question.
5. If several students raise their hands to answer, how do I decide who gets called on?
6. What is the best way to dismiss the class to the locker room or to their classroom teacher?

As you can see, most of the unwritten plan comes from questions the teacher should ask herself before the lesson starts to anticipate and prepare for possible events in each class segment. Other things are reminders of what to do or say as the class progresses, reducing the chance of forgetting important functions during the lesson.

Lesson Planning as Question-Asking

There are many useful ways to prepare a lesson plan and commit it to writing and memory. Remember, though, the primary purpose of the plan is to facilitate effective instruction by maximizing students' learning opportunities in class. In my work with teachers, I have found it useful to have them think of lesson planning as a series of questions that need to be asked—and answered—before a lesson begins. The question-asking process itself leads directly to the formulation of the plan. Once key questions have been addressed, the teacher should be adequately prepared for the lesson. Some key questions are listed in Figure 5.5.

Just by asking those key questions the teacher can have a good head start on a functional and effective lesson plan in every class, whether or not the plan is written on paper. I strongly suggest that novice teachers write out their lesson plans every time until those key questions become automatic from experience. One precaution needs to be stated here. Even when those key questions have been answered, there is always the possibility that things will change as the class proceeds and that the teacher will need to make new plans "on his feet" during class. This is called *interactive planning* to denote that the teacher is making decisions and taking actions by responding to unanticipated events in the lesson as they occur in "real time." Graham et al. (1993) found that expert teachers needed to use less interactive planning than novice teachers because the experts were better able to anticipate and plan for class events ahead of time. In effect, they asked and answered more and better key questions in their pre-lesson planning.

A Generic Lesson Plan Template for Physical Education

There are many possible ways to format and write a daily lesson plan for physical education instruction. While some instructional models will require specialized planning formats, most models use lessons plans that share several common characteristics. This allows teachers to use a generic *template* for lesson planning. A template functions well in most instances and can be based on the seven lesson plan components presented in this chapter. Figure 5.6 shows an example of one template. You will notice that the form is very open, with each section addressing one or more lesson plan components. Each section acts as a prompt, or an implied question, that directs the teacher to give consideration to that part of the upcoming lesson. The openness of the form allows the teacher ample room to write down plans and notes for each segment.

FIGURE 5.5   Key Questions for Lesson Planning in Physical Education

Lesson Context or Segment	Key Questions to Ask
Students	1. How many will I be teaching? 2. Which of them have special learning needs? 3. What is the typical developmental stage for this class? 4. What do they already know about this content?
Place in the unit	1. What have we covered already? 2. Are we on schedule to finish the unit? 3. What comes next?
Learning objectives	1. What objective/s from the unit plan need to be learned today?
Learning activities	1. What learning activities are scheduled for this time in the unit? 2. How many activities can be completed in this lesson?
Space and equipment	1. Where will each activity take place? What is my floor plan? 2. What equipment do I need for each activity? 3. Can I set equipment out before class? If not, how will students get it and return it? 4. How can I maximize equipment usage for the highest amount of student practice time?
Task presentations and task structure	1. Where will each task presentation take place? 2. What key cues will be given for each task? 3. How will I demonstrate the task to students? 4. How will each task be structured? 5. How long will each task be given? When will the students change tasks? 6. Where will each activity happen in the gym? 7. What are the performance criteria for each task?
Classroom management	1. How will class get started? 2. How will transitions be organized? 3. Do I need special rules for this lesson? 4. What are some potential safety hazards? 5. What is my time allocation for each class segment?
Teaching "jobs"	1. What special conditions exist that I need to alert students to? 2. What will I be doing while they are practicing? 3. Will some students need extra attention from me? 4. What might go wrong, and how will I handle it if it happens?
Closure and review	1. How much time will I need for it? 2. Where will it take place? 3. What needs to be reviewed? 4. Any last-minute announcements? 5. How do I dismiss the class in an orderly way?

FIGURE 5.6   Daily Lesson Planning Template for Physical Education

DAILY LESSON PLANNER

Teacher _____   Date _____   Class/Period _____

Lesson # _____ of _____ in unit   # Students _____   Location _____

Lesson content: _____

Today I would like to improve my teaching by: _____

Instant activity: _____   Set induction: _____

Equipment needed: _____

Learning objectives   Learning activities for each objective
1.   1.
2.   2.
3.   3.

Lesson Segments

Activity/Segment	Task Presentation	Cues	Structure	Time
1.				
2.				
3.				
4.				
5.				

(continued)

FIGURE 5.6   Continued

Floor Plan for Learning Activities

Assessment of student learning:

Suggestions for the next time I teach this lesson:

Summary

Good unit and lesson planning provides the best opportunities for effective teaching and learning to occur in physical education. As you will see in Chapter 6, an instructional model can be likened to a blueprint that provides the builder with a schematic picture of the end product of the project and guides the entire building process to completion. The unit and lesson plans work to operationalize the model's blueprint into an action plan for "getting the job done." But even with a good blueprint, something will not get built with poor planning. They must work together.

Two key concepts about planning were discussed early in this chapter. First, the purpose of planning is to promote the most effective instruction possible in any content unit. Second, the idea is not just to plan but to *be prepared* as best as possible for each unit and lesson. If planning is approached as a series of key questions to ask before each unit and lesson, the answers will lead the teacher to being prepared most of the time. With experience, these questions, along with the answers, will come automatically, greatly reducing the time needed to become prepared and giving the teacher greater confidence as units and lessons begin and greater effectiveness in reaching intended learning goals for students.

LEARNING ACTIVITIES

1. Select a class at any grade level and a physical activity content area. Conduct a complete contextual analysis in anticipation of teaching that class a ten-lesson instructional unit.

2. Using that same class and content area, complete a content analysis and listing. What will you include in the unit, and why did you choose each part of the content?

3. Make a complete outline for that same unit of instruction.

4. Write an annotated lesson plan for the first day of the unit, the fifth day of the unit, and the last day of the unit. Annotating means that you will make notes on the lesson plans that explain your decisions for each part of the lesson.

5. Share your unit and lesson plans with another physical education teacher and ask for her comments and feedback.

CHAPTER

6 Components and Dimensions of Instructional Models

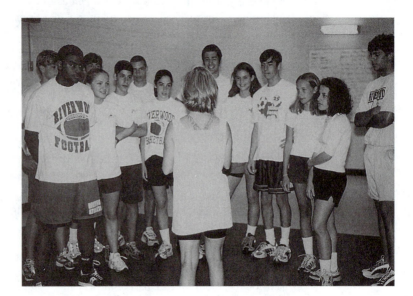

The word *model* has many different meanings, with several that apply to how a teacher might choose to instruct physical education. Model is often used to describe a good example of personal characteristics, such as a *model citizen* or a *model student.* It can have that same meaning for teachers when used to describe professional and pedagogical behavior that is viewed by others as highly effective and desirable. The word might also be used when some-one demonstrates, or shows, the way others should act or think—to *be a model* by example. That meaning can apply to teachers who display clear patterns of planning and instructional interaction that others can observe and emulate in their own teaching. Model can also be used to describe a *scaled-down replica* of a large object, like an automobile, airplane, or building. The scaled-down model allows the observer to more easily see, in miniature, what the larger object looks like from many perspectives without having the real object in hand. Instructional models also serve this same purpose for teachers by allowing the teacher to better understand a model's components and features before implementing the full version with students.

Instructional Models as Blueprints for Teaching Physical Education

For this book, the most important meaning for the word model is used in the way a blueprint functions as a plan for something to be built or procedures to be followed. The blueprint provides a detailed set of written and drawn plans, including instructions, measurements, locations, and materials that help the builder understand what the object will look like when completed. It allows for efficient and correct decisions to be made during the building process. The "builder" in this book is the teacher, who takes a blueprint (a model) and uses it to promote certain learning outcomes for students in physical education. All instructional models are based on a series of written plans that allow a teacher to understand what the model looks like, how it operates, and how it might be implemented for instruction.

Context plays an important role in the design and implementation of all models, whether they are models for teaching or blueprints for a building. Before a designer can begin to draw a blueprint, she must ask some important preliminary questions about what is to be built. Let's assume that an engineer wishes to draw plans for a new building. Before those blueprints are started, she will need to ask questions such as: What will the building be used for?, Who will be its primary users or occupants?, Where will it be located?, What is the construction budget?, and so on. These questions help to determine the context for the building design and ultimately how functional the building is for its owners and users. Context is just as important for teaching and must be considered as well in the selection and implementation of an instructional model for physical education. A teacher must be familiar with an instructional model and know how to change the model to fit the particular school setting, grade level, content, and class. It will be rare when a model can be used exactly as it will be described in this book, so it will be necessary for teachers to consider their context in selecting and implementing any one of the models presented here.

Advantages of Using Model-Based Instruction in Physical Education

There are many advantages to model-based instruction for physical education. Selecting and using the "right model for the right purpose/s in the right way" can lead to effective teaching at all times, regardless of content and class contexts. Model-based instruction can provide physical education teachers with several important advantages.

1. A model provides an overall plan and coherent approach to teaching and learning. All instructional models describe certain patterns of teacher and student instructional behaviors that effectively promote learning outcomes. Each model is a kind of master plan that helps a teacher make and carry out decisions that lead to student learning in a given unit.

Once a teacher has decided on the major learning outcomes for a unit and has taken the context into consideration, the selection of one or more teaching models that can help students best achieve those outcomes follows. If you will recall from Chapter 1, today's physical education programs can promote several types of student learning. Each type of learning outcome will require a different set of plans and strategies for working toward those goals. An instructional model provides a unique and coherent approach for reaching each goal.

2. **A model clarifies learning domain priorities and domain interactions.** Physical education programs today can strive for student achievement in any one or a combination of the major learning domains. A domain is a large category of related types of learning outcomes. Educators generally recognize three domains. The cognitive domain includes the recall of facts, the learning of concepts, and the ability to make decisions. It is usually demonstrated by verbal answers, written answers on tests, and problem-solving exercises. The psychomotor domain includes the learning of fine and gross movement patterns and other body motions. It is usually demonstrated through skilled movement or in the solving of generic movement problems. The affective domain includes one's feelings, attitudes, social interactions, and perceptions of self. For physical education, the affective domain usually refers to what one learns about self, others, and various forms of physical activity. It can be demonstrated by attitude questionnaires, personal interviews/conversations, verbal comments, self-efficacy, and through observable social interactions with others in the physical-activity setting.

Teachers usually attempt to have students learn in one or more of the major domains at all times, but one domain will likely have a stronger emphasis at the moment. If a teacher says, "I want my students to get better at tennis skills," he is prioritizing the psychomotor domain over the others. If another teacher says, "I am not terribly concerned about skills—I want students to explore each new activity and feel good about it," she is prioritizing the affective domain. Finally, if a teacher says, "I really want my students to learn the rules and history of soccer," he is setting the highest priority in the cognitive domain. It is also possible, and likely, that a teacher will strive for a balance of learning outcomes across all three domains within the same unit. Regardless of whether the domains are prioritized or balanced, the teacher must instruct in the most effective way for student learning to take place. Each instructional model to be presented in this book will clearly state which domain it is primarily designed for or if it is designed for a balance among learning outcomes. Knowing that for each model, a physical education teacher can easily select the most effective model/s for achieving stated outcome/s.

As discussed in Chapter 2, no activity promotes learning in a single domain, even when one domain is prioritized over the others. Students will always learn something in the other two domains that are not being emphasized at a particular moment. This is called a domain interaction. Just like each model as a domain priority, it will also have domain interactions that further help the teacher to decide which model is best for the intended learning goals in a unit. This interaction gives a model another aspect to its identity.

3. **A model provides an instructional theme.** By design, an instructional model represents a "big idea" for teaching and learning in a content unit. It is the unique way the teacher and students will operate within a model. For instance, the "big idea" about Peer Teaching (Chapter 11) is that students are responsible for teaching each other. The theme "I teach you, you teach me" represents the major plan for learning and can be used to help students better understand the way classes will be structured in that model.

If teachers and students understand that each model will call for different patterns of planning, decision making, responsibility, and learning activities, they will be more receptive to new ways of teaching and learning described in some of the models. By simplifying that with an instructional theme for each unit, teachers can regularly remind themselves and students that physical education class will be a bit different, and more interesting, than usual.

4. A model allows the teacher and students to understand current and upcoming events. The master plan in each model will become apparent to the teacher and students, providing a basis for understanding the purpose and sequence of events in the unit. All instructional models include features that allow the teacher to plan ahead and students to know where the learning plan is taking them. This understanding promotes increased student interest, cooperation, and managerial efficiency—all of which can enhance student learning.

5. A model provides a unified theoretical framework. All teaching models are designed from a unified theoretical framework that begins with assumptions about how learning occurs, the developmental needs of students, how the teaching setting should be managed, and what learning experiences/activities will lead to stated learning outcomes. If a teacher is aware of these assumptions and implements instruction within the model's theoretical framework, there is a much higher probability that the desired learning will occur.

6. A model has research support. All of the instructional models in this book have some level of research support for their effectiveness. Once a model has been developed from a unified theoretical framework, it is common for the developers and others to then conduct research on how best to implement the model with classes of students and to test the model's ability to promote the kinds of learning for which it is designed. Before selecting a model it is important for a teacher to become acquainted with the research that shows how best to use it and, more importantly, when it should not be used. That background information will be helpful in learning the best applications for the model, how it can be most effective, and knowing the model's limitations.

7. A model promotes a technical language for teachers. Every instructional model contains unique terminology used to describe its theoretical framework, design, and operations. We refer to that terminology as a *technical language,* from which all teachers have a shared meaning for words and terms applied in a model. That shared meaning allows designers, teachers, and students to communicate clearly and efficiently, increasing the potential for stated learning outcomes to occur. Teachers should be aware that some similar words and terms can have different meaning across models, so it is important to know what "language" is being spoken at a given moment.

8. A model allows for the relationship between instruction and learning to be verified. An instructional model will include a coherent pattern of decision making, managerial plans, instructional strategies, discrete teaching skills, in-class operations, learning activities, and assessment. All of these are designed for the primary purpose of increasing student learning of the stated outcomes. The model designers, in effect, are saying that if a teacher makes decisions and carries out instruction in a way that is congruent with the model's theoretical framework and design, it is more likely that students will learn what is intended. Since many teacher and student instructional behaviors can be observed and measured, as can many stated learning outcomes, it is then possible to examine this relationship within each model.

This can become a useful way to test the effectiveness of a model in any given application and can be used as the basis for making systematic revisions for the next time that model is used.

Those teacher and student operations and *ways to teach and learn* will be called *benchmarks* in this book. Each benchmark indicates a certain operation or in-class process that the teacher and/or students will try to follow in each model so that the model is implemented according to its design, leading to a greater likelihood of increased student achievement.

9. A model allows for more valid assessments of learning. Assessment of student learning in physical education has received increased attention in recent years, and many good new ideas have been developed (Wood, 1996). However, sometimes an assessment technique is developed with no clear directions for when and how a teacher might use it; the technique is simply a nice idea that each teacher must figure out how to use in their own classes. This decreases the chances that the assessment actually measures the intended learning outcomes in the correct (or valid) way. Every instructional model includes assessment techniques that are designed especially for that model and which are valid indicators of how well students learned in that content unit. Instructional models promote improved formative and summative assessments of learning by monitoring student achievement throughout a unit and at its completion. Many models will promote the use of alternative and authentic assessments, reflecting the unique domain interactions within them.

10. A model promotes teacher decision making within a known framework. Instructional models can help teachers to make decisions within a limited scope, defined by the model itself. Rather than decide "how to teach" from a long list of discrete skills, managerial schemes, styles, and learning strategies, the teacher will have a reduced range of choices based on the model's framework, design, context, and the unit content. This reduced range of choices can improve the congruency between decisions and actions within the unit, promoting more effective student learning.

That is not to suggest a teacher cannot use her own personal and creative options within a model-based instructional unit. In fact, how the teacher makes and carries out decisions within a model's framework will depend greatly on her pedagogical content knowledge (Shulman, 1987) and other professional expertise. As you will see in Part 2, each model will specify that certain instructional operations need to be completed within its framework. In only a very few instances will the model's design indicate that an operation must be done in just one way. In nearly all cases it will be the teacher who provides the innovation to implement each operation in the model for maximum effectiveness.

Components and Dimensions of Instructional Models for Physical Education

Each instructional model in this book represents a unique way for teachers to make and carry out decisions that lead to student learning in physical education. Although models can differ in many ways, it is possible to analyze each model from a common set of components and dimensions that serve to describe how each model works and when it might be used most effectively.

In Chapter 1 an instructional model is defined in this book as a comprehensive and coherent plan for teaching that includes assessment of student needs and abilities, statements of intended learning outcomes, teacher's content knowledge expertise, developmentally appropriate and sequenced learning activities, expectations for teacher and student behaviors, unique task structures, measures of learning outcomes, and mechanisms for assessing the faithful implementation of the model itself. That definition separates it from smaller, discrete teaching skills and less-complex teaching strategies—both of which are included in every instructional model. Before you learn each of the models in this book, it is important that you can understand how each model is designed and operates to promote student learning.

Each model is uniquely described through a combination of six components: (1) foundations, (2) teaching and learning features, (3) teacher expertise and contextual needs, (4) verification of instructional processes, (5) assessment of learning, and (6) contextual modifications. As shown in Figure 6.1, each component includes one or more dimensions that further describe each model's uniqueness.

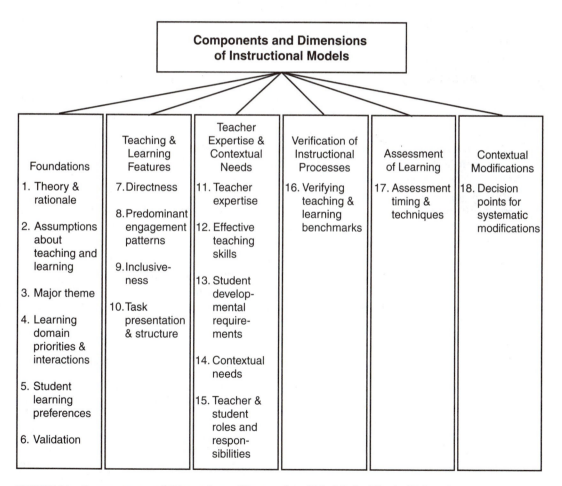

FIGURE 6.1   Components and Dimensions of Instructional Models for Physical Education

Component 1: Foundations

An instructional model is much more than the set of operations and learning activities in it. Each model is based on one or more learning theories that form the foundation for all aspects of the model. That theory is not always apparent to those who observe a model in action, but should be fully known to any teacher who selects a particular model for physical education.

Dimension 1: Theory and Rationale

Each model is based on an articulated learning theory that leads its designer to a rationale for why and when a model should be used and under what conditions it will be the most effective. In effect, it describes a relationship between one or more theories of learning and operations in the model that "make it work" for its intended purpose.

The theory and rationale explains to the teacher the central concepts behind the model, often indicated by the model's label (e.g., Cooperative Learning, Peer Teaching, Sport Education). Physical education teachers should clearly understand the "big picture" for each model they read about and consider for use in their classes.

What Does the Model Include?   Each model contains a different set of managerial plans, decisions, operations, learning activities, and assessments. A model also describes a set of roles and responsibilities for the teacher and students within it. Teachers need to be certain that they know what is expected of them and their students within each model and make sure that they can meet those expectations with pedagogical skills, content expertise, student management, and their own personal values for teaching.

What Does the Model Not Include?   Each model is designed to meet specific types of student learning needs. Therefore, it is important that a teacher does not make unrealistic expectations or misuse a model by setting up a mismatch between the theory, stated learning outcomes, and the model's capabilities. For instance, a model like Direct Instruction (Chapter 7) is designed to give the teacher a high degree of control over task structure, task progression, and learning activities. It offers only limited opportunities for students to make decisions in class. If a teacher wishes to have students participate regularly in interactive decision making in physical education, then Direct Instruction is not an effective model because it features limited student choice in class.

Dimension 2: Assumptions about Teaching and Learning

Little is known conclusively about the relationship between teaching and learning in gymnasiums and classrooms. An instructional model is based upon assumptions made by the model's designer; that is, if a teacher plans and implements instruction in certain ways, it should lead to somewhat predictable learning outcomes for students. While some assumptions can be strengthened with research, it is the job of the designer to set out those assumptions to teachers—in a sense, putting "his cards on the table" for potential users to make their own decisions on the validity of those assumptions. If a teacher shares most or all of the assumptions behind a particular model, that teacher is more likely to agree with and use the model in her teaching. As you can tell by now, there must be strong agreement between a designer's assumptions and the values held by a teacher who would use that model.

Theory goes one step past assumptions in that it is based on some preliminary evidence that an assumption is valid. Referring to instructional models, it means that some research evidence is available to indicate that the model is based on a good theoretical foundation. Typically, that evidence is gathered through research and then applied in the design of a given model. This theory represents an educated guess that the model *should* work, but is far short of demonstrating that it can and does work. Personalized Systems of Instruction (PSI, Chapter 8) were developed on a theory based in operant conditioning and behavior modification. Keller (1968) and his students carried that theory into their design of an individual learning model at the college level on their educated guess that it would be an effective way to promote increased levels of student knowledge in college introductory psychology courses. This guess was correct, and the PSI model developed from that theory.

It is important that teachers understand the assumptions and theories behind each instructional model. This does not mean a theory must be abstract and removed from the realities of teaching physical education to children and youth. Just the opposite is true, since a good theory must prove itself relevant and practical in a model that can be used in many contexts, across many grade levels, and for many types of movement content. Contrary to the popular view that theory has little to offer teachers in schools, *there is nothing more practical than a good theory* when used as the basis of an instructional model. Think about it!

Dimension 3: The Model's Theme

All instructional models are based on one major premise or theme that defines the model and makes it unique. That theme is used to summarize the most basic idea upon which the model is designed. A model's theme comes directly from its rationale and might also describe the major learning processes used in the model.

Dimension 4: Learning Domain Priorities and Domain Interactions

Each instructional model places a different emphasis on outcomes in the cognitive, psychomotor, and affective learning domains. That is, learning in one domain is more likely to occur than in other domains by the way the model is designed and the way students interact with the content. It is important not to view a model's domain priorities negatively when you disagree with them—it is simply a fact that each model is designed to emphasize different kinds of learning outcomes and should then be selected when those outcomes match the teacher's instructional goals. If not, a different model should be selected.

What Are the Model's Domain Priorities?   All of the models in this book are designed to promote learning in the three major domains. In physical education it is not possible to exclude any of the domains, but most of the models are based on a hierarchy of learning-domain goals. The Inquiry Teaching model (Chapter 12) places the strongest emphasis on learning in the cognitive domain, followed by the psychomotor and affective domains. In that model it is most important that students learn to "think first, then move." It is somewhat less important that students acquire motor skills without the underlying cognitive foundations. Affective learning is not ignored, but much less emphasis is placed on those outcomes than those in the cognitive domain.

A few of the models promote more balance across the three domains. As you will see in Chapter 10, the Sport Education model strives for student learning of motor skills, game rules, strategy, traditions, and personal interactions within team affiliation. Students can be in a learning activity that emphasizes one type of learning at any moment, but over the course of the whole unit all three domains receive balanced attention.

What Are the Most Likely Domain Interactions?   A domain interaction happens when emphasis is directly placed on one domain but learning still occurs in one or more of the other domains at the same time. Since it is not possible in physical education to exclude any of the domains in the learning process, teachers must recognize which domain interactions are most likely to occur in each model. In the Inquiry Teaching model (Chapter 12) students learn to develop thinking and problem-solving skills. Therefore, the model is best used when the cognitive domain has the highest priority in the unit. However, as students learn in that domain they will likely improve their movement skills as they use their bodies to explore possible answers—a result of the interaction between the cognitive and psychomotor domains. At the next level, this interaction will lead to increased self-efficacy and self-esteem outcomes in the affective domain. The domain interaction for this model will look like this:

Cognitive learning → Psychomotor learning → Affective learning

Domain interactions can serve to reduce some of the differences across models used in physical education and allow teachers to pursue multiple kinds of student learning in every model. So, while most models will have definite domain priorities, every model will have some interaction, which develops student learning in all domains.

Dimension 5: Student Learning Preferences

There has been much discussion in the educational literature about learning styles, which describe how each person best receives, assimilates, and acts upon perceptual stimuli in the environment (Dunn, 1996). The concept of learning styles, however, does not attempt to describe the conditions under which an individual student prefers to be engaged in learning. Since each instructional model essentially determines a unique learning environment (Joyce & Weil, 1996), the notion of *learning preferences* by Reichmann and Grasha (1974) works well within a model-based approach to instruction. Reichmann and Grasha (1974) identified three bipolar dimensions that determine a student's preferred learning environment: avoidant/participant (student attitudes toward learning), competitive/collaborative (views of teachers and/or peers), and dependent/independent (reactions to classroom procedures) (p. 214). Each dimension includes several pairs of descriptors that lead to a profile of each student's preferred conditions for learning. The design, operations, and types of learning activities within each model will generate an environmental profile for that model. The model will be most effective when its environmental profile matches that of the majority of students in a class. Figure 6.2 shows the dimensions and descriptors in the Reichmann and Grasha (1974) profiling scheme.

The attributes on the right side of the continuum should not be interpreted in a negative light—they simply reflect some students' preferences for how the learning environment is set up. Jonassen and Grabowski (1993) analyzed the bipolar ends of all three characteristics in the Reichmann and Grasha model to determine the kinds of teaching strategies and settings that would best suit each preference.

The *participant* student prefers class discussions, alternative assessments, individual learning activities, teachers who provide opportunities for analysis and synthesis, and enthusiastic task presentations.

The *avoidant* student prefers no required tasks in class, little interaction with the teacher and other students, self-assessment, and no tests.

FIGURE 6.2   Learning Preference Dichotomies

Participant	Avoidant
Strong motivation to learn course content	Weak motivation to learn course content
Likes to assume responsibility for learning	Likes to assume little responsibility
Participates with others	Prefers not to participate with others
Does what is required	Does what he/she wants

Collaborative	Competitive
Sharing	Competitive with others and self
Cooperative	Motivated to do better than others
Enjoys working with others	Enjoys competing
[PE] is a place for learning and interacting with others	[PE] is a competitive situation in which they must win

Independent	Dependent
Thinks for him or herself	Relies on teacher or others as source of information and structure
Works on his or her own	Needs others to provide direction
Will learn what is needed	Learns what is required
Will listen to others	Little intellectual curiosity
Strong self-confidence	Less self-confidence

The *collaborative* student prefers working in small groups, having student-designed activities, group projects, peer assessments, and interaction with the teacher.

The *competitive* student prefers direct teaching strategies, opportunities to ask questions in class, and teacher recognition.

The *independent* student prefers self-paced learning, independent study opportunities, student-designed activities, and indirect teaching strategies.

The *dependent* student prefers direct teaching strategies, teacher-directed assessments, and clear time lines for class activities and outside assignments.

Dimension 6: Validation of the Model

To be *valid* means that a model has shown it can be used effectively to promote certain types of learning in physical education. In other words, it works to help students learn what it is designed for in the contexts for which it is an appropriate way to teach. For teachers who have not used a model, the most important question is, "How do I know it can work to help my students learn what I want them to learn?" Validation can come from any or all of three sources: research, craft knowledge, and intuition.

Research.   There is a large body of research on instructional models. Most of it has come from other subject areas, but we also have research evidence for many models used in physical education. This research serves to describe optimal ways to plan and implement a model, or it can describe how effective a model is in promoting student achievement. Both kinds of research are important for teachers who will decide which model to use for certain outcomes and in certain contexts. Teachers can become familiar with a model's research base by reading research journals, searching the Internet, taking courses in instructional design, and by reading textbooks like this one that describe a model. Some models have entire books written about them that provide research evidence in support of their use.

Craft Knowledge.   Craft knowledge is derived from many teachers' shared experiences of using an instructional model. It is based on verbal and/or written communication among teachers about "what works" and "what doesn't work" when implementing a model of instruction. While research knowledge is more formal, and sometimes more valid, teachers more often rely on shared craft knowledge (their own and others') when deciding if and how to use a particular model. Craft knowledge of teaching decisions and actions that work well for many teachers and in many settings can rise to the level of *preferred practice* and become the accepted way of doing things within a particular model.

Craft knowledge is valuable because it is based on teachers' actual experience with a particular model, content, and context. Through craft knowledge a teacher can benefit from the experience of others and eliminate much of the trial-and-error when using a model themselves the first few times. Craft knowledge can come from many sources: one's own experiences, interactions at professional conferences, conversations with teaching colleagues, reading practitioner journals like *JOPERD* and *Strategies,* and by looking in physical education web sites like "PE Central" (http://pe.central.vt.edu/)

Intuitive Knowledge.   While research and craft knowledge are more tangible ways to validate the use of an instructional model, sometimes a teacher can select a model because the model appears to be a good way to instruct certain content in certain contexts. It just "makes sense" to instruct that way at a given time based on the teacher's general knowledge of the model and the learning goals for the content unit. Eventually, this will be replaced by craft knowledge as the teacher gains experience with the model over time or with research knowledge as the teacher reads more about the model. Basing an initial decision on one's professional intuition is an acceptable way to validate the selection of a model for the first time.

Component 2: Teaching and Learning Features

Each instructional model will include several features that give it an identity. These features in large part define what the model looks like for the teacher and students and make each model different from the others. These features come directly from the learning theory and assumptions upon which each model is based.

Dimension 7: Directness

The concept of directness has two parts. It can be used to describe the origin and type of verbal interactions between a teacher and students during instruction—who says what to whom. It can also be used to describe the nature of decision making and control during class. Because all models are based on different assumptions and views of how learning can be most effective, each model will, by design, lead to different degrees of directness. Models that are strong on the *direct* end of the spectrum (see Figure 6.3) give the teacher most or all of the responsibility for making decisions and initiating instructional interactions. Students are given few opportunities to make decisions and mostly receive information and directions from the teacher. Models that are strong on the *indirect* end of the spectrum allow students to make many decisions in class, to explore and be creative, and to initiate lots of questions and other interactions with the teacher. Models that promote high levels of teacher and student *interaction* are in the middle, since they feature shared decision making, control, and responsibility in physical education classes.

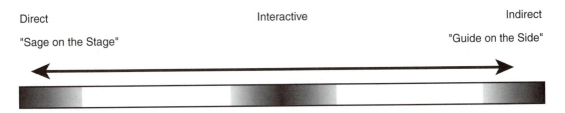

FIGURE 6.3   Direct-Indirect Continuum

Direct Teaching: "The Sage on the Stage."   Strongly direct teaching places the teacher at the center of control in class. The teacher is viewed as both the managerial and content authority in class. As the managerial authority, the teacher makes and oversees nearly all decisions about how students are organized, when practice segments start and stop, when learning tasks change, and what class rules are to be in effect. As the content authority, the teacher is viewed as the one who has the knowledge that needs to be transmitted to students according to decisions made solely by the teacher; thus, "The Sage on the Stage" label (King, 1992).

Direct teaching is also characterized by one-directional communication—from the teacher to students. The teacher makes decisions and informs the students what they will do or learn next while controlling the selection and pacing of class events. The students *receive* more than they initiate when teaching is strongly direct. Within some models it is used effectively to promote increased levels of student participation and high repetitions on skill practice.

Interactive Teaching.   In the middle of the direct-indirect continuum is interactive teaching, characterized by a balance between teacher- and student-centered instruction. Teacher and students have approximately equal responsibility for decisions and classroom operations. It is also characterized by frequent two-way communication between the teacher and students. Students are free to ask questions, offer suggestions, and have regular input into the functioning of lessons. The teacher will ask for, and act upon, students' suggestions and ideas in class.

Indirect Teaching: "The Guide on the Side."   Indirect instruction is found at the other end of the continuum, characterized by less teacher control of decisions and class events, more open-ended learning tasks, and more student-initiated learning tasks. Teachers at this end of the spectrum view themselves not as authorities but as *facilitators* of student learning—placing students, not themselves, at the center of the learning process. The major functions of teaching at this end of the continuum work to arrange the kind of learning environments that give students some direction and a task to accomplish, and then stand aside to monitor while students go about the learning process; thus, the "Guide on the Side" label (King, 1992).

While the indirect teacher still keeps a degree of decision making and control, the object of those decisions is to find ways to allow students to interact more freely with the content and each other—not necessarily with the teacher. For classroom management it means that students have input into the making of class rules and take more responsibility for their own behavior. Students make more of their own choices about how they will be engaged in learning tasks (e.g., selecting objects to throw or catch with, choosing the level of challenge they wish to pursue, and when to go on to a new task). Indirect teachers will promote more student thinking and creative movement exploration by posing questions and problems to students rather than telling (or showing) students how to move in certain ways. This kind of teaching also features the use of in-class or outside assignments in which the teacher gives students flexibility in managing their own learning processes. The teacher then serves as the main resource person to help students when they "get stuck" or need other assistance.

A model's designation as direct, interactive, or indirect is not determined by a single factor. It is determined by analyzing *key operations* within the model for their place on the direct-indirect continuum, to provide a profile of how direct or indirect each model is. Seven key operations will be used in this book to determine that profile (see Figure 6.4).

1. **Content selection:**   Who determines what is taught in the unit?
2. **Managerial control:**   Who is mostly responsible for classroom management?
3. **Task presentation:**   How do students receive task presentation information?
4. **Engagement patterns:**   How are student engagement patterns (re: space, groups, structure) determined?
5. **Instructional interactions:**   Who initiates the communications during learning tasks?
6. **Pacing:**   Who controls the starting and stopping of practice trials?
7. **Task progression:**   Who decides when to change learning tasks?

It is likely that a model will show varying degrees of directness across these seven key operations, but most of the operations will be at or near the same general area on the continuum. Therefore, the profile for each model can typically be described as mostly indirect, mostly interactive, or mostly indirect to reflect its overall place on the continuum.

It is tempting to prefer indirect teaching and interactive teaching over direct teaching. Direct teachers may seem like "authoritarians" while interactive and indirect teachers may seem like they would be "fun" for students to have. But it is not correct to pit these three ways of teaching against each other. Each way is effective in developing certain types of learning outcomes, and it is the wise teacher who can choose a direct, interactive, or

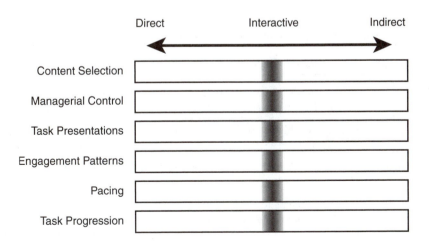

FIGURE 6.4   Direct/Interactive/Indirect Attributes on Key Instructional Operations

indirect model to more effectively promote those outcomes. It is possible that a teacher would teach one unit with a strongly direct model, the next unit with an interactive model, and a subsequent unit with a strongly indirect model.

Dimension 8: Predominant Engagement Patterns

The manner in which students interact with the learning content is called the engagement pattern. It is how they are involved in the learning process. The engagement pattern at any given time is strongly related to the learning activity and its task structure planned by the teacher. Engagement patterns can be defined by the degree of interaction with the content and by the grouping strategy used in the task structure.

Active Engagement.   The learning process is active when it involves direct personal participation by students. It is characterized by student movement, thinking, questioning, and decision making.

Passive Engagement.   The learning process is passive when students merely receive the content from other sources (usually the teacher) in the form of information given to them. It is characterized by student listening, watching, and reading. Figure 6.5 shows how students can be actively or passively engaged with some examples of content.

Active learning is not necessarily preferred at all times. Sometimes a teacher can use passive learning strategies to get large amounts of information to students quickly and effectively. The key question for the teacher here is, "How do I want students to know this content?" If cognitive knowledge is sufficient, then passive engagement will do fine. However, if the teacher wants students to learn how to think *and* move, then active engagement should be planned.

FIGURE 6.5   Passive and Active Engagement for Physical Education

Learning Outcome or Content	Passive Engagement	Active Engagement
Game rules	Reading rules in a book Hearing rules from the teacher	Officiating a game Explaining rules to others
Pitching a softball	Watching a teacher demonstration Viewing a CD-ROM	Practicing pitching drills Pitching in a game
Learning dance steps	Listening to step sequences from the teacher	Following the teacher's lead at "half speed"
Learning self-esteem	Listening to a definition of self-esteem Defining self-esteem on a test	Having success in a game or activity followed by reflection to develop a sense of self-esteem

Individual, Small-Group, or Whole-Class Engagement.   Part of the engagement pattern is determined by how students are grouped, if at all, for learning tasks. Some models rely almost entirely on individual participation in learning tasks; some are designed for participation in small groups or teams of students—all of whom share the responsibility for team achievement. Still other models are based on the whole class participating in the same activities at all times. Most models will have one or two predominant grouping strategies for student engagement.

Dimension 9: Inclusiveness

Physical education classes reflect the growing student diversity now found in almost every school in the United States. That diversity is based on nearly every conceivable combination of gender, race, religion, language, ethnicity, learning ability, and physical ability held by students in our society. With these differences in student demographics and abilities come differences in the needs, experiences, and preferences they bring with them to physical education class. Today's philosophy of inclusion challenges teachers to select content and instruct in ways that meet the educational needs of all students. Support for inclusion is legally mandated for girls by Title IX legislation and for students with disabilities by P.L. 94-142, The Education for All Handicapped Children Act of 1975 and the Individuals with Disabilities Education Act (IDEA) of 1997. But it is not just legislation that should compel physical educators to design inclusive content and instruction; we should strive to meet the educational needs of all children as part of our professional ethic.

The term *inclusive* is used to describe any class in which there are students with greatly differing needs and abilities all trying to learn at the same time. The dilemma for physical education teachers is that by addressing the needs of one or more groups of students in the inclusive class, they can reduce the opportunity for other groups of students to learn the content. If a teacher progresses quickly through a unit, it is more likely that only the skilled students will keep up while the lesser-skilled students fall further behind. If a teacher must take class time to communicate with a non-English-speaking student through a translator, attention is diverted from perhaps thirty-five or forty other children who also need the teacher's time and attention. If a teacher decides to use written task cards at learning stations, how will that affect students who cannot read at that level or who have reading impairments due to poor vision?

Each instructional model is based on some prerequisite abilities and experiences that students must have to be able to learn within the model. These prerequisites play a large role in determining if the model can meet the educational needs of all students in the inclusive class group. Students' learning preferences also determine how inclusive a model will be with any given group of students. Quite simply, students whose preferences match the kind of learning environment designed in the model will have a greater chance for success and will like the learning process being used. Students whose preferences do not match those in the model will likely not have that same degree of success and enjoyment. As a potential user of any instructional model, the teacher must be aware of which students can be served well by teaching that way and which students might be overly challenged in that model. Even more importantly, the teacher must ask herself if and how the model can be adapted to meet all students' needs.

Dimension 10: Task Presentation and Task Structure

Task Presentation.   As explained in Chapter 3, task presentation refers to those processes used to demonstrate skills and learning tasks to students (Rink, 1998). It is how students come to see and/or hear how to perform skills to be practiced in upcoming activity segments. It is an important part of every lesson, accomplished in many different ways across models. Some models will use just one or two task presentation strategies, while other models will use a number of them. Refer to Chapter 3 for more complete descriptions of these strategies for task presentation in physical education.

Teacher verbal lecture:	The teacher verbally communicates while students listen
Teacher-modeled demonstration:	The teacher provides his own model of the information
Combined lecture/demo:	The teacher models each piece of information as she tells it to students
Active demonstration:	The students follow as the teachers talks and demonstrates
Slow motion:	Similar to the active demonstration, but the students follow in slow motion
Peer-directed, verbal:	A student makes the verbal communication to another student, a group of students, or the whole class
Peer-directed, modeled:	A student provides a model for another student, a group of students, or the whole class
Task sheets:	Learning-task information is provided on sheets given to each student, and students read them individually
Station signs/sheets:	Each learning station has its own information sign or sheet that students read when they first arrive at the station

Task Structure.   A part of most task presentations will be a description of task structure to inform students how the learning task will be organized, how they will be grouped, how long it will last, what the performance criteria are, and what the expectations are for student conduct during the task. Refer to Chapter 3 for a more complete explanation of task structure. Like task presentations, each model will use certain kinds of task structures more than others, so it is not likely that a teacher would need to be prepared to use a large number of them in a content unit within one model.

Component 3: Teacher Expertise and Contextual Needs

Each instructional model represents a plan for action that will require certain conditions and resources for effective implementation. Teachers need to be aware of what is needed and consider those needs when selecting, planning, implementing, and assessing a model for physical education.

Dimension 11: Teacher Expertise

Like students, teachers need to possess certain kinds of knowledge, skills, and abilities to allow a model to work to its fullest potential. Knowledge about content is always important, regardless of the model used. Necessary pedagogical content knowledge—a combination of applied expertise about content, context, learners, and instruction (Shulman, 1987)—will change according to the model selected for each unit and class group. Of course, knowledge of each model used is important.

Since each model will include a unique repertoire of learning strategies and effective teaching skills, a teacher will need to be proficient in those called for in a given model. The Tactical Games model (Chapter 13) depends on a teacher's knowledge of games as learning settings, in particular how to sequence increasingly complex tasks from drills to modified games to full games. Those who will use the Inquiry Teaching model (Chapter 12) will need to have knowledge of students' cognitive development and strong skills in the use of questions as the primary teaching strategy.

Dimension 12: Needed Repertoire of Effective Teaching Skills

As you will recall from Chapter 4, there are many effective teaching skills that can be used to instruct physical education. That list is long, but the good news is that each instructional model will not require a teacher to use all of these skills within it. Each model's unique set of operations, managerial functions, task presentation strategies, and task structures will determine which teaching skills are needed most when using that model.

Dimension 13: Student Developmental Requirements

For instruction to be most effective, it must be matched to students' levels of developmental readiness. Developmental readiness refers to the students' ability to understand and follow directions, behave safely and responsibly, and have a reasonable chance to succeed at learning tasks. Instruction that matches student abilities in these areas is called *developmentally appropriate* instruction. If it matches little or not at all, it is considered to be *developmentally inappropriate* instruction.

For instruction to be developmentally appropriate, it must match students' readiness in four areas: (1) comprehension of verbal, written, and modeled information; (2) decision making and responsibility; (3) social/emotional maturity; and (4) prerequisite knowledge and skills. Figure 6.6 shows some examples of developmentally appropriate and inappropriate practice for physical education.

FIGURE 6.6   Developmentally Inappropriate and Appropriate Practices for Physical Education

Readiness Area	Developmentally Inappropriate	Developmentally Appropriate
Comprehension of information	Teacher uses words and terms that students do not know	Teacher uses only familiar words and terms when talking to students
	The teachers shows students an "adult" version of the task in the task presentation	Teacher asks a peer to demonstrate how the task should be performed by students of their age and ability
Decision making and responsibility	Students are told to work alone, without teacher supervision, but cannot stay on task	Teacher regularly monitors for proper engagement
	Teacher gives incomplete managerial directions and expects students to follow them correctly	Teacher gives simple and complete directions and checks for understanding
Social/emotional maturity	Unmotivated students work on individual projects with no supervision	Teacher provides students with a checksheet to remind them how to complete the project
	Students are asked to do peer teaching, but are rude to lesser-skilled students	Teacher shows peer teachers how to give constructive and supportive feedback
Prerequisite knowledge and skills	Teacher goes to advanced tasks before students have mastered basic skills	Teacher checks for student mastery before progressing
	All students do the same task, with the same task difficulty	Teacher uses intratask variation and "teaching by invitation"

Dimension 14: Contextual Needs

None of the instructional models in this book will work in all contexts. Student abilities and developmental readiness, teacher knowledge, content, length of the unit, equipment, facilities, and available learning resources must all be considered in selecting a model. At times, that analysis will lead a teacher to decide, "I can't teach that way in this situation." Failing to consider contextual needs for a model will cause the instruction to be less effective and perhaps even counterproductive in helping students learn stated goals. Contextual needs must be met for four important factors:

1. Instructional time
2. Facilities
3. Equipment
4. Learning materials

Students' age and development in each area will be a big factor in determining if instruction is developmentally appropriate. When abilities fall short (i.e., they are not ready yet) it can result in students misunderstanding through no fault of their own, fear for their own safety, frustration from the lack of any success, and immature reactions to comments from the teacher. When the instruction is way below the abilities of students (i.e., it is too simple or immature for them) it can lead to boredom, misbehavior, and a feeling that they are being insulted by the teacher. Developmentally inappropriate instruction, whether too easy or too difficult, can lead to seriously negative consequences including the loss of students' interest in physical education.

Related to the concept of developmental readiness are the prerequisite abilities needed by students within each instructional model. All models are based partially on expectations that students already have certain kinds of fundamental knowledge and performance abilities necessary to make the model work most effectively. A large part of the success of Cooperative Learning (Chapter 9) is based on the students' ability to contribute to a team effort by taking personal responsibility for one's role in shared learning processes. If a student does not have the ability to understand the concepts of teamwork, responsibility, and sharing with others he will not likely be a successful learner in that model. Several models rely on the use of written materials as a strategy for presenting learning tasks to students. Students who cannot read at or near grade level do not have the prerequisite skills to make that an effective way to explain learning tasks, which might prohibit the use of some models for those students.

Dimension 15: Teacher and Student Roles and Responsibilities

Each instructional model will call for teachers and students to take on a unique set of roles and responsibilities within it. It is important that everyone knows these roles and accepts responsibility for carrying them out in the unit. In general, this is related to the Directness dimension, defining who controls decision-making and many instructional operations in the model. Sport Education (Chapter 10) and other types of cooperative learning call upon the teacher to assume the role of resource person and facilitator, while students assume a large role in decision making and share responsibility for their team's learning. In Direct Instruction (Chapter 7) the teacher takes on the roles of instructional leader, the major source of task presentation, and the primary provider of instructional information (e.g., cues and feedback). Students take on a more receptive role, with their major responsibilities being to pay attention, follow directions, and stay engaged as directed by the teacher.

Managerial responsibilities can shift across models. In some models the teacher assumes nearly all control over class-management decisions and interactions. So, those teachers will expend considerable time and energy in "running class." In other models, students take responsibility for a large portion of class management, allowing the teacher more time to interact with students on content.

Component 4: Verification of Instructional Processes

It is important for a teacher to verify that she is implementing a model in the way it was designed. Each model is a plan of action that should lead to intended learning outcomes for students, so from time to time the teacher must ask herself, "Am I teaching according to the way the model was intended to be used?"

Dimension 16: Verifying Teaching and Learning Benchmarks

As indicated earlier, each model is designed for unique patterns of teacher and student behavior in class. In essence, those patterns distinguish each model from the others, so it is important that a teacher carries out the model in a manner that reflects an acceptable degree of adherence to its design. It will always be necessary to make some modifications, most often due to context, but those changes should not go against the basic assumptions in the model or cause major operations and features of the model to become unfamiliar.

Each model will have a series of *benchmarks*—patterns of teacher and student actions that should happen while using that model. These benchmarks help to remind the teacher of "how to teach" and "how students will go about learning" in that model, and can be used to verify proper planning and instructional procedures. There are several ways to monitor teaching and learning benchmarks in model-based instruction.

Systematic Analysis of Teaching and Learning Behaviors in Class.   Once a teacher knows what kinds of instructional patterns a model should foster (i.e., the benchmarks), these patterns can be analyzed by collecting data in live settings or from audio- or video-taped samples of classes. The behaviors to be analyzed should be those that reflect the model's benchmarks. For instance, the PSI Model (Chapter 8) is characterized by having very little class management time and many opportunities for the teacher to provide feedback to students (Metzler et al., 1989). It is quite easy to measure the amount of management time and teacher feedback in PSI classes, and to then establish that a teacher is implementing the model according to its design in those areas. Event recording, duration recording, and momentary time sampling can all be used to monitor certain kinds of teacher and student behaviors in physical education classes. Figure 6.7 shows how each technique can be used to verify different aspects of instruction.

Checklists of Benchmarks.   It is possible to make a list of teacher and student benchmarks and patterns that are indicative of each model, and to check off each time one of them is observed in class. The checklist can verify that a benchmark was observed, but cannot distinguish between correct and incorrect instances of the benchmark.

Rating Scales for Benchmarks.   A rating scale is similar to a checklist, with the added ability to render an evaluation of observed benchmarks. Each benchmark is followed by a series of evaluative criteria, such as "Poor," "Fair," "Good," and "Excellent" or a numeric scale of 1 to 10, with 1 being the lowest rating and 10 being the highest rating. The observer notes which benchmarks occurred in the class and circles the word or number that represents his judgment of the quality with which the benchmark was carried out.

Written Student Assessments.   Based on a model's unique benchmarks, it is possible to develop a short list of questions to which students respond. Students' answers can be a

FIGURE 6.7   **Systematic Analysis of Benchmarks**

Observational Technique	Used to Measure	Teacher Behaviors	Student Behaviors
Duration recording	The amount of time a defined behavior occurs in class	Management time Task presentation length Circulating in class	Management time Practice time Academic learning time On/off-task time Waiting time
Event Recording	The observed frequency of defined events	Teacher use of first name Feedback to students Cues given to students Questions Checking for understanding	Practice trials Success rate Feedback received Questions asked
Momentary time sampling	Occurrence/non-occurrence of behaviors at predetermined times in the lesson	Pedagogical moves Location in class	Percent of students on task at any moment Percent of students practicing at any moment Student success rate Appropriate task structure

good way for the teacher to verify that preferred instructional patterns were provided for the students. The questions can be open-ended or they can prompt students to circle or check from a series of possible replies.

Open Ended Questions
- How did you feel in your role of team coach? (Sport Education model)
- What were the two things you learned to do best in this unit? (Any model)
- What motivated you the most to stay on schedule during this unit? (PSI)
- Did you get to work things out on your own a lot in your field hockey unit? (Inquiry Teaching model)

Scaled Questions/Items
(Please circle the response that best describes your opinion)

The teacher was well organized in this unit. (Direct Instruction)	Disagree	Neutral	Agree
I improved my confidence in this unit. (Any model)	Disagree	Neutral	Agree

I really liked working with my team in this unit. (Cooperative Learning)	Disagree	Neutral	Agree
I was able to progress at my own pace all of the time. (PSI)	Disagree	Neutral	Agree

Component 5: Assessment of Learning

The most important criterion for determining the value of any teaching model is the degree to which it was effective in promoting students' achievement of the intended learning outcomes. Determining the effectiveness of a model is not a simple task since there can be several ways to describe and measure learning outcomes in physical education. Getting informative and valid assessments of learning takes time and the ability to state clear questions within that process.

Dimension 17: Assessment Timing and Techniques

The assessment of learning in model-based instruction involves the asking of six key questions that lead to the selection and use of proper assessment techniques in physical education.

What to Assess?   It is usually not possible to assess all of the learning that occurs in a unit of instruction since some of the outcomes are quite indirect and sometimes unintended by the teacher. It is possible, however, to identify the major learning outcomes that *should have* occurred in the unit and to develop simple and efficient ways to assess them. Therefore, the teacher should start by reviewing the list of major learning goals in the unit and to target several of them for assessment.

When to Assess?   Most instructional models are designed to include both formative and summative types of assessments. *Formative* assessments are those taken regularly during the content unit to provide interim feedback to teachers about how well students are learning as the unit progresses. This allows for changes to be made before the unit is finished. *Summative* assessments are taken at the end of the unit and are typically compared with learning scores at the start of the unit to measure the amount of student achievement across the unit's length, typically called the *learning effect.*

What Assessment Techniques Are Valid?   The construct of assessment validity is relatively easy to understand but often difficult to attain. It is the degree to which the information produced by the assessment technique accurately describes (i.e., measures) the learning being assessed. For example, if someone asks *how far* you ran in your workout today, you would say, "I ran two miles." You would not say, "I ran for twenty minutes," because that is not a valid way to describe the *distance* you covered in your run. Note that the italicized words match, giving strong validity to the way your run was "assessed."

Is the Assessment Procedure Practical?   One of the traditional problems with assessment in physical education is that it can take a long time to assess even a few learning outcomes from a unit. This is especially true for assessments in the psychomotor domain that require direct teacher supervision and students to take individual turns at performing the skill or task. There can sometimes be a conflict between the need to be practical and the need to maintain acceptable levels of validity. Some of the models in this book address both needs with "built-in" assessments as part of the model's basic operation. When this is not part of the model, there is no doubt that teachers face many problems of practicality when trying to assess student learning in physical education.

Is the Assessment Traditional or Alternative?   In the past few years there has been much debate about the value of traditional forms of student assessment in physical education. In this sense, *traditional* refers to fitness tests, skills tests, and written tests used as the primary means of assessing student learning outcomes. As the term indicates, these types of assessments have been in practice for many years. They have come under increased criticism from both teachers and assessment experts due to questions about validity, practicality, and student perceptions of them (Wood, 1996).

Alternative assessments differ from traditional techniques in their design, purpose, procedures, and the type of information they produce about student learning. Alternative assessment techniques typically do not produce numerical test scores or data on student achievement. Instead they produce other evidence that demonstrates student learning, such as in-class presentations, multimedia reports, group projects, peer teaching, and homework. Student performance on alternative assessments are evaluated with a *rubric* that is determined prior to the assessment (Hensley, 1997). The rubric describes both the expected completeness and quality of "work" that the student/s must submit as evidence of learning. Rather than a grade (i.e, "A" or "B") or a test score (i.e., 90 percent correct), the alternative assessment will indicate a level of performance (i.e., "Unsatisfactory," "Satisfactory," or "Excellent"). You can refer to Chapter 2 for a complete discussion and examples of alternative assessment.

Can the Assessment Be Authentic?   Authenticity is the degree of similarity between the type of learning demonstrated in the assessment and the way students will need to perform in realistic settings. For example, taking a written test on the biomechanics of soccer kicking is a valid way to assess student knowledge of that type of kicking performance but it is not very authentic. A more authentic assessment of soccer kicking would occur in the context of lead-up drills or competitive match play. This bit of realism makes it more authentic *when the goal of learning soccer skills is game performance.* Some models, like PSI, Sport Education, and Tactical Games feature highly authentic assessment techniques.

Component 6: Contextual Modifications

Most situations will not likely allow teachers to implement a model exactly the way it is designed "on paper." Contextual limitations, experience with using a model, and at times plain common sense will lead a teacher to make modifications to a model before and during a unit of instruction. However, changes should not be made thoughtlessly. Modifications should be planned systematically with the aid of process and achievement assessment information whenever possible.

Special precautions must be taken not to significantly alter the basic operations that make each model unique, or violate the learning domain priorities of the model. These two mistakes can lead to ineffective use of the model and incorrect thinking that "it doesn't work" when, in fact, a teacher changed too much of the model to allow it to work the way it was designed.

Dimension 18: Decision Points for Systematic Modifications

Some modifications will be suggested for each of the models presented in Part 2. These modifications will be made from a list of planning and decision areas a teacher could systematically change before and during a content unit as follows.

1. Managerial plan
2. Content coverage
3. Content progression
4. Instructional materials
5. Time allocation
6. Assessment techniques
7. Task presentation
8. Specific roles and responsibilities for teacher and students
9. Students' developmental stage

Notice that certain parts of a model cannot be modified: underlying theories of learning, basic assumptions, domain priorities, and domain interactions. They pertain to the basic foundation of a model, so changing them will cause the model to be something other than what it is designed to be.

If valid process and achievement information has been collected, it is easy to determine the effects of any modifications by comparing data from before and after the changes were made. For instance, if a new managerial plan (that fits the model's design) reduces the amount of class management time from 10 percent of class time to 3 percent, the teacher can say with confidence that the new plan is more effective and should remain in place.

Selecting an Instructional Model

The six components and the eighteen dimensions discussed in this chapter will serve only to generally describe how models are designed and how they operate. That is necessary but not sufficient information for a teacher who must select a model for an upcoming content unit in physical education. Perhaps the best way to select an appropriate model is to ask a series of questions that will lead to making the best choice. As the following diagram notes, sometimes the answers to a teacher's questions will identify more than one model that will be effective in a situation. In that case, the teacher should use professional experience, judgment, and personal preferences to make a choice. Refer to Figure 6.8 for a step-by-step process for selecting an instructional model for physical education.

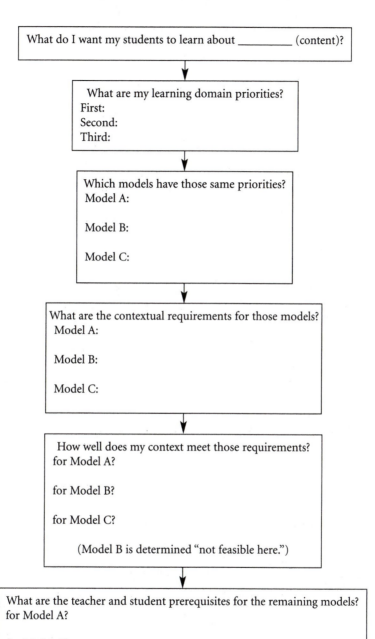

FIGURE 6.8   Selecting an Instructional Model for Physical Education

(*continued*)

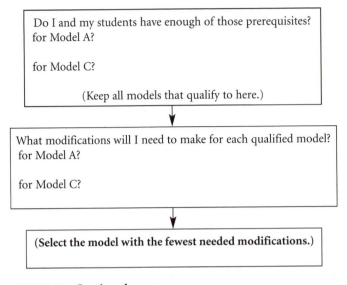

Do I and my students have enough of those prerequisites?
for Model A?

for Model C?

(Keep all models that qualify to here.)

What modifications will I need to make for each qualified model?
for Model A?

for Model C?

(Select the model with the fewest needed modifications.)

FIGURE 6.8   Continued

Note that the first two questions ask about the match between what the teacher wants students to learn and a potential model's designed learning-domain priorities. It is essential that this match is carefully considered so as not to expect something from an instructional model that it is not designed to do. Although questions about context are very important, they can be asked only after there is a good match with content, student learning goals, and the model's ability to develop them.

Summary

This chapter presented the major components and dimensions used to describe instructional models for physical education. A teacher who wishes to use model-based instruction can examine many models across these dimensions and use that information to select the model that will give students the best opportunity to learn the stated outcomes in an upcoming content unit. If you recall, instructional models are essentially tools that teachers can use to provide students with the most effective instruction possible in a given context. This chapter provided you with ways to look at each of the instructional models to be presented in Part 2 and to begin the process for choosing the "right tool for the right job" when teaching physical education to your students.

Now that you have the declarative knowledge for instructional models in physical education, Part 2 will help you acquire procedural and conditional knowledge for model-based instruction.

LEARNING ACTIVITIES

1. Analyze your own learning preferences according to the Reichmann and Grasha model presented in this chapter. What kind of learning environment suits you best? What kind of learning setting would give you the most challenge?

2. Individually interview five students from one class group to analyze each student's learning preferences according to the Reichmann and Grasha model. How many students are similar? How many are different and what are those differences?

3. Reflect for a moment on how you currently teach physical education. Then analyze your teaching according to each of the eighteen dimensions of model-based instruction presented in this chapter. From that analysis, write a profile of "how you teach" now.

4. Compare what you found in Activity 2 about students with how you described your own teaching in Activity 3 as it relates to learning preferences. How well do they match? What are the implications for student learning in your classes?

PART TWO

Seven Instructional Models for Physical Education

By now you should have a good understanding of what an instructional model is and why model-based teaching can be used to promote a wide range of learning outcomes in physical education programs at all grade levels and for all kinds of content units. However, you still might not have a good idea of what any one instructional model is, how to select a model for a content unit, how to implement a model the way in which it was designed, and how to know if the model is leading to the learning goals you have for your students. Part 2 will give you an extensive description of seven models that have shown to be effective in teaching physical education, along with some examples of how each model can be used for unit and lesson planning. This will take you from the sometimes abstract discussions in Part 1 to a clear picture of what a model actually looks like and how to use it in your teaching.

You will be reminded many times in Part 2 of the two most important things to understand about every instructional model in this book. First, each model is designed to promote certain types of student learning outcomes. No one model "does it all." If that were true, we would need only one model. Teachers who wish to have students become truly "physically educated persons" will have to use more than one model in their programs. Second, the effectiveness of a model is highly dependent upon the teacher using the model as it was designed—according to what you will learn as "benchmarks" that verify how well the model was implemented. Very simply, if the model is not followed according to its design, it will not work for its intended purpose.

Think of each model as a tool that is designed to help you do a certain job. If you select the right tool and use it in the way it is supposed to be used, you are more likely to get the job accomplished with more efficiency and effectiveness.

Each of the chapters in Part 2 presents an example of unit and lesson planning for that model. You will be able to find all of the model's design features and benchmarks in these examples, so it might be a good idea to refer to these examples as you go through each chapter. At some point you will need to understand each model well enough to use it in your teaching, as part of a methods course, during a field experience, or with your own students. That's when you will really learn model-based instruction! At that time, be sure to use the appropriate chapter in this book and the suggested readings for each model as good resources. All of these models have been field-tested and you can use the experiences of others to help you go from "method to models" in your teaching.

CHAPTER

7

Direct Instruction

Teacher as Instructional Leader

While not often identified formally as model-based direct instruction, it is likely that the vast majority of physical education teachers today use some recognizable version of what is known as direct instruction. For many years it was the single most predominant teaching approach in physical education—although not under that label. If you will recall from Chapter 1, there was a distinct method for teaching physical education that was dominant from around 1890 well into the 1970s. Oberteuffer and Ulrich (1962) referred to it as the *direct method,* characterized by the "teacher saying" and the "students doing." While this was not exactly the same as the Direct Instruction model, the method does bear enough resemblance that it can be misinterpreted as direct instruction by the uninformed observer.

161

That version of direct teaching is still used widely by physical educators, but it has given ground to some other teaching models that were developed in contrast to it and which are designed to promote other types of student learning outcomes.

It must be mentioned that Direct Instruction *the model* is not the same as the wide range of *direct teaching strategies* used in physical education today. While the model does incorporate many direct teaching strategies, it is further based on a series of defined steps, teacher decisions, and student engagement patterns as part of the model's design. Any number of direct teaching strategies might be used in other models presented in this book, but it becomes Direct Instruction only when a teacher plans and implements instruction according to the intentional design within this particular model.

As Baumann (1988) correctly notes, the Direct Instruction model was not developed by a single designer at a readily identifiable point in time. In reality, the model evolved from a constellation of classroom practices that research on teaching correlated with increased levels of student achievement, all of which shared some common instructional characteristics. Baumann notes that the model had at least three other labels (explicit instruction, active teaching, and teacher-directed instruction) until Rosenshine's (1979) label of *Direct Instruction* became the most common name for it. It was Rosenshine in 1983 who also delineated what was to become the most commonly accepted design and operations for this model. What will be presented in this chapter will be derived primarily from Rosenshine's (1983) conceptualization and design for the Direct Instruction model.

Overview

Direct Instruction is characterized by decidedly teacher-centered decisions and teacher-directed engagement patterns for learners. The teacher will have a distinct set of learning goals in mind; present students with a model of the desired movement, skill, or concept; and then organize student learning activities into segmented blocks of time, providing high rates of augmented feedback as learners practice each task or skill. Students are given only a few decisions to make and mostly just follow the teacher's directions in class and respond to the teacher's questions when asked. The purpose of this pattern is to provide the most efficient use of class time and resources in order to promote very high rates of student engagement in practice tasks and skills. The essence of the model is to give students as many supervised practice attempts as possible so that the teacher can observe these attempts and deliver equally high rates of positive and corrective feedback.

The unit content in Direct Instruction is divided into a series of sequential performance skills and knowledge areas. This is accomplished by a task analysis, leading to a list of content areas to be covered, as you learned in Chapters 2 and 5. Each skill and knowledge area will contain a set of specific performance tasks for students to practice and learn. According to Rosenshine (1983), Direct Instruction teachers perform a set of prescribed operations to promote student achievement (p. 336):

1. They structure the learning.
2. They proceed in small steps but at a brisk pace.
3. They give detailed and redundant instructions and explanations.
4. They ask a large number of questions and provide overt, active practice.

5. They provide feedback and corrections, particularly at the initial stages of learning.
6. They have a student success rate of 80 percent or higher on initial learning tasks.
7. They divide large academic tasks into smaller tasks.
8. They provide for continued student practice with a success rate of 90 to 100 percent so that students' responding becomes rapid, confident, and firm.

A class lesson can include from one to several designated tasks planned by the teacher. It is at the level of the lesson that Direct Instruction takes on its unique (but definitely recognizable) pattern for the teaching/learning process. Rosenshine (1983) identifies six steps in a Direct Instruction lesson (p. 338):

1. **Review previously learned material.** Each Direct Instruction lesson should begin with a brief review of the previous lesson. This is done as part of the teacher's *set induction,* or what is called the *anticipatory set* in the Hunter version of the model. This review should cover the most essential skills and concepts learned before. It serves four key functions: (1) it helps the teacher understand how much students retained from the previous lesson/s, (2) it allows students to bring that previously learned material into a more recent memory location, (3) it immediately establishes a learning environment by getting students to think, and (4) it provides a link between the previous and upcoming learning tasks.

2. **Presenting new content/skills.** Typically done immediately after the set induction, the teacher presents the new content (skills, knowledge, or concepts) that students will learn in the lesson. The new content is shown, or modeled, to students in a task presentation segment led by the teacher. The task presentation provides students with a verbal and/or visual description of what the new content is and how it should be performed. This gives students the "picture" or "idea" of what proficient performance looks like. Of course, that picture or idea must be a developmentally appropriate one for the students' age/stage.

3. **Initial student practice.** The task presentation leads directly into a structured practice segment, during which students take their initial steps toward proficiency. The practice task should allow for very high rates of student responding, with the teacher using direct monitoring in order to provide high rates of corrective feedback. The initial practice task should continue until students reach a success rate of 80 percent or higher for their attempts.

4. **Feedback and correctives.** The teacher's delivery of augmented feedback and corrective statements to students can be done concurrently with the early learning task/s or between each task in a practice sequence. The teacher may choose to reteach some of the key performance cues and even repeat some of the earlier learning tasks to ensure that students are ready to move on.

5. **Independent practice.** Once the teacher is confident that students have become proficient in the basic, supervised practice tasks, she can then plan for students to practice more independently. The teacher still designs the learning activities and leads the task presentations for them, but allows students to make their own decisions about pacing. This promotes even higher rates of student responding, since students do not wait for the teacher to cue and supervise their practice attempts. The goal is for students to achieve a 95 percent success rate on each independent task before the teacher moves on to a new task or content.

6. Periodic reviews. Direct instruction teachers will often plan to repeat previously learned tasks. This review helps the teacher check for student retention and alerts the students that new content is built from earlier content in the unit.

Even though Direct Instruction is still the predominant instructional model in U.S. schools, across all grades and subject areas, it has been criticized as other learning models have received increased attention—some from being designed in contrast to direct instruction (Baumann, 1988). Some criticism is legitimate, pointing out the well-recognized limitations of Direct Instruction—particularly its emphasis on lower learning-domain outcomes. On the other hand, some of the opposition is not valid, especially when opponents point to misuses of Direct Instruction and then attribute low student achievement to flaws in the model itself (Baumann, 1988). Morine-Dershimer (1985) states her support for Direct Instruction:

> Students are reinforced for correct responses, and incorrect responses are followed by corrective feedback, probing questions, or redirecting questions. Although the term direct instruction has suggested pupil passivity to some educators, the effectiveness of this [model] is in fact associated with the very active participation of students. The communication patterns in direct instruction clearly delineate both the content task and the participation task confronting pupils, and they place an obvious emphasis on the content-learning task. When the participation task is clear and fairly well routinized, as in direct instruction, then pupils can concentrate on learning content rather than on trying to draw inferences about shifting requirements for participation (p. 179).

As has been said many times, but bears repeating once again, every instructional model (in this book and elsewhere) is designed to promote certain kinds of student learning outcomes by following a well-defined set of operations and teaching/learning processes. As with all models, Direct Instruction will be effective when it is used for its intended purposes and implemented according to its prescribed plan. When a teacher has other purposes for instruction, or cannot implement the direct instruction model faithfully, he should simply look for a different model to use in that content unit.

Foundations of the Direct Instruction Model

Theory and Rationale

The set of teaching and learning strategies that evolved into direct instruction were derived from the operant conditioning theories of B. F. Skinner, the noted experimental behavioral psychologist. Many of the operations in Direct Instruction were extrapolated from research on laboratory animals, which demonstrated a clear relationship between learned behavior and its consequences. Essentially, responses that were followed by certain consequences, called reinforcers, increased the probability that the behavior would be emitted when the environmental stimulus was present again. Responses that were followed by other consequences, called punishers, would tend to decrease or not occur at all when the environmental stimulus was present again. This simple set of relationships was used by Skinner and his colleagues as the basis of several operations that could be used to get animals (and subsequently humans) to acquire long and complex sequences of learned behaviors. In the terminology of behavioral psychology, this process was called *behavior training* and included five main concepts: shaping, modeling, practice, feedback, and reinforcement.

The process of *shaping* occurs by determining the final outcome for the training procedure and then taking the learner through a series of small learning steps, or successive approximations, that lead to the eventual goal. At the start of the shaping process, the form of the skill to be learned might bear only a small resemblance to the final form. However, as the process continues, the learner will acquire skilled movement patterns that look more and more like the final desired outcome.

The use of *modeling* allows the learner to view or hear about a proficient example of the desired skill or movement. Having seen, heard, or read about the components of the modeled performance, the learner has a better frame of reference for what practice attempts should look like or result in. Of course, it is essential that the modeled performance is appropriate for the students' current developmental stage and readiness for the task.

Practice segments in Direct Instruction are highly structured and always have a *mastery criterion* with them. Having structure does not mean that they are dull or rigid—it means that the teacher makes explicit plans for every aspect of the learning task, including the task structure, the materials to be used, the time allocation, and student engagement patterns. Practice segments in Direct Instruction should be designed for very high rates of opportunities to respond (OTR), providing students with many repetitions of correct performance.

The high rates of OTR are matched by similar rates of *augmented feedback* provided by the teacher. Two kinds of feedback are preferred in Direct Instruction: positive and corrective. Positive feedback serves the dual purpose of reinforcing correct learning trials and giving the learner motivation to maintain task engagement. When the teacher does observe mistakes, he should be sure to tell the student not only that a mistake was made (negative feedback) but how to correct that mistake on the next try. That cue for the next trial turns negative feedback into corrective feedback that the learner can better use.

Reinforcement is provided at high rates in Direct Instruction, and not just for correct performance trials. Reinforcement is used contingently to reward many kinds of student behaviors: listening, good effort, staying on task, following directions, and paying attention to class rules and routines.

The basic rationale for Direct Instruction is quite straightforward, as alluded to earlier by Morine-Dershimer (1985). The teacher makes explicit plans for a series of class events that give the students a clear picture (model) of the desired performance outcome, which then leads into one or more teacher-directed learning activities that promote high levels of student engagement coupled with high rates of positive and corrective feedback. Each learning task must be performed to a stated level of mastery to bring the students one step closer (shaping) to the larger learning goals in the content unit. That rationale has proven to be highly effective in many grade levels and across nearly all school subject areas, including physical education.

Assumptions about Teaching and Learning

Assumptions about Teaching

1. The teacher is the main source of instructional content and decisions and should take a pronounced leadership role in the planning and implementing of classroom events.
2. The teacher should determine the unit content and place that content into a series of learning tasks through which students progress.
3. The teacher is viewed as the one who possesses the content knowledge that must be transferred to students by the most efficient and effective means possible. Therefore, teachers must have high levels of expertise in physical education content, as well as strong class-management skills.
4. The teacher can use her expertise to efficiently coordinate the complex environment in ways that allow for the best use of class time and resources, and maximize student engagement with the lesson and unit content.
5. The teacher serves as the instructional leader and can make the best decisions for planning and implementing student learning.

Assumptions about Learning

1. Learning occurs by making incremental progress on small tasks, which leads to the learning of larger and more complex skills/knowledge.
2. Learners must have a clear understanding of the learning task and its performance criteria prior to being engaged in a learning activity.
3. Learning is a function of the consequences that immediately follow emitted behaviors. Behaviors that are followed by reinforcers will tend to be maintained or emitted at higher rates; behaviors that are followed by no reinforcer or a punishing stimulus will tend to decrease or desist over time.
4. Learners need a very high rate of OTR in order to help "shape" their learning into the desired performance form or outcome. This assumption works against the criticism that Direct Instruction is a passive model for students; in fact, students need to have very high rates of engagement that allow movement patterns to become proficient and retained.
5. The high rates of OTR must be coupled with equally high rates of augmented feedback that inform the learner about the adequacy of learning trials.

Major Theme for Direct Instruction:
Teacher as Instructional Leader

"Teacher as instructional leader" is an accurate description of the most essential operation of the Direct Instruction model. Some precautions must be given along with that so that the teacher's actual role in this model is not misinterpreted. The teacher is the source and impetus for nearly all of the decisions made about content, management, and student engagement. There is a definite leadership function for the teacher; however, the purpose of that leadership is to allow students to have high OTR, high rates of needed feedback, and to make steady and positive steps toward learning the intended content. The Teacher is a *leader*, not an *authoritarian*. The teacher gives structure to the learning setting and the content progression, but it is the students who get the benefit of that structure by having much of the "trial and error" eliminated from the learning process.

Learning Domain Priorities and Interactions

Direct instruction is an achievement-based model of instruction, used most often for the learning of movement patterns and concepts. While it was developed initially to foster learning in the cognitive domain (e.g., reading and mathematics), it has been used in physical education primarily for learning outcomes in the psychomotor domain. The learning *domain priority* for direct instruction in physical education would most often be:

First priority:	Psychomotor learning
Second priority:	Cognitive learning
Third priority:	Affective learning

At times, the cognitive domain will have the highest priority, as in the learning of rules and concepts, but most often learning in that domain serves to facilitate what is being learned in the psychomotor domain. Students' thinking is fostered to help them learn motor-skill patterns more quickly and proficiently.

That description leads to the *domain interactions* that occur in direct instruction. In order to become proficient in learning tasks in the psychomotor domain, students must have some engagement in the cognitive domain. They must recognize, process, and learn concepts and strategies that are prerequisite to and concurrent with desired movement patterns. However, it is the teacher who first alerts the learners to these cognitive aspects, rather than having students struggle through a trial-and-error period. The affective domain is not directly addressed in this model. It is assumed that students will achieve positive affective outcomes through the processes of working diligently, experiencing regular success, and making steady progress toward learning goals.

Student Learning Preferences

Using the Reichmann and Grasha (1974) profile for student learning preferences, the direct instruction model will work most often for those students who are classified as avoidant, competitive, and dependent. As mentioned in Chapter 6, these labels should not be given a negative interpretation. They are used to describe how some students would prefer the instructional environment to be designed. The selection of content and the learning tasks are strongly teacher-directed and provide students with little personal choice of what and how they learn in physical education.

Validation

As stated at the beginning of this chapter, there is often a misunderstanding between the Direct Instruction model and any number of direct teaching strategies. A teacher using the model would follow most or all of Rosenshine's (1983) six operations presented earlier, in approximately that same order. A teacher using a direct instruction strategy might only use a task structure that places the teacher in control of the learning activity for the moment, without implementing the other components of the model as described by Rosenshine. That misinterpretation makes it difficult at times to provide an accurate validation for the Direct Instruction model. The following section on validation will be based as much as possible on discussions, research, and other evidence taken from sources that refer to the Direct Instruction model or an adequate simulation of it.

Research Validation.   The Direct Instruction model has been the object of much research in classroom-based teaching, particularly in reading and mathematics. These studies reported consistent, if modest, gains in student achievement when various forms of the Direct Instruction model were used as the primary teaching/learning process. It should be noted that these gains were realized most often on basic academic skills; the research in support of Direct Instruction's effectiveness with higher-order outcomes and with advanced students was somewhat less convincing. Still, it has been demonstrated to be very effective when used to teach certain academic content to students at certain stages of the learning process.

Research on Direct Instruction in physical education is more difficult to document, mainly because of the model/strategy problem discussed previously. While we have many studies that focused on direct teaching strategies, very few of them reported using direct instruction in the more formal sense of the model's definition and design. Even so, the large number of studies in physical education that used direct strategies does allow us to make some valid statements about the effectiveness of that approach to teaching.

The first descriptive studies of Direct Instruction in physical education indicated that students were likely to spend more time in class receiving information and waiting than practicing motor skills (Metzler, 1989). Also, physical education teachers typically gave low amounts of performance feedback to students. This, of course, is contrary to the model's design. To support the use of direct teaching strategies, interaction analysis research with the Cheffers Adaptation of the Flanders Interaction Analysis System (CAFIAS) instrument (Cheffers, Mancini, & Martinek, 1980) verified that many physical education teachers were able to fulfill the role of instructional leader by maintaining control of the flow of information in classes. While the descriptive research was not always complimentary of physical education teachers, that line of research did serve to draw attention to some teaching/learning process variables that showed promising links to student achievement. Foremost among these variables was academic learning time (ALT), defined as the amount of time a student spends in class engaged in appropriate learning activities with a high level of success (Metzler, 1979). Many studies in physical education helped to substantiate this link, and many teachers tried to design instruction that maximized the amount of ALT in classes. Most of these instructional methods were based on some version of the Direct Instruction model.

Rink (1996) identified several other connections between teacher and student process and student achievement in physical education within Direct Instruction (pp. 174–192):

1. Students who spend more time in good practice learn more
2. Practice should be appropriate to the goal of learning and the individual student
3. Students who practice at a reasonably high success level learn more
4. Students who practice at a higher level of cognitive processing learn more
5. Effective teachers create an environment for learning

6. Effective teachers are good communicators

7. Good content development can increase learning

Again, these relationships are important because they have all been established with teachers who used some form of direct instruction in physical education, and provide strong research validation for direct instruction strategies, if not the model itself.

Experimental research has yielded many promising results related to Direct Instruction in physical education. Intervention studies have shown that it is possible to successfully change many process variables that increase the likelihood of students' learning in physical education. For instance, it is possible, and relatively easy, to increase the rate of teachers' feedback, to improve class and time management, to increase student OTR, and to increase levels of ALT within the Direct Instruction model (Metzler, 1989). So, while the descriptive phase of research on Direct Instruction showed that many physical education teachers did not apply the model as designed, the experimental phase demonstrated that improvements were fairly simple and generalizable.

Craft Knowledge Validation. Physical education teachers have been using some form of Direct Instruction for nearly one hundred years, attesting to its ability to help students acquire skills and knowledge efficiently and effectively. This longevity and its current widespread usage is further evidence that teachers consider it to be one of the "tried and true" ways to teach movement skills and concepts to students of all ages and skill levels. While it is no longer the only way to teach physical education, the fact that so many teachers continue to use direct strategies (if not the Direct Instruction model itself) provides strong validation for this approach to teaching and learning.

Intuitive Validation. The basic operations of the Direct Instruction model make a compelling case for why it makes sense to use it for instruction: (1) content is broken into a series of small steps that students master on their way to the eventual, larger learning goals; (2) the teacher provides the students with a model of how the skilled movement should look, along with key performance cues to increase proficiency; (3) students get very high rates of OTR and ALT, along with high rates of teacher feedback; and (4) students must demonstrate mastery of learning tasks before they can pursue subsequent tasks on the content listing. When the goal is to learn basic skills and concepts, this approach makes good sense to many teachers, providing strong intuitive validation for the use of Direct Instruction in physical education.

Teaching and Learning Features

Directness

The following figure describes each section of the directness profile for direct instruction as it is used for physical education (as shown in Figure 7.1).

1. *Content selection.* The teacher maintains complete control of content decisions in the Direct Instruction model. He decides what will be included in the unit, the order of the learning tasks, and the performance criteria for students' mastery of the content. The students receive that information from the teacher and follow along during the unit.

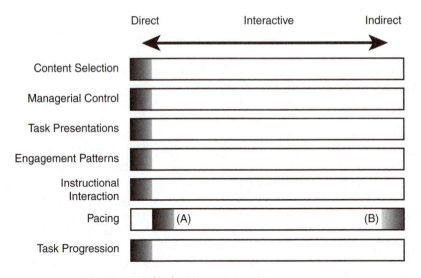

FIGURE 7.1   **Directness Profile for Direct Instruction**

2. *Managerial control.* The teacher determines the managerial plan, class policies/rules, and specific routines for the instructional unit. This control is maintained to provide maximum efficiency for class operations.

3. *Task presentations.* The teacher plans and controls all task presentations in Direct Instruction. However, this does not mean that the teacher is always the model; other students or audio-visual materials can be used to give learners visual and verbal explanations of the upcoming skill or learning task.

4. *Engagement patterns.* A wide variety of student engagement patterns can be used in Direct Instruction for physical education: individual practice, partner practice, groups of all sizes, stations, and whole-class instruction. However, it is the teacher who decides which pattern will be used for each learning task.

5. *Instructional interaction.* Nearly all instructional interactions are initiated and therefore controlled by the teacher in Direct Instruction. The teacher is the major source of augmented feedback and directs all of the question-and-answer class segments. This does not mean that students are forbidden to ask questions—only that the teacher will have predetermined times in which student questions are solicited.

6. *Pacing.* The teacher maintains firm control of the pacing of student practice trials, especially initial learning tasks. The teacher might even choose to deliberately cue each practice trial at the beginning of a learning sequence by telling students when to start and stop each attempt (A). This allows the teacher to monitor every trial to provide a better analysis of students' skill attempts. Later the teacher might say, "Practice your overhand serves ten times," or "Practice only overhand serves for the next five minutes," and let students determine when to start each trial (B). Note that the teacher still decides how many tries or how long students will get to practice.

7. *Task progression.* The teacher makes all determinations about when students will move from one learning task to the next. These determinations are made according to the teacher's criterion for task mastery (e.g., 90 percent correct). Once most or all of the students have met that criterion, the teacher moves the class to the next learning task.

Predominant Engagement Patterns

Direct Instruction uses many types of student engagement patterns, determined by the task structure the teacher chooses for each learning activity. Students can practice alone, with partners, in small groups, in large groups, or as a whole class. Stations are often used as well. The only common feature is that it is the teacher who decides on the engagement pattern and then gives students directions for how to organize and maintain the pattern.

Inclusiveness

When used according to the model's design (Rosenshine, 1983), Direct Instruction is inherently inclusive. All students see the same task presentation; practice the same learning tasks; get high rates of OTR, ALT, and augmented feedback; and progress to the next learning activity together. However, since content progression is determined at the class level, it is possible that lesser-skilled or slower learners will not have mastered one learning task before they are moved along with the rest of the class to the next task. So, they are included, but their need for more practice at the current task is not met by the teacher's decision to move all students to the next task in the unit. Direct Instruction teachers can plan for multiple groups in class, based on learning rate, but this occurs less often than is desired in physical education. "Teaching by invitation" is a good strategy for promoting more inclusiveness in planned learning activities in classes with a wide range of learner aptitude and experience.

Task Presentation and Task Structure

The effectiveness of Direct Instruction hinges on the teacher's planning and implementation of task presentations and task structure. Since the task presentation is the vehicle for providing students with the description of how to perform the skill/task proficiently, it is essential that the task presentation gives a clear picture of how to perform the task successfully. Task structure is equally critical since it allows students to clearly understand the organizational components of the learning activity and promotes the efficient use of class time, leading to higher rates of OTR and ALT for students.

Task Presentation. While it is possible to use instructional media such as CD ROMs and videotapes for making task presentations, the Direct Instruction teacher will most often serve as the model in order to maintain more control of the flow of information to students. Student models can also serve this function, but it is important that the modeled performance is exactly what the teacher wants the other students to see. Since the Direct Instruction model promotes high rates of OTR, students must not be practicing the wrong performance cues and then need to have that learning be "undone" and replaced later with correct performance patterns. Because of that, a Direct Instruction teacher will most often serve as the model in task presentations.

Task presentations are given to all students in a class at one time. The teacher must be sure to check for student understanding frequently in order to be confident that students comprehend the model and performance cues they have been given. It is also possible to use the *active demonstration strategy* that has students moving along with the teacher's model as performance cues are stated. The teacher can then see if students really do comprehend the task presentation before they begin to practice.

Task Structure.   As mentioned earlier, Direct Instruction can use a wide variety of learning activities with different task structures planned for them. Regardless of which task structure is selected, it is critical that students understand how the activity will be organized and the accountability system in place for it. If students do not understand the task structure, the teacher will need to repeat the directions, losing momentum and OTRs in the lesson.

Several structures can be used for the initial learning tasks:

1. Individual practice in self-space
2. Individual practice in repetitive drills
3. Teacher-led practice (e.g., following along with dance steps, slow-motion of skills)
4. Low-organizational games

There are many structures that can be used for subsequent learning tasks and independent practicing:

1. Partner practice (e.g., throwing back and forth, kicking to each other)
2. Station tasks
3. Circuits and obstacle courses
4. Complex drills
5. Lead-up games
6. Minigames

Learning tasks in Direct Instruction can use any number of visual aids and markers to help students practice the task as designed and to increase OTR as much as possible. Lines drawn on the floor to denote proper spacing, cones used as path markers, targets on the wall that indicate accuracy, and mechanical devices that return balls all assist students in maintaining the desired performance parameters and getting more OTR in physical education.

Teacher Expertise and Contextual Needs

Teacher Expertise

Direct Instruction teachers will need to have several particular areas of expertise in the proposed knowledge base presented in Chapter 2.

Task Analysis and Content Listing. Direct Instruction features learning content that is broken into small units and sequenced into a series of progressive learning tasks. Teachers will need to be able to complete detailed task analyses that are used to construct the learning task sequences through which students progress. Once the task analyses are complete, the teacher will need to know how much content can be learned in a unit, determining the content listing. This requires knowledge of content and students' learning abilities.

Learning Objectives. Direct Instruction strives for student achievement of stated learning goals, written in the form of performance objectives. Teachers will need to be able to write objectives that include challenging yet attainable performance criteria for students.

Physical Education Content. To provide effective task presentations and give students usable performance feedback, it is essential that Direct Instruction teachers know the content being taught to students. That knowledge must come in two forms: the ability to model proficient skill performances in a task presentation and the ability to observe students' movement skills in order to provide high rates of specific, corrective feedback. Because the Direct Instruction teacher is the source for nearly all unit content, there is no substitute for strong content expertise in the unit being taught.

Developmentally Appropriate Instruction. To lead students through a series of learning tasks with performance criteria, the Direct Instruction teacher must know the developmental abilities of her students. Teachers must be able to communicate task presentations at a level that matches students' cognitive abilities, and provide clear directions for task structure. This also applies when the teacher observes students as they are practicing. The teacher must know the range of developmentally appropriate responses that students can make at that stage so that expectations for performance are matched with student abilities.

Effective Teaching Skills Applied to Direct Instruction

Much of the research on effective teaching in physical education has been derived from teachers using some semblance of the Direct Instruction model. Therefore, the link between teacher and student in-class behaviors and student achievement is substantiated more with Direct Instruction than with any other model presented in this book. In fact, the model itself was originally built upon many repeated findings in process-product research in numerous subject areas, including physical education (Rink, 1996).

If you will recall, one of the most important variables in effective teaching is academic learning time, which is the amount of time students spend engaged in appropriate learning tasks with high levels of success (Metzler, 1979). Very simply, students who accrue more ALT are more likely to acquire the stated learning objectives of the moment, so if we observe and measure ALT we can have a good approximation of how much student learning is happening in a lesson. All of the effective teaching skills discussed in this section have a known effect on ALT rates in direct-instructed physical education, so we can be more confident about their contribution to student achievement in Direct Instruction than in other teaching models. Teachers who make decisions and instruct in ways that raise student ALT are considered to be more effective Direct Instruction teachers.

Planning.   Because the teacher maintains control of nearly all instructional operations in Direct Instruction, there is a premium placed on unit and lesson planning. At the unit level, the teacher will need to determine the content listing and makes plans for every learning task students will pursue. This involves the task presentation, task structure, time allocation, space and equipment needs, content progression, and assessment. At the lesson level, Direct Instruction depends heavily on the maximum use of class time and other teaching resources, facilitated by careful and detailed planning for each lesson.

Time and Class Management.   The most effective Direct Instruction teachers are those who can maximize allocated time in class to provide students with high rates of OTR and ALT. The Direct Instruction teacher must be able to orchestrate many aspects of the learning environment—aspects that are always complex and sometimes at odds with one another. Class events and planned segments must flow smoothly from one to the next, and students must become engaged in learning activities quickly and correctly—all under the teacher's lead.

Task Presentation and Structure.   Task presentations are key segments in every Direct Instruction lesson. Students must be given a clear picture of the upcoming skill, movement, or concept so they can try to perform it correctly in the learning activity. The same goes for the task structure. It is essential that students understand the organization of the learning task so they can become engaged in it quickly and correctly, promoting high rates of OTR.

Graham (1988) states eight dimensions of an effective task presentation and structure for physical education:

1. Making instructions explicit
2. Emphasizing the usefulness of the content being presented
3. Structuring new content
4. Signaling students' attention
5. Summarizing and repeating information
6. Checking for understanding
7. Creating a productive climate for learning
8. Presenting accountability measures

Teachers can monitor their task presentation skills by using the Qualitative Measure of Teaching Performance Scale (QMTPS) (Rink & Werner, 1989). The QMTPS rates a teacher on seven dimensions of task presentation: clarity, demonstration, appropriate number of cues, accuracy of cues, quality of cues, appropriate focus, and specific congruent feedback. It results in a total QMTPS score that indicates a teacher's ability to plan for and present effective task descriptions to students. Gusthart, Kelly, and Rink (1997) validated the QMTPS instrument for use with Direct Instruction teaching, linking total QMTPS scores with increased levels of student achievement.

Communication.   Clarity is the key communication skill for direct instruction teachers. Task presentation, task structure, and feedback must be given to students in ways that they can comprehend and then use the information. This can be facilitated by checking for understanding frequently and repeating information not understood by students the first time.

Instructional Information. The flow of instructional information in Direct Instruction is most often one way. The teacher initiates the communication and students listen or watch. The teacher will ask questions, but they are used mostly for clarification about previous information. The most essential kinds of instructional information are verbal and modeled cues given in the task presentation, and two types of augmented feedback given during learning activities—positive and corrective.

Review and Closure. A good Direct Instruction lesson will be "bookended" at the start and finish. The class begins with a review of the previous lesson and a set induction. It ends with a well-planned review and closure. The first review and set induction allows the students to get focused on the lesson content; the culminating review and closure ties together what was learned in that lesson and ends the lesson in an orderly manner. During the review the teacher can reinforce learning cues, highlight aspects of students' performance, ask questions, and preview the next lesson's content. The closure alerts students that "PE is over for the day" and brings them into the exit routine.

Student Developmental Requirements

Student developmental ability must be addressed in two primary areas: comprehension of task presentation and task structure information, and readiness for planned learning tasks. The teacher must be sure to use vocabulary that students can understand and to model age/stage appropriate examples of movement performance. Once the teacher has been careful to match the level and complexity of task information to students' comprehension levels, students will be able to use that information quickly and correctly in their practice attempts. The selection of learning activities also has developmental issues to address. The activities must allow students the opportunity for many repetitions on tasks with a moderate level of difficulty. This type of engagement allows students to accrue high rates of Academic Learning Time, which promotes increased achievement in physical education. Teachers can check for understanding frequently and monitor students' understanding of task presentation and task structure information by simply watching what happens in the first minutes of a learning activity.

Contextual Needs for Direct Instruction

Direct Instruction can and has been used in every conceivable physical education context. It can be used to teach virtually all movement content to students at any age and developmental level. The main contextual consideration is to be able to provide students with high rates of OTR, so it is necessary to have sufficient amounts of equipment and enough activity space to reduce or eliminate student waiting time in class.

Teacher and Student Roles and Responsibilities in Direct Instruction

Each instructional model will have certain operations that need to be completed to make the model function according to its design. Some of these operations are carried out by the teacher; others are carried out by one or more students. The following table shows the major operations within the Direct Instruction model, and indicates who is responsible for completing them during each lesson.

Operation or Responsibility	Who Does It in Direct Instruction
Starting class	The **teacher** begins class by calling all students together for the set induction.
Bringing equipment to class	The **teacher** makes a list of needed equipment and brings it to class. Students can assist in setting up the equipment.
Dispersing and returning equipment	The **teacher** gives students directions for how and where to set up equipment. Students can assist by returning the equipment to a designated place at the end of class.
Roll call (if needed)	The **teacher** can call the roll or use an alternative method to save time.
Task presentation	Planned and implemented by the **teacher,** who most often provides the performance model for students to observe.
Task structure	Planned for and directed by the **teacher.** Students get instructions from the teacher and carry them out.
Assessment	The **teacher** determines the performance criteria for each learning task and monitors student achievement. Assessment can be made in a variety of ways, but typically occurs through the teacher's informal observation of students' performance.
Content progression	By monitoring student performance, the **teacher** determines when a learning activity ends and when students move on to the next one.

Teaching and Learning Benchmarks for Direct Instruction

Teachers who use Direct Instruction can learn the benchmarks for the teaching and learning behavior patterns that should be consistently evident in the model. Monitoring and adhering to these benchmarks ensures that the teacher is using the Direct Instruction *model* and not simply a series of direct instruction strategies in physical education. The teacher and student benchmarks presented are a combination of those suggested by Rosenshine (1983) and others derived from process-product research on teaching in the past two decades.

Teacher Benchmarks

Benchmark	How to Verify
Unit content is broken into a series of small learning tasks, leading to larger learning goals.	Review the teacher's task analysis, content listing, and content progression prior to the start of the unit.
Review previous day's content.	Review teacher's lesson plan to include a review of the previous lesson and a set induction.
Present a clear and effective task presentation.	1. Monitor with QMTPS. 2. Observe students as they begin to practice. Are they doing the task correctly? Did the teacher check for understanding?
Present a clear task structure.	Observe students as they begin to practice. Are they engaged in the way described by the teacher? Did the teacher check for understanding?
Use a brisk pace through content progression.	1. Teacher plans a series of small learning tasks. 2. Teacher has quick transitions between planned class segments.
Teacher provides high rates of positive and corrective feedback.	Record the frequency and types of augmented feedback given to students by the teacher.
Learning tasks have a mastery criterion.	1. Check lesson plan. 2. Verify that 80–100% of students have mastered the previous task.
Regular content reviews are made.	1. Check the unit plan. 2. Record the timing and focus of each review made.

Student Benchmarks

Benchmark	How to Verify
Students understand task presentation.	Count the number of students who are practicing the skill/movement/concept as it was described by the teacher.
Students understand task structure.	Count the number of students who: a. Are engaged according to the teacher's direction b. Have modified the task c. Have withdrawn from the task
Students have high rates of OTR.	1. Count the number of practice attempts (if frequency is the best indicator of OTR). 2. Measure how much actual practice time students get (if time is the best indicator of OTR).
Students have high rates of ALT.	Monitor a sampling of students with a valid ALT-PE recording instrument.

(continued)

Student Benchmarks Continued

Students get high rates of positive and corrective feedback.	When counting the teacher's feedback, note which student/s receive each one. The feedback should be distributed among all students in the class.
Initial student practice is directed by the teacher.	Check task structure and content progression.
Later student practice includes some independent practice.	Check task structure and content progression.
Students have mastered content.	Students complete and pass regular assessments that match the teacher's stated learning goals.

Assessing Learning in Direct Instruction

The Direct Instruction model calls for frequent assessment of student learning, usually done for each planned learning task. Rosenshine (1983) recommends that students achieve a success rate of 80 percent on initial learning tasks and 90 to 100 percent on the later learning tasks in a content unit. This means that students do not necessarily take quizzes or skills tests in physical education; rather, they practice a task until they have achieved the criterion success rate set by the teacher. Success rates can be monitored with formal and informal assessment techniques.

Informal Assessment

A Direct Instruction teacher can informally monitor student success rates with some practical strategies that take very little time and record keeping:

1. Have students practice in blocks of task trials and then stop the class when all students have finished one block. If each block is five trials and the criterion success rate is 80 percent (four out of five), the teacher can ask, "How many of you were able to get four or five correct that time?" If not enough students reached the criterion success rate, the task is continued. If all or nearly all students got four of five correct, the teacher then moves to the next task.
2. The teacher can monitor a sampling of students as the class practices a task and count the number of successful and unsuccessful trials each selected student completes. When all or nearly all of the sampled students have reached the criterion rate, the teacher then moves to the next task. It is important that the sampled students are representative of the entire class, meaning that the sample should include students from various skill ability groupings in the class and an equal number of boys and girls.

Formal Assessment

Informal strategies are typically very practical but run the risk of providing the teacher with potentially false information about student success rates on learning tasks. Formal strategies tend to be more systematic, objective, and rigorous but do present some feasibility problems for physical education. The following are examples of practical formal assessment methods:

1. Students are given cards on which to record successful and unsuccessful skill attempts for each learning task. When students have reached the criterion rate, they turn the card into the teacher for his records. When enough students have turned in their cards, the teacher moves on to the next task.
2. Periodic, brief performance quizzes are given to students and immediately scored by the teacher. These quizzes can be written, oral, or skill-based. When all or nearly all students reach the criterion score, the teacher moves on to the next task.
3. Students' skills can be observed by the teacher with a checklist of key performance cues. When all or nearly all students have demonstrated proficiency, the teacher moves on to the next task.
4. Student peer observers can be used in the previous assessment strategy in place of the teacher.

Because Direct Instruction is a mastery approach, it is essential for the teacher to document that students have achieved the criterion success rate or performance score before progressing to the next learning task. The behavioral shaping feature of Direct Instruction will not work if students do not master each successive approximation to the eventual performance outcome. If allowed to proceed without mastery, students will at some point "get stuck" on a new learning task because they have not demonstrated adequate proficiency of lead-up tasks.

Selecting and Modifying Direct Instruction for Physical Education

As mentioned at the start of this chapter, Direct Instruction has been used in physical education for many years to teach nearly all content to all grade levels of students. The selection of Direct Instruction depends more on the teacher's learning goals for a content unit than any other factor. Direct instruction is designed to teach basic movement skills and concepts, and it does that more effectively than any other model in this book. However, when the teacher wants student learning at higher levels (cognitive or psychomotor), or primarily in the affective domain, then Direct Instruction will not be the most effective model in those units. Direct Instruction would seem to be best suited for certain types of content units in physical education:

1. Individual sports (beginning and intermediate levels)
2. Team sports (beginning and intermediate levels)
3. Recreational activities (bowling, horseshoes, darts)
4. Dances with prescribed steps (line, square, folk, etc.)
5. Aerobics (all kinds that require teacher cuing for students)
6. Repetitive exercises (calisthenics, stretching, weight training)
7. Combatives (noncompetitive)

Grade-Level Adaptations

As mentioned, the most effective use of Direct Instruction will depend more on the stated learning goals for a content unit than the grade levels of students. If the Direct Instruction teacher correctly selects unit goals that are fostered through Direct Instruction, then she needs only to make the instruction developmentally appropriate for the students she will teach. Figure 7.2 presents an analysis for selecting Direct Instruction and making grade level adaptations for it.

FIGURE 7.2   Grade-Level Adaptations for Direct Instruction in Physical Education

Grade Levels	Select Direct Instruction?	Possible Adaptations
Preschool	Yes	1. Reduce verbal cues in task presentations. Use more modeling and have students mimic. 2. Use only teacher-led tasks. 3. Provide feedback as encouragement—not corrective information. 4. Make questions very simple—yes/no answers. 5. Use more general performance criteria.
Elementary	Yes	1. Simplify task presentation and structures. 2. Use mostly teacher-led tasks. . 3. Make questions simple. 4. Repeat instructions and check for understanding every time. 5. Use less stringent performance criteria, but do expect some proficiency before moving to new tasks. 6. Cover less content by giving students more time on each task.
Middle school/ Junior high	Yes	1. Couple verbal information with teacher demonstrations in task presentations. 2. Use a combination of teacher-led and independent practice tasks. 3. Teach for developmentally appropriate performance proficiency. 4. Increase corrective feedback. 5. Use higher-order questions to help students learn underlying concepts.
High school	Yes	Use the full Direct Instruction model.
College/adult	Yes	Use the full Direct Instruction model.

A Sample Unit for Direct Instruction

Unit content:	Tennis
Grade level:	10th
Students:	36 (18 boys, 18 girls) Varied skill levels, mostly beginner
Resources:	5 tennis courts A tennis racquet for each student 70 tennis balls 2 volleying walls
Length of unit:	15 class periods
Length of class:	42 minutes of instructional time each period

Content listing and schedule:		
	Class 1	Introduction to tennis (history, famous players) Basic safety procedures Equipment and clothing Stretching for tennis
	Classes 2–3	Serving
	Classes 4–5	Forehand drive shot
	Classes 6–7	Backhand drive shot
	Class 8	Returning service
	Class 9	Rules, scoring, and strategies for singles play Lead-up game (serve and return only)
	Class 10	Net play Singles matches
	Class 11	Singles matches
	Class 12	Rules and strategies for doubles play Doubles lead-up game
	Class 13	Half-volley shot Doubles matches
	Class 14	Singles and doubles matches
	Class 15	Final test Singles and doubles matches

Sample Lesson Plan for Direct Instruction

Class 6: Introduction to Backhand Drive Shot

Class Segment	Task Presentation	Task Structure	Assessment
Set Induction: Ask students who their favorite players are. Tell students that all good players need to be able to use a variety of offensive shots, including the backhand.		Grouped around teacher (1–2 minutes)	They know forehand—now, what is a backhand shot?
Review of previous skills (forehand)	Ask students to mention five major parts of the forehand drive shot. Tell them that those parts are also included in the backhand shot, just "in a mirror image," so they already have a good start on the backhand.	Question and answer (1–2 minutes)	Checking for understanding
Introduce and demonstrate the stance, grip, swing, point of contact, and follow-through for the backhand drive.	Teacher demo with verbal cues	1. Students in self-space 2. Listen to teacher and follow along in slow motion (active demonstration) 3. Students then practice without teacher cues (and without ball) at half-speed (4–5 minutes). Teacher circulates and observes.	Students perform 5 consecutive backhand strokes at half-speed, correctly.
Introduce self-toss	1. Review from forehand 2. "Same thing, other side"	1. Students in self-space 2. Practice making tosses from "ready position." Do not hit the ball. (5 minutes)	Students make 5 consecutive correct self-tosses to backhand side.
Hitting into fence	Teacher demo of ready position, self-toss, and contact into fence (no specific target)	1. Students in self-space around perimeter fence. Be 20 feet from the fence (designated by cones). 2. Practice self-toss with ball contact for 10 minutes. Students hit when they are ready and it's safe.	At the end of 10 minutes, try 10 self-tosses. Criterion is 9 of 10 that hit the fence.

Sample Lesson Plan for Direct Instruction   Continued

Class 6: Introduction to Backhand Drive Shot

Class Segment	Task Presentation	Task Structure	Assessment
Interim review	1. Teacher calls class together 2. "What is happening when you hit the ball?" 3. Teacher uses students' responses to review earlier task presentation and performance cues.	(2–3 minutes)	
Hitting to a target on the court	1. Teacher demo of ready position, self-toss, contact point, and (new concepts) aiming line and trajectory. 2. Teacher demos a backhand shot to a target (left service box on opposite side of net).	1. 6–8 students per court. 3–4 hit to their left side; other 3–4 hit to their left side from the other side of the net. 2. Self-toss and hit to the designated target. 3. Practice for 10 minutes. Students hit when they are ready and it's safe.	At the end of 10 minutes, try 10 self-tossed backhand shots to the target. Criterion is 8 of 10 that clear the net and hit in the target area.
Interim review	1. Teacher calls class together. 2. "What is happening when you hit the ball?" 3. Teacher uses students' responses to review earlier task presentation and performance cues.	(2–3 minutes)	
Return to previous task		(5 minutes)	At the end of 5 minutes, try 10 self-tossed backhand shots to the target. Criterion is 8 of 10 that clear the net and hit in the target area.
Final review and closure	1. Teacher again reviews the major parts of the backhand drive shot, providing a demo. 2. Teacher "pinpoints" one student who has good form. 3. Teacher previews the sequence of learning activities for the next class. 4. Dismissal	1. Students follow along in slow motion in self-space.	1. Teacher observes and provides individual feedback

Summary

Even though physical education teachers do not often use the full and formal model of Direct Instruction described in this chapter, several forms of Direct Instruction have been common in our field for over one hundred years. That longevity, along with the strong research evidence of its effectiveness, provides good support for its continued use in many settings, grade levels, and movement content areas for physical education. However, it must be recognized that Direct Instruction has come under criticism in the past decade as other contrasting models have been developed for our field. To be fair, it should be noted that Direct Instruction will be less effective when chosen as the model to pursue student learning that is incongruent with its foundational learning theories and applied in ways that do not match its intended design. But that observation will be the same for every instructional model, and you should keep that in mind as you learn about the other models in Part 2 of this book.

It is also important that you do not interpret the amount of control retained by the teacher in this model as rigid or militaristic. Direct Instruction can be flexible, supportive, and very positive. It provides students with increased time to learn lesson and unit content, along with high rates of teacher monitoring and instructional interaction, particularly performance feedback. All of those contribute to higher levels of student achievement in physical education—one of our most valued learning outcomes.

SUGGESTED READINGS

Baumann, J. F. (1988). Direct instruction reconsidered. *Journal of Reading Behavior, 31,* 714.

Rosenshine, B. (1983). Teaching functions in instructional programs. *Elementary School Journal, 83,* 335–350.

CHAPTER

8 Personalized System for Instruction

Students Progress as Fast as They Can, or as Slowly as They Need

One of the most often-mentioned goals of teaching is to provide individual instruction to every student in the class. It is also one of the least frequently achieved goals of teaching. Large classes, inadequate time, limited equipment and facilities, and a typically wide range of student abilities all work against teachers who attempt to plan and implement individualized learning programs for students. From another perspective, it should be noted that nearly all instructional strategies and models are simply not designed for individual instruction and are able to give only well-intended but unsuccessful attempts at personalizing instruction in physical education. Some models are more successful than others, but only one model begins and proceeds from the notion that truly individualized instruction is not only possible but attainable. That model is called a Personalized System for Instruction, or PSI. It is also known as the *Keller Plan,* after its developer, Fred Keller.

PSI was developed by Keller and his graduate students at the University of Sao Paulo, Brazil, in the early 1960s and refined a few years later at Arizona State University (Keller & Sherman, 1974). Faced with teaching Introductory Psychology to sections of over 300 students, it was immediately clear to Keller that the traditional lecture approach would not meet the needs of his undergraduate students. Keller had come from the research tradition of applied behavior analysis, which focused on observing and teaching as few as one subject at a time, so he set out to design an instructional model that would provide an individual learning program for all students. The educational world was introduced to PSI in the provocative article, "Goodbye, teacher!" (Keller, 1968). You can imagine how readers, especially teachers, would have reacted to just the title of the article. Now imagine the reactions of those same people as they read Keller's design for instruction that placed the teacher at the periphery of the instructional process and suggested that students could learn more by the teacher being *less* involved in the direct transmission of content!

After the initial article, Keller moderated his plan a bit, recognizing that he had underestimated the role of context and student motivation in his plan (Keller & Sherman, 1974). The biggest problem with his original plan was that he considered time (for instruction) to be unbounded. That is, PSI was first designed to give students unlimited time to learn, not bounded by the constraints of class periods and academic terms. Eventually accepting that time is rarely unbounded in education, he modified some of the radical claims for learning effects attributable to PSI. Notice that he did not change his claim for PSI's ability to provide individualized instruction for every learner—only that some students would simply "run out of time" in the term before they achieved all that was intended. The strong research history on the effectiveness of PSI in every subject and across nearly all age groups of learners bears this out. Lowry and Thornburg (1988) published a summary of research on PSI that included over 1500 references from 1968 to 1988.

The use of PSI in physical education has been limited but has great promise as an effective instructional model for nearly all movement content and across most grades, particularly at the secondary levels. Siedentop (1974) was the first to introduce the possibility of PSI as an instructional model for physical education, but referred mostly to cognitive content for college students. The most complete implementation of PSI in physical education for activity instruction can be found in the *Personalized Sport Instruction Series,* written by Metzler and Sebolt (1994). That series contains complete PSI units for golf, tennis, racquetball, and volleyball. Although designed for college-level activity courses, such units can easily be adapted for use in any grade from middle school upward, as will be shown later in this chapter.

Overview

PSI is designed to allow each student to progress at his/her own pace through a sequence of prescribed learning tasks. The learning tasks are derived from a task analysis for each of the skills and knowledge areas to be covered, determining the content listing for the entire unit. Every learning task module includes information on task presentation, task structure, error analyses, and performance criteria given to students in a written and or mediated format. The key is that teachers do not provide this information to students in person—students read materials or view video samples for that information. This feature frees the teacher from having to spend her time in class on these functions, allowing her to have much more instructional interaction with students. As a student completes a learning task to its stated performance criteria, he then moves on to the next task on the list, without depending on the teacher for permission or directions.

When used in large classes in which the teacher has designated assistants, PSI as it was designed by Keller relies on proctors to review unit exams, assist students with logistics, and provide one-on-one tutoring for students (Keller & Sherman, 1974). These proctors could be teaching assistants, teachers' aides, or advanced students. In most applications for physical education in schools the availability of proctors is limited, but there are other ways to provide that function for students. These ways will be discussed later in this chapter. Because there are few, if any, teacher-directed task presentations, PSI instructors use interactions with students to provide motivation and instructional information (e.g., feedback and one-on-one tutoring).

PSI relies heavily on a *unified plan* for the content unit; there are no daily lesson plans. Students progress individually through the sequence of learning tasks and simply begin each lesson where they left off from the previous lesson. The teacher needs only to be aware of which tasks will be attempted in the upcoming lesson and provide the necessary equipment for student engagement on them. The functions of providing students with information about class management, learning tasks, and assessment are carried out with a course workbook and instructional media (typically videotapes). Students read and follow the course workbook as much as possible; the teacher provides only needed clarification and details not covered in the workbook.

The basic design goal of PSI is to allow students to be independent learners and at the same time allow the teacher to use high rates of interaction with students who need it. It has shown to be a highly effective model for student achievement in the psychomotor and cognitive domains.

Foundations of PSI for Physical Education

Theory and Rationale

The first ideas for PSI were developed within the area of applied behavior analysis. This branch of psychology holds that human learning occurs as a result of interactions between a person and the external environment. Certain consequences of behavior, called reinforcers, increase the likelihood of a behavior being emitted again. Other consequences, called punishers, tend to decrease the likelihood of the behavior being emitted. A science of human behavior is based on these and other relationships between people and their environment. B. F. Skinner was among the first psychologists to use behavioral theory in the design of instruction for school subjects. His "teaching machines" were able to deliver positive reinforcement to learners who made correct answers by pressing buttons, touching screens, or pulling levers. This rudimentary design allowed the teacher to determine the questions and correct answers, but gave the key functions of content presentation, feedback, and reinforcement to the machines for delivery. That important step led to the development of a larger role for the teaching environment (besides the teacher) in the teaching/learning process.

Keller was a colleague of Skinner and an experimental behavioral psychologist who shared the same theory about the role of the environment in the teaching/learning process. If it was the complete environment, and not just the teacher, that led to human learning, then it was possible to design environments that could promote student learning with or without a direct role for the teacher. Keller and Sherman (1974) acknowledge that PSI is based on four features that provide students with a rich schedule of reinforcement, not often available within other models:

1. The ability to view creative and interesting learning materials
2. Regular, tangible progress toward the course goals
3. Immediate assessment of learning
4. Individual attention from the instructor

Assumptions about Teaching and Learning

Assumptions about Teaching
1. Many teaching functions, especially task presentation and task structure, can be provided through printed, visual, and audio media (that is, not the teacher).
2. The teacher's primary function is to interact with students for learning and motivation, not to manage the class. Class management operations can be communicated to students in print and carried out by students with little teacher direction.
3. Student participation and learning is most effective when it is largely independent of the teacher.
4. Planning decisions are made from data collected on student learning.
5. It is not only desirable but possible to design truly individualized instruction.

Assumptions about Learning
1. Student learning can occur with little dependence on the teacher.
2. Students learn content at a different rate.
3. Students have differing aptitudes for learning content.
4. If given enough time and/or trials, nearly all students can achieve the stated goals of instruction.
5. Students will be highly motivated and responsible as independent learners.

Major Theme for PSI: Students Progress as Fast as They Can, or as Slowly as They Need

The basic design of PSI provides each student with a complete set of instructional materials that includes management information, task presentations, task structures, learning activities with performance criteria and error analyses, and assessments. Students then proceed through the sequence of learning activities, completing each one to the stated performance criterion before moving on to the next activity. Students are allowed to progress at their own pace, according to their aptitude for learning the unit content. Students with higher skill, more experience, and better aptitude can progress as quickly as they can through the content. Students will lower skill, less experience, and lower aptitude can take the time needed to complete each activity, since there are no group- or class-level progressions. Therefore, the theme for PSI is *students progress as fast as they can or as slowly as they need* (Metzler & Sebolt, 1994).

Learning Domain Priorities and Interactions

PSI is a decidedly mastery- and achievement-based instructional model. Mastery-based instruction means that students must meet the performance criterion on the current learning task before they can proceed to the next task in the sequence. Achievement-based instruction means that the instruction is focused strongly on student learning outcomes that are demonstrated through overt student performance, either in the cognitive or psychomotor domains. For physical education, it is most often the latter domain in which student learning is demonstrated. Therefore, the learning *domain priorities* for PSI are typically:

First priority:	Psychomotor learning
Second priority:	Cognitive learning
Third priority:	Affective learning

The *domain interaction* for PSI works in the following manner. Students must use their cognitive abilities to comprehend the written and visual media used for task presentations and task structures. They must also use those abilities to devise some learning strategies for completing learning tasks. However, that learning occurs to facilitate performance in the psychomotor domain, in which most performance criteria are stated. Some learning tasks are designed for performance in the cognitive domain, such as comprehension quizzes, strategy tests, and rules tests, but the majority of performance criteria are written for the psychomotor domain. The domain interaction does not ignore affective learning, but it is not directly addressed in the PSI model. Students who are able to progress at their own pace enjoy that feature and feel a strong sense of accomplishment as they move from one mastered task to the next. This promotes high levels of independency and student self-efficacy—both desired outcomes in the affective domain.

Student Learning Preferences

Using the Reichmann and Grasha (1974) profile for student learning preferences, PSI will most often work best for students who are classified as avoidant, competitive, or dependent. As mentioned in Chapter 6, these labels should not be given a negative interpretation. They are used to describe how some students would prefer the instructional environment to be designed. While PSI gives students independence in how they progress through learning tasks, the list of tasks is determined solely by the teacher, providing students with little latitude on what and how they learn in physical education.

Validation

Research Validation.   PSI has received extensive and mostly consistent research support as an effective instructional model, perhaps more so than any other model to be presented in this book. Over ten years ago, Lowry and Thornburg (1988) cited over 1500 research articles that described how to implement PSI and how effective it could be in a wide variety of content areas: earth science, mathematics, writing, physics, chemistry, health, psychology, and many others. Most of the completed research has been in grades from middle school through college. Some research has been completed on the effectiveness of PSI for teaching physical education. In a summary of the literature in personalized instructional materials, Annarino (1979) reported results from several studies completed in which personalized instruction was compared to other approaches in teaching physical education. The key point in his review was that the PSI and PSI-like techniques were always shown to be at least as effective as other teaching methods, and often more effective. Metzler and his graduate students at Virginia Tech completed a series of studies on the effectiveness of authentic PSI materials used in college basic instruction programs. Metzler (1984) compared how students spent time in tennis classes while using PSI and Direct Instruction. The PSI students had higher rates of content engagement, skill practice time, academic learning time, and success at learning tasks. In a follow-up study, Metzler (1986) reported similarly positive results for student process, along with a more important finding that the PSI students scored significantly higher learning gains over the students who had Direct Instruction. In an analysis of teacher processes in PSI, Metzler, Eddleman, Treanor, and Cregger (1989) reported that PSI teachers spend less than 1 percent of class time in management, almost no time giving task presentations, and provide almost three times as much feedback as non-PSI teachers.

Cregger (1994) designed an animated PSI-Computer Assisted Instruction (PSI-CAI) module for students learning spare conversion in a college bowling course. Students who used the PSI-CAI module showed increased learning gains over another group that received a traditional Direct Instruction approach. Interestingly, the CAI group did not show significant gains over a group of students who received that same PSI information on spare conversion from a packet of written text and graphics, suggesting that the format of the PSI media is less critical than the design itself.

Research on PSI has consistently demonstrated its effectiveness in promoting high levels of student achievement, but that support has not been unanimous. A few reports suggest that PSI will work better for students who are self-disciplined and independent learners; the lack of task progression structure allows students to procrastinate, thereby reducing achievement and risking lower grades (Sherman, 1974). It should be noted that most of the research that does not support the effectiveness of PSI points to factors that are not design flaws—they are human application errors and contextual factors that cause the model not to work for some students, while others apply themselves and show large learning gains with PSI (Sherman, 1974).

Craft Knowledge Validation.   The fact that PSI has been used in almost every content area and has generated a huge amount of literature on how to implement it provides good evidence for craft knowledge validation. If it was not effective, and if it was not adaptable to so many content areas, it would not have received so much attention in the educational literature. Its continued use for over thirty years is strong evidence that many kinds of teachers like it, can use it, and can see demonstrable gains in student learning. PSI was never a fad!

I have used PSI in my teaching of physical education activity courses for nearly twenty years. After becoming familiar with this model in a graduate instructional design course, I soon faced the "PE version" of Fred Keller's dilemma: how to provide personalized tennis instruction in classes with sections of more than fifty students of varying ability (and with five teaching courts!). I designed some rudimentary PSI materials which over the years have evolved into a four-course PSI series for physical education (Metzler & Sebolt, 1994) used in many universities across the country. During that same time, many of my undergraduate students have designed and used PSI units for middle-school, junior-high, and high-school instruction—demonstrating that PSI can be adapted in many grades and for much of the movement content in physical education programs.

Intuitive Validation.   As I began this chapter, I stated that individualized instruction has been a long-standing goal for physical education teachers. All teachers know that some students learn faster than others, that students come to physical education with varying levels of skill and experience with the unit's content, and that the most effective teaching occurs one-on-one with a student. All of these realizations provide strong intuitive evidence that Personalized Systems for Instruction can be an effective way to teach physical education in many settings. In addition, PSI's strong emphasis on achievement-based learning in the psychomotor domain matches many teachers' expressed domain priorities in a large number of physical education units.

Teaching and Learning Features

Directness

The following list describes each part of the Directness Profile for Personalized Systems for Instruction as it is used for physical education (as shown in Figure 8.1).

   1. *Content selection.* The teacher maintains complete control of the content and its sequencing in PSI. She decides what will be included in the unit, the order in which

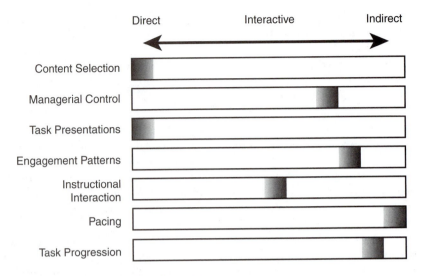

FIGURE 8.1   **Directness Profile for PSI**

learning tasks will be sequenced, and the performance criteria used to determine mastery of each task. Students simply receive the content and task listing from the teacher and pursue them in the order given.

2. *Managerial control.* The teacher determines the managerial plan, class policies, and specific procedures in the PSI model. However, once these are determined, students assume a large degree of responsibility in implementing class management in each lesson.

3. *Task presentations.* In a true PSI design, the task presentations are given to students via written and/or video displays. The teacher produces or adopts instructional media that show students how to do each task, how to correct errors, and how to set up each task for engagement. This allows students to be independent of the instructor, facilitating individual progression through the content.

Some PSI designs (Metzler & Sebolt, 1994) use one whole-class task presentation by the teacher to start the unit, then have small-group presentations by the teacher as students begin each new skill or knowledge area in the unit. In these cases, the teacher's role in the task presentation process is more direct, as shown in Figure 8.2.

4. *Engagement patterns.* Students practice independently from the teacher and other students nearly all of the time in PSI. Most learning tasks are designed for individual practice; a few are designed for partner or small-group engagement. Regardless of the design, students are typically engaged independently from the teacher's direction.

5. *Instructional interaction.* Because a PSI teacher has very few managerial responsibilities in class, he is able to provide students with high levels of instructional interaction, especially about content. Metzler et al. (1989) observed rates of teacher feedback at over three per minute during PSI units, more than three times that typically reported in physical education research. But it is not just feedback; PSI students can request "tutoring time" with the teacher that allows for high levels of verbal interaction in class.

6. *Pacing.* Simply put, each student determines her own pace at which she is engaged in learning tasks and will progress through the unit content. Students make their own choices about when to start and stop practicing, how many trials they attempt, and how long to take between trials. They are held accountable for achieving each task's performance criterion, but not for the process of getting there.

7. *Task progression.* In a different way, students also control their own pace through the unit content by how fast their ability and effort allows them to move through the task sequence. They can go "as fast as they can, or as slowly as they need." Admittedly, some students cannot progress as fast as they'd wish, but by and large it is the student, not the teacher, who controls task progression.

Predominant Engagement Pattern

As the model's name would indicate, PSI uses individual practice engagement almost exclusively. Each student is on his or her own to get the task presentation information, set up the practice area, and monitor achievement. At some times, it will be necessary for paired practice, such as rallying in tennis, making and returning serves in badminton, or pitching to a batter in softball. Poole, Sebolt, and Metzler (1997) designed noncriterion lead-up games, called "challenge tasks," for volleyball in which students play reduced-team (e.g., three vs. three) games that focus on discrete skills just learned in the learning sequence. These challenge tasks allow students to practice newly acquired skills in small-sided and simple games that develop tactical awareness and applications.

Inclusiveness

PSI's focus on individual student achievement makes it a highly inclusive model for teaching physical education. All students are able to participate and progress through the sequence of learning activities according to their own abilities, so no one is excluded by being "left behind" when teachers base task progressions on a time-allocation plan. Lower-ability learners can take the time they need to demonstrate mastery on each task. Higher-ability students can progress according to their own pacing as well.

PSI also allows the teacher time to identify and work one-on-one with those students who need more extensive instructional interaction. Since students know what they are supposed to be doing at all times, the teacher can spend several minutes with one or a few students who need extra attention—without losing managerial control of the class.

Task Presentation and Task Structure

The most important feature of PSI is that it allows students to be largely independent of the teacher in the management of class operations and progression through learning activities. The idea is not to have the teacher carry out the many routine operations in class that take away from instructional time with students or reduce students' active engagement. In order to accomplish that, the model uses some unique approaches to providing students with information about task presentation and structure.

Task Presentation.   Information about tasks that is typically provided to students by lecture and/or demonstration are given to students in PSI with written and visual media. Recall the most important functions of task presentation: (1) to give students a "picture" of the correct way to perform a task or skill, (2) to provide learning cues on key elements of the skill, and (3) alert students to common errors that occur when practicing that skill. In most instances, this information is given to the entire class, with the teacher serving as the model. In PSI, the modeling operation of task presentation is most often provided to students by instructional media—some combination of written text, photographs, illustrations, videotapes, and CD ROMs. Each student reads/views a presentation as she is ready to begin a new learning task, separately from other students in class. She informs the teacher that she is ready, gets and reviews the mediated task presentation and structure information, and then proceeds to practice the task on her own.

Written Text.   Most students cannot get sufficient task presentation information from reading text only. The transfer from reading to a "mind's picture" of a psychomotor skill is too abstract for all but a few learners, so text must be supplemented with visual displays.

Photographs.   Pictures of models performing a skill can be helpful for many learners. Photographs can show good detail and can be superimposed with text and graphics for added information. The limitation of photographs is that they are just snapshots that portray one brief instant of skill performance in each frame.

Illustrations.   These work the same as photographs when used as single frames, but have the added potential to show movement through animation of body parts and sequential motions. Superimposing text and graphics also adds to the amount of information illustrations can provide learners.

Videotapes.   One of the best ways to show task presentations are videotapes that have both visual and audio information on them. It is quite simple for a teacher to record a task presentation for each learning task and to then have students view the tape when they begin a new skill or task in the PSI sequence. Teachers should not worry about achieving professional quality production on these tapes—they are meant to be "homemade" and will work fine as long as students get the needed information from them. Many commercial instructional videos are available but must be carefully selected to provide the exact task presentation needed by the teacher. Cost is also a prohibitive factor.

CD ROMs. More and more physical education teachers are getting personal computers in their gym offices. If a computer is available, it is possible to use a CD ROM in much the same way as videotape to provide task presentation information. Again, many commercial products are on the market, and are usually priced lower than videotapes. CD ROMs are also much faster and more durable than tapes. If your school has the capacity to make CD ROM recordings, you can do what was suggested with videotapes—make a recording of yourself giving each task presentation for students to view when it is time.

If none of these kinds of media are available, the teacher can use a modified approach for PSI task presentation. In the past, I have used one whole-class live task presentation for **only** the very first skill in the course (e.g., forehand drive in tennis). All students then begin to progress individually through the forehand task sequence. When a small group of students have finished that sequence, I then give the second task presentation (e.g., backhand drive) to them, and they move on while the rest of the class is still working on the forehand. That scenario is repeated as small groups finish one skill sequence and need a new task presentation. I would caution teachers that this approach has the potential to undermine the PSI model by taking up the teacher's time with too many "minipresentations" at the cost of time with students who are practicing. But, it can be a practical alternative to producing or purchasing instructional media.

Task Structure. PSI uses a list of sequenced learning activities within each of the skill and knowledge areas in the unit's content listing. For example, in a tennis course there would be a list of learning activities under each area to be included in the unit: forehand drive, backhand drive, serving, returning serve, volleying, rules, scoring, and strategy. Each learning task includes the needed task presentation information, error analyses, performance criteria, and details about task structure. The task structure information should include:

1. Needed equipment
2. The practice space requirements or specific location
3. Arranging the learning task (e.g., where to place targets, where to hit from, needed assistance from partners)
4. Performance criteria for accuracy, consistency, time, etc.
5. Directions for pursuing the task, including safety
6. Procedures for verifying completion of the task (self-check, partner check, instructor check)

Poole, Sebolt, and Metzler (1996) use six different kinds of tasks for PSI units: (1) readiness drills, (2) comprehension tasks, (3) criterion tasks, (4) challenge tasks, (5) quizzes, and (6) game or match play. Each type of task has a different structure.

Readiness Tasks. Students receive the task presentation and then spend a short period of time in noncriterion engagement to get the feel of objects, implements, and movement patterns. They simply hit, throw, catch, run, jump, or shoot for a few minutes to become familiar with space, objects, and equipment.

Comprehension Tasks. Students demonstrate that they have understood the key elements of the task presentation by making a brief display for the teacher (e.g., showing the correct grip in golf, using the proper form for soccer trapping, performing the correct stance and swing for a badminton serve). The teacher observes each student's display with a short checklist of key elements; when those elements have been correctly demonstrated, the student proceeds to independent practice. A sample checklist for the overhead volleyball serve is shown below.

Key Element	Demonstrated	Practice a Bit More
1. Proper stance, 2 feet behind the baseline	✓	
2. High and accurate toss	✓	
3. Contact ball at nearly full extension	✓	
4. Proper arm speed at contact		✓
5. Proper follow-through, one step onto court	✓	

Criterion Practice Tasks. Most practice tasks in PSI are criterion tasks, in which students must demonstrate mastery of the current skill to standards established by the teacher. Students practice these tasks until they are ready to be monitored for mastery. Criteria can be set for accuracy, consistency, time, distance, speed, or attained score. More will be presented on these tasks later in this chapter.

Challenge Tasks. Since proficiency for most criterion tasks is demonstrated in isolated and sometimes static drills, there is a need for students to extend their mastery to the next level of complexity. Challenge tasks are lead-up and modified games that are used to allow students to practice combinations of skills acquired in two or more criterion tasks. Some examples of challenge tasks are:

1. Tennis: Serving and returning games (no volleying)
2. Soccer: "Keep away" or three vs. three in a small area and with a small goal
3. Basketball: Two-on-two half-court games
4. Volleyball: Three vs. three with a "no spiking" rule

Quizzes. Some content areas will develop students' knowledge of game history, rules, scoring, and strategy. In PSI students typically learn that content by reading it or by viewing videotapes or CD ROMs. Once they have studied the material, they must pass a quiz to a stated performance criterion.

Game or Match Play. Once students have completed all of the content areas in the unit, they progress to playing games or matches. Students who finish all of the unit's content modules faster get more class days of play. Students who take longer often appreciate the extra time to develop their skills, knowing they will be more prepared for competition when that time comes. Getting to the game stage is a motivating factor for many students, regardless of their skill levels.

Non-Mastery Attempts. As mentioned previously, a student practices a skill task or studies a knowledge task until she thinks she is ready to be monitored for mastery. At that time, either the instructor or a peer will watch as she attempts to meet the criterion stated in the task structure. If met, she moves on to the next task. If the criterion is not met, she resumes practice until she once again feels confident and takes a second mastery attempt. The same goes for nonmastery attempts on tests and quizzes—they can be taken over without penalty. *Mastery attempts can be repeated as many times as needed for the student to complete the performance criterion.*

Verifying Proficiency. In small classes it is possible for the teacher to be the witness for all mastery attempts. In larger classes it is a good idea to have designated students or practice partners serve as monitors for some of the lower-level tasks in a course content area. However, it is important that the teacher retain his role as witness for the final task in each content module, because completion of that task signals that the student is ready to move on to a new module in the unit.

As mentioned, students can get task presentation information from a variety of sources; task structure information comes from written and visual directions. An example of a PSI criterion learning task is shown in Figure 8.2. The example contains directions for students to get all of the needed task presentation and task structure information. When a student is ready for this task she reads the directions, watches the task presentation, gathers the needed equipment and proceeds—with no dependence on the teacher.

PSI Course Workbook. All managerial operations, instructional materials, learning tasks, and assessments in a PSI unit are explained to students in a *course workbook* that they read as the unit begins and then refer to on an as-needed basis. The manual should include the following kinds of information:

1. Attendance policies
2. Class rules and disciplinary plan
3. Dressing-out policies
4. How to get and return equipment
5. Grading plan and applicable policies
6. Procedures for starting each class
7. Complete content list and all PSI learning tasks with performance criteria
8. All required readings (rules, strategies, history, etc.)
9. Student progress chart for completed tasks

FIGURE 8.2   Task Presentation and Task Structure for a Badminton Skill

High Deep Serve for Badminton

1. View the videotape segment for the high deep serve. Be sure to note the applicable rules and the key elements for this important badminton skill.

2. Equipment: racquet, 10 shuttles, 2 small cones, pencil for recording scores

3. Mark off a line 8 feet from the back boundary of the opposite service return box and put 1 cone there on each side. The resulting rectangle is your **aiming area** for this task. Set up for your serves in the proper position in the service court. Practice your high deep serves in blocks of 10 shots, keeping a record of how many shots in each group have a high trajectory and land in the aiming area. When you are ready, have your partner witness and score your mastery attempt. When you reach the criterion, have your partner initial and date in the designated areas.

   1. Position: Serving position in appropriate box
   2. Aiming area: Marked rectangle in opposite service return box
   3. Trajectory: High
   4. Shuttle: Self-tossed, with legal contact
   5. **Criterion: 8 of 10 in aiming area, two sets from both service sides**

From the Right Service Side
Practice this task in blocks of 10 serves. Record the number of successful high deep serves for each block on the **Personal Recording Form** below. When two block scores reach or exceed 8 out of 10, have your partner initial and date in the space provided.

Block 1	Block 2	Block 3	Block 4	Block 5	Block 6	Block 7	Block 8	Block 9	Block 10
___/10	___/10	___/10	___/10	___/10	___/10	___/10	___/10	___/10	___/10

Your partner's initials and date: _____

From the Left Service Side
Practice this task in blocks of 10 serves. Record the number of successful high deep serves for each block on the **Personal Recording Form** below. When two block scores reach or exceed 8 out of 10, have your partner initial and date in the space provided.

Block 1	Block 2	Block 3	Block 4	Block 5	Block 6	Block 7	Block 8	Block 9	Block 10
___/10	___/10	___/10	___/10	___/10	___/10	___/10	___/10	___/10	___/10

Your partner's initials and date: _____

(continued)

FIGURE 8.2   Continued

Common Errors on the High Deep Serve and Their Correction

1. *The serve does not go straight*
   Make sure your footwork is correct on set-up (point your front foot to the target).
   Change your swing path to be more vertical (straight up in the air).

2. *The serve goes too long*
   Use a little less power and wrist action.
   Increase lifting action on the serve to get higher trajectory.

3. *Inconsistent shots, no set pattern for errors*
   Recheck all key elements by yourself without striking the shuttle.
   Practice this serve with no target until you gain more consistency.

Teacher Expertise and Contextual Needs

Teacher Expertise

Teachers who use PSI will need to have particular strengths in several areas of the proposed knowledge base presented in Chapter 2.

Implementing Developmentally Appropriate Instruction.   The main building blocks for PSI are the individualized learning tasks pursued by students. From a managerial standpoint, students must be able to comprehend directions with little teacher guidance, so the teacher must know the appropriate level at which to write those tasks. From an instructional standpoint, the teacher must be knowledgeable about students' ability in the cognitive and psychomotor domains so that the performance criteria for tasks can be set at attainable, but not simplistic, levels.

Learning Objectives.   Since PSI relies on the sequence of mastery-based learning tasks, teachers must be able to write clear and concise learning objectives—often in the Mager (1984) format. Learning objectives must be written at the behavioral level in the psychomotor and cognitive domains.

Task Analysis and Content Progression

Each content module in a PSI unit will contain a sequence of learning tasks progressing from simple to complex. PSI teachers must have strong knowledge of how to analyze skills into component parts and then sequence those parts into a coherent learning progression.

Assessment.   As shown in Figure 8.2, each PSI learning task contains an assessment component, most often expressed as a performance criterion. PSI teachers will need to know how to establish the criterion for each task and the best way to assess performance abilities in an ongoing *formative* plan. While it is possible to write authentic assessments for PSI tasks, such as the Game Performance Assessment Instrument (Griffin, Mitchell, & Oslin, 1997), most tend to be static assessments of discrete student knowledge in the cognitive and psychomotor domains. The PSI teacher must know how to write performance assessments into the task structure itself.

Effective Teaching Skills Applied to PSI

A teacher will apply effective teaching skills in unique ways while using a Personalized System for Instruction in physical education.

Planning.   PSI requires a substantial amount of planning at the unit level. The managerial plans, content listing, task analyses, learning activities, task presentation materials, and performance criteria must all be designed and produced for the student workbook before the unit can begin. A PSI teacher will need to see the unit's "big picture" clearly in mind in the planning process. On the other hand, daily lesson planning is simple in PSI. Since the unit plan contains all of the plans for each learning activity, the teacher needs only to determine what equipment is necessary for an upcoming lesson and arrange to have that equipment ready for class.

Time and Class Management.   Time management is easy in PSI. Since students know exactly what they are to do in every class, and all of the task information is in their workbooks, the teacher does not have to monitor or make managerial decisions in class. The same goes for class management, as students have all necessary information at their disposal in the workbook. Essentially, the information in the student workbook runs the class for the teacher, so the teacher's skill in designing and writing the student workbook is critical in PSI.

Task Presentation and Structure.   Most or all task presentation and structure information is provided to students through instructional media and written in the students' workbook. A PSI teacher needs to know how to select and/or produce these materials so that students can use them without asking the teacher for clarification or added information. Designing the student workbook is greatly facilitated by a teacher's skill and knowledge with word processing and other information technologies.

Communication.   Writing is the key communication mode in PSI. The teacher decides what information students will need in the unit and writes that into the students' workbook. Therefore, good writing skills *at the students' level of comprehension* are needed in PSI.

Instructional Information.   Because the teacher is free from nearly all managerial functions in PSI, there is more time in class to interact with students on skill development, strategy, and game/match performance. Metzler et al. (1989) found that PSI teachers give over three times the amount of feedback to students than teachers who use Direct Instruction. That is possible because PSI can lower class management to approximately 1 percent of class time—the rest of which can be used to interact with students. So, PSI teachers must have good skills in observing student performance and providing many different kinds of feedback so that feedback does not become "stale" and ineffective. The increased opportunity for interaction also calls for good questioning skills so that a PSI teacher can get students to think independently when they are practicing individualized learning tasks. Students will benefit more from PSI if they can reach a point of *learning how to learn* without the teacher.

Review and Closure. Because students can be practicing many different learning tasks in the same lesson, it is not possible to provide a whole-class review. In addition, there is no need to review managerial operations each time because all of the managerial information should be contained in the students' workbook. So, PSI lessons typically have no planned review and closure; when class ends the students return their equipment, turn in their workbook to the teacher, and leave.

Student Developmental Requirements

PSI is a unique instructional model with some different developmental needs for students in physical education.

Reading. PSI students will need to be able to read the managerial and task information in their personal workbook. The teacher can write that information for the average reading ability in the class, but less-than-average readers will be challenged. PSI should not be used with students who have poor reading ability, regardless of their grade level.

Technology. There are many technologies that can be used to present PSI task and structure information besides printed media. Videotapes, CD ROMs, and computer-assisted instruction can all be used for that purpose. Students will need to be able to operate any such technology used in a PSI unit.

Personal Responsibility. As you know by now, the key design feature of PSI is individual student learning with very little direct guidance by the teacher. PSI students must be mature enough to make good decisions about how they spend their time in class. They must also be able to assume the responsibility of monitoring their own practice and verifying their own task mastery when self-checks are allowed.

Asking for Help. Although PSI features individualized practice, that does not mean students have no one to turn to for help when they need it. Students who get "stuck" on a task or have sustained difficulty in any way need to take the initiative to use the designated attention signal to alert the teacher to come over and work with them. PSI teachers should tell students what the attention signal is and be watching for it in class.

Contextual Needs for PSI

PSI can be used in almost any physical education setting. It is not limited by facility or environmental factors. The main contextual requirement is that there is enough room for all students to be practicing individually, without having to wait. There is also a need to have enough equipment so that all students can be practicing their current learning task. PSI can actually require fewer of each object or implement in many instances. For example, in a PSI golf unit, some students might be putting, some might be chipping, some might be hitting short irons, and others might be using drivers—all at one time—so it is not necessary to have enough of each type of club for every student in the class. However, it is important to have a sufficient number of objects (e.g., balls, shuttlecocks, bean bags), as the individualized structure will allow students to make a large number of practice trials.

Teacher and Student Roles and Responsibilities in PSI

Each instructional model will have certain operations that need to be completed to make the model function according to its design. Some of these operations are carried out by the teacher; others are carried out by one or more students. The following table shows the major operations within the PSI model, and indicates who is responsible for completing them during each lesson.

Operation or Responsibility	Who Does It in PSI
Starting class	Each **student** starts to practice when he/she arrives. There is no teacher-led starting procedure.
Bringing equipment to class	The **teacher** checks to see what tasks will be practiced in class and brings the needed equipment.
Dispersing and returning equipment	**Students** get the needed equipment for their next learning task and return it when finished.
Roll call (if needed)	**Students** keep their attendance in their workbook. The **teacher** verifies it after each class.
Task presentation	**Students** read or view the task presentation information as they begin each new task.
Task structure	**Students** set up each new task according to the directions in their workbook.
Assessment	**Students** verify mastery of each task in their workbook. Some tasks can be self-checked, some can be partner-checked, and some can be teacher-checked.
Monitoring learning progress	**Students** decide if they are going fast enough to complete the unit on time. The **teacher** monitors their progress periodically by checking workbooks.

Teaching and Learning Benchmarks for PSI

Teachers who use PSI can learn the benchmarks for their own and student behavior patterns. The following teacher and student benchmarks verify that the PSI model has been designed and implemented with an acceptable degree of faithfulness, increasing the likelihood that the stated student learning outcomes will be achieved.

Teacher Benchmarks

Benchmark	How to Verify
PSI course materials are clear to students.	Monitor the number and types of questions students ask after reading/viewing information in their workbooks.
Teacher has very low percentage of managerial time in class (less than 2%).	Use a stopwatch to measure how much management time a teacher uses in class.
Teacher has very high rates of individualized instructional interactions in class.	Audiotape a lesson and count the number of cues, feedbacks, and questions directed to individual students.
Performance criteria for tasks are set at appropriate levels of difficulty.	Direct students to practice tasks in blocks (e.g., 10 trials) and to record the number of successful trials in each block. If most students reach mastery after one or two blocks, the task is too easy. If many students get "stuck" on a task, it is too difficult. Adjust the task or its performance criteria accordingly.
The teacher should not spend too much time witnessing and verifying mastery attempts.	Count the number of times the teacher witnessed mastery in each class. If that takes away from instructional time: (1) design more self- and partner-checked tasks, or (2) appoint some dependable students as temporary witnesses until the backlog is gone.
The teacher should make few or no task presentations.	Count the number of task presentations made in class. If that takes away from instructional time with individual students, design and produce media-based task presentations.

Student Benchmarks

Benchmark	How to Verify
Students understand written or visual task presentation.	1. Check for understanding. 2. Design brief comprehension tasks that direct students to demonstrate key elements from the task presentation. 3. Note the number and pattern of students' questions.
Students are staying on-task.	Periodically monitor and count the number of students who are on task in class.
Students can properly set up learning activities from the written task structure information.	Observe several students setting up learning stations. Note how long it takes each one to set up and how correctly it is done.
Students do not make "inappropriate progress" (i.e., cheat on verifying mastery).	Review students' progress charts each day, looking for faster-than-expected progress.
Students make self-paced progression.	Monitor the number of managerial questions students ask the teacher. Too much reliance on the teacher slows down students' progression.
Student progression is more or less even.	1. Have students complete "practice blocks" to monitor tasks that are too easy or too difficult. 2. Students can "loop back" to review previous tasks when they experience long periods of failure on the current task.

Assessing Learning in PSI

Assessing student learning in PSI is mostly automatic; that is, it occurs every time a student completes each learning task according to the specified performance criteria. If the task structure has directed students to record the number of successful trials in each "practice block," then the teacher can easily know how many trials it took each student to reach mastery on every task. This built-in assessment feature can provide the teacher with useful information:

1. It lets the teacher know if tasks are too easy or too difficult. From this the teacher can make adjustments, delete a task, add a task, or combine tasks.
2. It can be used to calculate the average number of trials students need on each task.
3. It can be used to determine the range of trials to mastery (the fewest and the most).
4. It lets the teacher identify students who are going too slow and need extra attention.

This continuous assessment feature is also beneficial to students:

1. They get regular knowledge of results and can tell when they need extra help from the teacher.

Student Progress Chart for Badminton

	1	2	3	4	5	6	7	8	9	10	11	12	13	14
Match Play											X	X	X	X
Pass rules and scoring quiz										X				
Final challenge task										X				
Backhand drop									X					
Forehand drop									X					
Overhead smash									X					
Backhand drives								X						
Forehand drives								X						
Challenge task for clears							X							
Overhead clears						X								
Backhand drive clear						X								
Forehand drive clear					X									
Serving challenge				X										
High deep serve			X											
Short low serve		X												
Stretching	X													
Class Day	1	2	3	4	5	6	7	8	9	10	11	12	13	14

Student's Name: Robert Weir   Class Period for P.E.:   3rd

FIGURE 8.3   A Student's Personal Progress Chart for Badminton

2. They can project if they are on schedule to complete the course.
3. Reinforcement for success is frequent and predictable.

Figure 8.3 shows an example of a student progress chart for a PSI badminton unit. As the student completes each listed task, he puts an "X" in the box across from that task in the column above the class in which it was accomplished. Notice that the sequence of learning activities starts at the bottom of the page, so if the X's were connected they would form a line graph that represents that student's learning pace in the unit. The student and teacher can then see with one glance if the student is making satisfactory progress in the unit.

Selecting and Modifying PSI for Physical Education

PSI can be used in many physical education settings for a wide variety of content. It is particularly effective for activities that can be broken into discrete skills or knowledge areas that should be learned in a definite sequence. It can be designed for units that have a strong emphasis on learning outcomes in the psychomotor domain, along with some outcomes in the cognitive domain. I would recommend the following types of content for using PSI in physical education:

1. Individual sports
2. Team sports
3. Recreational activities (bowling, horseshoes, Frisbee)
4. Dances with prescribed steps (line, square, folk, etc.)
5. Personal fitness concepts
6. Personal fitness programs

Grade-Level Adaptations

PSI will be more effective with students who have the prerequisite abilities discussed earlier in this chapter. Students must be able to read and follow directions, make responsible decisions about pacing and engagement, and ask for help when they need it. Figure 8.4 presents an analysis for selecting PSI and making grade-level adaptations for it.

FIGURE 8.4   Grade-Level Adaptions for PSI in Physical Education

Grade Levels	Select PSI?	Possible Adaptations
Preschool	No	
Elementary	No	
Middle school/ junior high	Yes	1. Reduce the number of learning tasks. 2. Simplify the task presentations or have the teacher make them. 3. Make performance criteria simple and attainable but still at an appropriate mastery level. 4. Teacher sets up learning stations for students. 5. Use task cards with pictures at each station. 6. Simplify the management system.
High school	Yes	1. Designate higher-skilled and dependable students to assist novices or slow readers. 2. Use video-based media for task presentations. 3. Use more teacher-checked tasks.
College/adult	Yes	None needed. The full PSI design can be implemented.

Summary

Perhaps the biggest problem with the PSI model occurs when a teacher wishes to implement individualized instruction but fails to follow the Keller plan faithfully. Because PSI is so unique, it is important that physical education teachers do not compromise its design. Siedentop (1974) cautioned physical educators about ways in which the PSI model could be compromised to (a) cause it to violate Keller's design enough to make it something other than PSI, and (b) result in reduced student achievement (pp. 118–119):

1. Reducing performance criteria to nonmastery levels (e.g., five successful out of ten, rather than seven)
2. Delaying students' attempts at mastery due to "backlogs"
3. Reducing the number of tasks (and performance assessments)
4. Attempting to limit cheating by structuring group performance assessments

The PSIS courses mentioned earlier (Metzler & Sebolt, 1994) offer some valid adaptations. Cregger and Metzler (1992) analyzed the PSIS volleyball course and determined that its few modifications fully complied with the key PSI design features. Teachers were using faithful versions of PSI and students were engaged in a manner consistent with PSI learning processes. In that way the full potential of PSI can be realized for students in physical education.

A Sample Student Workbook for PSI*

Introduction Section

Hello, and welcome to your **badminton class**! That's right, your badminton class. This personal workbook includes almost everything you will need to learn the game of badminton and become a proficient beginning-level player. Of course, your instructor Mrs. Canning will play an important part as you progress, but most of what you will need is contained in your personal Workbook. Your badminton class will be taught this term using the **Personalized System for Instruction (PSI)** model.

The key design feature of the PSI is that it allows for individualized learning and progression through the course. Think back to other classes you have taken: some students learn faster than others. That is a fact in all learning situations. Depending on the individual learning rate, some students become frustrated if the course goes too fast. Others become bored if the course goes too slowly. Either way, many students become disinterested, reducing their enjoyment of the course. For badminton, the most harmful result of frustration or boredom is that students are not given a proper chance to learn the game and to enjoy it as a regular part of their activity schedule. Whether you are a "bare beginner" or currently have some badminton experience, the PSI design will allow you to progress "as

*Adapted from Metzler, M., & Sebolt, D. (1994). *The personalized sport instruction series: Instructor's manual.* Dubuque, IA: Kendall-Hunt. Used with permission.

fast as you can, or as slowly as you need." Keep that little motto in mind as you become familiar with this workbook and progress through your badminton class this term.

Another point to keep in mind is that PSI is *achievement oriented*. That means it is intended to help you learn the necessary skills, strategies, and rules for beginning badminton play. I guarantee you will be a better player at the end of your PSI class than you are now!

As you will see, your improvement will come in a way that is different from most other courses you have taken. You will be asked to assume more responsibility for your own learning than ever before. Remember, all of the instructional material is included in your **Personal Workbook.** It will be up to you to learn the contents of the workbook, become familiar with the PSI system, attend class regularly, follow class policies, and work diligently toward completing the course sequences. It has been my experience that students enjoy taking a large role in their own learning, and appreciate the individualized plan of the PSI. I know that you will, too.

Your Role in PSI Badminton.   Your role in PSI badminton can be summarized easily: become familiar with and follow the Personal Workbook as an independent learning guide. You will not need to depend on Mrs. Canning for content and managerial information. But when the Workbook is not sufficient, or specific learning information is needed, you should be sure to *ASK MRS. CANNING FOR HELP!* Your Personal Workbook will provide nearly all the information needed to complete the course. So, if you can progress without the instructor's direction, the system is designed to let you. If you need extra help, Mrs. Canning will be free to provide it for you. She will show you a "Help Signal" for getting her attention in class.

Your Instructor's Role in PSI Badminton.   Mrs. Canning has the important role of *facilitator* in your PSI badminton course. Your Personal Workbook will provide most of the content and management information you will need. That gives your instructor more time to interact with students who need individual attention. There will be just one large-group demonstration throughout the entire course, and very little time spent organizing routine class "chores." Nearly all of the instructor's time will be available to facilitate your learning on an individual basis.

Skill and Knowledge Unit Sequences.   Your PSI badminton course contains a predetermined amount of learning content, divided into a number of course modules. Each module will have a series of learning tasks, which together form the unit sequence. There are two types of modules: **Performance Skill** and **Badminton Knowledge.** Performance skill modules focus on the major psychomotor performance patterns needed by students to play badminton. The badminton knowledge module contains information on basic game rules and badminton etiquette.

PSI Course Management and Policies.   The purpose of this section is to inform you about some of the ways in which the PSI system can give you increased control over your own learning. Some of the course management and policies will come from this Workbook. Others will be communicated to you by your instructor. Be sure that you are familiar with all course management routines and policies.

Dressing for Class.   You will need to have proper clothing and footwear in order to participate comfortably and safely in your badminton class. I suggest that you wear lightweight, loose-fitting clothes that will not restrict your range of motion (shorts, t-shirts, loose windbreaker, etc.). Specialized clothing and badminton shoes are not necessary.

Equipment.   You will need to have a badminton racquet for class each day. The school has enough racquets for all students, but you are welcome to bring your own, if you wish. Mrs. Canning will provide all other equipment needed for your badminton course.

Depositing and Distributing Student Workbooks.   Mrs. Canning will collect all students' Workbooks at the end of class, and bring them to class the next day.

Practice Partners.   Some of the learning tasks will call for you to practice with a partner and be checked-off by him/her. Any classmate can be your partner for most tasks. A few tasks will specify that both partners are at the same place in the task sequence.

Starting Class
1. Arrive at or before the stated class time
2. Locate your own Student Workbook and equipment
3. Be sure to check off the correct day for your attendance
4. Complete your stretching and warm-up routine
5. Find a practice partner (if needed at that time)
6. Begin to practice the appropriate learning task in your sequence

Note that you can begin as soon as you arrive. Except for the first day of instruction, the instructor will not wait to begin the class with all students together. **Getting out of the locker room quicker will allow you extra time to practice your badminton skills.**

Self-Checks, Partner Checks, and Instructor Checks.   Each learning task in PSI badminton requires that your achievement of mastery is documented (checked off). Some of the tasks can be checked off by you, some must be checked off by a partner, and some must be checked off by Mrs. Canning. Items are checked off by the appropriate person initialing and dating the designated area after each checked task.

Instructor-checked tasks will require that you practice for a period of time prior to Mrs. Canning watching your attempt at mastery. When you are ready, indicated by a series of successful trial blocks, signal her to observe your criterion test. If you do not reach the stated criterion, you can return for more practice and signal her again at a later time. There is no penalty for not making a criterion. You can try as many times as it takes to be successful.

You may find it helpful to alert Mrs. Canning at the beginning of a class in which you anticipate needing her observation and checking. That will allow her to be on the lookout for your signal.

Attendance Checking.   Your personal workbook has a log for showing your attendance each day. Initial the appropriate box each day. Mrs. Canning will do the roll from your log, so be sure to initial the correct place each day. Students who forget to do this will be counted as "absent" for that day.

Pass/Fail Grading.   The PSI badminton course has 14 learning tasks in it. Students must complete 10 of the 14 activities to receive a passing grade.

Match Play.   You cannot advance to badminton match play until you have completed all 14 learning activities in the course, including a passing score of at least 70% on the rules and scoring quiz.

Using Your Time Effectively.   Your PSI badminton course is made up of a series of predetermined learning tasks. Your course has 14 class periods with 55 minutes in each class. It is important for you to know your own learning pace, and to make **steady** progress toward completing all course requirements. Therefore, you will need to learn how to best use your time in class, and to accurately project completion of PSIS badminton before the end of the term.

PSI Badminton Learning Content.   This section will describe how the PSI course learning content is designed. It is important that you know how the system works, so that you can take advantage of its individualized learning features. The course learning content is included in two kinds of learning modules: **Performance Skill** and **Badminton Knowledge.**
   Each *Performance Skill* Module will include the following:

1. A written **introduction** to the skill
2. **A videotaped demonstration** of the proper skill techniques. When you are ready for a new skill, get the proper tape and watch it on the VCR located in the gym. Be sure to pay extra attention to explain the **key performance cues** highlighted on the tape.
3. Simple **comprehension and readiness tasks** to develop initial skill patterns
4. An **error analysis and correction section** for self-analyzing common mistakes
5. **Learning tips** for increased proficiency
6. **Criterion tasks** for demonstrating skill mastery in each sequence
7. **Challenge tasks** for developing tactical applications of skills in modified competitive situations
8. A **Personal Recording Form** for selected tasks, used to record successful practice trials

The *Badminton Knowledge* Module will include:

1. A **reading** on the basic rules of badminton and badminton game strategy
2. A **knowledge quiz** to test your understanding of the rules and strategy

Charting Your Progress.   The last page of your PSI Badminton Workbook includes your **Personal Progress Chart.** Mrs. Canning will show you how to correctly label the chart. At the end of each class period in the course, put an "X" in the box across from each task you completed—above the correct class period number. As the days go by, you will begin to see how your individual learning pace projects your successful completion of all course learning tasks.

Ready . . . Set . . . Go!! This brief introductory section, combined with additional information from Mrs. Canning, will allow you to use the PSI Badminton system to your full advantage, learning badminton at your own pace. Because PSI Badminton is a complete system for learning the game, it might take you a little time to become familiar with this approach. However, remember that Mrs. Canning is there for you when you have questions about the system, and when you need individual attention for learning.

A Sample PSI Course Module: Badminton Serves

The following module is taken from a PSI badminton course. It includes learning activities for short low serves, high deep serves, and a challenge task. Once students have read the course manual and understand the PSI management scheme, they would begin on task 1 and proceed according to the sequence.

1. Short Low Serves. First, view the videotape on the low short serve. Be sure to pay special attention to the key elements needed for skilled performance.

Performance Cues
1. Court position: Near center line, 2–3 feet from the short service line
2. Aiming area: 1–2 feet over the opposite short service line, backhand side preferred
3. Grip: Forehand or underhand
4. Footwork: Forehand set-up
5. Contact point: Between 3 and 4 o'clock (vertical, lifting upward)
6. Wrist action: Firm
7. Trajectory: Low, as close to the net as possible
8. Power/speed: Low
9. Follow-through: Short

Comprehension Task. Find a partner and demonstrate to each other the proper performance cues for the short low serve *without hitting the shuttle.* Be sure to provide feedback to each other for correct and incorrect performance cues, until both of you can execute this shot correctly.

Learning Tips
1. Hold the feather of the shuttle with your thumb and index finger of your non-striking hand. The tip of the shuttle should point down.
2. Release the shuttle straight down as your racquet is coming forward.
3. With your firm wrist, try to lift the shuttle over the net and into the aiming area.
4. Be sure to complete your follow-through, even this short one.

Readiness Drill

1. From the correct court position in the service area attempt 40 short low serves from each service side. Do not be concerned with a specific aiming area at this time. Use these shots to gauge the proper contact point, power, and trajectory for the short low serve.

If you are experiencing difficulty with the readiness drill, please refer to the **performance cues** and review each cue as presented. If you are still having difficulty, ask Mrs. Canning to assist you in applying these techniques.

Common Errors and Their Correction

1. The serve does not go straight
   - Make sure your footwork is correct on set-up
   - Change your swing path to be more vertical (straight up in the air)
2. The serve goes too short or into the net
   - Use a little more power (but do not add more wrist action)
   - Increase lifting action on the serve
3. The serve goes too far into the service return box
   - Reduce power and wrist action
   - (**Do not** move back in your service area)
4. Inconsistent shots, no set pattern for errors
   - Recheck all performance cues without striking the shuttle
   - Continue the readiness task until you gain more consistency

Criterion Task (Self-Checked).   Choose a service box and the proper service return box for this task. Mark off a parallel line 3 feet past the opposite short service line. The resulting rectangle is your aiming area for this task. Set up for your serves in the proper position in the service court. Practice your short low serves in blocks of 10 shots, keeping a record of how many shots in each group of 10 have a low trajectory and land in the aiming area.

1. Position: Serving area in appropriate box
2. Aiming area: Marked rectangle in opposite service return box
3. Shuttlecock: . Self-tossed, with legal contact
4. Criterion: 8 of 10 in aiming area, two sets from both service sides

From the Right Service Side:
Practice this task in blocks of 10 serves. Record the number of successful short low serves for each block on the **Personal Recording Form** below.

10	10	10	10	10	10	10	10	10	10	10	10

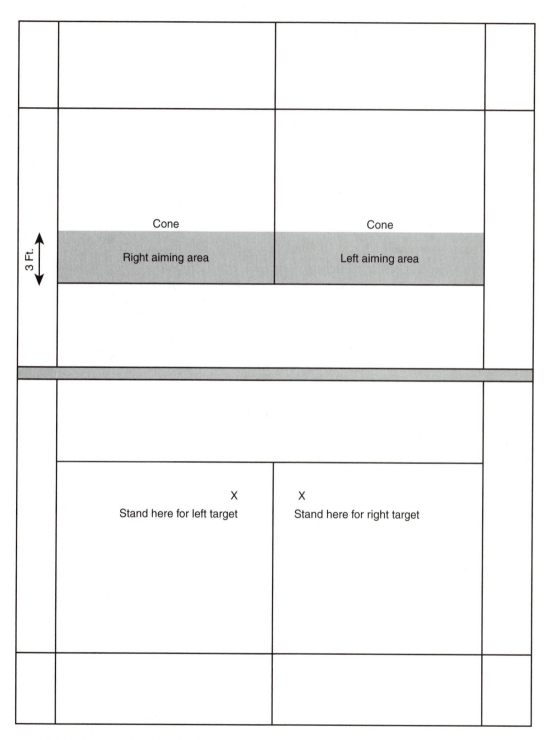

CRITERION TASK #1   Targeting for Short Low Serve

From the Left Service Side:

Practice this task in blocks of 10 serves. Record the number of successful short low serves for each block on the **Personal Recording Form** below.

10	10	10	10	10	10	10	10	10	10	10	10

Initial and date your completion of the performance criterion _____

2. High Deep Serves. First, view the videotape on the high deep serve. Be sure to pay special attention to the key elements needed for skilled performance.

Performance Cues

1.	Court position:	Near center line, 2–3 feet from the short service line
2.	Aiming area:	(Singles) Between the long service line for doubles and the back boundary line; backhand side preferred
		(Doubles) Less than 2 feet inside the doubles' long service line; backhand side preferred
3.	Grip:	Forehand
4.	Footwork:	Forehand set-up
5.	Contact point:	Between 3 and 4 o'clock (vertical, moving upward)
6.	Wrist action:	Full, with hard upward extension
7.	Trajectory:	High, over the top of your opponent's outstretched racquet
8.	Speed/power:	Full
9.	Follow-through:	Full

Comprehension Task. Find a partner and demonstrate to each other the proper performance cues for the high deep serve *without hitting the shuttle.* Be sure to provide feedback to each other for correct and incorrect performance cues, until both of you can execute this shot correctly.

Learning Tips

1. Hold the feather of the shuttle with your thumb and index finger of your non-striking hand. The tip of the shuttle should point down.
2. Release the shuttle straight down as your racquet is coming forward.
3. Use an upward, full wrist action to hit the shuttle high and deep into the aiming area.
4. Be sure to complete your follow-through.

Readiness Drill

1. From the correct court position in the service area attempt 40 high deep serves from each service side. Do not be concerned with a specific aiming area at this time. Use these shots to gauge the proper contact point, power, and trajectory for the serve.

If you are experiencing difficulty with the readiness drill, please refer to the **performance cues** and review each cue as presented. If you are still having difficulty, ask Mrs. Canning to assist you in applying these techniques.

Common Errors and Their Correction
1. The serve does not go straight
   - Make sure your footwork is correct on set-up
   - Change your swing path to be more vertical (straight up in the air)
2. The serve goes too long
   - Use a little less power and wrist action
   - Increase lifting action on the serve to get higher trajectory
3. Inconsistent shots, no set pattern for errors
   - Recheck all performance cues without striking the shuttle
   - Continue the readiness drill until you gain more consistency

Criterion Task (Partner Checked).   Choose a service box and the proper service return box for this task. Your aiming area will be the rectangle formed by the singles side boundary, the center service line, the back boundary, and the doubles back service line. Have a partner stand in the middle of the service return box with his/her arm stretched and racquet reaching overhead. Set up for your serves in the proper position in the service court.

1. Position: Serving position in appropriate box
2. Aiming area: In designated aiming area
3. Trajectory: Over partner's outstretched arm and racquet
4. Shuttlecock: Self-tossed, with legal contact
5. Criterion: 7 of 10. Two sets from both service sides

From the Right Service Side:
Practice this task in blocks of 10 serves. Record the number of successful high deep serves for each block on the **Personal Recording Form** below.

10	10	10	10	10	10	10	10	10	10	10	10

From the Left Service Side:
Practice this task in blocks of 10 serves. Record the number of successful high deep serves for each block on the **Personal Recording Form** below.

10	10	10	10	10	10	10	10	10	10	10	10

Have your partner initial and date your completion of the performance criterion _____

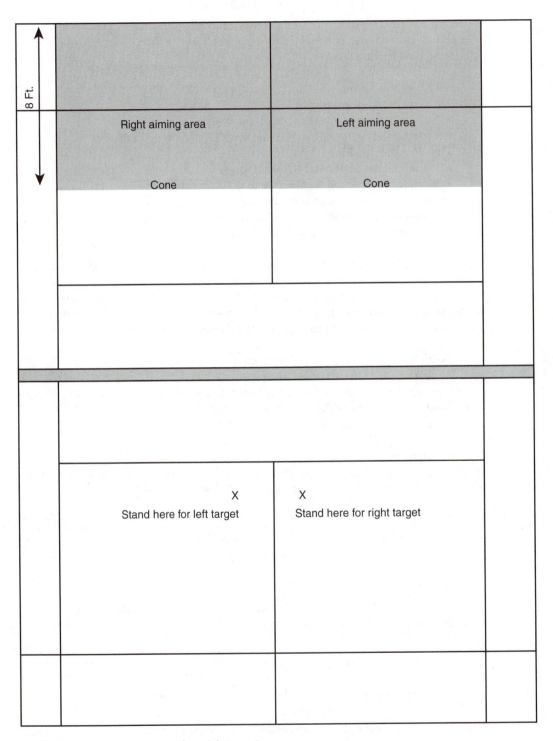

8 Ft.

Right aiming area

Left aiming area

Cone

Cone

X
Stand here for left target

X
Stand here for right target

CRITERION TASK #2   Targeting for High Deep Serve

3. Serving Challenge Drill (Instructor Checked).   Refer to the targeting set-up on the next page, which includes five aiming areas and their designated points. Note that the targeting is mirrored from the right and left sides, reflecting a right-handed opponent's orientation. Any serve landing outside the legal service return box results in 0 points. The large area in the middle results in 1 point (because serves landing in that area can easily be returned with attacking shots). Choose one service box from which to hit your serves, and set up the diagonal service return box according to the layout. Practice serves in blocks of 10 shots, hitting 5 low short serves and 5 high deep serves in each block. *Subtract 1 point from any 2- or 3-point serve that does not have the proper trajectory.* Example: a 3-point deep serve is reduced to 2 points, due to a low trajectory.

1. Position: Serving position in appropriate box
2. Aiming area: As designated for each type of serve.
3. Trajectory: Correct for each type of serve
4. Shuttlecock: Self-tossed, with legal contact
5. Criterion: Score 20 or more points on one block from each side (30 points maximum)

From the Right Service Side:
Practice this task in blocks of 10 serves. Record the number of points scored in each block on the **Personal Recording Form** below. (Maximum score in each block is 30).

30	30	30	30	30	30	30	30	30	30	30	30

From the Left Service Side:
Practice this task in blocks of 10 serves. Record the number of points scored in each block on the **Personal Recording Form** below. (Maximum score in each block is 30).

30	30	30	30	30	30	30	30	30	30	30	30

Instructor's initials and date _____

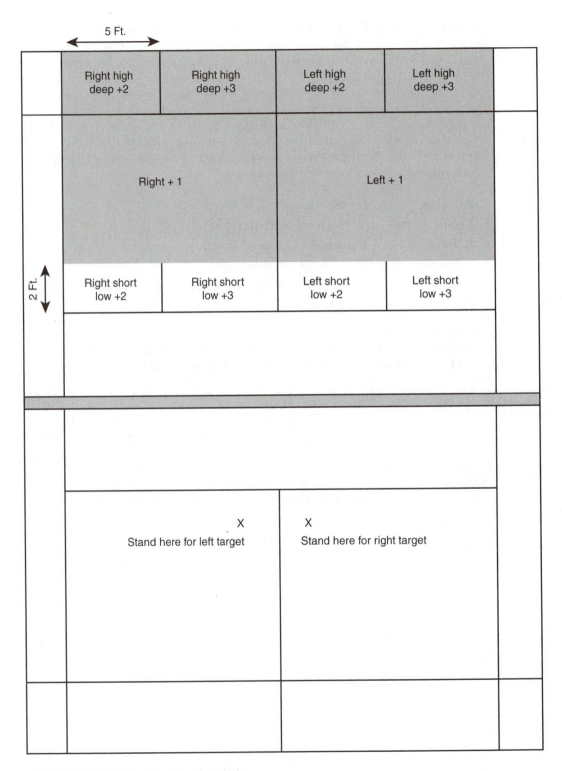

CHALLENGE DRILL #3   Targeting for Serving

SUGGESTED READINGS

Keller, F., & Sherman, J. G. (Eds.) (1974). *The Keller plan handbook.* Menlo Park, CA: W. A. Benjamin.

Metzler, M., & Sebolt, D. (1994). Instructor's manual for the Personalized Sport Instruction Series. Dubuque, IA: Kendall Hunt. (This series includes PSI courses for college-level instruction in golf, tennis, racquetball, and volleyball. All student workbooks can easily be adapted for use in middle/junior and high schools.)

Sherman, J. G. (Ed.). (1974). *Personalized system of instruction: 41 Germinal papers.* Menlo Park, CA: W. A. Benjamin.

9

Cooperative Learning

The Group Has Not Achieved until All of Its Members Have Achieved

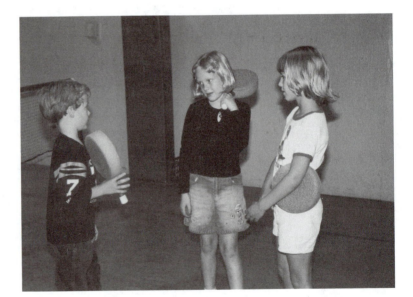

One of the major dilemmas facing all teachers is how to engage all students in the learning process at the same time, without allowing one or a few students to dominate the classroom interaction and learning opportunities. Consider this scenario: Mrs. Lesh asks her fifth-grade class, "Who can show me three important things to do when you are throwing a ball?" Several students who have answers immediately raise their hands. Mrs. Lesh calls on Bob, who says, "Make sure you step with your opposite foot," and he shows the rest of the class how to do that part of the throw. The teacher then calls on Mara, who says, "You need to follow through to your target," while she demonstrates the proper technique. Finally, Mrs. Lesh calls on Maddie, who adds, "You should turn your opposite shoulder toward your target when you start, like this," as she also shows the other students the correct form. Acknowledging all three as good answers, Mrs. Lesh continues to the next part of her task presentation. This is a very common scenario that could take place in almost any physical education lesson at any grade level. But, on a closer look, it raises a few important questions about this approach to teaching. First, it becomes competitive, as students who have answers raise their hands to vie for the teacher's attention and the chance to be "in the spotlight" for a moment. Secondly, when these students raise their hands, it is likely that the other students will stop trying to come up with answers of their own, in effect becoming passive learners for the moment. As a result, students who do not have an answer right away do not learn for themselves—they are actually taught by those students who do have answers. Thirdly, this approach does not allow students to interact with each other, promoting a kind of isolation among them even while being very close to each other. Now, that is not to say this approach is bad—only that it contains some features that open the door to thinking about other possible ways to structure the learning environment. One such way is represented by the Cooperative Learning model, developed in the early 1970s and now being used in many schools, at all grade levels, and for every subject area in the curriculum, including physical education.

Cooperative Learning is not really a model by itself. It is a set of teaching strategies that share key attributes, the most important being the grouping of students into *learning teams* for set amounts of time or assignments, with the expectation that all students will contribute to the learning process and outcomes. The word *team* takes on the same meaning as it does in sport—all members work to achieve a common goal. In this model, that common goal is the completion of a learning task given to them by the teacher. The task can require them to base their achievement on intragroup performance (trying to be the best team they can be), intergroup performance (competing with other teams), or shared-group performance (learning content so that they can teach it to the rest of the class).

The Cooperative Learning model was developed and initially researched at Johns Hopkins University in the mid-1970s. This development was led by Robert Slavin and was first reported in a series of research and topical articles in education journals. It is now one of the most recognized instructional models in education worldwide. Slavin's early label for the model was Student Team Learning (STL) and changed a bit later to Cooperative Learning (CL) as the scope of the model expanded. Slavin (1983) states that STL/CL is based on three concepts: team rewards, individual accountability, and equal opportunities for success:

1. *Team rewards.* The main building block in STL/CL is a task given to each team by the teacher. All teams can be working on the same task or different but related tasks. Either way, the teacher includes one or more stated performance criteria that teams must meet, along with the reward to be received by those teams who meet the standard. Rewards can be cumulative points, classroom privileges, public recognition, or grades.

2. *Individual accountability.* Another key part of the learning task is the specification that all team members' performance is included in the team score or assessment. Therefore,

all students must contribute to the team's effort, and so it is important that all members learn and achieve to their fullest potential. This requirement leads to regular peer teaching within groups as higher-ability students interact with lower-ability students to increase the whole team's performance. That peer teaching becomes a large factor in the model's ability to promote high levels of social learning within teams.

3. *Equal opportunities for success.* The process of selecting student teams is critical in STL/CL. The model calls for small groups of students (four to six per team) who are as heterogeneous as possible, and for all teams to be equal in their total performance abilities. Student learning teams should be established for a mixture of gender, skill levels, previous experience with the content, cognitive ability, and motivation. This diversity within teams serves to promote social learning outcomes within the model. Balancing teams on performance ability promotes fair competition and increases student motivation. Once that balance is achieved, and with the stipulation that all team members' performance counts, there is a greater likelihood that all students will have an equal chance to be successful and that each one's contribution will be valued by other team members.

Slavin first called his instructional technique Student Team Learning (Slavin, 1977). As more techniques were developed under the three main concepts just discussed, a larger and more inclusive name was given to the model—Cooperative Learning (Slavin, 1983). That label is the one now used most often by Slavin and many other proponents worldwide, so that will be the label used in this book, even when referring to developments prior to 1983.

It is also important to note the difference between Cooperative Learning (the model) and collaborative learning (various group-learning strategies). The Cooperative Learning model stipulates that the three major design concepts must be present to call it by that name. The model also includes a number of recognized learning task structures that adhere to these concepts and have been validated by research. Cooperative Learning also includes six procedural elements that give the model much of its identity and uniqueness (Cuseo, 1992):

1. Intentional group formation
2. Continuity of group interaction
3. Interdependence among group members
4. Individual accountability
5. Explicit attention to the development of social skills
6. Instructor as facilitator

On the other hand, collaborative learning techniques represent a less formal and enduring structure. They feature small groups that are together usually for only a short time, most often for reasons related to management, not social and performance learning. Collaborative structures can be characterized as "students learning alongside or assisting one another," while cooperative techniques can be characterized as "students learning with and for each other."

Overview

As mentioned, Cooperative Learning is a set of related instructional strategies that share the common attributes given by the primary developer Robert Slavin (1983): team rewards, individual accountability, and equal opportunity for success for all students. However, given that all of the strategies used in Cooperative Learning have these common attributes as well as established procedures for instruction, it is possible to regard them as a formal instructional model, as will be done in this book. Again, these attributes and procedures differentiate Cooperative Learning from other collaborative or small-group instruction.

Eileen Hilke (1990) lists the major instructional goals for Cooperative Learning: (1) to foster cooperative academic cooperation among students, (2) to encourage positive group relationships, (3) to develop students' self-esteem, and (4) to enhance academic achievement (p. 8). From these goals it is clear that Cooperative Learning is both achievement-based and process-based. Achievement-based means that the model is designed to foster student mastery of the instructional unit's content, whatever it may be. A strong emphasis is placed on student learning. Process-based means that the ways in which students interact with each other in order to learn the content is equally important, and in fact facilitates each student's achievement. It is not that "students must learn to cooperate" but that "students must cooperate to learn."

The process of learning is facilitated by five essential elements of Cooperative Learning, according to Johnson, Johnson, and Holubec (1994, p. 27–34):

1. *Positive interdependence among students.* Students must understand that all members of the cooperative team are needed for the whole team to achieve its goals. Each team member brings to the group unique talents, knowledge, experience, and skills that can help the team. This array of talent might also lead to intellectual conflict within a group, which then occasions more opportunities for social learning to occur.

2. *Face-to-face promotive interaction.* The team structure can cause students to support, facilitate, and reinforce the work of teammates—to "root them on" as sport team members would do for each other. Team members soon realize that all members of the team must achieve to their fullest potential for the team to reach its shared goals, so it is best for the team to "pull together" and take a genuine interest in the achievement of all members.

3. *Individual accountability/personal responsibility.* Cooperative Learning works best when all students in the group contribute their fair share. Now, that does not mean all students get the same score on assessments. Rather, it means that all students participate fully in the group process and learn as much as their own abilities allow. In order to do this, the teacher must set expectations for student participation in their groups and find ways to assess each student's participation. In addition, all performance assessments must include individual student scoring in some way so that every student's learning counts. This type of accountability promotes increased levels of personal responsibility by students.

4. *Interpersonal and small-group skills.* Student achievement in Cooperative Learning is highly valued. Just as highly valued is the learning of interpersonal skills displayed in the team dynamics. There is an emphasis placed on knowing and trusting team members, good communication, mutual acceptance and support, and conflict resolution. What social learning students do not bring to their team as the process begins must be learned as the cooperative experience is lived.

5. *Group processing.* To further emphasize the value placed on social learning, the teacher must regularly get students to reflect (process) their shared team experience. This processing should be a planned part of each lesson, particularly in the early part of a Cooperative Learning unit. This is when the teacher takes an active role in teaching students how to work well in groups in order to reach their shared goals—both academic and social. The key strategy here is that the teacher should not directly tell students how they should behave and interact with teammates. The processing should be more indirect, to foster thoughtful student reflection in this area of learning.

The formal Cooperative Learning model includes a recognized set of instructional strategies that can be used within it—once again, it is not just "putting students in small groups to learn next to each other." A strategy can be used for a short learning task (one or two lessons), an extended learning task (three to five lessons), or an entire unit. Due to the time it takes to establish groups and to assign a Cooperative Learning task, it is not recommended to use more than one strategy in a lesson. Some Cooperative Learning strategies are designed for specific subject areas other than physical education and will not be mentioned here. Those that would seem to be most effective in physical education are presented later in this chapter.

According to Johnson, Johnson, and Holubec (1994, pp. 37–48), the cooperative learning teacher has six major role functions. As you can see, some directed instruction is used to make groups and set the learning task in motion; from there, the teacher assumes a mostly indirect role in this model.

1. *Specify the instructional objectives.* The teacher must specify the academic objective/s for the assigned task. What content is to be learned and what are the stated performance criteria? The teacher must also specify the social skills objectives that inform students what it means to have good group interactions and process as they work together in teams.

2. *Make preinstructional decisions.* Cooperative Learning teachers must make a number of plans before units and lessons begin in order to facilitate students' interactions on teams: give each team a clear understanding of its assignment, inform teams of the performance criteria in place, announce how much time they will have to complete each assignment, and let them know what instructional resources (equipment, space, etc.) they will have to work with. Other decisions must be made about how teams will be selected, how learning will be assessed, and how social skills will be monitored. Undoubtedly, this model requires preunit planning that eventually allows the teacher to set the cooperative process in motion.

3. *Communicate task presentation and task structure.* There must be a delicate balance between the amount of information needed by students to get going on the assigned task, and giving too much performance or background information on how to complete the task. In many cooperative tasks there will be more emphasis placed on task structure (space, equipment, time, teams, and criteria) than task presentation. When in doubt about the amount of information to give about task presentation, it might be a good rule of thumb to give less than one might suspect. This leads teams to be a bit more resourceful and to figure out on their own when they need more information from the teacher—and then ask for it.

4. *Set the cooperative assignment in motion.* Once the teacher has selected teams, informed the class of the upcoming assignment, and provided the task structure, she will simply tell students to "get going" on the assignment. Students should be given only enough information to allow them to understand the assignment, without indication of how to complete it. When teams are first engaged in the task, it will take some time for teams to frame the problem embedded in the assignment and to get organized for its solution. The teacher needs to closely monitor this period to make sure that teams are moving in the right direction.

5. *Monitor the cooperative learning groups and intervene as necessary.* As teams are engaged in the assignment, the teacher will monitor to see if the teams are working cooperatively. Note that this does not mean the teacher monitors for progress on the assignment; that will take care of itself if teams are using all of their resources and if all team members are contributing to the best of their ability. Interventions by the teacher should happen only when a team is not working cooperatively. These instances then become "teaching moments" for the development of social skills teamwork and the basis of the processing that occurs at the end of each class.

6. *Evaluate learning and processing interaction.* Assessment in Cooperative Learning takes place in two areas: the quality and quantity of student learning and the effectiveness of team interactions. The teacher establishes assessments and criteria for both outcomes. It is more likely that the assessment of learning will be more summative once teams complete each assignment. The assessment of team interactions must be formative and quite regular so that periods of ineffective interaction will be fewer and shorter.

Cooperative Learning has received an enormous amount of attention in recent years, both from supporters and critics. That attention has resulted in the discussion of the advantages and disadvantages of Cooperative Learning strategies as they are used in the formal sense of the model being described in this chapter. McCaslin and Good (1996) summarize both sides of the debate over Cooperative Learning:

Advantages
1. Cooperative assignments simulate the way most people work outside of school, by sharing work to "get the job done."
2. Subject matter knowledge is increased as the sum of a group's expertise is always greater than that of any single member.
3. Students learn dispositions about shared tasks and group challenges.
4. Group members serve as developmentally appropriate models for each other.
5. Students learn to manage and use human resources.
6. Students come to value shared academic work more than working in isolation.

7. Students develop a greater understanding of self and others from the shared work.
8. Students can make choices that regulate the pace and process of learning.

Disadvantages

1. If group members focus too much on the product of the assignment, and not the process, they become too product-oriented and miss the other major purpose of the model.
2. When all students in a group share misconceptions, there is no way to change those misconceptions because there is little content interaction with the teacher.
3. When more emphasis is placed on process than achievement, students can value "getting along with others" more than "working with others to achieve a stated goal."
4. There is a danger of one or more students in each group becoming authority figures in place of the teacher.
5. Higher achievers can come to feel more pressure to make disproportionately more contributions than other students.
6. There is a risk of some students learning to be "social loafers," either intentionally or unintentionally.
7. Students who try hard but make a lesser contribution to the team's achievement may feel ashamed or become defensive.
8. Some students may limit their own contributions (and learning) to allow other students more chances to contribute.

Read over the advantages and disadvantages again. You will note that the advantages are part of the model's design; the disadvantages occur when the model is not applied correctly, and can all be avoided or reduced by careful teacher planning and monitoring of the group process. In that sense, Cooperative Learning is no different than any other model in this book: when implemented according to its design, there is a strong likelihood that the model will work to promote the kinds of student learning it is designed for. If applied incorrectly, the model will not work as intended, but that should not be regarded as a design flaw and cause teachers not to use it when called for. Rather, teachers should be aware of these potential problems and plan accordingly to reduce or eliminate them from the model.

Foundations of the Cooperative Learning Model for Physical Education

Theory and Rationale

Deutsch (1949) suggested that there are three main goal structures in education: individualistic, competitive, and cooperative. Models like PSI (Chapter 8) are highly individualistic—students work on their own to achieve learning objectives and have very little interaction with others, including the teacher. Models like Direct Instruction (Chapter 7) and Inquiry Teaching (Chapter 12) are highly competitive in the sense that students must assert themselves to gain the teacher's attention, to obtain resources needed to learn content, and are sometimes assessed relative to other students' achievement. Cooperative Learning models are well represented in this book by the one described in this chapter, Sport Education (Chapter 10), and Peer Teaching (Chapter 11). The basis of these models is to have students learning with, from, and for each other through a structured interdependent relationship. The achievement of academic learning goals is a high priority, but no more important than social learning processes and skills. Clearly, the Cooperative Learning model has its foundation in Deutsch's third group of structures.

The design of the Cooperative Learning model is based on the convergence of four major sets of theories: motivational, cognitive, social learning, and behavioral. This is somewhat unique, as most other models are derived from just one or two theories about learning. However, all of these theories play equally key roles in the design and operation of the model.

1. *Motivational theory* is used to create structures that get teams to recognize that the only way the team can reach its goals is for all of its members to contribute and achieve. That prompts individual students to give their best, and initiates group interactions to meet shared goals.

2. *Cognitive theory* is used to provide students with developmentally appropriate cooperative learning tasks that give teams the right amount of challenge to accomplish team goals. If the task is too easy, the team does not need to use all of its resources to achieve the goal. If the task is too difficult, team members will eventually become frustrated, leading to dissent and even withdrawal from the task.

3. *Social learning theories* are incorporated into the model when learning occurs by listening to and watching other team members. The process becomes reciprocal as one student makes progress and then shares that learning with others, most often by showing and explaining to them. Teachers contribute to the social learning agenda of the model when they watch for positive and negative instances of social skills and use them at "teaching moments" to highlight desired and undesired interaction skills.

4. *Behavioral theory* is used to provide a relationship between cooperative processes, student on-task engagement, and the rewards of team achievement. Good cooperative tasks make it clear to students what social skills (behaviors) are needed in that situation, what the learning goals are, and what the consequences are for achieving or failing at the assigned task. Note that students are not directly informed about how to complete the task—only the parameters under which that task will be pursued.

The rationale behind the Cooperative Learning model is straightforward, as explained by its principle designer, Robert Slavin (1990):

> . . . cooperative structures create a situation in which the only way group members can attain their own personal goals is if the group is successful. Therefore, to meet their personal goals, group members must help their group mates to do what helps the group to succeed, and perhaps more important, encourage their group mates to exert maximum effort (pp. 13–14).

The careful selection of groups that stay together for a longer period of time and the structuring of group tasks to promote academic and social learning outcomes are the major differences between Cooperative Learning according to the model and simply placing students in small groups for a single learning task in class. That must be kept in mind as you learn more about this model and use it in your teaching in physical education.

Assumptions about Teaching and Learning

Assumptions about Teaching

1. The teacher's main role is to serve as facilitator of students' academic and social learning.
2. The teacher can take on the role of facilitator only after he directly establishes the setting, structure, and parameters of group tasks. That is, the model begins with directed instruction, and then becomes very indirect once teams become engaged in their assigned task.
3. The teacher is the key person to monitor for and teach students reflective processes for social learning.
4. The teacher must seek a balance between the social and academic learning goals. Within that balance, the process of social learning is just as important as the academic product/s of learning.

Assumptions about Learning

1. Cooperative structures promote higher levels of social and academic learning than individualistic or competitive structures.
2. Groups can, will, and *must* work cooperatively to achieve personal and shared objectives.
3. Team learning works best when groups are heterogenous on all key factors, and the same groups are maintained over several class periods or an entire unit.
4. All group members have something to contribute to the achievement of the group's goals.
5. Learning tasks must specify criteria for individual accountability, and all members' performances must count in the team's assessment score.
6. "Social loafing" can be, but is not automatically, a part of the group process. Parameters must be stated to ensure that all team members contribute to the group's achievement.
7. Groups of students can organize themselves to pursue and complete an assigned task.

Major Theme for Cooperative Learning: The Group Has Not Achieved until All of Its Members Have Achieved

It sounds impossibly altruistic to express this theme for any instructional model. The realities of life and differences among students' abilities would seem to work against the goal (and the theme) that all students must achieve in order for the entire group to be considered successful. Nonetheless, that theme expresses one of the most important ideas behind the model, and its designers hold that as a reachable goal for every application of cooperative learning. Achievement within this theme does not imply that all students in a group will get the same score on assessments or take on the same role in completing group assignments. Rather, achievement is defined as being a responsible team member, developing one's potential to its fullest, and making the best contribution possible to the team's success.

Learning Domain Priorities and Interactions

Cooperative Learning is designed to promote increased levels of student achievement, mediated by small-group interactions and social skills. The former cannot happen if the latter does not occur, making the learning of progroup social skills a prerequisite to individual and group learning. That makes the *domain priorities* for Cooperative Learning a bit complex, as the affective domain will always share the highest priority with the major objective of the assigned learning task. For instance, if the assigned task has a primarily cognitive learning focus, the domain priority would be:

First priority (shared):	Affective and cognitive
Third priority:	Psychomotor

If the assigned task has a primarily psychomotor learning focus, then the domain priority would be:

First priority (shared):	Affective and psychomotor
Third priority:	Cognitive

To complicate matters even more, it should be mentioned that in physical education a good Cooperative Learning task will challenge students equally in all three domains, requiring good group interaction and reflection (affective), an appropriate degree of intellectual rigor (cognitive), and the eventual demonstration of skilled movement (psychomotor). When this happens, all three domains receive approximately the same level of emphasis and development. If students or groups cannot learn in all three domains equally well, they will not be successful at the assigned task.

The *domain interactions* for Cooperative Learning tasks then become equally complex when all three domains are shared. The interaction is not linear—learning in one domain does not follow from the other domains. Rather, all three domains take on a reciprocal relationship among them—learning in any one domain is dependent on learning in the other two domains. For instance, in order to achieve in the psychomotor domain, students in each small group must have good interpersonal skills (affective) and good problem-solving abilities (cognitive). This reciprocity must occur at all times within all domains.

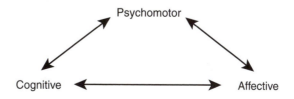

This relationship is the basis of the entire model and underscores the need for students to cooperate *not just to get along* but to learn. The design feature in the model also emphasizes that the process of learning is just as important as the products of learning.

Student Learning Preferences

Using the Reichmann and Grasha (1974) profile for student learning preferences, Cooperative Learning will most often work best for those students who are classified as participant, collaborative, competitive, and independent. Students must be collaborative as members of a learning team, trying to achieve the team's immediate goals. Students will be competitive in those task structures that involve periodic competition with other teams in some other learning tasks.

Validation

Research Validation.   If you will recall, the Cooperative Learning model is actually a set of learning strategies that share some common attributes and procedures that set them apart from more simple group-based learning activities. The Cooperative Learning strategies recognized as part of the model also share one other feature: they all started as experimental learning designs and were developed from systematic research in schools and school-simulation settings. In most of the models presented in this book, the model was first designed and then researched. For Cooperative Learning, the strategies were designed and developed from research findings until those findings began to shape each of the strategies over time. This is a very powerful way to validate an instructional model because the research actually leads to the development of the model, rather than being used to "see how it works" after the model has been designed "on paper."

Cooperative Learning has been the focus of an enormous amount of research studies in the past two decades. In his review of more than one hundred studies, Slavin (1995) summarized the major research findings about cooperative learning:

1. In 64 percent of the studies, the Cooperative Learning groups had significantly better achievement gains than counterparts who had some other form of instruction.
2. Students in Cooperative Learning groups improved cross-racial relationships significantly more often than students in control groups with traditional methods.
3. Students in Cooperative Learning groups improved cross-handicap relationships significantly more often than students in control groups with traditional methods.
4. Cooperative Learning can be successful with students at every grade level and in all subject areas.

Despite the wealth of research on Cooperative Learning in so many subjects area, little of it appears to have been generated from physical education settings. Grinseki (1996) cites only a handful of studies on the formal Cooperative Learning model in physical education. The results of these studies are generally supportive of Cooperative Learning's ability to promote fitness improvement and positive social interactions in young children and a reduction in negative social interactions. An interesting study by Yoder (1993) found that Cooperative Learning in a dance unit improved both social learning and achievement.

The effectiveness of the Cooperative Learning model has been validated in hundreds of studies in almost every school subject area. The fact that only a few studies have been completed in physical education likely reflects the newness of the model in our subject, and should not be taken to question the potential for the model in our field. Given the similarity of findings in so many subjects so far, there is no reason to believe that Cooperative Learning cannot be validated from research for use in physical education. In fact, the strong similarities between Cooperative Learning and the Sport Education model, with its own early impressive research record, is a likely predictor for future findings on Cooperative Learning in physical education.

Craft Knowledge Validation. The record of craft knowledge validation for Cooperative Learning is very similar to that of its research validation. That is, the model has an extensive and impressive record of use in many school subject areas and across every grade level from elementary to college. Thousands of teachers have used the model and have refined its instructional strategies for many situationally specific applications (Slavin, 1995). This validates not only the model's effectiveness, but its adaptability for many settings and subject areas. A study by Stevens and Slavin (1995) had five entire elementary schools use cooperative learning across several subject areas for two years, with positive results for many types of students. The key point here is that the teachers at each of these schools voted unanimously to be trained in the use of Cooperative Learning and to implement the model for two full school years. That is strong evidence that these teachers were familiar enough with Cooperative Learning before the study began to commit to its use for an extended period of time.

Craft knowledge validation for Cooperative Learning in physical education is not widespread. Grineski (1996) states that very few physical education teachers use the formal Cooperative Learning model. Instead, they use some form of small-group-based learning activity that they might misconstrue as Cooperative Learning. However, one physical education teacher in San Diego does use the Cooperative Learning model, and reports excellent results in the improvement of social skills in her diverse, low-SES school (Mercier, 1993). Just as with research validation, craft validation for Cooperative Learning in physical education can be based on its impressive success in many other subjects until such time that it is used more widely in physical education. There is no reason to believe that this model cannot work for hundreds of teachers, just as it did for Mercier.

Intuitive Validation. With the team sport background of so many physical education teachers, it should be simple to let this model "make sense" in our subject area. Nearly all of us have experienced and recognize the role of team effort in the achievement of shared and individual goals in sport settings. We have all rooted on teammates, let our own success hinge on the success of others, and pulled together for the common good of the team. We also know that the team is only as strong as its weakest link, or player—so we all try to help every other member perform to her fullest potential. If you apply all of these reasons to why sport team members need to work together in assigned group tasks in physical education, you come up with a strong rationale for the Cooperative Learning model. It makes sense that any group of students will achieve more when they work together than when they work individually, and that their social development is greatly enhanced by that process—giving strong intuitive validation for the use of Cooperative Learning in physical education.

Teaching and Learning Features

Directness

The directness profile for Cooperative Learning is based on three different patterns that occur during lessons. The model is very direct as the teacher decides what the assigned task will be, selects teams, explains the parameters for completing the task (e.g., available time and other resources), and sets criteria for performance and social skill behaviors. The model becomes student-centered during the time teams are engaged to complete the task. It then becomes highly interactive as the teacher processes the learning of social skills with students during and at the end of each class. To clarify how this determines the directness profile for Cooperative Learning, Figure 9.1 indicates how each component of the profile can change according to the three major structures in a cooperative lesson. More complete explanations are given as follows:

1. *Content selection.* This component of the Cooperative Learning model is very direct. The teacher determines the series of tasks that teams will pursue in the unit and communicates them to students. A formal content listing is difficult to determine ahead of time because the teacher cannot often predict the needed social learning skills in advance. These needs will become apparent as teams work on the assigned tasks. The academic content is

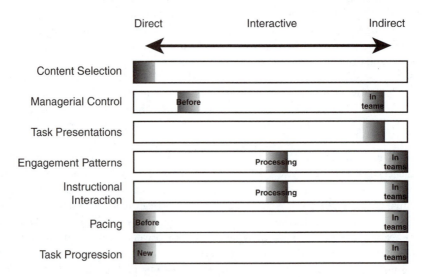

FIGURE 9.1   Directness Profile for Cooperative Learning

also difficult to list ahead of time because each task will likely be large enough to contain many academic outcomes within it. The content listing is usually represented by the series of learning tasks the teacher will assign to groups as the unit progresses. That process is almost always teacher-directed.

2. *Managerial control.* Managerial control is strongly teacher-centered prior to the teams starting their engagement on the learning tasks. The teacher selects the teams, decides what resources will be available, determines the amount of time to be allocated for each task, and decides the parameters within which teams must work. Once the teams begin to pursue the task, this control shifts quickly to the students within each cooperative group. They make decisions about how to organize themselves, how to divide the work to be done, and how to use their available time and resources.

3. *Task presentations.* There are no task presentations by the teacher in cooperative learning. Rather, the teacher sets the stage by explaining the assigned task and the ground rules teams must follow in their pursuit of it. After that it is up to students, in their groups, to explain to each other what needs to be done and how to do it. It is expected that teams will use peer teaching as their main mode of instructing.

4. *Engagement patterns.* There are two primary engagement patterns in this model. One of the patterns is strongly student-directed, occurring among students in each of the cooperative teams. They decide who takes the lead at any given time and establish their own engagement plans for getting the task completed. The other pattern is interactive, as the teacher uses questions to develop students' social skills. To be the most effective, this process should allow students time to reflect on their current behavior patterns and to come up with their own solutions when they are not working cooperatively in groups.

5. *Instructional interactions.* With the two distinct engagement patterns there will be two types of instructional interactions with Cooperative Learning. The interactions will be the same two types as the engagement patterns: almost totally student-directed as teams work on the assigned tasks, and interactive when the teacher is attempting to develop students' social skills. While students are working in their teams, the teacher takes on the roles of facilitator and primary resource person. The teacher facilitates the cooperative processes, getting teams to work to their fullest capacity; the teacher also serves as the "resident expert" when teams need advice or need someone to listen to their ideas. The most effective Cooperating Learning teachers are those who can facilitate the learning process without providing teams with too much information or assistance on completing the task.

6. *Pacing.* After the teacher has introduced the learning task and informed teams how long they will have to complete the task, the pacing of instruction is strongly student-centered. In their teams, the students decide how much work needs to be done and how long they plan to spend on each part of the task. The teacher would intervene only when a team's plan will obviously not allow them to finish on time.

7. *Task progression.* The teacher decides when a new task will be assigned. As with pacing, once the teams are working together, each team determines the steps needed to complete the task and when to consider each part of the task finished. Having a work plan and evaluating it regularly is a key part of the cooperative learning process.

Predominant Engagement Patterns

Except when the teacher is introducing a learning task and processing for social skill development, the Cooperative Learning model uses only one engagement pattern: groups of four to six students working in teams for an extended period of time. All of the strategies used in cooperative learning are initially based on that configuration; at times two or more groups will merge, but only temporarily.

Selecting Team Members.   The placement of students into teams is one of the most important functions for the teacher in the Cooperative Learning model. Notice that I said it is a teacher function, not to be delegated to students. That is because the team selection process must serve several key purposes in the model in order to promote the most effective academic and social learning possible. The primary considerations are for diversity within teams and for fairness across teams (when teams will be competing with each other). Having diversity within a team promotes the awareness of others' talents, personalities, and perspectives, as well as providing a wider range of resources with which to work on the assigned task. The major factors for achieving diversity should include: previous experience in the content area, gender, skill ability, cognitive ability, learning style, race, ethnicity, willingness to take leadership or to follow, and student behavior. Each teacher might have other factors on which to base decisions.

The process of assigning students to teams should be done privately by the teacher and then announced in class or posted. Because some students might misunderstand the larger purposes being served by the selection process, it is not a good idea to make team selection a public event or to liken it in any way to picking up sides for a game. We are all aware of the potential harm that can occur with that type of selection process. Once the teams are made, the teacher should make students aware of the human resources and talent on each team, and not allow students to focus on perceived shortcomings of their team or to overly analyze the composition of other teams. Therefore, it is helpful for the teacher to begin the cooperative process right away by informing the class of how and why teams were selected and to get teams working together as soon as possible.

Inclusiveness

The Cooperative Learning model is designed to allow every student to be included in the team process. This is achieved in three ways. The team selection process just described ensures that all teams are heterogenous, comprised of students with diverse abilities, motivations, and personalities. That diversity promotes interaction among all types of students. Secondly, all members are accountable for making a contribution to the team's success, so there is strong motivation for students to support, encourage, and teach each other to meet the team's goal. This promotes fuller participation by all team members. Thirdly, the team's success is more likely when it recognizes and uses the full range of talent among its members, promoting an appreciation for any contribution that helps the team achieve its goal. Therefore, it is in the team's best interest to find ways to include, not isolate, students with unique abilities and talents.

Slavin (1995) cites several studies that support the potential for Cooperative Learning in promoting greater awareness, appreciation, and inclusion for diverse student groups:

> Cooperative learning increases contact between students, gives them a shared basis of similarity (group membership), engages them in pleasant activities together, and has them work toward common goals (p. 66).

This statement highlights one of the strengths of the Cooperative Learning model—it is purposely designed to be inclusive and to make every student's contribution count. The teacher's group processing procedures can be used to teach students how to be inclusive of all team members, taking inclusion one large step past just "learning next to one another" to "learning with, from, and for each other."

Task Presentation and Task Structure

The Cooperative Learning model is actually a group of related teaching strategies that share a common purpose, procedures, and student engagement patterns. This section will describe the major learning strategies and explain how each one can be structured for physical education instruction.

Task Presentation. There is no task presentation in Cooperative Learning in which the teacher shows students how to set up and perform learning tasks. It is up to each team of students to organize themselves for the assigned task and to determine their own solutions to the "problems" inherent to the task. In that way, the model is very different from nearly all other models in this book. The teacher does take time to *frame* the learning task in a way that allows students to understand what the task is, without informing students how to complete the task (that is, not teaching them). The teacher should include several things when framing the task:

1. Announce membership for all teams and explain how teams were selected.
2. Announce how long teams will have to complete the task.
3. Announce which learning strategy will be used for the task.
4. Inform teams of any ground rules to be in effect.
5. Let teams know what resources will be available to them and how shared resources will be divided among all teams.
6. Explain the learning objectives and how they will be assessed.
7. Explain objectives for social learning and how they will be assessed.
8. Explain the teacher's role as facilitator.
9. Inform teams of any products that should be generated from the task (such as posters, portfolios, team records).
10. Explain the rules for team competitions when used with some strategies.

Task Structure. There are many recognized organizing strategies that can be considered part of the formal Cooperative Learning model. Five of these strategies can be adopted for the kinds of content and outcomes typically taught in physical education programs. Each strategy has its own unique task structure that is explained to students as part of the task presentation.

Student Teams—Achievement Divisions (STAD).   First developed by Robert Slavin (Slavin, 1980), students in a class are placed in noncompeting teams. All of the teams are given the same assigned learning task and needed resources for it. The teacher allocates a set time period for teams to initially learn and practice, typically fifteen to twenty minutes. The teacher is available during this time to clarify the task or to serve as another resource for teams. At the end of the time period, all members of each team compete an assessment task on the knowledge or skill just learned. That assessment could be in the form of a short quiz, a skills test, or any type of performance test that covers the content just practiced. The scores for all team members are summed to get a team score. Team scores are announced and the teacher interacts with the class to discuss the cooperative process and make suggestions for improved group interactions. Teams are then directed to return to practicing the same task again, with an added emphasis on cooperation and improving the scores of every team member. A second time period is allocated, after which all team members complete the assessment task again. Two goals are stated for the second practice period: all individual members and the team as a whole should beat their first score. Obviously, succeeding at the first goal automatically achieves the second goal. Team grades are assigned, based on the amount of improvement in the total team score from the first to second assessment. It should be noted that only a team grade is given, so that students who can improve between assessments are motivated to help (teach) other students do the same.

Orlick (1982) uses two variations of STAD in physical education, called Collective Score. Scores can be summed for entire classes, or they can be summed for entire schools. Both variations expand the scope of Cooperative Learning so that more students are working for and supporting each other.

Team Games Tournament (TGT).   The initial structure of TGT is similar to that of STAD. Students are placed in teams, presented with the assigned learning task, and given a set period for the initial practice or knowledge acquisition. All members of every team complete an assessment at the end of the practice period. At this point, TGT begins to differ from STAD. In TGT, the first, second, third, and fourth highest scores on each team are compared to the corresponding ranked scores from all other teams—first against first, second against second, and so on. Each winning score earns that team a predetermined number of points, which allows all students to contribute to their team's success, regardless of ranking. A second round of practice is scheduled, which usually results in increased interaction and support on each team. The assessment is given again, and ranked scores are compared again—with points awarded in the same way. The winner of the TGT is the team with the most points at the end of the game. It is possible to keep teams intact for many assigned tasks and to make the tasks progressively difficult over time. It is not necessary to keep students on the same task for more than two practice and assessment periods.

Team-Assisted Instruction (TAI).   This strategy is a combination of Cooperative Learning and Personalized Systems for Instruction, described in Chapter 8. After teams are selected, a list of learning tasks with performance criteria is given to all students. The list contains a progression on one or more skills and knowledge areas, going from easy to more difficult. Team members may practice the tasks individually or with the assistance of other members. When a student has completed a task to its criterion performance level, another team member checks that off and the first student moves to the next task. Team performance can be assessed in one of two ways. The teacher can give points for the number of tasks each team completes each week, or a final assessment task can be given to all team members independently, with the summed scores used for awarding points and the team grade.

Jigsaw. Students are placed in teams and assigned to learn one part of a skill, knowledge area, or game. For example, in a tennis unit, one team can be assigned to learn the components and cues for the forehand drive, another team can be assigned to learn the backhand drive, another team can be assigned to learn game rules and scoring, and so on. All teams are given a set period of time to learn their component and to then take the role of teacher when the whole class moves to that segment of the unit. Assessment is based on the quantity and quality of the team's instruction to the class.

In a variation of the jigsaw strategy, members of each team can be assigned to learn different components so that each member becomes an "expert" on that topic or skill. "Expert groups" are formed by having students from different teams who learned the same topic/skill meet to share what they have learned individually. Once they have done that, each "expert" goes back to his original group to teach his own teammates what he has learned. The jigsaw strategy and its variations share one key feature—at some point in time students will instruct other students through peer teaching.

Group Investigation. This strategy is used to have teams cooperate to produce and share the results of their learning. Teams are selected and the task is assigned. The time period for group investigation is typically longer, perhaps as long as three weeks, with the expectation that students will work on it in class and outside of class. The task is presented as a group project, part of which requires each team to present what they learned in some form of media: posters, collages, a videotape, computer-generated graphics, or a written report. The media production serves two purposes: it is the self-contained evidence of each team's learning and it is shared with other teams for their learning. Assessment is completed from a scoring rubric presented to students before the group investigation begins and results in a single grade being given to each team.

Teacher Expertise and Contextual Needs

Teacher Expertise

Teachers who use the Cooperative Learning model will need to have particular strengths in several areas of the proposed knowledge base presented in Chapter 2.

Learners. One of the key functions in this model is the selection of heterogeneous teams that are mixed in several ways: skill level, previous experience, gender, race/ethnicity, communication skills, leadership abilities, and willingness to contribute to the team's efforts. That means the teacher will have to know each student on all of these dimensions and be able to select teams that reflect a diversity of talent and a diversity of team dynamics. While it is not possible to make all teams balanced on all dimensions, the overriding criterion is to provide all teams with an equal chance of succeeding at the assigned task.

Learning Theories.   The Cooperative Learning model is based on a combination of four major learning theories: cognitive (during team problem solving), behavioral (in meeting performance criteria), motivational (in mutual support among teammates), and social (learning by observing and interacting with team members). The teacher will need to recognize which theory is most prominently at work within each part of the model and facilitate that kind of learning at the appropriate time.

Task Analysis and Content Progression.   The task analysis in Cooperative Learning must represent a learning progression in all three domains. Therefore, the teacher must be able to plan progressions not only for motor skill performance and cognitive learning, but for the social/affective domain as well. The teacher will need to consider the progression from simple to complex learning in the affective domain, just as she does for the other two domains.

Developmentally Appropriate Instruction.   It is possible that teams of students can be ready for the academic challenges inherent to an assigned task in the psychomotor and cognitive domains, but not be ready for the types of social and cooperative interactions needed to make the team work successfully. As the teacher determines the task analysis and progression through assigned tasks, he must ask himself, "Are the students ready for the types of cooperative interactions needed to work well together on these tasks?" To design developmentally appropriate Cooperative Learning, the teacher will need to be certain that students can make good choices and assume the kinds of responsibilities needed to be contributing members of teams.

Assessment.   All assigned cooperative learning tasks are assessed for performance and cooperative learning process. Performance assessments are made regularly during and after assigned tasks. Teachers must know how to design interim assessments during tasks that are directly targeted on the key performance outcomes, and which can be completed and scored quickly to determine team points and new objectives. Performance assessments must also be designed for the end of assigned tasks to determine team points and grades. Even though cognitive and psychomotor performance is assessed, the cooperative model relies on alternative, authentic assessment techniques.

Teachers must also know how to design assessments for social skills observed within and between teams during cooperative tasks. The teacher should explain her expectations to students for team interactions, and monitor (assess) those interactions during assigned tasks. This can be done with the use of checklists and critical incident reports that represent the types of social learning outcomes sought by the teacher.

Establishing and Maintaining the Social/Emotional Climate.   The effectiveness of the Cooperative Learning model is determined to a great extent by the regularity and quality of student interactions on teams as they pursue assigned tasks. This requires teacher expertise in three related areas: establishing a positive environment, being able to detect ineffective patterns that lead to a negative environment, and the ability to teach students how to change a negative climate to a positive one. The tricky part is that the teacher should not dictate to students how they should act toward each other so that students behave well to avoid being punished by the teacher. The teacher should establish some ground rules and select teams in a way that will set the cooperative process in motion, and then allow students to discover how they can best work in their teams to meet their goals. The teacher monitors as teams work on tasks, noting interactions that lead toward a positive or negative climate in class. Positive interactions are noted and reinforced through public recognition at the end of class. Negative interactions are *processed* at the end of class through a reflective analysis led by the teacher. The purpose of processing is to locate the source of the problems and to get students to reach solutions on their own, in their respective teams.

Physical Education Content. The indirect, facilitative type of instruction used for Cooperative Learning tasks calls for the teacher to know physical education content in ways that differ from more direct kinds of instruction. In Direct Instruction, the teacher's content expertise is shown by the ability to demonstrate proper techniques (during task presentations) and to analyze students' practice attempts. In the Cooperative Learning model, the teacher's expertise is shown by the ability to frame appropriate, challenging, and creative assigned learning tasks, and the ability to recognize diverse ways in which teams can reach solutions to the problems embedded in those tasks. "Knowing your stuff" takes on a unique meaning in Cooperative Learning and other models that use facilitative, indirect approaches to student learning.

Equity in the Gym. One of the founding principles of Cooperative Learning is to promote equal opportunities for success for all students (Slavin, 1995). There is an assumption that all members of a team can contribute to its success if each one is allowed to let his/her unique talents be used in the team effort. The teacher's expertise is needed to select teams and design tasks in which individual students are held accountable in assessments, both for performance achievement and social learning outcomes. There is no expectation that all team members will contribute equal amounts of skill and knowledge, but there is every expectation that all team members will contribute their fullest effort to the team's success.

Effective Teaching Skills Applied to Cooperative Learning

A teacher will need to develop a unique repertoire of effective teaching skills for using the Cooperative Learning model.

Planning. Much of the planning in cooperative learning comes at the unit level in determining the tasks given to teams and classes. The teacher will have to make several decisions ahead of time for each task:

1. What are the problems posed within each task? What cognitive, psychomotor, and social learning challenges will the task include?
2. Which Cooperative Learning strategy will work best for this task?

3. How will teams be selected? What factors will determine the size and heterogeneous mix on each team?
4. How long will teams have to complete the task?
5. What resources will be made available to teams for the task?
6. What performance outcomes or products will be produced by each team?
7. How will each team's performance and social learning be assessed?
8. What will the teacher's role be as teams work on the task?

Once all of these questions are answered, the teacher can select teams and present the learning task to all teams. At that time, planning becomes an interactive process as the teacher looks for things that need to be adjusted as teams work on the assigned task. When an assigned task will last for more than one class period, the teacher can plan a short briefing each day to give students feedback on their teamwork and to assess progress to that point.

Time and Class Management.   The teacher's major time management decision is how long to allocate for each assigned task. Some tasks will be brief, perhaps ten to fifteen minutes. Other tasks, such as those using group investigation, can last for several lessons, including time outside of the physical education period (library work, using the Internet, writing reports).

Classroom management in Cooperative Learning is largely the responsibility of students once they are in teams and working on tasks. Each team can decide how to pace itself and how to apportion the allocated time. The teacher does play a key, if indirect, role by monitoring student interactions within teams and using the reflection process to help teams be more efficient and effective. The Cooperative Learning teacher will need to be skilled in recognizing poor team interactions and knowing how to help teams become more productive without making directed interventions.

Task Presentation and Task Structure.   The skills needed for these key functions are similar to those stated for the planning process in this section. There is no task presentation as it is used in many other models (in which the teacher shows students how to perform the skill correctly). Instead, the teacher selects teams, "frames" the assigned task, and directs teams to "go." The needed skill here is to give teams enough information to start working on the task without giving them clues on how to complete the task.

Task structure in Cooperative Learning is determined by which strategy is selected for each assigned task. All of the strategies presented earlier in this chapter promote certain types of interactions and performance outcomes. The Cooperative Learning teacher will need to know the design and procedures for each strategy and select the best strategy for each situation.

Communication.   The Cooperative Learning teacher will need to give teams clear and specific information when framing a task and explaining the strategy to be used for it. It will be helpful to check for understanding often during the explanation, as well as in the first few minutes of team engagement.

Instructional Information.   The Cooperative Learning teacher will need to be skilled in providing two types of instructional information: explanations as tasks are framed and questioning during reflective processing. As mentioned, it is important that students (in teams) get a clear and detailed explanation of the assigned task and the cooperative strategy to be used for it. The better they understand the task, the more likely they are to become appropriately engaged right away.

The teacher's use of questions during times of reflection on the cooperative process is an essential skill. When the teacher observes that one or more teams are not working well together, she should not use directive statements to correct the situation. Instead, the teacher engages teams in a reflective exercise to get them to understand the nature of the problem and to devise their own course of action. That is part of the social skill learning process, and students' ability to find ways to make each team function to its maximum potential is one of the main goals in the model.

Review and Closure.   Cooperative Learning lessons should end with the teacher leading an interactive reflection process to let teams know how well they worked together that day. The teacher monitors teams while they are engaged, noting instances of positive and negative interactions. Again, remember that the process is indirect and interactive, with the teacher using questions rather than direct statements to get students to think about how well they worked as teams.

Student Developmental Requirements

Because of the three-way emphasis on cognitive, psychomotor, and social learning (affective), it is important that students are developmentally ready for Cooperative Learning in all three domains. Again, that does not mean students must have existing skills or knowledge prior to using this model—only that they are *ready* to learn in this way. The cognitive requirements of the model call for students to be able to understand the mostly general directions given to them about the task and to be able to participate in the group problem-solving process. The psychomotor requirements will depend on the complexity of that component in the assigned task. The most important developmental question is whether students will be able to teach each other the necessary skills and strategies needed to be successful in the task. The developmental issues regarding the learning of social skills are perhaps the most critical, given that social learning is just as important as each team's performance in the model. Are students ready and able to take on the individual and shared responsibilities needed for their team's success? Can they learn what it means to be part of a group and to support the efforts of all team members? If that *potential* is not there, then the teacher should not select Cooperative Learning as the unit's model because the needed "chemistry" is absent and the model will likely lead to failure and frustration, defeating the main objectives in the model's design.

Contextual Needs for Cooperative Learning

Cooperative Learning can be used in any setting in which students have the ability to learn how to work cooperatively. Notice that I did not say that students must *already* have good social learning skills. Since those skills are a major outcome in the model, it is necessary only that students are *ready to learn how* to contribute to a group's success. Once that condition is satisfied, Cooperative Learning can be used for its designed purposes in almost any physical education setting at any grade level. Equipment and facilities needs are determined by the nature of the assigned task, so teachers can easily plan tasks that can be accomplished with their existing resources. Perhaps the single greatest contextual need is to have enough allocated time for groups to complete assigned tasks, especially when using strategies like group investigation. However, when that amount of time is not available, any of the other strategies can be used.

Teacher and Student Roles and Responsibilities in Cooperative Learning

Each instructional model will have certain operations that need to be completed to make the model function according to its design. Some of these operations are carried out by the teacher; others are carried out by one or more students. The following table shows the major operations within the Cooperative Learning model, and indicates who is responsible for completing them during each lesson.

Operation or Responsibility	Who Does It in Cooperative Learning
Content listing	The **teacher** decides what is to be learned, in the form of assigned tasks given to student teams.
Team selection	The **teacher** selects teams to ensure the maximum amount of diversity and heterogeneity on all teams.
Task "framing" and problem-setting	The **teacher** explains the assigned task to all teams, based on the formulation of a problem that student teams will need to pursue or solve.
Bringing equipment to class	The **teacher** brings to class what each team states they need for the assigned task.
Task structure	The **teacher** decides the task structure in the form of a defined cooperative learning strategy that provides the ground rules for student engagement.
Engagement patterns	**Students** on each team decide how they will organize themselves to pursue the assigned task.
Problem mediation	Initially, problems are mediated within teams by **students.** If that is not successful, the **teacher** mediates through a reflective process.
Performance assessment	The **teacher** designs all performance assessments, typically in the form of a scoring rubric. **Students** on each team decide how their team will work to achieve the best possible score on each assessment.
Social-skill assessment	The **teacher** decides the criteria for group interactions and monitors students as they work on their teams.
Instructional processes	**Students** on each team decide and implement their own peer-teaching plan as they pursue the assigned learning task.

Teaching and Learning Benchmarks for Cooperative Learning

Teachers who use the Cooperative Learning model can learn the benchmarks for their own and student behavior patterns. The following teacher and student benchmarks verify that the Cooperative Learning model has been designed and implemented with an acceptable degree of faithfulness, increasing the likelihood that the stated student learning outcomes will be achieved in all three domains.

Teacher Benchmarks

Benchmark	How to Verify
Teacher selects heterogenous and equitable teams	1. The teacher lists the criteria used for making selections. 2. The teacher shows a plan for how each student was assigned. 3. The teacher asks students for their feedback on selections.
The teacher selects an appropriate assigned learning task.	1. The task has stated time limits and procedures. 2. The task can be completed by all teams in the allocated time. 3. The task requires a contribution by all team members. 4. The task requires teams to be challenged in all three domains.
The teacher selects an appropriate Cooperative Learning strategy.	1. The task is one of the recognized cooperative strategies, and not simply "grouped learning." 2. The task provides a challenge to students to learn in all three domains.
The teacher frames the assigned learning task.	1. The teacher provides sufficient information about the task, without giving clues for completing the task. 2. Teams become engaged right away, indicating that they understand the task and its structure.
Teacher serves as a facilitator during tasks.	Monitor the number and types of interactions initiated by the teacher. The teacher should use indirect statements and questions, and only when interaction is initiated by students
Teacher monitors and processes for social learning outcomes.	1. Teacher includes a planned segment to process for social learning outcomes. 2. The teacher uses few, if any, direct statements in this segment.
Teacher designs assessments for performance and social learning.	1. Check the teacher's plan for these components. 2. Assessments should be designed for team achievement, with each team member having individual accountability.

Student Benchmarks

Benchmark	How to Verify
Students view teams as being fair.	Students are asked for their comments on the selection process and indicate no objections.
Students understand the assigned task.	1. Teams begin to work on the task right away. 2. Teams ask few clarification questions of the teacher.
Students understand the cooperative strategy in place.	1. Teams begin right away to allocate time and other resources for the task. 2. Teams quickly formulate a "plan of attack." 3. Teams follow the procedures given for completing the task.
Teams share the work and the accountability across all members.	1. Teams assign individual members to specific "jobs." 2. Teams chart the contributions of each member. 3. Teams complete peer evaluations of other members.
Teams use peer teaching to improve performance, and publicly support each member's efforts.	Monitor the type and frequency of interactions within teams.
Teams show improvement on performance assessments.	Compare assessment scores over time.
Teams show evidence of social learning.	Teacher or peers use critical incident reports or checklists to identify instances of positive and negative social behaviors.

Assessing Learning in the Cooperative Learning Model

Since the learning domain priorities in the Cooperative Learning model are typically shared across all three major domains, it is important that the teacher assess student learning in ways that give equal attention to all of these kinds of outcomes. The authenticity of assessments in the Cooperative Learning model will reflect the nature of the assigned learning task given to students. If the task is designed to develop rather standard kinds of psychomotor skills and content knowledge, then the assessment can be mostly traditional (i.e., a skills test or a written test). If the assigned task strives for more complex and applied outcomes, then the assessment should be more authentic and alternative. Either way, the assessment is likely to be "homemade" by the teacher because the assigned learning task will be the same—designed by the teacher to match the specific student abilities, content, and context of the unit.

The Cooperative Learning teacher has several options for assessing outcomes in the psychomotor domain:

1. Short skills quizzes that require students to complete a certain number of trials to a stated criterion (e.g., the number of successful shots to a target, the number of made foul shots, the number of completed passes)

2. Timed completion of an event or task (e.g., elapsed time for the 200 meter run, time taken to complete an obstacle course, the time needed to achieve a certain number of successful trials)
3. Accuracy tests (e.g., score on and end of arrows, percent of made shots, distance from a target)
4. Consistency (e.g., number of made shots in a row)
5. Standardized skills tests

Recall that strategies like STAD and TGT require teams to practice for a set amount of time and then complete an assessment of that learning. These assessments should be directly related to the task just practiced and be completed very quickly. Most often the teacher can simply ask each member of all teams to make a certain number of attempts (shots, kicks, throws) and to record the number of successful attempts. Each team's score is the sum of all members' scores. These simple "quizzes" can be used to monitor each student's progress (remember that the model calls for individual student accountability) and to assess the effectiveness of teams' peer teaching.

Assessment in the cognitive domain is similar to that in the psychomotor domain when the assigned task focuses on relatively simple outcomes, such as recall knowledge. The teacher can use homemade quizzes to assess students' knowledge on such things as game rules, procedures, and strategy. Such assessments are most likely to be used in STAD and TGT. Again, the quiz should focus on the content just studied and allow students to complete it in a few minutes. Quizzes can be made up of several kinds of questions and items:

1. Multiple choice
2. Fill in the blanks
3. "What if . . ." questions
4. Definitions and terminology

More sophisticated assessment techniques will be used when the cooperative strategy is more complex and strives for higher-order learning outcomes. This refers to strategies like jigsaw and group investigation, in which student learning is multidimensional, representing several types of knowledge. Because these strategies are more likely to be authentic learning experiences, they should then be assessed with alternative and more authentic techniques. This typically leads the teacher to develop a scoring rubric that is given to the teams at the same time the learning task is assigned. The scoring rubric should include:

1. Parameters for what the learning should produce (a portfolio, video, collage, or lesson to be taught to other students)
2. A delineation of each level of quality for the completed work, and a clear description of the features that make up each level. For example, a group investigation on the history of the Olympic games will be assessed at four levels: Olympian (lowest), bronze medalist, silver medalist, and gold medalist (highest). The teacher then describes the characteristics of each category so that teams can know what it will take to reach each level of quality in the product they generate.
3. A scoring sheet and written report that the teacher completes for each team's work and gives to them for their review

The Cooperative Learning model also calls for assessing student learning in the affective domain, represented by intrateam interactions such as peer teaching, verbal support for teammates' efforts, cooperation, leadership/followership, and problem solving. Assessing these kinds of processes can be a bit tricky, but it is possible for the teacher to use several strategies to get a handle on the development of students' social skills:

1. Regularly monitor each team as it works together, making notes on positive and negative instances of social interactions. This is called critical incident reporting.
2. Use a checklist of positive and negative social interaction items to monitor the frequency and patterns of those interactions.
3. Have each team compile a log of its work (who did what part/s).
4. Have each team complete a daily journal of its group work, noting positive and negative instances of group process.
5. Use the end-of-class processing time to allow students to make comments on the group process.

Teachers who use the Cooperative Learning model will need to keep in mind that the process of team learning is just as important as the academic outcomes of team learning, so that social learning skills must always be monitored in some way, either formally or informally.

Selecting and Modifying Cooperative Learning for Physical Education

Because the Cooperative Learning model promotes outcomes in all three domains, it can be used for a wide variety of goals and content in physical education. This model will be effective in many content areas of physical education:

1. Team sports
2. Dual- and small-team recreational activities
3. Dance
4. Personal fitness
5. Personal fitness concepts
6. The learning of sport history
7. Current trends and issues in sport and physical education
8. Group initiatives and Project Adventure
9. New Games

Grade-Level Adaptations

Developmentally appropriate versions of Cooperative Learning can be used across many grade levels in physical education. Figure 9.2 presents an analysis for selecting cooperative learning and making grade level adaptations for it.

FIGURE 9.2   Grade-Level Adaptations for Cooperative Learning in Physical Education

Grade Levels	Select Cooperative Learning?	Possible Adaptations
Preschool	No	
Early elementary	Yes	1. Use teams of no more than three. 2. Do not use interteam competitions. 3. Make tasks short. 4. Do not use explicit performance assessments. Use checklists.
Upper elementary	Yes	1. Do not use interteam competitions. 2. Make tasks short. 3. Use simple scoring rubrics for performance assessment.
Middle school/junior high	Yes	None needed, if assigned tasks are developmentally appropriate.
High school	Yes	None needed, if assigned tasks are developmentally appropriate.
College/adult	Yes	None needed.

Summary

While the field of physical education has been slower than some others to adopt the theory and practice of Cooperative Learning, it would appear that this model can be invaluable in the process of promoting the multidimensional outcomes expressed in the NASPE (1995) standards for P–12 programs. It strives for a true balance among outcomes in all three major learning domains, and when implemented correctly can accomplish that very well. The key is that physical education teachers must recognize the difference between "students learning alongside each other" (i.e., grouped learning) and "students learning with, from, and for each other" (cooperative learning). The Cooperative Learning model begins with an emphasis on teacher-centered decisions in the planning stage and the presentation of assigned learning tasks. However, once a task is assigned, the model becomes very much student-centered as they negotiate the dynamics of team learning and pursue their common goals. The model changes to an interactive mode at the end of each lesson as the teacher guides students toward a better understanding of the group process. This model, perhaps more than any other in this book, requires a teacher to use a broad range of real-time communication, observation, and decision-making skills to promote the types of learning intended in the model.

It is my prediction that as more physical education teachers at all levels adopt the broad learning goals reflected in the NASPE (1995) standards, the Cooperative Learning model (true versions of it, not grouped instruction) will become one of the most widely used instructional models in physical education. That prediction is based on Cooperative Learning's impressive record for promoting social and cognitive learning outcomes in other subjects, and the obvious carryover potential in promoting similar kinds of outcomes in the psychomotor domain. It would seem to be very much a "model for the times."

Sample Unit Plan for Cooperative Learning

Unit content:	The Summer Olympic Games
Grade level:	Middle school (7th grade)
Students:	34 students
	17 boys, 17 girls
	Varied cognitive and psychomotor skill abilities
	Varied familiarity with the Olympic games
Resources:	Sufficient equipment for sports/events included in the unit
	Reference books in teacher's office
	Multimedia technology in school library
	Internet access in the school technology lab and library
Length of unit:	15 class periods
Length of class:	Block scheduled, with 105 minutes of actual learning time each period

Class	Content to Learn	Cooperative Learning Strategy

1	1. Overview of the unit
	2. Assessment of student knowledge of the Olympics
	3. Selection of 5 cooperative teams by the teacher
	4. Framing of first cooperative task. Each team assigned to research one of the following:
	  a. Ancient Olympic games
	  b. Modern summer Olympic games history
	  c. Organization of Olympics
	  d. The Olympic oath
	  e. Current list of summer Olympic sports
		4. Group investigation
		Criteria:
		  a. Must be written and then presented to the rest of the class
		  b. Must use at least one text and one Internet resource
		  c. All team members must contribute
		  d. Due at the start of class 3

Continued

Class	Content to Learn	Cooperative Learning Strategy
2	Work on group investigation in the gym, library, or technology lab	
3	1. Present group investigation to the class 2. Teacher will check for understanding to determine nonteaching students' knowledge on each topic	

4	1. Each team can select a country it will represent–one team per continent
	2. Learning about each country:
	  a. Language (common words related to the Olympics)
	  b. Political system
	  c. Economic system
	  d. Common customs
	  e. Role in Olympic history
		1. Order of continent selection will be random (restriction: cannot pick the United States)
		
		2. Jigsaw: 1–2 members of each team pick one of the areas (a–e) to research and become the "expert/s" on
		  a. Experts work independently on their country, then meet with other experts to discuss how countries are different or similar on those characteristics
		  b. Due by next class

5	Jigsaw teaching: 1. Each expert teaches his/her team about that topic for their country 2. Experts on the same topic teach the entire class, noting similarities and differences	
6–7	Learning summer Olympic sports/events 1. Track and field (sprints, relays, long jump)	1a. Student Teams—Achievement Divisions (STAD) 1b. Team Games Tournament (TGT)
8–9	Learning summer Olympic sports/events 1. Modified decathlon	1a. STAD 1b. TGT
10–11	Learning summer Olympic sports/events 1. Archery	1. TGT
12	Learning summer Olympic sports/events 1. Modified weight lifting	1a. STAD

(continued)

Continued

Class	Content to Learn	Cooperative Learning Strategy
13	Learning summer Paralympic sports/events 1. Boccia	**1a.** STAD **1b.** TGT

14	Capturing the Olympic spirit	Learning together:
		1. Each team plans and makes a multimedia presentation to "capture the essence" of the Olympic spirit
		Criteria:
		  a. Must use at least three types of media
		  b. Final collage must reflect the true spirit of the Olympic and Paralympic games
		  c. Each team must prepare a narrative to teach their collage to the rest of the class
		  d. All team members must participate and contribute to the collage
		  e. Collages and narratives to be presented in next class

15	Presentation of teams' collages on the Olympic spirit	Assessment into four "medal categories" Gold Silver Bronze Olympian

Lesson Plan for Class #6: Track and Field Events (sprints, relays, high jump)

Equipment needed:	relay batons stopwatches tape measures
Stations needed:	50-yard sprint area with lanes 200-yard relay area with lanes 5 marked long-jump areas

Framing the Task	Task Structure and Sequence	Assessment
50-yard sprint. Teacher discusses rules, procedures, skills, and strategy for this event	STAD 1. Teams have 10 minutes to practice starts and strategy. 2. At the end of 10 minutes, all members of each team run a timed 50-yard sprint. The team score is the TOTAL time for all members.	2. Each member's time is recorded on a team score sheet. All scores are summed to get the TOTAL team score.

Continued

Framing the Task	Task Structure and Sequence	Assessment
	3. Teams have 10 more minutes to practice and peer teach for reduced times.	3. Teacher observes for social interaction and group process.
	4. At the end of 10 minutes, all members of each team run a timed 50-yard sprint. The team score is the TOTAL time for all members. Goal: Reduce the times for all members and the total team score.	4. Assessing team achievement: Gold medal: reduce total by more than 10%. Silver: Reduce total by 5–9%. Bronze: Reduce total by 1–4%. Olympian: No reduction or an increase.
200-yard relay (4 × 50). Teacher discusses rules, procedures, skills, and strategy for this event.	STAD 1. Teams have 10 minutes to practice starts, baton passes, running order, and strategy.	
	2. At the end of 10 minutes, each team runs a timed 200-yard relay. The team score is the ELAPSED time.	2. Each team's time is recorded on a score sheet.
	3. Teams have 10 more minutes to practice and peer teach for reduced times.	3. Teacher observes for social interaction and group process.
	4. At the end of 10 minutes, each team runs a second timed 200-yard sprint. The team score is the ELAPSED time. Goal: Reduce the team's relay time.	4. Assessing team achievement: Gold medal: reduce time by more than 10%. Silver: Reduce time by 5–9%. Bronze: Reduce time by 1–4%. Olympian: No reduction or an increase in team's time.
Running long jump. Teacher discusses rules, procedures, fouls, skills, and strategy for this event.	TGT 1. Each team practices for 15 minutes to work on form, skills, and distance.	
	2. At the end of 15 minutes, all members of each team make two measured jumps. Only the best jump is kept.	2. Jump scores are ranked from 1 (longest) to 5 (shortest) on each team and listed on a large poster.
	3. Teams compare the jump rankings, 1 to 1, 2 to 2, 3 to 3, and so on.	
	4. Teams have 10 more minutes to practice.	4. Teacher observes for social interaction and group process.

(continued)

Continued

Framing the Task	Task Structure and Sequence	Assessment
	5. All students make two more jumps, keeping the best jump. All students ranked "1" (from the first assessment) are compared with others of the same ranking. Same for "2s", "3s", etc.	**5.** Assess for: **a.** Team point totals **b.** Individual improvement **c.** Team improvement on total score
	5th place = 1 team point 4th place = 2 team points 3rd place = 3 team points 2nd place = 4 team points 1st place = 5 team points	
	The team with the highest number of points wins the TGT.	
Review and Processing	Teacher has recorded and shares instances of good teamwork and peer teaching.	
	Teacher interacts with teams that were not successful, getting them to reflect on the social learning process and skills.	
	Teacher queries the class on what key elements they needed for each event. How did they teach these to each other?	

SUGGESTED READINGS

Grineski, S. (1996). *Cooperative learning in physical education.* Champaign, IL: Human Kinetics.

Johnson, D. W., Johnson, R. T., & Holubec, E. J. (1994). *The new circles of learning: Cooperation in the classroom and school.* Alexandria, VA: Association for Supervision and Curriculum Development.

Slavin, R. E. (1988). *Student team learning: An overview and practical guide* (2nd ed.). Washington, DC: National Education Association.

Slavin, R. E. (1995). *Cooperative learning: Theory, research, and practice* (2nd ed.). Boston: Allyn and Bacon.

CHAPTER

10 The Sport Education Model

Learning to Become Competent, Literate, and Enthusiastic Sportspersons

The teaching and learning of many forms of institutionalized sport have been central parts of U.S. physical education for over one hundred years. Many of the earliest school programs started on a sport foundation, stemming from the huge popularity of sport in American culture, from both the participant and spectator's perspective. The traditional benefits from participation in sport (skill, strategy, cooperation, and healthy competition) were often used as the curricular objectives for teaching sport at all grade levels. The United

States loved sporting activity, in all of its many new forms, so our schools were quick to use that as a primary vehicle for achieving three key goals of the 1918 Seven Cardinal Principles of Education (worthy use of leisure time, health and safety, and ethical character) (Van Dalen & Bennett, 1971). That vehicle and these goals remained the cornerstones of U.S. physical education for more than fifty years afterward.

It is clear that the place of sport in the physical education curriculum is being reduced at the same time sport participation is still showing steady growth in our society. The growth among population groups that had typically been denied access to sport participation (girls, women, people with disabilities, and older adults) is nothing short of phenomenal today. Concurrent with that expansion is the growth of familiar sport organizations (such as youth sports, interscholastic sports, community leagues) and structures (such as private clubs, community recreation centers, and instruction-for-pay) that provide participation opportunities for anyone who wishes to do so and can afford the costs. It is still clear that Americans love to participate in sport; it is also clear that they less often turn to physical education programs to get a positive sport experience. That is a sad reality for the many physical educators who grew up and started their careers in the sport model. However, there is a curriculum and instruction model that is designed to provide students of nearly all ages with positive, educational, and lasting sport experience as part of the school physical education program. Sport Education, developed by Daryl Siedentop (1998), is ". . . designed to provide authentic, educationally rich, sport experiences for girls and boys in the context of school physical education" (p. 18). According to Siedentop, the Sport Education model has strong implications for curriculum and instruction, so it represents a dual-functioning model. The most salient curricular implication is that sport becomes the organizing center for the physical education program: everything that is taught and learned is accomplished in the context of developmentally appropriate forms of sport. As an instructional model, "its purposes are best achieved through combinations of direct instruction, cooperative small-group work, and peer teaching . . ." (Siedentop, 1998, p. 18), designed within a comprehensive approach to the teaching and learning of sport.

You should be alerted that the model to be presented in this chapter is not used to teach *sports, per se* (such as flag football, basketball, soccer, and tennis), although students will certainly learn much about each sport form offered within this model. Rather, it is designed to teach the concept and conduct of *sport,* a much broader set of goals that includes: team affiliation, fairness, etiquette, traditions, appreciation, strategy, values, structure, and of course the inherent movement patterns that are part of every sport form included in the physical education program. These lofty goals separate Sport Education from simply *learning to play* flag football, basketball, soccer, tennis, etc. These goals, and the processes that teachers use to accomplish them within the model, give Sport Education a unique look as it is carried out in physical education, allowing students to learn about sport from many perspectives through authentic participation.

Overview

The basic structure of Sport Education is adapted from the familiar model of organized sport leagues, with one major exception. Think for a moment about what you would need if you were starting a competitive sport league. What roles and jobs need to be carried out? You would need: players, coaches, officials/referees, score keepers, trainers, administrators, and support staff (managers, groundskeepers, etc.). You would also need: practice time, a schedule (with playoffs), league rules, equipment, and facilities. All of these features, and others, provide the structure that allows students to experience and learn from their participation in sport.

Now, here is the exception within the Sport Education model. In the structure just described, children and youth most often learn sport from only one perspective—that of player. They rarely get to have a broader sport experience from which they can learn the many other facets of sport in order to reach a fuller understanding and greater appreciation for the entire scope of our sport culture. In addition, their experience is very directive—the coach makes nearly all of the decisions and the players are expected to comply with the coach's directions. In Sport Education, all students are players, but they also learn (not just "take on") one or more of the other roles needed to make the league operate. Their experience base is broadened as they learn the skills, decisions, customs, and responsibilities that go with these roles in the league structure. For example, a student does not just "call balls and strikes" in a game to fill that need for the moment. Rather, she *becomes an umpire* in the fullest sense of that term, by learning all of the things needed to do that job well for an entire league season.

Students in the Sport Education model take active roles in making decisions that determine the structure and operation of the league—they are not passive participants. For instance, students who become part of the "league council" are given autonomy in deciding things like rules modifications, team selection procedures, scheduling, and conflict resolution. Students who become coaches are responsible for team selection, position assignments, practice planning, and game strategy. Students who are on the support staff make sure that the playing area is set up properly and that the needed equipment and gear is ready. In effect, students are not just in a league for a season. They *become the league* in many ways that can provide a deeper, broader, and positive educational sport experience.

Siedentop (1994) cites three major goals for the Sport Education model: to develop competent, literate, and enthusiastic sportspersons (p. 4).

1. A competent sportsperson has sufficient skills to participate in games satisfactorily, understands and can execute strategies appropriate to the complexity of play, and is a knowledgeable games player.
2. A literate sportsperson understands and values the rules, rituals, and traditions of sports and distinguishes between good and bad sports practices, whether in children's or professional sport. A literate sportsperson is both a more able participant and a more discerning consumer, whether fan or spectator.
3. An enthusiastic sportsperson participates and behaves in ways that preserve, protect, and enhance the sport culture, whether it is a local youth sport culture or a national sport culture. As members of sporting groups, such enthusiasts participate in further developing sport at the local, national, or international levels. The enthusiastic sportsperson is involved.

Siedentop (1994) cites ten specific learning objectives for the Sport Education model (pp. 4–5):

1. Develop skill and fitness specific to particular sports
2. Appreciate and be able to execute strategic plays in sports
3. Participate at a level appropriate to students' development
4. Share in the planning and administration of sport experiences
5. Provide responsible leadership
6. Work effectively within a group toward common goals
7. Appreciate the rituals and conventions that give particular sports their unique meanings
8. Develop the capacity to make reasoned decisions about sport issues
9. Develop and apply knowledge about umpiring, refereeing, and training
10. Decide voluntarily to become involved in after-school sport

As you can see, the Sport Education model attempts to educate students in all aspects of the sport culture by providing them with more than one active role (player plus "duty role/s"). Once students have had positive sport experiences in physical education, it is hoped that they will extend their participation and involvement beyond the physical education program.

Sport Education has six key features that give it a unique identity (Siedentop, 1994). As you will see, each of these features is an adaptation of a characteristic of organized sport.

1. *Seasons.* Sport Education uses seasons rather than the more traditional content units of physical education. A season implies a longer time period that includes a practice period, a preseason, a regular season, and a postseason with a culminating event. Sport Education seasons should be a minimum of twenty lessons when possible (Grant, 1992).

2. *Affiliation.* Students remain members of the same team for the entire season. This extended affiliation promotes many of the affective and social development objectives within the model by allowing team members the opportunity to work toward common goals, make group decisions, experience success and failure as a group, and fashion a group identity for itself.

3. *Formal competition.* Students make many of the decisions that determine the structure and operation of the season. They can modify game rules to promote fairness and better participation. A formal schedule of competition allows each team and its players to make short-term and long-term decisions for the season. The competition schedule provides teams and players with an ongoing focal point for their practices and preparation.

4. *Culminating event.* The season ends with a culminating event that could take many forms: a round-robin tournament, a team competition, or individual competition. This event should be festive and allow all students to participate in some capacity (except only as spectators).

5. *Record keeping.* Games provide lots of opportunities to make records of performances that can be used to teach strategy, increase interest within and among teams, pub-

licize results, and assess student learning. Records can be simple or complex, depending on the ability of students to keep and comprehend them. By making the records public, they help to provide a backdrop for the competition schedule, such as when the top defensive team is getting ready to play the top offensive team. Game statistics can be used by coaches and players to analyze their own team strengths and those of their opponents.

6. *Festivity.* Sporting events are known for being festive. Teams have names that become part of their tradition and add to the lore of the sport. Playing venues are colorful and often decorated with signs and banners. While at a somewhat smaller scale, so as not to detract from the event itself, Sport Education teachers try to make their seasons and competitions as festive and celebratory as possible.

Sport Education makes a direct effort to reduce and eliminate some of the negative characteristics that have become associated with sport in our society:

1. Competition is used as a means of getting students to develop their skill, knowledge, and strategy. It is an educational tool, not an end in itself.
2. Everyone participates as a player and in an assigned role. It is not exclusionary in any way like many sport experiences that allow only the best players an opportunity to participate.
3. Students are given an active, not passive, role in determining the context and structure. They learn to make decisions that are normally given to adults in sport settings.
4. Students can decide to design and play developmentally appropriate versions of sport—not necessarily the adult versions often imposed on them.
5. Because it occurs in an educational setting, the teacher has the ultimate responsibility of keeping the goals and conduct of Sport Education in line with the school and program's most important mission—teaching children. There should be no mixed messages and misplaced priorities like those that can occur in interscholastic and youth sport leagues.

The Sport Education model relies heavily on cooperative learning strategies in which teams (coaches and players together) are given much of the responsibility to get prepared for the season. The teacher and the league council (made up of students) decide the basic structure for the season, and how teams will be determined. Once in teams, students work cooperatively to determine their needs for the season, how their team will be organized, and how they will prepare for the season. They work out practice schedules, position assignments, substitution plans, and game strategy. Even though one student is designated as "coach," his role is to coordinate the team's efforts, not *run* the team. Much of the teaching on a team comes in the form of peer teaching, as teammates help each other learn the skills and strategies needed for the team's success. The amount of cooperative learning responsibility and peer teaching given to students will depend on their developmental readiness for their nonplaying roles. As you will see in the example of Sport Education at the end of this chapter, sport education can be modified for students as young as fourth grade and still maintain many of the model's key features.

Foundations of Sport Education
for Physical Education

Theory and Rationale

The underpinnings of Sport Education can be found in some of Daryl Siedentop's earlier writings on philosophical issues in the field of physical education. *Physical Education: Teaching and Curriculum Strategies for Grades 5–12* (Siedentop, Mand, & Taggart, 1986) contains references and a rationale for what would eventually become this curriculum and instruction model a few years later. Siedentop recognizes sport as a form of play, which is given a special place in societies that span both history and the globe. Because play is such a fundamental human endeavor, it is essential that societies pass down (through teaching) that activity from one generation to the next. Other forms of play include music, art, and drama, which share many of the same core characteristics as sporting activities in our culture.

The rationale for Sport Education is quite simple and direct. If sport, as an accepted form of play, is a valued part of any society, it is the society's responsibility (and in its best interest) to find ways to formalize the process of how people come to learn and participate in the sport culture. Quite simply, we must teach each new generation our sport culture, and one of the best places to do that is within the school curriculum. Certainly, children and youth can and do learn the sport culture in many other ways and places (youth sport, church leagues, private tutoring, playgrounds, and at home), but the best place to provide a broad-based, educational, and egalitarian sport experience is through our schooling system. Therefore, Sport Education is designed as a way to pass down our sport culture in a way that features sport's most positive characteristics.

Assumptions about Teaching and Learning

Assumptions about Teaching

1. The teacher needs to use a combination of strategies to facilitate the varied learning goals in the Sport Education model. These strategies include direct instruction, cooperative learning, peer, and small-group teaching.
2. The teacher should serve primarily as the major resource person in Sport Education seasons, rather than be in direct control of every learning activity.
3. The teacher should guide students to make decisions that reflect the inherent values, traditions, and conduct of sporting activities.
4. The teacher should plan for and facilitate students' opportunities to take on and learn the responsibilities within nonplaying roles in a Sport Education season.

Assumptions about Learning

1. With proper guidance and facilitation, students can take on many decision-making and other responsibilities in the Sport Education season. Opportunities for student learning will occur as they engage in the processes of making and carrying out these decisions.
2. Students can work cooperatively within the team structure to set and reach group goals.

3. Active, rather than passive, participation is the preferred way to learn sport.
4. Students can determine developmentally appropriate forms of sport for themselves, but sometimes need the teacher's guidance to do so.
5. The Sport Education structure provides a truly authentic sporting experience that can generalize to participation in other settings.

Major Theme for Sport Education: Learning to Become Competent, Literate, and Enthusiastic Sportspersons

The designer of the Sport Education model, Daryl Siedentop, succinctly states he intends for the model to promote the development of competent, literate, and enthusiastic sportspersons (Siedentop, 1994, p. 4). He goes on to say that the model should teach students of all ages to become *players* in the fullest sense of the word. A player is someone who comes to know sport from a variety of perspectives, makes sport participation a central part of his/her life, and who derives deep personal meaning from sporting activity. Think of something that you are really enthusiastic about in your own life. Perhaps you have a hobby, can play music, have a favorite sport, or have come to know something "inside out." More than likely you reached that point through an initial interest that allowed you to become knowledgeable and proficient. Eventually the activity became a very important part of your life. That level of meaning is what Sport Education strives to instill in physical education students, and is reflected as the major theme for the model. Students will not simply *play a game*—they will learn the sporting traditions embedded in the game and the structure of the sport itself until they reach the point of being competent, literate, and enthusiastic sportspersons.

Learning Domain Priorities and Interactions

Sport Education strives for student learning outcomes that cut across all three major learning domains. Although from time to time learning in one domain will be the primary objective, there will be a balance across all three domains as the Sport Education season goes from beginning to end. The three-part theme of the model makes that point clearly; competence refers to the ability to discern and execute skilled strategic moves (psychomotor, with strong cognitive support), being literate refers to one's ability to comprehend and appreciate a sport form and culture (cognitive), enthusiastic refers to making sport a central part of one's life and daily activity (affective). All of these domains must be addressed by the teacher when planning a Sport Education unit (called a "season") so that ample learning opportunities are provided for each area of students' development. Because students will have many different types of learning activities, with shifting domain priorities for each one, it is not appropriate to make a firm list of domain priorities, as was done with other models. Rather, it is more helpful for teachers to understand what types of learning are fostered in each part of the Sport Education model and to make sure that students get a balance of domain emphases across the season. The following table shows how domain priorities can shift across various times in a Sport Education season.

Learning Activity	Temporary Domain Priority
Making organizational decisions	1. Cognitive 2. Affective
Preseason practice (as player)	1. Psychomotor 2. Cognitive 3. Affective
Preseason practice (as coach)	1. Cognitive 2. Affective 3. Psychomotor
Learning duty roles (umpire, scorekeeper, trainer, etc.)	1. Cognitive 2. Affective 3. Psychomotor
Working as a member of a team	1. Affective 2. Cognitive 3. Psychomotor
During competitive games (as a player)	1. Psychomotor 2. Cognitive 3. Affective
During competitive games (as a coach)	1. Cognitive (strategy and tactics) 2. Affective (team leadership) 3. Psychomotor

Determining *domain interactions* within the Sport Education model is even more complicated due to the many unexpected events and "learning moments" that can occur during a sport season. For instance, as a team of students is working cooperatively to prepare for the competitive part of the season, they will need to address all of the complex dynamics that come into getting ready: skill development, team cohesion, analysis of team strengths and weaknesses, position assignments, and assumption of leadership roles. The development of skills might need to be supported by the analysis of player abilities; the development of team cohesion might be fostered by negotiating clear role definitions and position assignments. And, because the teacher takes on a less-direct role once the teams are in the preparation stage, it is difficult for the teacher to always recognize and change domain interactions for all teams in class.

Even though the teacher takes on a less-direct role in Sport Education, he must still remain a keen observer of the many complex events that will occur during the season—and recognize when domain interactions are not contributing to the students' development at the moment. When recognized, the teacher can suggest that students need to be looking at the bigger picture, and that the team's success is more likely if they learn to approach sport from multiple perspectives.

Student Learning Preferences

Using the Reichmann and Grasha (1974) profile for student learning preferences, the Sport Education model will most often work best for those students who are classified as participant, collaborative (on their team)/competitive (toward other teams), and independent. Although at first glance it appears a bit contradictory, students do need to be cooperative and competitive in the Sport Education model. They must recognize times when the team must work cooperatively to achieve its goals, one of which is to compete well against opponents. The Sport Education model also provides opportunities for students to learn to be cooperative and competitive at the appropriate times and in appropriate ways.

Validation

Research Validation. Because of its reliance on three different teaching models (Cooperative Learning, Direct Instruction, and Peer Teaching), the Sport Education model can draw general validation from the research base on each of those models. In addition, there has been a growing body of research that has been generated directly from the Sport Education model itself. This line of research has begun to provide descriptions of the model's effectiveness across many grade levels, sport content, and geographical locations.

Carlson and Hastie (1997) examined the student social system within Sport Education seasons in an Australian high school. The social system pertains to how students interact with the teacher and their classmates as they pursue planned learning tasks in class. Carlson and Hastie found that students were favorable toward the Sport Education model, especially those aspects that allowed them more responsibility and interactions with their peers (as teammates). Most students reported that they liked the added dimension of being teachers (as coaches) and having to learn their duty job roles. In a follow-up study of a middle school speedball season, Hastie (1998) reported three major findings in support of student perception of Sport Education: (1) students prefer the activity of the duty job roles over the passivity of having to wait on the sidelines to play again, (2) students valued the opportunities for social development promoted by continuing team membership, and (3) students expressed a preference for getting their instruction from peer teachers (as coaches and teammates) over the typical teacher-directed instruction.

At this stage, there has been little research on the effectiveness of Sport Education related to student achievement and performance. One of the few studies was completed by Hastie (1998), in which he monitored the efficiency of play early and late in an Ultimate Frisbee season. Efficiency is determined by monitoring key playing skills that have positive and negative results (caught passes, dropped passes, etc.), and can be used as a measure of playing performance. In this small-scale study of just one team, two-thirds of the players, and the team as a whole, showed significant improvement in their efficiency indexes in the latter part of the season. Although quite promising, this study provides only a small, preliminary picture of the effectiveness of Sport Education in skill and tactical development.

Craft Knowledge Validation.   Developmentally appropriate versions of the Sport Education model are now becoming more commonplace in physical education programs—attesting to the model's effectiveness in promoting its major goals in many situations. In the authoritative text on the model, Siedentop (1994) provides field-tested examples at elementary grades (soccer, gymnastics, basketball, volleyball, and track and field), middle schools (volleyball), and high schools (fitness, rugby, and tennis). In other adaptations, Hicks (1998) used sport education for a fourth-grade Ultimate Frisbee season, and Watts (1998) designed a Sport Education unit for sixth-grade pickleball. Bennett and Hastie (1997) used the model within a collegiate physical activity course. In my own college teaching, I have implemented Sport Education units in volleyball, softball, and three-on-three basketball.

Sport Education has also been implemented at broader levels. Dugas (1994) described a Sport Education curricular track at the Louisiana School for Math and Sciences that included over twenty different units across four distinct seasons. Many schools in Australia and New Zealand have adopted the Sport Education model as well. Grant (1994) reports that twenty-one schools in New Zealand began to use the model on a trial basis. The trial was so successful that over 150 schools had adopted the model for their entire programs by 1994. Similar growth was reported in Western Australia by Alexander, Taggart, and Luckman (1998), starting with fifty-three teachers and growing to over one hundred teachers one year later. It should be mentioned that both the New Zealand and Australia thrust in Sport Education was endorsed and supported in part by their respective regional education agencies, allowing faster and more effective dissemination of the model along with some funding for the necessary staff development.

The list of teachers, schools, and entire school districts that have now used the Sport Education model continues to grow at an impressive rate. Surely part of that growth is attributable to demonstrable student learning observed by teachers who use Sport Education. Some evidence to that effect has been provided by published anecdotal records of teachers who have used the model. Alexander, Taggart, and Thorpe (1995), Carlson and Hastie (1997), and Grant (1992) all report strongly positive experiences by Sport Education teachers and their students.

Intuitive Validation.   Sport has been used for over one hundred years as a primary vehicle for reaching many of the major programming goals for physical education. The educational potential of the sporting experience is enormous if it can be structured and implemented at the appropriate developmental level for students, and if the more positive features of sport are properly emphasized and learned. Perhaps this new model of something that physical educators have practiced for a century is so attractive because it allows teachers to get back to their roots and revisit sport as an educational pursuit—without many of the negative practices which have come to pervade other sport settings (i.e., youth sport, interscholastics, and college sports).

Teaching and Learning Features

Directness

Figure 10.1 shows the Directness Profile for the Sport Education model when used in physical education instruction.

1. *Content selection.* Teachers have two options for deciding which sport will be offered in a Sport Education season. One option is direct; that is, the teacher makes the decision and informs students. The second option is to offer students a range of choices and let them select the sport for each season. This option becomes interactive as the teacher advises students about each possible choice while also considering contextual factors.

2. *Managerial control.* The teacher makes most of the initial managerial decisions that give the Sport Education season its overall structure: how teams will be selected, which nonplaying duties will be needed and how students get assigned to them, how long the season will last, how to prepare equipment and facilities, and overall "ground rules" for the season. After these decisions are made and communicated to students, the students assume nearly all control for putting them into operation. Students will plan and carry out many of the day-to-day managerial tasks during the season.

3. *Task presentations.* Most of the task presentations for skill and strategy development will take place in the context of team practice sessions before and during the season. This

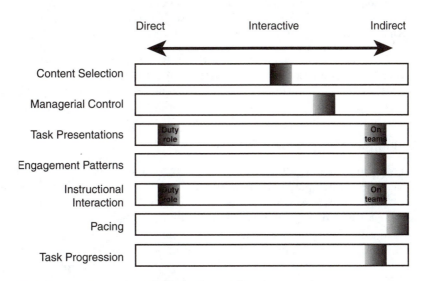

FIGURE 10.1   Directness Profile for Sport Education

will likely take the form of peer teaching and group cooperative learning—conducted by students. Task presentations for duty roles will be carried out by the teacher in the form of miniworkshops for each needed job (training officials, showing managers how to prepare the field, explaining scoring rules to statisticians, etc.). Because most students will have little or no experience in these roles, and time will be short, teacher-directed instruction is the most effective way to teach roles to students at the start.

4. *Engagement patterns.* Like task presentations, students' engagement patterns will differ for their playing and nonplaying roles. As members of a team, students will be engaged in peer and small-group cooperative learning tasks. Each team is given the responsibility of getting itself ready for the season, so members must be able to make group decisions and take a very active role in teaching their teammates. In their nonplaying roles, students will be engaged as active participants as they learn the knowledge, skills, and procedures for each assignment. Initially, they are likely to get direct instruction from the teacher to become familiar with the rudiments of each job. After that, they will get lots of on-the-job learning as they carry out their assigned duties during competitions. Most of that interaction will come with other students in the game context.

5. *Instructional interaction.* Most of the instructional interactions will take place between students as they work on teams in peer- and small-group cooperative learning activities. One or more students on each team will be designated as the captain or co-captains, and will assume many of the teaching functions. The teacher will be available as a resource person, but most of the instruction is conducted with student-to-student interaction.

6. *Pacing.* Team members will decide what is needed to prepare for the competitive season and make up a preseason plan. They can also decide how much time they need for their preparation, giving them total control of pacing before and between games.

7. *Task progression.* Much the same as pacing, teams make decisions about the order for practice tasks as they prepare for the season and between games. The content listing for each team in the class might be somewhat different, depending on the specific abilities of their players.

Predominant Engagement Patterns

According to Siedentop (1994) there are three predominant engagement patterns for learning activities in the Sport Education model: direct instruction, cooperative learning, and peer teaching. *Direct instruction* is most often used by the teacher to train students for duty roles. This can be done in miniworkshops that focus on each assigned role and allow students to gain a beginning knowledge to carry out their assigned responsibilities. Time is usually short for this, so a directed kind of engagement from the teacher to student is quite effective. Once students are trained, they are engaged in authentic role assumption learning before, during, and after each duty time. That is, they learn what needs to be done to get ready a contest, carry out an active role during the contest, and are responsible for any postcontest work that needs to be done. They are not just temporary workers—they actually *become* that role when they are not playing on their team. *Cooperative learning* occurs regularly within each team as players and coaches make and carry out the many decisions needed to help the team reach its goals. This process tends to be very democratic, since there is no central authority figure present at most times. Conflict resolution may be needed from time to time, but that too becomes part of the cooperative learning process. *Peer teaching* is used frequently so that higher-skilled members of a team can help lesser-skilled members improve—thereby facilitating the whole team's achievement. Students quickly recognize that a team is only as strong as its weakest link, so it is in everybody's interest to help lesser-skilled members improve, and the best resource for doing that is other team members.

Inclusiveness

Sport Education is inherently designed for inclusive physical education instruction. Since all students must be players on a team, everyone is automatically included at that level. If the teacher has been careful to make sure that all teams are balanced across skill levels, experience, and gender, then all teams must work equally well to ensure that members can contribute to their full potential, promoting inclusion at the most important level—among students themselves. According to Hastie (1998), three features of Sport Education directly benefit marginalized students: small teams that need everyone's contribution for success, the affiliation with a continuing team that promotes a sense of cohesion and belonging, and regular practice that allows lower-skilled students to improve over the course of the season.

All students do not come to physical education with the same interest and abilities to play the game in season. This can often be a source of student dissatisfaction and isolation that can work against an inclusive environment. However, since all students take on a non-playing role they can negotiate for, they can be active sport participants from a second perspective—and make valuable contributions to the operation of the season. Since all students must take on a duty job, there is no playing of favorites in the assignment of these roles—everyone must do it, which also promotes an inclusive environment in physical education.

Task Presentation and Task Structure

Due to the use of direct, cooperative, and peer teaching strategies, task presentation and task structure in Sport Education will vary. These operations will also vary across grade levels, depending on students' developmental readiness; in lower grades the teacher will likely need to take on a direct role more often than with older students. However, the design of the model supports indirect and cooperative learning activities to the highest degree possible for students in a given class. When in doubt, the teacher should start by giving students a reasonable amount of autonomy and then make adjustments only when that is shown not to be effective.

Task presentation and task structure will be greatly influenced by any modifications made in the game being played, decided by the students and the teacher before the season begins. For instance, a typical modification for soccer is to have reduced-size teams, such as three-person or four-person teams. Flag football can be played with four to six players per team, and three-on-three basketball works very well. These modifications greatly reduce the complexity of the games for students, as well as the time needed to prepare for the season. This translates into fewer learning tasks that students need to master or refine before and during the season.

Task Presentation

Teaching Players. In the full version of the Sport Education model, the teacher arranges for teams to be selected, oversees the organization of the season, and lets each team work cooperatively to determine what learning needs to take place and how it will get achieved. The task presentation function is left up to each team and its leaders to determine and carry out. In some situations it might be necessary for the teacher to plan a short period of direct instruction tasks for the whole class before teams are selected. This ensures that all students have a basic level of proficiency, and it can facilitate the team-selection process. Once teams are selected and working together, the teacher can train one or more students on each team to plan and implement task presentations for other students. This will be the first step in the use of cooperative and peer teaching strategies.

Teaching Duty Roles. The teacher is more likely to take a direct instruction approach to teach students their assigned support duties for the season. There can be several "jobs" to teach, and limited minutes in which to teach small groups of students the skills, knowledge, and responsibilities for each job. The teacher can use a "clinic" strategy in which students are given direct information and modeled task presentations for doing each job correctly. These are basically "how-to" minisessions. Guest speakers can also be used for this same purpose: other teacher/coaches in the school, certified game officials and statisticians, and the school's trainer, for example. Instructional videos and other visual materials can be used for this same purpose.

Task Structure

Teaching Players. The structure of learning tasks in Sport Education will be similar to those used by sport coaches in practices and game preparations. When together as a team, each group of students will essentially be practicing like any other competitive team. The range of task structures could include warm-ups, "chalk talks," drills, conditioning exercises, run-throughs of plays and defenses, scrimmages, and strategy sessions—all designed by the team leaders and implemented with cooperative or peer teaching strategies. Jones and Ward (1998) suggest that the teacher devise the general practice schedule and needed routines and then let students make specific plans within the teacher's time frame.

Teaching Duty Roles. The task structure for teaching students the various duty jobs can also have a familiar look, based on how people come to learn the important support roles in sport. Referees should first know the rules, and can get that information from the teacher, videotapes, CD ROMs, or guest speakers. Taking and passing a rules test should be one criterion for that job. Next, they will need to learn procedures and techniques for refereeing the sport—typically by viewing correct models in a simple-to-complex progression. The student referees can then practice their own techniques under the supervision of the mentor/teacher, perhaps while teams are in scrimmages. Soon the referees will be ready to officiate a full game, which then becomes the task structure for that learning progression—a quite authentic structure at that! Similar task structures and progressions can be planned by the teacher for all duty jobs in the Sport Education season.

Teacher Expertise and Contextual Needs

Teacher Expertise

Sport Education teachers will need to have expertise in many of the knowledge areas discussed in Chapter 2. The teacher's expertise is brought to bear on the delivery of what Knop and Pope (1998) call "educative sport" in physical education—a merging of the competitive sport structure and developmentally appropriate instruction (p. 47).

Learners. Sport Education students must be able to learn three very different roles: player, teammate, and the assigned duty/job. Each role makes different demands on students' psychomotor, cognitive, and affective abilities. The Sport Education teacher must be well aware of how much students will be able to learn in each role and to not let expectations exceed those levels.

Developmentally Appropriate Instruction. Closely related to knowledge about learners is the teacher's ability to promote developmentally appropriate versions of sport for each physical education class. The Sport Education model rarely implies that students must learn "full" or "adult" versions of sport (Siedentop, 1994). Game structures are simplified, rules are modified, record keeping is kept at a level students can follow and get down on paper, the teacher ensures a positive and safe environment, and duty assignments match students' maturation levels—all so that students can learn sport at their current stage of development.

Physical Education (Sport) Content. Even though the teacher takes a more indirect role in Sport Education, his knowledge of the sport form (game) in season is invaluable. The teacher must not only know the sport from a player's perspective, he must also know each of the various duty jobs, the sport's organizational structures, and its customs. Since most of the decisions will be made by students as the season progresses, the teacher must be able to see the big picture and anticipate potentially harmful situations before they occur. All of that comes from knowing the sport well and from many perspectives.

Equity. Sport does not work well when equity issues are not fully addressed and resolved. In fact, if left alone, inequitable sport will become miseducative and counterproductive to its own goals and objectives. The kind of inequities I am referring to are those created when the sport environment allows one group of students more access to full participation than other groups of students. This inequity is based on differences related to gender, ethnicity, and ability. The Sport Education teacher must be able to anticipate, recognize, and adjust inequitable situations so that all students get a similar chance to participate and learn through sport. Equity can be promoted by making rules and policies that give all students a fair chance to participate, such as:

1. All players must play every position (each game or on a set schedule).
2. Team rules are voted upon by all members.
3. All players get to play the same amount of time each game.

Related to the issue of equity is fairness of competition. Once again, the teacher must use her knowledge of students, the game, and democratic process to select fair teams for the season. And, the teacher must be ready to make adjustments when the teams are obviously not balanced for competition. Some suggestions could be:

1. Make provisions that all teams must have the same number of boys and girls on them, according to how many of each gender are in the class.
2. Have students rate their own skill levels, and make provisions that teams will be balanced on that factor, as well as on gender.
3. Allow all students to review the teams before they are finalized and indicate if they think the teams are fair.
4. Allow a limited "trading" procedure shortly after the season begins, allowing each team to change only one player from their current roster. All "trades" must be approved by a majority of members of both involved teams.

Assessment.   Sport Education relies heavily on authentic assessment of students' performance, knowledge, and behaviors. In one sense, Sport Education is entirely authentic because it always provides students with a realistic context (the season) in which they prepare and apply their abilities. Teachers can design systems to monitor players' game play, to be used by the trained statisticians to create records of each player's performance on key aspects. By keeping these records over the course of the season, a clear picture is formed to assess each player's performance. Checklists can be made to assess students' performance of duty jobs—much like a job description. The teacher can observe a student as he is doing his job and check off each completed part. Watts (1998) had students check themselves each day after their jobs were completed, freeing the teacher to do other things as class ended.

The key source of assessment knowledge in Sport Education is the ability to recognize the most important aspects of playing and duty job performance. Once a teacher has these identified, she can then design self-made systems for monitoring performance in the most authentic way—as students apply their own knowledge and skill in the context of the season and competitive events.

Social/Emotional Climate.   If you will recall, one of the key features of Sport Education cited by Siedentop (1994) is that it should be festive. The festive nature of sport should emphasize the positive, allow all students to participate and enjoy, strive for keen and fair competition, and promote the highest standards of good sport behavior. The Sport Education teacher must know how to arrange the social/emotional climate in the sport season to allow these things to happen and to prevent the opposites from occurring.

At times the teacher will find himself being mentor, arbitrator, coach, parent, sport psychologist, and cheerleader—all for the purpose of creating a positive climate in the Sport Education season.

Effective Teaching Skills Applied to Sport Education

With the combination of direct instruction, cooperative learning, and peer teaching, the Sport Education teacher will use a wide range of effective instructional skills in the model. The key point to understand is that each skill will be applied spontaneously in most cases, as the teacher addresses situational needs during the season.

Planning. Most of the planning occurs after the teacher and/or students have decided which game will be played in the Sport Education season. This will lead to an intense period of formal planning for the teacher, followed by a longer period in which plans must be made as the season progresses. The initial planning period will determine the overall structure of the upcoming season and will include many considerations:

1. How long will the season last?
2. What equipment and facilities will be needed?
3. What modifications, if any, will be made in the game?
4. What will be the competitive format?
5. How will teams be selected?
6. What duty jobs will be needed and how will students be selected for them?
7. How will students be trained for duty jobs?
8. If there is to be a "Sport Council," how will it be selected?
9. What is the season's schedule?
10. How will playing and duty job performance be assessed?
11. How will each lesson/practice be structured?
12. What kind of award system will be in place?

Once the overall structure has been determined and teams are preparing for the season, the planning will shift from formal to an as-needed and sometimes unpredictable basis. Jones and Ward (1998) suggest that the teacher plan only an outline for each class and allow teams to make their own preseason and practice structure. The teacher's job is to know what teams will need each day and make sure those resources are provided. Once the competitive schedule begins, the teacher's main planning responsibilities are to organize the duty students (some of whom bring the needed equipment and prepare the space), allocate time for games, and prepare assessment materials. Beyond that, little can be planned for; most of the teacher's decisions and actions will be determined in real time as class events unfold.

Time and Class Management. The teacher needs to provide the overall plan for each class and competitive event, but most of the class management will be left to students once practices and the season begin. The teacher's main responsibility is to ensure that schedules are being met so that the season does not fall behind its original plans.

Determining Developmentally Appropriate Roles.   As mentioned, most of the task presentations and structures will be determined by students as each team prepares for the season. However, the teacher still maintains the responsibility for training students for duty jobs that are essential to the operation of the season. The key thing for the teacher to remember is that students are being trained for roles typically assumed by adults in most sport settings: coaches, managers, trainers, and score keepers. The teacher must be knowledgeable of how much of each role students can learn and the best way to teach it to them. Many times, tasks cannot be presented in "official" or adult versions; they must be presented to students in terms they can understand and relate to. Similarly, most students will not be able to perform the technical aspects of a job like a trained adult, so the teacher will need to show them developmentally acceptable ways to "get the job done."

Communication.   Sport Education teachers need to be effective at both direct and indirect communications to students. Teachers will be more direct when they are explaining the organization of the season and when they are training students for duty job roles. Much of that communication is similar to what is used in direct instruction.

Teachers will also need good indirect communication skills, most often in the form of questions. Once teams are practicing and once students are in duty jobs, it is better to use a problem-solving approach to learning—prompted more by questions than by direct statements or instructions.

Instructional Information.   As mentioned with task presentation and task structure, the operations for providing students with instructional information will differ when learning as players and learning duty job roles. As players, nearly all of the instructional information will come through cooperative learning and peer teaching. Students (as coaches and teammates) will observe each other perform and provide the needed guidance and feedback to promote proficiency. In their duty job roles, most of the instructional information will come from the teacher who is typically both the trainer and supervisor.

Review and Closure.   The review and closure segments serve familiar purposes in Sport Education lessons. In the preseason the teacher can make general comments about how teams are progressing and answer questions from individual students and teams. The teacher can also preview the next day's lesson to allow teams to interact out of class if they wish to. During the competitive part of the season, the review and closure segment is used to summarize the major events and outcomes and to give deserving players and teams public recognition for good play and good sport behaviors. Hicks (1998) used "Good sports checkers" in her fourth-grade Ultimate Frisbee season, and had the monitors make brief reports of positive and negative sport behaviors at the review. When entire teams went the whole lesson with no observations of negative sport behavior, a smiley face was placed on a poster and they were given an extra point in the season's standings. The closure part of the lesson can be time for the assigned duty students to gather up and store the equipment in its proper place, while the rest of the students are dismissed or take a rest break.

Student Developmental Requirements

Sport Education will be effective in a wide range of grade levels if the teacher matches the complexity of the season's organization with students' abilities to assume the responsibilities of nonplaying roles (coaching and duty jobs). With lower grades, the teacher will need to retain more control of the managerial system and many of the instructional interactions. This can be accomplished with more direct instruction that does not place unrealistic demands on students as they learn the sometimes complex roles of coach and duty jobs. As students' maturity levels increase at higher grades, students can take on more responsibility for their own learning, and that of others on their team. They can also assume a larger part of the managerial system in the sport education season.

Because Sport Education is new for so many teachers and their students, there are few guidelines to follow when determining the readiness level of students. In elementary grades, it is best that a teacher experiments with Sport Education in increments by giving students increasing roles in the model—and interacting with students often to get their feedback about the process. Secondary students should not have problems with the implementation of the full Sport Education model, although the teacher will have to acclimate them to this new way of participating in physical education class.

Contextual Needs for Sport Education

To implement Sport Education with an acceptable version of the model, contextual considerations must be made about resources, students, and the competition format. At some point all three become related and must be given an "OK" by the teacher before deciding if Sport Education is an appropriate way to instruct a content unit.

When considering resources, the teacher must be sure that sufficient time (lesson days), equipment, and space is available to allow the model to work properly. Grant (1992) advocates no fewer than twenty lessons be allocated for a sport education season. While this seems excessive when compared to the current length of most physical education units, this model relies heavily on the cumulative benefits derived from extended practice, many scheduled competitions, and longer affiliation on teams. Teachers will need enough equipment and space to allow all teams to practice at one time and to hold concurrent games when the number of teams warrants that. Demands for these two types of resources can be reduced by using small-sided teams (e.g., three-on-three basketball, four-vs.-four soccer) and modified rules (e.g., 4 inning softball games).

Teacher and Student Roles and Responsibilities in Sport Education

Each instructional model will have certain operations that need to be completed to make the model function to its design. Some of these operations are carried out by the teacher; others are carried out by one or more students. The following table shows the major operations within the Sport Education model, and indicates who is responsible for completing them during each lesson.

Operation or Responsibility	Who Does It in Sport Education?
Deciding the sport for each season	The **teacher** can decide or give **students** a list of choices they can select from.
Organizing the season	The **teacher** provides the basic structure and then lets **students** determine specific rules and procedures. Typically, students elect a "Sport Council" that makes many of the rules for the season.
Selecting captains and teams	The **teacher** establishes some ground rules and lets students (or the Sport Council) determine procedures.
Determination of rules and game modifications	**Students** (the Sport Council) can make suggestions for the teacher to approve.
Organize and conduct team practices	**Student coaches/captains.** The teacher can be used as a resource for this.
Prepare teams for competitions and coach them during games	**Student coaches/captains.** The teacher can be used as a resource for this.
Train students for duty jobs	The **teacher** serves as the key resource. Outside personnel (e.g., certified officials) can also be used.
Bring equipment, prepare the playing area, return equipment	**Student** managers.
Officiate games	**Student** referees.
Keep score and maintain season records	**Student** statisticians.
Assessment of learning	1. **Student** coaches/captains evaluate their players. 2. **Student** statisticians can analyze players' performance with game stats.

Teaching and Learning Benchmarks for Sport Education

Since Sport Education uses a combination of direct instruction, cooperative learning, and peer teaching, it can be difficult at times to determine just what the teacher and/or students should be doing to implement the model according to its design. However, the benchmarks shown on the following tables can be used within the general framework to help Sport Education teachers know if they are staying within the parameters of the model.

Teacher Benchmarks

Benchmark	How to Verify
Teacher provides the overall structure for the season.	1. Review the teacher's unit (season) plan. 2. Review the teacher's goals and objectives.
Teacher interacts with students to determine specific season structure, rules, and game modifications.	1. Review teacher's unit (season) plans. 2. Interview a small group of students to get their perspective.
Teacher assigns students to duty jobs or allows students to determine them.	1. Review teacher's unit (season) plans. 2. Interview a small group of students to get their perspective.
Teacher supervises the selection of teams for competitive balance.	1. Review teacher's unit (season) plans. 2. Interview a small group of students to get their perspective.
Teacher trains students to perform duty jobs proficiently.	1. Review teacher's unit (season) plans. 2. Teacher writes a "job description" for each duty role. 3. Teacher designs and implements assessments for all jobs.
Teacher promotes cooperative learning when teams are practicing and competing.	Observe the teacher's interactions with students. Are the interactions mostly indirect, with a problem-solving approach?
Teacher arbitrates disputes.	Observe teacher's interactions when disputes arise.
Teacher plans for player performance assessments.	1. Review teacher's unit (season) plans. 2. Teacher designs assessments for key performance objectives; assessments can be implemented by the teacher and/or student coaches.
Teacher promotes enthusiastic participation.	1. Review teacher's unit (season) plans. 2. Teacher maintains a list of plans and ideas for keeping students enthusiastic.

Student Benchmarks

Because students take on the roles of player and a duty job, separate benchmarks are needed to verify each type of participation. The following tables show some useful benchmarks for each role.

Player Benchmarks	How to Verify
Players are competent	1. Performance on teacher-designed assessments of game skills and knowledge. 2. Use the GPAI (Griffin, Mitchell, & Oslin, 1997) to assess game performance.
Players are literate	1. Players can pass a test on rules, history, and game traditions. 2. Players demonstrate nuances of the game (clothing, selection of equipment, etiquette, appreciation of quality performance).
Players understand strategy	1. Teams can plan and implement appropriate strategy and tactics from a cooperative approach. 2. Players can interpret a scouting report. 3. Players can correctly analyze game-summary statistics.
Players are enthusiastic	Observe to monitor events that represent enthusiastic participation (cheering, celebrating, on-field hustling).
Players work cooperatively on their teams	Monitor interactions on teams with event-recording systems.
Players display good sporting behavior	1. Monitor games for examples of positive and negative sporting behavior. 2. Appoint students to duty jobs as "good sports checkers"; they record instances of good sporting behavior and make brief reports at the end of class.

Duty Job Benchmarks	How to Verify
Students can select their own duty jobs (or are informed why not).	Interview students after jobs have been assigned. Do they feel that they were given a chance to get the job they wanted?
Students are knowledgeable.	1. Students receive training in all duty jobs. 2. All students pass a written or oral test on their specific job.
Students can perform the skills of their duty job.	1. Students receive training in all duty jobs. 2. All students pass a practical/performance test on their specific job.
Students can carry out duty jobs will little supervision from the teacher.	1. Each duty job has a daily checklist for all responsibilities. 2. Teacher observes and records students as they complete each job (spot checks are OK). 3. Teacher monitors the number and types of questions students have about their jobs as the season progresses.
Students can resolve conflicts during duty jobs (e.g., officiating) independently.	Teacher monitors the number and types of disputes brought to him or the Sport Council.

Assessing Learning in Sport Education

Assessment in Sport Education must include outcomes for students in two key roles during the season: as players and in their duty jobs. Assessment in both must reflect the major goals of the Sport Education model: to be competent, literate, and enthusiastic participants (Siedentop, 1994). In order to properly assess these goals, it will be necessary to use a variety of assessments, most of which should be authentic in nature.

Assessing Players

Learning to be players in sport requires several types of knowledge and abilities: basic skills, knowledge of rules and strategies, game performance and tactics, team membership, and good sporting behavior. Some of these types can be assessed in traditional ways, but most of them will require the teacher to design innovative, authentic assessments to monitor student learning:

1. *Basic skills* can be assessed with simple checklists implemented by student coaches and teammates. One player can perform the skill while the other observes for key performance cues completed to a stated level of proficiency.

2. *Knowledge of rules and strategies* can be assessed with short written tests or quizzes that cover the main body of rules to be used in the season. It is important that the rules being assessed match the way in which the rules will apply to the competition. It makes little sense to assess students on the official game rules when modified rules and competitions will be used in the season.

3. *Game performance and tactics* can be assessed in a few ways, but it is important that the assessments take place during actual games. Game statistics taken by the duty job score keepers can be used as one type of assessment when they accurately reflect the performance requirements of each player's position. Checklists can be made for each player (by position) that represent good performance, and other duty job score keepers can observe for them as the game progresses. A version of the Game Performance Assessment Instrument (Griffin, Mitchell, & Oslin, 1997) can be devised for the game being played, and duty job students trained to use it. The GPAI is a checklist system that monitors a player's positioning, execution, decisions, and involvement to determine an overall "Game Performance Index." Since it is used only during games, it is a highly authentic assessment technique.

4. *Team membership* can be assessed by observing interactions between players and the student coach throughout the season. A checklist of behaviors that reflect positive participation on the team can be devised, with team members filling it out on themselves and each other periodically. The teacher can review these reports in order to avoid potential problems and reinforce good team membership contributions.

5. *Good sporting behavior* can be assessed in at least three ways. A list of good sporting behaviors can be compiled for the particular sport by the teacher and the students before the season begins. Teams can complete the checklist during the preseason in much the same way as the team membership checklist—on themselves and fellow team members.

Teams can complete the checklist on other teams at the end of games during the season. Hicks (1998) trained students in the duty job role of "good sport checkers" during games. The good sport checkers watched from the sideline and recorded each instance of positive sporting behavior they saw or heard from either team. They would record things like, "The Bulldogs walked over right after the game to shake hands with the Eagles," "Jimmy (Hawks) helped Paul (Yellowjackets) up when he fell during the game," or "Melissa told Craig (team-mates), 'good job, keep trying' when he missed his first three shots." The recorders would then make brief reports after all of the games were completed for that class.

Assessing Learning in Duty Job Roles

Students trained to do duty jobs must show adequate knowledge of their job, how to execute the necessary procedures, and most importantly, how to fulfill the decision-making responsibilities during actual competition. Each kind of knowledge will call for a different assessment technique.

Job Knowledge.   Job knowledge must be assessed before the season begins to ensure that students have the rudimentary knowledge for each assigned job. Officials must know the rules and how to conduct a competition, score keepers must know the definitions of key performance statistics, managers must know how the playing area should be prepared (lined, measured, cleaned), what equipment is needed for a game, and how to check that the equipment is functioning properly. The student coaches must have the broadest scope of knowledge: how to evaluate players' abilities, how to assign positions, how to conduct practices, and how to devise game strategies. All of these areas of knowledge can be assessed with written and/or oral tests before the season begins. If students do not possess this fundamental knowledge when the season begins, things can get off to an uneven start and take several classes to be cleared up.

Execution of Techniques.   All jobs require students to execute certain techniques that reflect competent performance and make the games operate smoothly. Officials need to know how to signal calls, coaches need to know how to signal time-outs or plays to their team, score keepers need to know when and how to make accurate records, and managers need to know how to use tools and equipment safely and efficiently. This knowledge can be assessed by asking students to demonstrate techniques as the teacher uses a checklist to note key parameters of the task. These techniques can be assessed in static tasks (simply demonstrating for the teacher) and during preseason games that allow the teacher to make corrections right on the spot.

Authentic Assessments during Games.   In the final analysis, it is important that students can carry out their assigned duty jobs during actual games. That represents the most authentic assessment of their knowledge, techniques, and decision making in an assigned role. The teacher can devise a short checklist for each duty job and use it to monitor students' performance during games. It would also be possible to have each student fill out the checklist after each match for a self-assessment.

Selecting and Modifying Sport Education for Physical Education

Sport Education is one of the few instructional models presented in this book that was developed exclusively for physical education programs. Siedentop (1994) and others (Tannehill, 1998) describe many examples of how Sport Education has been implemented at every grade level from middle-elementary to college. It has been shown to be a viable instructional model for a wide variety of sport forms:

1. Individual sports (regulation and modified)
2. Team sports (regulation and modified)
3. Fitness programs
4. Olympic-based festivals

Grade-Level Adaptations.   Sport Education can work in any setting in which the students are able to assume a developmentally appropriate amount of decision making and other responsibilities in order to foster the many outcomes embedded in the model. Adaptations must be based on the students' abilities as players (performers and team members) and their abilities to assume the duty job roles that are critical to the functioning of the sport education season. Sport education will not be effective in reaching its overall goals if the teacher must take a direct role too often. Figure 10.2 shows how to implement the Sport Education model for various grade levels in physical education.

FIGURE 10.2   Grade-Level Adaptations for Sport Education in Physical Education

Grade Levels	Select Sport Education?	Possible Adaptations
Preschool	No	
Early elementary (1–3)	No	
Upper elementary (4–5)	Yes	1. Teacher decides much of the season's structure. 2. Modification of game rules and procedures (shorter games, small-sided games). 3. Teacher supervises team selections and the decisions of the Sport Council. 4. Student duty jobs are simple to learn and carry out. 5. Teacher organizes team or whole-class practice sessions each lesson.
Middle school/junior high	Yes	1. Modification of game rules and procedures. 2. Teacher monitors decisions of the Sport Council.
High school	Yes	None needed
College/adult	Yes	None needed

Summary

The effectiveness of the Sport Education model can be a "moving target" as it requires the teacher to make many on-the-spot decisions that cannot often be anticipated—much like sport competition itself. It is a complex balancing act with the teacher facilitating student responsibility and learning without inadvertently allowing some of the miseducative aspects of sport to emerge during the season. The teacher can guide and monitor the structure of the season, but much of the Sport Education process happens in the minute-to-minute interactions between team members and opponents, leaving the teacher to make an instant judgment as to whether those interactions promote or inhibit the development of competent, literate, and enthusiastic participation. Knop and Pope (1998) summarize it well:

> A complete sport education program should teach students how to compete, how to win and lose, how to understand the sport culture, how to prepare for participation, and how to analyze sport in a variety of settings . . . For this to occur, all students need to have opportunities presented in a safe, controlled environment. The responsibility for selecting, planning, sequencing, and delivering this kind of [instruction] falls on the teachers' shoulders. At the same time, teachers must build student accountability into the plan and determine how to reward student involvement in their own learning (p. 48).

Despite some of the criticisms directed at competitive sport at all levels, the educational potential of positive sport experience remains powerful. There are few human endeavors that can promote the variety of learning and developmental activities inherent to sport. The Sport Education model should be viewed as a means to take back the most positive attributes of our sport culture in order to teach them to the next generation of sport participants—children and youth.

A Sample Sport Education Unit (Season)

The following example of a sport education unit was developed by Donna Wright, physical education teacher at Hickory Flat Elementary School in McDonough, GA, and used with her gracious permission. As you will see, the students in this example are fourth graders, at about the lowest grade that I would recommend for selection of the Sport Education model. And, as you will see, Wright made several developmentally appropriate adaptations in her season that would not have been necessary with older students. I chose this example because Donna was able to make these adaptations and retain enough features to keep it recognizable as Sport Education, and more importantly, to promote the varied kinds of learning outcomes inherent in the model's design. If the Sport Education model can be faithfully implemented with fourth graders, there is no reason to believe it cannot be equally effective at all higher grade levels in physical education.

Sport season:	Ultimate Frisbee (developmentally appropriate version)
Students:	22 4th graders, 11 girls and 11 boys
Location:	Medium-sized gym, carpeted floor
Class periods:	15

Length of periods:	30 minutes of instruction	
Equipment:	Frisbees	
	Pinnies (4 different colors)	
	Small cones to mark boundaries	
	Whistles for referees	
	Posterboard and markers	

Season's plan

Lesson #	Focus	Learning Activities
1	Introduction to sport education Introduction to Ultimate Frisbee	1. Explanation of unit format: Jobs Practice Assessments Sportsmanship board Objectives 2. Overview of the unit plan 3. Introduction to disk throwing skills 4. Captain and team selection (see note 1)
2	Throwing skills	1. Review throwing cues (see note 2) 2. Throwing drills 3. Partner-assessment of throwing skill (see note 3)
3	Throwing for accuracy	1. Review throwing cues, and practice 2. Partner-assessment of throwing accuracy (see note 4)
4	Catching skills	1. Describe catching cues (see note 5) 2. Partner-assessment of catching (see note 6)
5–6	Introduction to rules and strategy	1. Description of common strategies 2. Strategy lead-up drill 3. Introduction to rules and procedures (see note 7)
7	Duty jobs	1. Students select non-playing roles 2. Explain each duty job to students 3. Job-assignment board (see note 8) 4. Forms for duty jobs (see note 9)
8	Scrimmage games	Two ten-minute games are played with all students involved as players and in their duty job roles. Teacher interacts with captions and duty job students to help them.
9–14	Non-elimination tournament (see note 10)	1. 3 teams (two play each game while one is "on duty") 2. Cumulative point scoring for whole tournament (no wins and losses) 3. Extra points can be earned for good sport behavior seen by "checkers"
15	"Season finale"	1. Written test 2. Student questionnaire 3. Awards for all teams

Note 1.   The teacher picked three students to be team captains. The captains met with the teacher and the rest of the class to discuss how teams would be selected. The teacher discussed the overall purposes of the unit and the need to have fair teams with equal numbers of boys and girls on each team. After that the captains selected teams in a private meeting. Once teams were selected, each team had a meeting to choose their colors and a mascot. The team names were the "Bulldogs," "Hurricanes," and "Eagles."

Note 2.   The teacher made a poster that had 5 key cues for throwing the Frisbee disk:

1. Four fingers under the rim, thumb on top
2. Reach across your body (hug yourself with your throwing arm)
3. Outer edge of the disk tilted slightly down
4. Release disk toward your target
5. Follow through by pointing to your target

The teacher gave the class a demonstration of the proper throwing technique, highlighting the cues on the poster. Several copies of the poster were made and hung around the gym as reminders. Students were given time to practice their throwing in their teams, with directions to help each other to improve.

Note 3.   After the practice time was over, members of each team observed their teammates throwing the disk 10 times. A partner-assessment checklist was used to help the observers give their teammates better feedback on their throwing skill.

Thrower's name _____

Cues to watch for	#1	#2	#3	#4	#5	#6	#7	#8	#9	#10
Four fingers under the rim-thumb on top										
Reach across your body										
Tilt the outer edge										
Release disk toward target										
Point to target on follow through										

Note 4.   Six stations were set up around the gym. Each station had a different distance and a different sized target for students to throw the disk through. Students rotated through the stations as teams, helping each other improve accuracy. Teammates observed each other and recorded accuracy on the sheet shown next.

Check Sheet for Target Throwing Accuracy

Thrower's Name _____

Place an "X" for each "hit"

	Throw #1	Throw #2	Throw #3
Station 1			
Station 2			
Station 3			
Station 4			
Station 5			
Station 6			

Note 5. The teacher made a poster that had 3 key cues for catching the Frisbee disk:

1. Keep your eye on the Frisbee
2. Reach your arms toward the Frisbee
3. "Give" with the Frisbee as it hits your hands (bring it into your body)

The teacher gave the class a demonstration of the proper catching technique, highlighting the cues on the poster. Several copies of the poster were made and hung around the gym as reminders. Students were given time to practice catching in their teams, with directions to help each other to improve.

Note 6. After the practice time was over, members of each team observed their teammates catching the disk seven times. A partner-assessment checklist was used to help the observers give their teammates better feedback on catching skill.

Check Sheet for Successful Catching

Catcher's Name _____

Place an "x" for each successful catch (if you think it was a bad throw, mark nothing and do it over)

THROW 1 _____

THROW 2 _____

THROW 3 _____

THROW 4 _____

THROW 5 _____

THROW 6 _____

THROW 7 _____

Note 7. The teacher introduces basic rules for ultimate Frisbee, along with the modifications to be made for her 4th grade students. The most important rules are written on a poster, and several copies are hung around the gym to remind students.

Ultimate Frisbee Rules for Hickory Flat School

1. Only one person can touch the Frisbee at a time
2. No more than two steps allowed after a running catch
3. No guarding the thrower
4. If the Frisbee hits the floor or goes out of bounds, possession goes to the team that did not throw the Frisbee
5. All games continue for the specified time limit (set each day, depending on available time once a class arrives to the gym)

Note 8. The teacher described the duty jobs to the class and explained the specific responsibilities for them. Captains had already been selected at this time. Each team was responsible for supplying a full complement of duty students when it was not playing. Each team decided among themselves who would assume each duty role. Brief job descriptions were written on a poster, which was hung near the place in the gym where the teacher organized the day's games.

Job Descriptions for Non-Playing Duties

Captain:	Help make fair decisions and report to Ms. Wright. Captain is also responsible for turning in all paperwork for his/her team.
Co-Captain:	Takes the place of the Captain when the Captain is absent.
Scorekeeper:	Keeps score of all points made by each team, and operates the flip-card scoreboard.
Referee:	In charge of enforcing all rules and procedures for starting and playing games.
Good Sport Checkers:	Uses a recording sheet to make notes of instances of observed good and bad sport behavior.
Statistician:	Records all completed passes (who threw it and who caught it). Also records points scored.
Retrievers:	Stand on the sideline to retrieve Frisbees that go out of bounds.

Note 9. Forms Used for Duty Jobs. A "Job Assignment" sheet is filled out by each duty team, to remind students of who is doing each job during an upcoming game.

GAME: Bulldogs vs. Eagles

Scorekeeper   _____

Referee   _____

Good Sport Checker   _____

Statistician for Bulldogs   _____

Statistician for Eagles   _____

Retriever   _____

Retriever   _____

Statistician's Sheet

GAME: Bulldogs vs. Eagles (Circle the team you are recording for)

Statistician's Name _____

Place an "x" for each successful throw and catch by each player

Player	Catches	Throws

Good Sports Checker Sheet

Recorder's Name _____

Make a note on any bad sports behaviors you see or hear.

Team:

Team:

Make a note on any good sports behavior you see or hear:

Team:

Team:

Note 10.

1. The class had three teams. Two teams would play each game and the third team carried out the duty roles. Games lasted 8–12 minutes, depending on available time.
2. The teacher started each tournament day by updating the points accumulated by each team, and reminding students of how to do each duty job.
3. Once the teacher gave the "OK," the playing teams warmed up while the duty team prepared for the game (got the equipment, placed the cones on the field, distributed pinnies to teams, and obtained their needed duty role sheets).
4. Teams got points for each touchdown scored, and also for each instance of good sport behavior recorded by the "checkers."
5. The referees were given complete authority in making calls during a game. The teacher did not overturn any calls, but did give corrective feedback privately to referees when mistakes were made.
6. At the end of each lesson, the teacher brought all of the teams together for a "Post-Game Report" which included
   a. Statisticians, reports
   b. Reports by Good Sports Checkers with points added to each team's cumulative total
   c. Overall comments by the teacher on the quality of play (group feedback)
   d. Preview of the games for the next class

SUGGESTED READINGS

Siedentop, D. (1994). *Sport education: Quality PE through positive sport experience.* Champaign, IL: Human Kinetics.

Tannehill, D. (Ed.). (1998). Sport education. Two-part feature presented in the *Journal of Physical Education, Recreation & Dance,* May (Vol. 69, No. 4) and June (Vol. 69, No. 5).

CHAPTER

11

Peer Teaching Model

I Teach You, You Teach Me

Think back to when you were a child, trying to learn all of the many things children learn outside of the formal schooling process. Besides your parents, who were your most frequent teachers? Most likely they were your friends, playmates, and siblings who first taught you many of the basic social, communication, cognitive, and psychomotor skills that you took into and through your early years in school. If you were like me, you learned how to play sports, ride a bicycle, jump rope, sing songs, and play games like hopscotch by being told how and shown by your siblings and friends. It is rare for adults to be around while children play during the day in their neighborhood, so children rely on each other to teach them how to do the many things they learn as they grow up. Even in the formal school process, you probably still learned much from your fellow students, although most of your academic teaching was carried out by your teachers. We have long recognized that children can teach other children, and that in some ways peer teachers can be as or more effective than adult teachers. Wagner (1990) presents a history of peer teaching that begins as early as the classical Greek period with Aristotle and extends uninterrupted into modern educational settings. Peer teaching takes many forms and is conducted under a variety of labels, but its most fundamental feature is clear: to structure a learning environment in which some students assume and carry out many of the key operations of instruction to assist other students in the learning process.

Like direct instruction (Chapter 7), the Peer Teaching model evolved from a number of teaching strategies that shared a common feature, in this case students helping students to learn. Many of these peer teaching strategies were developed as variations within direct instruction approaches, so the basic operations of peer teaching and direct instruction are often similar, differing mainly in who carries them out in class.

Three concepts related to the Peer Teaching model need to be clarified and kept in mind throughout this chapter. First, the Peer Teaching model obviously relies on strategies that use students to teach other students, but it becomes the Peer Teaching model only when a teacher plans for and follows a model-based approach, as will be presented in this chapter. Second, peer teaching is not the same as partner learning, in which students are paired together for one or more learning activities, and learn "side-by-side." To qualify as peer teaching, one student must be given the explicit responsibility of carrying out several key instructional operations normally assumed by the teacher. There must be a clear tutor-learner role delineation, even though these roles can be reversed on a regular basis. Third, peer teaching is not to be misinterpreted as cooperative learning (Chapter 9) on a smaller scale. True, cooperative learning does feature students teaching other students, but the Cooperative Learning model uses a very different overall plan and places students into small "teams" that stay together for an entire content unit.

The most recognizable version of peer teaching in physical education is Mosston and Ashworth's (1994) Reciprocal Style, in which one student is designated as the "Observer" (the tutor) and the other student is designated as the "Doer" (the tutee). While this style does maintain the most essential feature of peer teaching, it is meant to be used as a temporary task structure, and is not usually designed as the only instructional strategy in a content unit. Physical education teachers have been using this strategy for many years, but it is not quite the same as the Peer Teaching model to be presented in this chapter.

Overview

As mentioned, the Peer Teaching model can be considered a variation of direct instruction. As you learned in Chapter 7, direct instruction places the teacher in charge of making and implementing nearly all content, managerial, task, and instructional decisions in a unit and lesson. In the Peer Teaching model, the teacher retains control over all of these same elements except one—instructional interactions that occur during and after students' learning trials. That important responsibility is delegated to students, called tutors, who have been trained to observe and analyze other students' practice attempts.

Terminology in the Peer Teaching model can sometimes be confusing. To reduce the potential for confusion, let's differentiate between four terms that will be used frequently in this chapter:

1. *Tutor:* Someone temporarily assigned the role of teacher
2. *Learner:* Someone who is practicing under the observation and supervision of a tutor
3. *Dyad:* A tutor-learner pair
4. *Student:* The general term used to describe students in class when they are not in the role of tutor or learner

The Peer Teaching model is based on an accepted trade-off to help reduce the problem of too little teacher observation of practice attempts and limited feedback received by students. Actual student opportunity to respond (OTR) in class is for all intents cut in half in the Peer Teaching model, since each student spends approximately half of the activity time as a tutor and half of the activity time practicing as a learner. However, when they are in the learner's role, each student in effect has a private tutor to observe and analyze each practice attempt—increasing the effectiveness of that learning time. And, when in the tutor's role, the student is cognitively engaged in a way that can increase her own comprehension of the task, thereby contributing to improved practice when it is her turn to do so. Even though students get fewer OTR in peer teaching, the increased effectiveness of practice time will allow the teacher to cover more, not less, content in a unit of instruction.

Proponents of peer teaching also point to the social learning that occurs within the model. Both members of the dyad become dependent on each other in ways that do not occur in other teaching models. The tutor must pay close attention to the task presentation and task structure given by the teacher, apply good concentration when observing skill attempts, have good verbal communication skills when giving cues and feedbacks, and be sensitive to the abilities and feelings of his temporary charge. The learner must be willing to accept the tutor's comments, ask questions when the tutor is not clear, and practice diligently under direct observation of each attempt. As students alternate between these two roles in class, they begin to develop a reciprocal relationship based on a shared level of responsibility not given to them in most other teaching models.

The Peer Teaching model also has great potential to enhance students' cognitive development in physical education. To be a good tutor, a student must know the key performance cues and understand the relationship between those cues and the outcome of each practice attempt. Using golf as an example, it is not helpful for the tutor to simply state the obvious, "Your shot went to the right, not down the middle." The tutor must be able to identify the source of each mistake and provide good learning cues for the next attempt: "It went to the right because you lifted your head on the backswing, and that caused you to open the club face. Be sure to keep your head down throughout the whole swing next time." In essence, the tutor is developing problem-solving skills that can improve his own level of understanding and performance of movement skills in physical education.

One of the things that makes peer teaching an instructional model and not just partner learning is the degree to which the tutors are prepared and trained for their role as teacher-of-the-moment. In order for the model to be the most effective, the teacher must help tutors to understand and carry out the operations for which they will assume responsibility. It is not simply telling one student to "go teach" another student. A good training plan for the tutoring role should include:

1. Clarification of the learning objectives
2. Expectations of tutors (what they should do, what they should not do)
3. Task presentation and check for understanding
4. Task structure and check for understanding
5. How to communicate errors to learners
6. How to provide praise appropriately
7. How to practice safely
8. How to assess mastery or task completion
9. Knowing when to ask questions of the teacher

It is important to keep in mind that the Peer Teaching model calls for the tutors to lead only a small portion of the instructional process; the teacher retains much of the decision making and leadership, much as with the Direct Instruction model. Research by Ellis and Rogoff (1986) suggests that many students are not capable of seeing the big picture in a content unit, nor are they able to orchestrate more than a small portion of the complex learning environment. Tutors can carry out some of the teacher's plans for instructional operations, but the tutors are rarely able to make those plans on their own. Ellis and Rogoff report that tutors could handle only two of the three key instructional components typically carried out by the teacher: task management, instructional information, and social management. Therefore, the role of the tutor is probably best limited to receiving directions from the teacher and acting as the teacher's proxy in tasks with limited time and complexity. However, that limitation should in no way dissuade a teacher from selecting the Peer Teaching model in physical education. The nature of many physical education learning activities and the tutor's ability to "be the teacher's eyes, ears, and voice" in the direct observation of the learner's practice attempts can serve a vital role in the learning process.

Greenwood, Carta, and Kamps (1990) compared the advantages of teacher-mediated and student-mediated instruction and found that peer teaching fared quite favorably (see Figure 11.1).

This analysis makes it clear that students can benefit greatly from engagement in the Peer Teaching model, despite some of the stated disadvantages. Actually, many of the disadvantages will be reduced or eliminated completely the more times a teacher uses this model and is able to anticipate some of the problems inherent to it. In the end, the Peer Teaching model comes with the same stipulation as every other model presented in this book. That is,

FIGURE 11.1 Comparing Teacher-Mediated and Peer-Mediated Instruction

Teaching Factor	Teacher-Mediated	Peer-Mediated
Advantages		
Pupil/teacher ratio	High	Low
Engaged time	Variable	High
Opportunities to respond	Low	High
Opportunities for error correction	Low	High
Immediacy of error correction	Delayed	Immediate
Opportunities for help and encouragement	Few	Many
Opportunities for both competitive and cooperative learning experiences	Few	Many
Motivation	Teacher support	Peer plus teacher support
Disadvantages		
Peer-training requirements	Few	Many
Quality-control requirements	Few	Many
Content coverage	Good	Variable
Peer selection	Not required	Required
Curriculum adaptations	Few	Many
Costs	High	Low
Ethical concerns	Few	Increased

when the model is selected to match a unit's learning goals, meets the contextual demands for the content unit, and is implemented according to the model's design, it will be an effective way to increase student achievement on stated learning goals in physical education.

Foundations of the Peer Teaching Model in Physical Education

Theory and Rationale

To the degree that the Peer Teaching model is based on direct instruction, it shares much of the theory and rationale of direct instruction. That is, it is a mastery-based model that strives for high rates of student OTR, high rates of augmented feedback (from tutors, not the teacher), and a brisk, teacher-led pacing through unit content. This way of structuring the teaching-learning process is based on theories and principles of training developed by B. F.

Skinner and other behavioral psychologists. However, the main feature of peer teaching—having students teach each other—is derived from quite different theories on human learning, most notably those on social learning, cognitive development, and constructivism.

Social learning theory states that humans learn by interaction with their environment, especially interactions with other people. We learn from other people by imitating them, listening to them, talking to them, and by observing the results of their own behavior, according to social learning theorists like Albert Bandura (1977). This theory is strongly based on operant psychology, with the added emphasis on the role of other humans in the learning process. The formalization of student-to-student interactions in the Peer Teaching model recognizes the important role other people play in our own learning.

The theories of noted cognitive developmentalist Jean Piaget also contribute to the rationale behind the Peer Teaching model. Piaget theorized that humans progress through a series of stages in the development of intellectual abilities. We develop cognitive schemas that allow us to give meaning and structure to the world around us, and we progress through these stages in a rather predictable manner, based on physiological and environmental factors. According to the cognitive learning theories, students who engage in shared learning develop problem-solving skills that foster intellectual development by requiring both tutor and learner to "figure out" more than they would in teacher-directed instruction. Just placing a student in the role of teacher/tutor presents an entirely new set of intellectual and social challenges that must be met in order to fulfill that role well.

Constructive learning theory lends a third contribution to the theories that support the Peer Teaching model. Social constructivists place a strong emphasis on the process of learning, especially those processes that foster a democratic environment and allow students to use what they already know as the basis of interactions with peers (Joyce & Weil, 1996). Therefore, they would be closely aligned with the one feature of the Peer Teaching model that separates it from direct instruction. However, the social constructivists would be much at odds with the rest of the Peer Teaching model.

The fact that the Peer Teaching model draws from three different learning theories can be problematic for teachers who have strong beliefs for one view of learning over the others—unless they can recognize the commonalities among those theories and not allow the differences to deter them. The strength of the model is actually derived from these commonalities as they are merged for the benefit of student learning in all three domains: the psychomotor, the cognitive, and the affective.

The underlying rationale for the Peer Teaching model is rather simple. The teacher is able to use her content, managerial, and supervisory expertise to make the major planning decisions in a unit of instruction. Because of the inability of one teacher to observe and provide feedback on the large number of learners' practice attempts that can occur in physical education, students are trained and assigned to carry out these functions as tutors to other students (learners) who are engaged in practice attempts. The practicing learners get the benefit of increased instructional interactions that lead to improved learning. While carrying out the functions of teacher, the tutor is engaged intellectually and socially in ways that offer development in the cognitive and affective domains. It is a win-win-win situation for all involved.

Assumptions about Teaching and Learning

Assumptions about Teaching

1. The teacher must retain control over many decisions related to unit content, class management, task presentation, and content progression in order to maximize the use of time and other resources.
2. The teacher can train tutors to carry out the key function of providing learners with instructional information.
3. The peer teaching dyad fosters development in all three domains.

Assumptions about Learning

1. Learning in the psychomotor domain is facilitated by the increased monitoring and feedback provided by tutors.
2. Learning in the cognitive domain is facilitated for the tutors as they observe, analyze, and instruct practicing learners.
3. Affective/social learning is facilitated for both students in the dyad as they assume differentiated roles in the teaching-learning process.
4. Tutors and learners develop problem-solving skills by having to work cooperatively to assist each other in completing assigned learning tasks.

Major Theme for Peer Teaching: I Teach You, You Teach Me

As you already know, the basic task structure in the Peer Teaching model is for students, in pairs, to alternate in the roles of tutor and learner after the teacher has provided the task presentation. Essentially, one student assumes the role of teacher and one assumes the role of learner for a short period of time, and then switch roles at the teacher's direction. Neither one is the tutor or student on a permanent basis, so from both points of view, "I teach you, then you teach me and we both learn different things together."

Learning Domain Priorities and Interactions

Because students will assume two very different roles in the Peer Teaching model, it is necessary to discuss learning domain priorities and interactions from both perspectives. The model fosters learning across all three domains, but the type of learning that occurs will depend on which role a student is fulfilling at a particular moment.

As learners, students will be engaged primarily in the psychomotor domain as they practice motor skill attempts in learning activities. It is possible for a teacher to use peer teaching for the learning of cognitive concepts, but that is viewed as a somewhat inefficient strategy since all students can be learning the concepts at the same time and gain nothing from peer instruction. So, the domain priorities for the learner in the Peer Teaching model are typically:

First priority:	Psychomotor domain
Second priority:	Cognitive domain
Third priority:	Affective/social domain

The second and third priorities for the learner are often reversed, as the learner interacts with the tutor to learn listening, trust, and other affective/social skills within the dyadic relationship. The *domain interaction* for the learner in the Peer Teaching model works this way: he must accept and process verbal and modeled (cognitive) information from the tutor in order to master the current psychomotor task. These processes have an "overlay" of affective/social interaction between the tutor and the learner that determines the atmosphere for these communications, and impacts the learner's ability to master the task of the moment.

Students will have different domain priorities as tutors in the Peer Teaching model. They will focus primarily on the cognitive components of the task: understanding the key performance cues given by the teacher, understanding the task structure demands, observing the learner's skill attempts for errors, and communicating the results of each skill attempt back to the learner in the form of feedback and cues for the next try. In trying to learn and carry out the momentary responsibility as the *teacher,* tutors are also strongly engaged in the affective domain—learning about themselves and the needs of the learner. While it is possible for the tutor to acquire some cognitive knowledge that can help her when it is her turn to practice, that link places the psychomotor domain third for the tutor in this model. So, the domain priorities for the tutor in the Peer Teaching model are typically:

First priority:	Cognitive domain
Second priority:	Affective/social domain
Third priority:	Psychomotor domain

The *domain interaction* begins for tutors in the cognitive domain as they acquire all of the task and content information needed in the role of teacher. It is when they provide instructional information to the learner that they must draw on affective/social and psychomotor knowledge to do that effectively. If the tutor is not sensitive to the learner's abilities and feelings, the learner is likely to ignore or reject the tutor's interaction. If the tutor cannot provide reasonably close models of the learner's mistakes and/or proper cues for the next trial, the learner will make slow or no progress. So, the tutor's cognitive knowledge will be the source of interactions with the learner, delivered through a combination of affective/social and psychomotor abilities.

Student Learning Preferences

Because of the dual roles assumed by students in the Peer Teaching model, the profile for learning preferences will be somewhat different for the tutor and the learner. Based on the Reichmann and Grasha (1974) scheme the tutor will most likely prefer the participant, collaborative, and independent attributes of the model. The learner will most likely prefer the attributes of participant, collaborative, and dependent. The tutor prefers the independent attribute because he is given lots of responsibility and decision making. The learner prefers being dependent on another person for information and task structure, much the same as direct instruction.

Validation

Research Validation.   It is somewhat difficult to establish the research validation for peer teaching because the feature of "students teaching students" occurs in several models of instruction. Some research reports on peer teaching will include any strategy that has this feature, even if it takes place in another model, such as cooperative learning. In a brief review of peer teaching, Foot, Morgan, and Shute (1990) report that peer teaching (used in various models) has been shown to be effective in increasing achievement in several subject areas such as mathematics, science, and language arts.

Little research has been completed on peer teaching in physical education. In our field, the most notable version of peer teaching is Mosston and Ashworth's (1994) Reciprocal Style. While many other styles have been given much research attention, we know very little about the effectiveness of the Reciprocal Style.

Craft Knowledge Validation.   As noted by Wagner (1990), teachers have been using some form of peer teaching for over 2000 years, starting with Aristotle and the ancient Greeks. The fact that this strategy has been practiced for such a long time, and has been developed into a more formal instructional model in the past thirty years, provides strong evidence that teachers in all subject areas find it to be feasible and effective for many learning goals. Again, this is not the same as placing students in learning pairs, but rather the more formally operationalized plan and decisions that get one student to *teach another* for a period of time.

Teachers have found peer teaching to be highly effective in adaptive physical education settings by having a higher-skilled student take on the role of individual tutor for a student with learning disabilities (Houston-Wilson, 1997; Webster, 1987). However, the higher-skilled student does not receive reciprocal instruction, often making this a one-way street for learning—although the higher-skilled student does learn important lessons about communication and others' needs.

It is difficult to determine how much true peer teaching occurs in physical education today. It is likely that teachers use this as a temporary *strategy* in many kinds of learning tasks, and do not sustain it across many learning tasks and entire content units. Most physical education teachers probably practice this under the name of the Reciprocal Teaching Style, described by Mosston and Ashworth (1994).

Intuitive Validation.   It is clear that a physical education teacher cannot provide the amount of direct observation and instructional information needed by every student as they practice movement skills and concepts in class. There are simply too many students for one teacher, or even one teacher and a teacher's aide. It is also clear that students at nearly all grade levels can comprehend the necessary performance cues, observe them as other students execute them, and provide feedback on each practice attempt. Since many students can carry out a limited range of key teaching operations in class, it makes good sense to use them as additional teaching resources for physical education—increasing learning levels for both learner and tutor in the dyad. By formulating this strategy into a formal model of instruction, it improves the design and implementation of this powerful way to teach in physical education, making a good case for intuitive validation.

Teaching and Learning Features

Directness

Figure 11.2 shows the directness profile for the Peer Teaching model as it is used in physical education.

1. *Content selection.* The teacher maintains complete control of the content and its sequencing in the Peer Teaching model. He decides what will be included in the unit, the order in which learning tasks will be sequenced, and the performance criteria used to determine mastery of each task. All students—tutors and learners—simply receive the content listing from the teacher and proceed through it.

2. *Managerial control.* The teacher determines the managerial plan, class policies, and specific procedures that students follow in the Peer Teaching model. The tutors are given a small degree of managerial responsibility within instructional tasks, such as arranging the practice area, orienting the learner to the task, and monitoring for safety.

3. *Task presentations.* These occur at two levels. The first level is controlled by the teacher as she informs the tutors of performance cues, task structure, and mastery criteria—and checks for understanding. At the next level, it is controlled by the individual tutor who relays that information to his/her learner to initiate practice on the assigned task. At both levels the task presentation is quite direct.

4. *Engagement patterns.* The teacher determines the assignment of students to each role and the rotation plan within each task. Obviously, the predominant task structure is dyadic, but it is possible to use groups of three when the class has an uneven number of

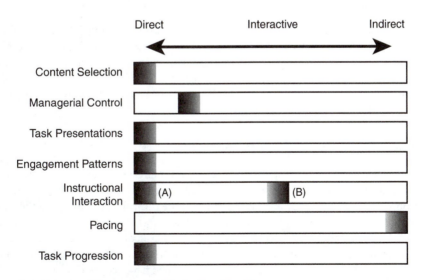

FIGURE 11.2 **Directness Profile for Peer Teaching**

students. Students alternate between the role of tutor and the role of learner according to the teacher's plan.

5. *Instructional interaction.* Two paths are used for instructional interactions in the Peer Teaching model. The first path is between the teacher and the tutors of the moment. Initially that interaction is quite direct: the teacher gives tutors the needed task presentation and task structure information, checks for understanding, and then lets them pursue their role (A). After that, the teacher interacts only with the tutors, *not the learners,* except on rare occasions. The teacher's communications with the tutors should be interactive, using questions more often than direct statements to develop the tutors' observation, analysis, and communication skills (B). The idea is to promote problem-solving skills, and not to simply use the tutor as a "conduit" to the learner. For example, if the teacher observes that a learner is not doing the correct step in a dance sequence, she should not make a comment to the learner. Instead, the teacher should ask the tutor to "watch carefully" to see if the learner is making any mistakes, and then get the tutor to identify the incorrect movement pattern and communicate that to the learner.

The second path is between the tutors and the learners. It will also be highly interactive, as they work cooperatively to structure and pursue assigned learning activities (B). The tutor is free (and expected) to make comments to the learner and to ask questions. The learner is expected to do the same. The tutor should provide the learner with all of the information usually given by the teacher during learning activities. Cues, guides, feedbacks, questions, and encouragement should all occur at very high rates before and after each practice attempt.

6. *Pacing.* Once the teacher has given the task presentation and task structure information to the tutors, and the tutors relay that to the learners, the learners can begin to practice at their own pace. Along with the tutor, the learner determines when each practice attempt will begin and how long it will last.

7. *Task progression.* The teacher decides the content listing for each unit and when learning activities will change within it. The teacher also decides when each student switches from tutor to learner and vice versa. However, it is possible for the teacher to state a performance criterion for each task and allow student pairs to go to the next task on their own once they both have completed the current task. This can reduce management time significantly.

Predominant Engagement Patterns

As the name of the model states, the predominant engagement pattern in peer teaching is the dyad, or pair. When the number of students dictates, it is possible to place them in groups of three, with each one taking a turn as the tutor. The teacher gives the task presentation and task structure information to the tutors, who in turn relay that information to the learners. Once the learners have completed the task, or the teacher decides it is time, the students switch roles. It should be mentioned that the student who practices second should need a bit less time to complete a task, since she will have acquired some knowledge of the task and its performance cues while being the tutor.

Inclusiveness

The Peer Teaching model can accommodate a wide range of student ability levels and previous experience with the content, making it highly inclusive. Students with low ability levels get more monitored practice tasks and have the opportunity to learn in the role of tutor. Students with higher ability can refine their skills with the added monitoring and information given by the tutor and develop increased analytic skills when it is their turn to tutor.

It must be emphasized that the Peer Teaching model is not to be used with higher-skilled students always serving as tutors for lesser-skilled students. There must be reciprocity in the process: "I teach you, you teach me."

Task Presentation and Task Structure

The dyadic arrangement in the Peer Teaching model increases the efficiency of practice for the learner and gives the tutor an opportunity to develop movement skill analysis knowledge. It also provides both students in the dyad the opportunity to develop personal, social, and verbal communication skills. All of these benefits come within some limitations placed on the key operations of task presentation and task structure when the Peer Teaching model is used in physical education.

Task Presentation. The process of providing the tutors with task presentation information is quite direct in this model: the teacher shows the tutors a model of the skill or task to be practiced, along with the key performance cues they must relay to the learners and watch for during each practice attempt. It is essentially the same as the Direct Instruction model. It is very important that the teacher regularly checks for understanding to make sure the tutors know what and how to give instructional information to the learners. The teacher can use instructional media for giving the task presentation to the tutors, such as CD ROMs, videotapes, drawings, and photographs.

The teacher has a few options when it is time for the tutors and learners to switch roles, since that group will already be aware of the task and its key performance cues:

1. Before the students switch, the teacher can ask the tutors to repeat all of the performance cues to their partners.
2. The teacher can conduct a brief task presentation himself, checking for understanding often.
3. The teacher can ask the new tutors to recall what they just learned, wanting to hear them cite the key performance cues for the task they will be teaching.

Task Structure. The dyad pattern limits the kinds of task structures that can be used with peer teaching to those that allow one student to be practicing while another student observes. Drills, self-space tasks, stations, and brief in-class cognitive tasks are typically the kinds of task structures used in peer teaching.

The teacher can develop simple observational checklists to be used by the tutors as they watch each learner's practice attempts. The checklist would show all of the key performance cues and allow the tutor to check off each time he sees the learner perform a cue correctly. This strategy is especially useful for younger students who might forget one or more of the key cues from the task presentation.

Teacher Expertise and Contextual Needs

Teacher Expertise

Physical education teachers who use the Peer Teaching model will need to have particular strengths in the proposed knowledge base presented in Chapter 2. Many of these areas are similar to those needed for direct instruction, but with a slightly different slant to address the needs of both the tutor and the learner.

Implementing Developmentally Appropriate Instruction.   Teachers must address developmental issues that pertain to the learner's need to be engaged safely in meaningful tasks, with high rates of OTR. It benefits neither the learner nor the tutor to have too much waiting time between practice attempts. The teacher must ensure that the learner can comprehend the task presentation and task structure information, and that the level of task difficulty matches the learner's stage of development. The learner must also be willing and able to accept both praise and criticism (in the form of negative performance feedback) from a peer.

There are more issues about developmental appropriateness that pertain to students in the role of tutor. The teacher must ask herself if tutors have the intellectual ability (to comprehend task information and monitor practice attempts), the needed level of responsibility (to assume some of the teacher's functions), the communication skills (to provide accurate feedback and cues), and the maturity (to work for the benefit of the learner) necessary to be "the teacher for the moment." If tutors are not developmentally ready for their role, the model's key feature will not work, greatly reducing its effectiveness.

Task Analysis and Content Progression.   The teacher must know the movement skills or concepts to be learned in the unit and be able to break each one into its component parts so that a sequence of learning tasks can be formulated and presented to students. Students then progress through this sequence of tasks, alternating as tutor and learner throughout the unit.

Assessment.   Tutors most often serve as the assessors in the Peer Teaching model. They observe learners' skill attempts and help verify mastery of each learning task. The teacher's assessment expertise occurs by designing and communicating assessment techniques to the tutors, such as the observational checklists. Other alternative assessment strategies are possible in the Peer Teaching model, depending on the tutor's observational and communication skills.

Social/Emotional Climate.   The Peer Teaching model relies heavily on the moment-to-moment interactions between the tutor and the learner. It will not work if both members of the dyad are not comfortable in these roles, and care about each other's learning. It is up to the teacher to create an atmosphere that allows both members of the dyad to feel secure in this arrangement and be willing to work for the benefit of others when it is their turn as tutors. The tutors must be sensitive to the learner's abilities and needs, especially when the learner is having difficulty and the needed feedback is not positive. The learners must be aware that the tutors can make mistakes and do not have the same level of expertise as their teacher—and that negative feedback is not meant personally. The teacher can promote a positive climate by having regular discussions with the class, reinforcing examples of good tutor and learner role behavior, and by reminding all students of the shared responsibility that occurs in the model.

Effective Teaching Skills Applied to Peer Teaching

The needed repertoire of effective teaching skills in the Peer Teaching model will be similar to those used in the Direct Instruction model, except for some interactions with the tutors as they work with learners.

Planning. The Peer Teaching model calls for the teacher to break unit content into discrete tasks that lead.to identified learning objectives. The teacher will need to plan for all aspects of these tasks so that the tutors and learners can become appropriately engaged quickly once the teacher completes the task presentation.

Time and Class Management. The Peer Teaching model requires some extra attention to how time is allocated to lesson segments and how transitions are managed. Because students alternate between the roles of tutor and learner, there are typically more transitions during classes—and the potential loss of momentum. Teachers must establish routines and procedures for these times to ensure that little practice time is lost when changing activities and roles. Particular attention must be given to providing students with approximately equal amounts of time in each role.

Task Presentation and Task Structure. These are critical areas of effective teaching skills for the Peer Teaching model. Teachers must make good task presentations to the tutors and check for understanding often, so that the tutors know what to look for as they observe the learners and can provide helpful comments. Task structure is equally important, since the teacher will leave it to each pair of students to set up the learning environment and become engaged in the task as the teacher intends. If the teacher has provided tutors with good information about task presentation and task structure, the tutors will be more effective as they assume their temporary teaching responsibilities.

Communication. Verbal communication is used most often in peer teaching, as the teacher informs the tutors about the task presentation and task structure. The key point to remember is that the teacher must communicate well enough so that the tutors can *teach* the content to the learners, so it is important to check for understanding frequently.

Instructional Information. In this model, once the dyads are engaged, the teacher interacts only with the tutor—and in a very indirect mode. Because the teacher is trying to develop the tutor's analysis and communication skills, the primary mode of interaction is based on questions that promote problem-solving abilities. The teacher should not say things like, "Billy is not using the correct grip on the bat. Go and show him how to do it correctly." Instead, the teacher might say, "I think Billy is having some problems with his swing. Watch his next try carefully and see if you spot an error in his grip." Billy (the learner) takes another swing, after which Debbie (the tutor) says to the teacher, "He has a gap between his top hand and his bottom hand—I'll go tell him." The teacher says, "Not just yet. Why is that not a good way to hold the bat?" Debbie thinks for a moment and replies, "Because it causes him to lose control and miss the ball." The teacher acknowledges that correct answer and then says, "Good, now go and tell him how to fix it, and keep watching so he does not do it again."

Review and Closure.   The review segment of a lesson that uses the Peer Teaching model must address all of the kinds of learning that occurred in class: what students learned as they practiced, what they learned when they taught, and what they learned while interacting with their partners. All of these are related at some level, and the teacher must tie them together for students to see the "big picture" of what happens when they take turns teaching each other in physical education class.

Student Developmental Requirements

The Peer Teaching model can be used with students across a range of developmental stages. It is a matter of recognizing how much responsibility they are capable of assuming in the role of tutor and not exceeding those expectations. That will depend on the tutor's ability to comprehend task presentation and task structure information, to communicate with the learner, and to interact with the learner in a caring, supportive manner. Young tutors, or those with lesser abilities, can be given a limited number of performance cues to monitor, or even just one. Tutors who can handle an increased level of responsibility can be given a larger part of the teaching role.

Contextual Needs for Peer Teaching

The main contextual need in peer teaching is having sufficient space and equipment for half of the class to be practicing at one time. That requirement cannot be compromised in this model. Beyond that, the Peer Teaching model can be used for a wide variety of movement content and in nearly every kind of activity area in schools. It is especially effective with large classes, since it provides every practicing student with his/her own tutor for the moment and requires only enough equipment and space for half of the class for any learning activity.

Teacher and Student Roles and Responsibilities in Peer Teaching

Each instructional model will have certain operations that need to be completed to make the model function to its design. Some of these operations are carried out by the teacher; others are carried out by one or more students. The following table shows the major operations within the Peer Teaching model, and indicates who is responsible for completing them during each lesson.

Operation or Responsibility Who Does It in Peer Teaching?

Starting class	The **teacher** starts the lesson.
Bringing equipment to class	The **teacher** brings the needed equipment to class.
Dispersing and returning equipment	Each **partner group** gets the equipment needed for the activity and returns it when finished.
Roll call (if needed)	The **teacher** calls the roll.
Task presentation	The **teacher** shows and describes each movement skill or concept to the tutors. The **tutors** then show and describe each movement skill or concept to the learners.
Task structure	The **teacher** explains the task structure to the tutors. The **tutors** then explain the task structure to the learners.
Instruction interactions	**Path 1:** The teacher uses questions to interact with the tutors. **Path 2:** The tutors provide the learners with cues, guides, feedback, and encouragement.
Assessment	The **teacher** determines how each task will be assessed. The **tutor** assesses the learner (e.g., with a checklist).
Monitoring learning progress	The **teacher** determines when it is time to go on to new content.

Teaching and Learning Benchmarks for Peer Teaching

Because students assume two different roles in the Peer Teaching model, it is necessary to identify a set of benchmarks for each role and that of the teacher. The following teacher, learner, and tutor benchmarks verify that the Peer Teaching model has been implemented with an acceptable degree of faithfulness, increasing the likelihood that the stated learning outcomes will be achieved.

Teacher Benchmarks

Benchmark	How to Verify
Unit content is broken into a series of small learning tasks, leading to larger learning goals	Review the teacher's task analysis, content listing, and content progression prior to the start of the unit.
Review previous day's content	Review teacher's lesson plan to include a set induction that covers this.
Present a clear and effective task presentation to tutors	1. Monitor with QMTPS. 2. Observe learners as they begin to practice. Are they doing the task correctly?

(continued)

Teacher Benchmarks Continued

Benchmark	How to Verify
Present a clear task structure	Observe learners as they begin to practice. Are they engaged in the way described by the teacher?
Use a brisk pace through content progression	1. Teacher plans a series of small learning tasks. 2. Teacher has quick transitions between planned class segments and role changes within learning activities.
Teacher primarily uses questions to interact with tutors during learning activities	Record the frequency and types of questions directed by the teacher to tutors.
Learning tasks have a mastery criterion	1. Check lesson plan. 2. Use written assessments to verify learners' mastery.
Regular content reviews are made	1. Check the unit plan. 2. Record the timing and focus of each review made.

Learner Benchmarks

Benchmark	How to Verify
Learners understand task presentation	Count the number of learners who are doing the skill/movement/concept as it was initially described by the teacher.
Learners understand task structure	Count the number of learners who: a. Are engaged according to the teacher's directions to tutors. b. Have modified the task. c. Have withdrawn from the task.
Learners have high rates of OTR	1. Count the number of practice attempts (if frequency is the best indicator of OTR). 2. Measure how much actual practice time learners get (if time is the best indicator of OTR).
Learners have high rates of ALT	Monitor a sampling of learners with a valid ALT-PE recording instrument.
Learners get high rates of positive and corrective feedback	Record and analyze the tutors' feedback to learners.
Learners have mastered content	Learners complete and pass regular assessments monitored by tutors.

Tutor Benchmarks

Benchmark	How to Verify
Tutors comprehend task presentation	1. Count the number of correct answers when the teacher checks for understanding. 2. Monitor each tutor's task presentation to the learner, noting correct and incorrect information. It is possible to use the QMTPS for this.

Tutors comprehend task structure	1. Count the number of correct answers when the teacher checks for understanding.
	2. Allow pairs to set up the learning environment and the learners to begin to practice. Scan and count the number of learners who:
	  a. Are engaged as directed by the teacher.
	  b. Have modified the task.
	  c. Are off task.

Tutors provide high rates of positive and corrective feedback	Monitor the type and rate of feedback from the tutor to the learner.
Tutors and learners work cooperatively	Monitor interaction patterns within dyads.
Tutors can analyze movement skills/concepts correctly	Teacher and tutor use an identical checklist while observing the same learner and compare records after each attempt.

Assessing Learning in Peer Teaching

It is recommended that peer teaching be used for discrete learning activities that can be pursued with individual student engagement patterns: the learner practices while the tutor observes. That feature lends itself to using peer teaching for the learning of relatively simple movement patterns and concepts that can be viewed by the tutor as the learner practices them. More dynamic engagement patterns, such as competitive games, do not allow many opportunities for the tutor to interact with the learner while the action occurs—although it is possible for them to interact once the game has paused or stopped. By design, the Peer Teaching model allows many opportunities for a tutor to observe a learner who is engaged in repetitive and relatively simple movement activities in a static situation—making the use of observational checklists most appropriate for assessment purposes.

Checklists are widely used as assessment devices in Peer Teaching because it is easy for the tutor to watch performance in the psychomotor domain and then record which parts of the movement or skill were performed correctly. The teacher trains the tutor on what to watch and how to determine if a movement or outcome is correctly executed. The key is to match the number and complexity of checklist items with the tutor's ability to discern them in motion.

Checklist assessment techniques can help both the learner and the tutor. The learner benefits from having specific feedback on each component of her performance, while the items on the checklist remind the tutor of the key performance cues for the task when it is his turn to practice.

Selecting and Modifying Peer Teaching for Physical Education

The Peer Teaching model can be used in a wide range of settings and content areas in physical education. The major consideration for using peer teaching is the level of student learning the teacher wishes to achieve, rather than the content itself. For example, peer teaching can be used effectively in all individual and team sports, but should be limited to noncompetitive learning activities because the dynamics of game situations rarely allow students to interact in the tutor-learner roles. Therefore, peer teaching would be an appropriate model for beginner and intermediate levels, but not for advanced students who will be engaged in competitive games more often. Recognizing that feature of the Peer Teaching model, I would recommend it for the following types of physical education content units:

1. Movement skills and concepts
2. Individual sports (noncompetitive emphasis)
3. Team sports (noncompetitive emphasis)
4. Recreational activities
5. Dances with prescribed steps (line, square, folk, etc.)
6. Personal fitness concepts
7. Personal fitness training programs
8. Aquatics (swimming and diving)

Grade-Level Adaptations

The Peer Teaching model will be more effective once student developmental levels can accommodate the full range of observational, communication, and problem-solving abilities needed by the tutor. However, it is possible to greatly reduce the number and complexity of role requirements for tutors and use the Peer Teaching model with some lower grade levels. Figure 11.3 shows some grade-level adaptations for using Peer Teaching in physical education.

Summary

Students are one of the most underused resources in teaching today. Children teach other children every day during playtime around the house and neighborhood, but yet most instructional strategies and models are designed for only one (adult) teacher who cannot provide all students with regular observation and feedback during practice time. To the degree that students are mature and skilled enough to assume some of the necessary functions of instruction, they can be used as an in-class "teacher corp" to help their peers and themselves achieve more in physical education. The Peer Teaching model is designed to do just that, promoting learning outcomes in all three domains and across a variety of physical education content.

This chapter concludes by repeating one of the early precautions for the Peer Teaching model. It is more than simply placing students in pairs and having them learn along

FIGURE 11.3   Grade-Level Adaptations for Peer Teaching in Physical Education

Grade Level	Select Peer Teaching?	Possible Adaptions
Pre-school	No	
K–3	No	
4–5	Yes	1. Give task presentation to all students at once, eliminating the need for tutors to do it. 2. Have the tutors watch for one key element at a time. Add more as the tutors' observational skills increase.
Middle school/junior high	Yes	1. Limit the number of key elements the tutors will look for (no more than three or four). 2. Use simple checksheets to remind tutors of what to watch for. 3. Train students on how to be good, sensitive communicators.
High school	Yes	None needed. The full Peer Teaching model can be implemented.
College/adult	Yes	None needed. The full Peer Teaching model can be implemented.

side each other for a short period of time or even a few learning tasks. It becomes, and remains, the Peer Teaching model when the teacher plans for, prepares, and monitors students to assume the role of tutor on nearly every learning task in the unit. Only then will the full range of student learning outcomes be achieved through this model.

Sample Unit for Peer Teaching

Unit content:	Personal fitness
Grade level:	8th
Students:	28 (14 boys and 14 girls)
Equipment:	Jump ropes Dyna-bands 4 multistation weight-training units Outdoor track Fitness trail behind school Heart-rate monitors Sit and reach boxes 1 computer with Fitnessgram software loaded on it
Length of unit:	12 classes
Length of classes:	42 minutes of instructional time

Content Listing and Unit Schedule

Class	Topic or Fitness Area	Learning Activities
1	1. Health-related fitness 2. How to be a good "Personal trainer"	1. Overview of HRF by teacher 2. Selection of partners for the unit. Teacher explains the structure of peer teaching, with suggestions for how to be an effective tutor (called "personal trainer" in this unit). 3. Both partners complete HRF assessment and enter on Fitnessgram software. 4. All students write a "Personal Fitness Profile" with goals for the unit.
2	Warming up and stretching	1. Teacher explains purposes of warming up and stretching to personal trainers while learners walk around the gym. 2. Teacher explains to the personal trainers how to stretch safely (major "dos" and "don'ts"). 3. Teacher demonstrates stretching routine for this unit to the personal trainers. 4. Teacher gives each dyad a handout with 8 stretches on it. 5. Dyads teach each other the stretches.
3–6	1. Determining target heart rate zone for exercise 2. Cardiovascular fitness	1. Personal trainers watch a video on THR and then teach it to their partners. 2. Teacher instructs personal trainers on: 　■ Jump rope techniques 　■ Fitness trail exercises 　■ Pacing for endurance running 3. Personal trainers then teach their partners all of the techniques and concepts. Dyads then make and complete a series of exercises for rope jumping, fitness trail, and distance running.
7–10	Muscular strength	1. Teacher instructs personal trainers on a strength-building exercise on multi-station machines. 2. Personal trainers teach the exercise to their partner. 3. Students switch roles and the personal trainers get instruction on another exercise and then teach it to their partners. Students alternate as personal trainers and learners until they have learned 6 safe exercises on the multi-station machines. 4. All students make a personal plan for strength building on all 6 exercises. Students alternate between personal trainers and learners. The personal trainers observe the learners for correct technique, safety, and spotting.

(continued)

Class	Topic or Fitness Area	Learning Activities
11	Flexibility	1. Teacher instructs all students on how to use the sit-and-reach box. 2. Students review their scores on the sit-and-reach test. 3. Teacher explains one exercise for increasing lower-back flexibility to personal trainers. The personal trainers teach the exercise to their partners. Students switch roles to learn another exercise. This process is repeated for 2 more exercises. 4. All students take the sit-and-reach test again with their partners making the recordings. Partners help each other analyze improvements in scores from the class 1 pretest.
12	Abdominal strength	1. Students review their scores on the bent knee sit-up test. 2. Teacher explains 1 exercise for increasing abdominal strength to personal trainers. The personal trainers teach the exercise to their partners. Students switch roles to learn another exercise. This process is repeated for 2 more exercises. 3. All students rest and then take the bent knee sit-up test again with their partners making the recordings. Partners help each other analyze improvements in scores from the class 1 pretest.

Lesson Plan for Class 2

Teaching area:	Auxiliary gym, with mats on floor
Content:	Warming up and stretching for exercise sessions
Equipment:	None
Materials:	Stretching handout
Objective:	Students will learn and teach their partners 8 safe exercises to use at the start of all exercise sessions in this unit.

Lesson Segment	Time	Procedures
Set induction	2 minutes	1. Explain to students that they will get the most out of each exercise session if they follow some established plans and procedures each time. 2. The first part of all exercise sessions is the warm-up and stretching segment to: ■ Reduce injuries ■ Warm up muscles 3. Today you are going to learn and teach each other 8 good stretches.

(continued)

Lesson Segment	Time	Procedures
Purposes of warming up	30 minutes (total)	1. Learners walk around the gym for a general body warm-up. 2. Teacher explains 5 general safe and unsafe points to look for while stretching. 3. Learners and personal trainers switch. The second group of personal trainers is told the 5 safe and unsafe points by the teacher. The teacher introduces them to stretch 1 (the hamstring stretch), explaining its purpose, the muscles being stretched, the correct technique, and common errors to watch for. Personal trainers then teach the hamstring stretch to their partners. The teacher observes the personal trainers, using questions as the major kind of interaction. 4. Learners and personal trainers switch. While the learners continue to practice the hamstring stretch, the teacher instructs the personal trainers on stretch 2 (wall stretch for calf muscles), explaining its purpose, the muscles being stretched, the correct technique, and common errors to watch for. Personal trainers then teach the wall stretch to their partners. The teacher observes the personal trainers, using questions as the major interaction. This alternating routine is used for the remaining stretches to be used to start each class.
Assessment	8 minutes	1. The teacher passes out a handout that has illustrations for all 8 stretching exercises learned in class. The illustrations have no text on them. 2. In their dyads, partners identify each stretch by name and write down: ■ The muscles being stretched ■ Three key elements of correct technique ■ Two "safety concerns" to watch for
Review and closure	2 minutes	1. Teacher calls on dyads in turn to explain what they wrote for each stretch. 2. Teacher asks the other students, "Is that correct?" and "What else should you know about that stretch?"

SUGGESTED READINGS

Foot, H. C., Morgan, M. J., & Shute, R. H. (eds.) (1990). *Children helping children.* Chichester, England: John Wiley & Sons.

Mosston, M., & Ashworth, S. (1994). *Teaching physical education* (4th ed.). New York: Macmillan. Note: See Chapter 5, The Reciprocal Style (style C).

CHAPTER

12

Inquiry Teaching

Learner as Problem Solver

As you will recall from Chapter 1, teacher-directed instruction became the predominant approach to teaching physical education in the late 1800s. That method went unchallenged for over sixty years, even as physical education programs began to shift away from sport-centered content. The first and perhaps biggest challenge to teacher-directed instruction emerged in the 1960s from a fast-growing and vocal group of advocates for programs based on the development of intellectual ability, problem solving, and generic movement skills. Such programs were labeled *movement education* and have since become the basis for a large number of physical education programs, most notably in the elementary grades. Some teachers retain the original movement education label, while others use the broader term of *movement-based physical education* to denote the philosophy, content, and teaching methods to which they adhere. By whatever label, any program that has *movement* in its name shares some common characteristics that are relevant to this book of instructional models.

As mentioned, the "movement movement" (Locke, 1970, p. 208) was perhaps the first significant programmatic shift from sport-centered curriculums in physical education. The major learning outcomes in sport-centered programs are the development of skills, knowledge, and tactics needed for proficiency in a given game form (e.g., basketball, soccer, hockey). The content of any program is the list of sports to be taught during the school year. Teachers instruct by showing and telling students how to be proficient performers and then giving students time to practice under the teacher's supervision. Of course, you know this as the Direct Instruction model from Chapter 7. But the content of movement education was quite different, at times even in direct contrast to sport-centered programming. Taken from a variety of sources, the major purposes of movement-based programs would be:

1. The development of basic and generic movement skills that may or may not be precursors to those needed in more complex sport forms. In other words, it is OK if the learned movement does not have any direct application to a known sport. It is also OK if it does.
2. The development of problem-solving and other intellectual abilities as they apply to human movement.
3. The development of expressive and creative movement.

It was clear to the advocates of movement-based programs that the traditional, teacher-directed instruction would not work to help students achieve these goals. As you know, differing objectives should lead to differing kinds of instruction. While the content of movement-based physical education remains a prominent force in our field today, for the purposes of this book the most important outcome from the "movement movement" was the development of a new array of teaching strategies used to teach students. The method for movement-based teaching has been given several names: problem solving, exploration teaching, child-centered teaching, discovery teaching, and indirect teaching. Regardless of the name used, all forms of movement-based instruction share one important characteristic. Rather than the teacher showing and telling students how to move, the teacher uses a series of questions to prompt student engagement in both the cognitive and psychomotor domains. Essentially, the teacher asks a question that leads to some type of student thinking, which in turn leads to a "movement answer" displayed by students. The types of questions can vary, as can the types and level of student thinking and movement answers.

Because questions are at the heart of this kind of instruction, the term *inquiry teaching* will be used in this chapter to describe this array of strategies that can be defined as an instructional model. The unique characteristics of question-based teaching, and the many recognizable strategies included within it, formulates a coherent set of procedures that teachers can use to promote student thinking, problem solving, and exploration in physical education. And, while these strategies were originally developed for movement-based programming, they can be used effectively to teach a wide range of physical education content today.

The Inquiry model described in this chapter shares some similarities with other models in this book, most notably cooperative learning and tactical games. Those models use problem-solving teaching strategies—as does the Inquiry model. However, there are many differences that make the Inquiry model unique. Cooperative learning is based on the team structure for learning activities. Inquiry teaching uses many kinds of structures, but most often relies on individual student thinking. Because of the scoring rubrics used by the teacher and communicated to students in the Cooperative Learning model and the situation-based activities in the Tactical Games model, these models typically lead to a narrower range of answers and movements. Inquiry teaching can be used to have students explore a wide range of answers (both cognitive and psychomotor), especially creative ones that are "not obvious."

All physical educators use questions in their teaching. Question-asking is a basic pedagogical skill. However, using questions from time to time does not constitute teaching by the Inquiry model. It becomes inquiry teaching when entire units of instruction are based on such strategies, and question-asking is used nearly exclusively as the method of developing students intellectually, physically, and emotionally in physical education. Like all other models in this book, using something "a bit" or "from time to time" does not qualify as model-based instruction. As you will see in this chapter, inquiry teaching is more than asking students a question and "letting them go at it." When done according to the model described here, inquiry teaching is just as engaging for the teacher as it is for students, and requires specific kinds of planning and pedagogical skills that are quite different from other models.

Overview

There is no formally designed Inquiry Teaching model in physical education. The model to be presented in this chapter is really an amalgam of a number of inquiry- and problem-solving strategies that physical educators have been using for many years under many different names:

1. Indirect teaching
2. Problem solving
3. Exploration teaching (Barrett, 1970)
4. Guided Discovery (Mosston & Ashworth, 1994)

Because each of these terms describes one or more strategies that are used for short periods of time in classes, they do not comprise a model for teaching in and of themselves. In order to form them into an actual model of teaching, their most common characteristic (using questions to guide learning) will be used as the basis of the Inquiry model presented here. The design of the Inquiry model owes a large debt to these strategies, but as you will see, the Inquiry teaching model is more encompassing than any one of them.

Perhaps the most important feature of inquiry teaching is that student learning occurs in the cognitive domain first, and at times exclusively. Students are asked questions that get them to think to themselves or with one or more peers. Cognitive learning is sometimes the only type of achievement sought by the teacher. More typically, however, the cognitive engagement is used as the prerequisite or stimulus for answers expressed in the psychomotor domain: students think first, then express their answer through some type of movement. The interaction between the cognitive and psychomotor domains will depend on the kind of student learning sought by the teacher.

There are a number of ways to classify the development of student learning, and thus the types of questions used, in the inquiry model. One of the most common schemes is Bloom et al's (1956) taxonomy, which has six levels of cognitive knowledge. Based on the kind of knowledge sought with the learning activity, the teacher would emphasize questions at one level more than others, and make sure that students had the prerequisite knowledge for that task. Bloom's taxonomy can be used to differentiate between lower-order and higher-order knowledge, based on their position in the taxonomy. Lower-order learning includes: *knowledge* (recognition and recall), *comprehension* (translation, interpretation, and extrapolation), and *application* (using previous knowledge to solve problems). Higher-order learning includes: *analysis* (explanation of parts and function), *synthesis* (creativity used to make something new), and *evaluation* (judging the worth or merit of something). A teacher would target the level of knowledge being developed in a given learning activity and use questions to students that would promote verbal and movement answers at that level. You should be aware that higher-order questions are not necessarily better than lower-order ones; the appropriateness of a question is determined by the degree to which it matches the targeted knowledge level and promotes that kind of student learning.

Some entire physical education curriculums are strongly based on inquiry teaching. Movement education, educational games, and skill themes (Graham, Holt/Hale, & Parker, 1998) all promote the development of students' intellectual abilities, which then work to help students be expressive, creative, and skillful in the psychomotor domain. These curriculums are used in many schools in the United States and abroad, most often at the elementary grades. The roles of teacher-as-question-asker and learner-as-problem-solver are central in these programs, making inquiry teaching an effective model for them. But, as you will see in this chapter, the Inquiry model can also be effective with a wider range of content and in all grade levels.

Foundations of the Inquiry Teaching Model

Theory and Rationale

The Inquiry model to be described in this book is based on a number of recognizable cognitive learning theories, each of which might suggest slightly different teaching strategies and learning activities in physical education. Among some of the theories that contribute to the inquiry model are Bruner's (1961) theory of discovery learning, Ausubel's (1968) meaningful reception learning, and, very recently, constructivism—espoused by many contemporary educational theorists. Because of its current prominent place, constructivism will be used here as the major theory that contributes to the Inquiry model. Actually, there are many constructivist viewpoints, but they all share some common grounds, outlined in the next section.

Assumptions about Teaching and Learning

Assumptions about Teaching

1. The main pedagogical function of the teacher is to stimulate student thinking, which then leads to development in the psychomotor domain.
2. Questions are used as the most prominent type of discourse from the teacher to students.
3. The teacher is a facilitator of student learning, someone who prompts students with carefully thought-out questions that promote student exploration and creativity.
4. Teacher questions should match students' intellectual abilities.
5. The teacher's role is a combination of direct and indirect instruction. It is direct when the teacher plans for and leads students into a certain kind of engagement with the content. It is indirect once the teacher has prompted students into thinking about and exploring movement problems to solve.

Assumptions about Learning

1. Learning occurs best when the learning activity has personal meaning to the student.
2. Learners enter an activity with multiple sources of prior knowledge that they use to construct new knowledge and meanings.
3. Learning in the psychomotor domain is preceded by learning in the cognitive domain.
4. Learning is essentially a problem-solving process, in which the learner uses prior knowledge and meaning to create solutions that can be expressed verbally and/or through physical movement.
5. Like all other kinds of learning, cognitive development occurs best when the complexity of the problem-solving task closely matches the learner's developmental abilities.

Major Theme for the Inquiry Model: Learner as Problem Solver

Although there are many recognized inquiry-based teaching strategies used in physical education today, they all share one common characteristic: they approach learning as a problem-solving process. The teacher "frames" the problem by asking a question, gives students some time to create and explore one or more plausible solutions, and then asks students to demonstrate their solutions as evidence that learning has occurred. Typically, the problem must be solved in the cognitive domain before students can formulate the "movement answer" that shows they understand the key concept and have solved the problem posed by the teacher's question. Tillotson (1970) indicates that the problem-solving process has five steps (pp. 131–132):

1. *Identification of the problem.* The teacher knows the concepts that students need to learn, the skills to be mastered, and how to prompt students with well-planned questions that lead students through a well-planned sequence.
2. *Presentation of the problem.* The teacher asks one or more focused questions that "frame" the learning task and its embedded problem for students.
3. *Guided exploration of the problem.* The teacher observes students as they attempt to solve the problem, providing cues, feedback, and facilitative questions.

4. *Identifying and refining the final solution.* The teacher uses these cues, feedback, and facilitative questions to refine the students' thinking and to lead students to one or more plausible solutions.

5. *Demonstration for analysis, evaluation, and discussion.* Once they have completed the task by devising a solution to the problem, students (individually or in groups) demonstrate their solutions to the rest of the class. These demonstrations serve as prompts for the teacher and other students to analyze—not to be critical, but to allow the rest of the class to benefit from their thinking and moving.

Tillotson's basic description obviously places problem solving at the organizing center of the teaching and learning process, nicely formulating the theme of "learner as problem solver" for the inquiry model presented in this chapter.

Learning Domain Priorities and Interactions

The Inquiry model is strongly based in the cognitive domain, even for physical education instruction. Students are prompted into some level of thinking by the problem given to them by the teacher, solve the problem cognitively, and then fashion a movement answer. Typically, the *domain priorities* for the inquiry model will be:

First priority: Cognitive learning
Second priority: Psychomotor learning
Third priority: Affective learning

However, many teachers who use inquiry teaching will place affective learning ahead of psychomotor learning to promote students' self-awareness, exploration, creativity, and self-esteem. The cognitive domain is always given the highest priority, but after that the teacher wishes to help students feel good about themselves in the movement environment—more so than trying to develop skilled movement patterns. The rationale is to provide students with stimulating and positive movement experiences that will lead to increased enjoyment and additional participation.

The *domain interaction*, then, will depend on which domain the teacher gives the second priority for each learning activity. For example, if the teacher is trying to get students to problem solve and then demonstrate skilled movement after some "thinking time," then learning in the cognitive domain should facilitate learning in the psychomotor domain. Affective learning then occurs when students feel good about their ability to "think better and move better." If the teacher wants to promote affective learning as the second priority, then student thinking can lead to any number of creative solutions that allow students to feel good about "thinking and moving," even if their motor answers are not highly skilled or proficient.

Student Learning Preferences

Using the Reichmann and Grasha (1974) profile for student learning preferences, the Inquiry model will be most effective with students who are classified as participant, collaborative, and independent. It must be emphasized that this profile best applies when students are engaged in the problem-solving process—not at those times when the teacher is "framing" the problem to be solved. That framing will often take on many attributes of the Direct Instruction model, as the teacher controls the pacing of the lesson and the interactions with students.

Validation

Research Validation. As you will recall, the Inquiry Teaching model presented in this chapter is an amalgam of several strategies that rely on the teacher to frame and ask questions, and the students to "think, then move." Siedentop (1991) calls this *teaching through questions.* Mosston and Ashworth (1994) have the most recognized label, *Guided Discovery.* Harrison, Blakemore, Buck, and Pellett (1996) call it *inquiry learning* but describe it more as a one-time strategy than as a complete model, as shown here. Even though inquiry teaching, in these forms and others, has been part of physical education instruction for many years, we have little research verification that it can promote the kinds of achievement stated by its proponents. One of the very few studies was completed by Schempp (1982), in which students (grades one through five) were placed in shared decision-making groups for eight weeks. At the end of that time, the students showed significantly higher scores on originality, elaboration, and a total "creativity composite" over students who were instructed with teacher-centered decision making.

One version of inquiry teaching, called *critical thinking* (McBride, 1992), has some research support behind its use in physical education. Ennis (1991) reported that elementary students were able to develop better cognitive-analytic skills within a unit taught with the critical thinking approach. McBride and Bonnette (1995) found that critical thinking skills could be increased in nonphysical educational settings, such as a sports camp.

Some of the lack of research support for the Inquiry Teaching model can be attributed to the variety of teaching strategies that use questions but do not fully match the Inquiry model. Some of the gap can be attributed to the large numbers of practitioners who began to use inquiry teaching as part of movement-based programming, and chose to validate it through the accumulation of craft knowledge—not waiting for firm support in the research literature. Teaching-as-question-asking became "the way they taught," and they simply carried on with it.

Craft Knowledge Validation. Inquiry-based teaching has been prominent in physical education for nearly forty years. Under several different names and procedures, teacher-as-question-asker has been the main pedagogical approach used by a large number of teachers in the United States and abroad, particularly in Great Britain. Entire programs have been designed and implemented for physical education content that is most effectively taught exclusively or in large part with inquiry-based instruction, such as:

1. Movement education
2. Educational gymnastics
3. Skill themes (Gallahue, 1996; Graham, Holt/Hale, & Parker, 1998)
4. Group initiatives and New Games
5. Dance

The prominence of these and other types of physical education programs indicates that many teachers use some form of inquiry instruction, even if not the Inquiry model presented in this chapter. Many teachers use Mosston and Ashworth's (1994) Guided Discovery style in their lessons, expanding the number of teachers who are familiar with this approach. This widespread use of inquiry teaching in physical education gives strong support for its effectiveness in promoting students' thinking, creative movement, and self-esteem—all three of which appear to be growing as goals for contemporary physical education instruction. While research validation in physical education is lacking, it is difficult to ignore the fact that so many teachers use inquiry- and problem-solving approaches in their gyms.

Intuitive Validation.   Intuitive validation for the Inquiry model comes from a combination of motor learning principles and the common sense use of Bloom's taxonomy. Motor learning experts will agree that cognition plays a fundamental role in psychomotor learning. Learners must have basic cognitive abilities in order to comprehend and carry out the demands of nearly all movement tasks. In the strictest sense, we must think (consciously or unconsciously) before we move. There is much disagreement on the manner in which these domains interact in a given situation for a learner and the exact way that cognitive development contributes to motor development (Rink, 1996).

If you will recall, Bloom's taxonomy in the cognitive domain is based on a hierarchy of learning categories, starting with simple recall and advancing to evaluation. Each stage of cognitive development requires the learner to be engaged in increasingly complex and difficult tasks, which then implies differing teaching strategies. So-called lower-order learning can be accomplished with mostly direct techniques: the teacher shows and/or tells students, who then attempt to recall or reproduce what they have just observed. So-called higher-order learning is typically pursued with mostly indirect techniques in which students attempt to synthesize previous knowledge, create new knowledge, or make value judgments. These higher-order outcomes cannot be effectively achieved with direct techniques; the teacher must find ways to *facilitate* student learning without providing students with actual answers. It then stands to reason that inquiry teaching can be used for these purposes, providing a sound rationale and validation for its use in many kinds of physical education instruction and content.

Teaching and Learning Features

Directness

The directness profile for the Inquiry model as it is used in physical education is shown in Figure 12.1. Note that while such teaching is often called *indirect,* it falls on the direct side of the profile in several categories. As you can see, the teacher retains control over nearly all of the instruction, but does give control to students on one key category: engagement patterns. Once the teacher frames the problem and students begin to think and move, it is students who determine how they will be engaged as they explore possible answers. While this is only one characteristic in the total profile, it does allow the model to work as it is designed, providing students with the kind of engagement needed for cognitive development.

1. *Content selection.* The content in the Inquiry model is most often cognitive knowledge, concepts, and movement patterns the teachers wants students to learn, contained within each of the problems to be solved. The teacher determines all of the content in this model by deciding what will be taught (explored, solved, etc.) in the unit and each lesson.

2. *Managerial control.* The teacher determines the managerial plan and specific class procedures in the inquiry model. When managerial tasks overlap with learning tasks, such as in how to set up learning stations, selecting equipment, and making teams, the teacher allows students to make some decisions.

3. *Task presentations.* Task presentations are used to frame the problem that students will be asked to solve in the learning task. Task presentations take the form of questions that the teacher communicates to stimulate students' thoughts and movement. The teacher will have a content progression planned for each class, and uses the task presentation/questions to move students through that progression. It is important to note that the task presentation should provide students only with enough information to clarify the task and its parameters; the teacher should stop short of giving students information that he wishes students to learn for themselves. So, although the task presentation leads to student-centered engagement, the teacher still retains control over this function in this model.

4. *Engagement patterns.* Once the teacher has framed the problem, students are given much of the control in pursuing the solution/s, especially for higher-order cognitive tasks.

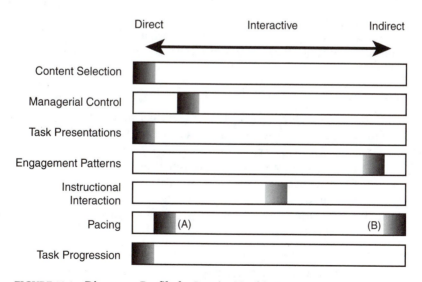

FIGURE 12.1   Directness Profile for Inquiry Teaching

Students can explore possible solutions, work with other students, try new things, change equipment, or change body positions as they attempt to "think through" the problem of the moment.

5. *Instructional interactions.* The Inquiry model is highly interactive once students become engaged in the solution of problems, particularly when the problem is complex or has several steps. The nature of this interaction is interrogatory, not didactic. That is, the teacher uses questions, not direct statements, in order to actively stimulate student thinking and the exploration of movement patterns.

6. *Pacing.* The teacher determines the overall pacing in the unit and each lesson. She decides when new tasks (problems) will begin and how much time will be allocated for each one (A). Students determine the pacing within the time allocated for each task by deciding how long they need to think about solutions, how many times to practice possible solutions, and by determining when they are finished with a task—that is, when they have the problem solved (B).

7. *Task progression.* The teacher determines the list and sequencing of learning tasks for the unit and each lesson. This progression should lead students toward increasingly complex problems to solve, developing cognitive, psychomotor, and affective abilities. Students might be asked periodically, "What do you think should come next?", but the teacher retains control by guiding students to an answer he has already determined to be correct or appropriate.

Predominant Engagement Patterns

The Inquiry model can use many different engagement patterns as students pursue solutions to the problem framed by the teacher. Students can "think and move" individually, in pairs, in small groups, in temporary teams, in large groups, and even as an entire class. The most appropriate engagement pattern will be determined by the complexity of the problem and the degree to which the teacher wants students to interact with others in its solution.

Inclusiveness

Inquiry teaching is highly inclusive. Once the teacher frames the problem and communicates it to students, all students have an opportunity to think about a solution and fashion their own cognitive and movement answers. And, if the teacher is trying to foster inductive thinking, almost every answer that students can come up with is acceptable. There are few wrong answers that can be used to exclude students who do not understand the concept or movement pattern to be mastered. Everyone gets a chance to "think and move," and there is something in nearly every answer for which every student can be reinforced by the teacher and classmates.

Task Presentation and Task Structure

As defined in this book, inquiry teaching leads students through a series of planned learning tasks in which they attempt to solve one or more problems "framed" by the teacher in the form of a question. The problem is almost always given verbally by the teacher, although some print and visual media can be used, such as task cards, cue cards, and CD ROMs. Once the problem has been framed, the teacher signals the students to begin "thinking and moving" within a stated task structure. You should be aware that many of the problems within inquiry teaching are small ones that students can solve quickly. Because of this, there will often be many task presentations (questions) used rapidly within a single task structure.

Task Presentation.   Task presentations in the Inquiry model look very different from those used for more direct instructional models. In the Inquiry model, the teacher does not show and explain a concept or movement to the class and then ask students to reproduce it. Actual teacher demonstrations are rarely used, and only when it is clear that the students cannot solve the problem on their own after "thinking and moving." Essentially, the task presentation has two main components: framing the task and asking a question.

The teacher should provide students only with enough information to allow them to understand the task and the problem to be solved. Once that is done, the teacher signals students to begin "thinking and moving." Framing the task means to put it into some context and give students a point of reference. It can also include words that modify the task or increase the level of complexity. The last part of the framing process is to simply ask students a question to indicate the cognitive and/or movement problem they need to solve in the immediate task. The following is an example of framing the task and asking the questions for a short series to develop second graders' concepts of balancing and balancing skills.

TEACHER: What does it mean to 'balance'?

STUDENTS: To be able to stay up without falling or losing your place.

TEACHER: When do you use balance?

STUDENTS: When we walk and run.

TEACHER: Are those the only times? How about when you kick a ball, or throw a ball, or spin yourself around? What happens if you lose your balance while doing those things?

STUDENTS: We will fall down.

TEACHER: Yes. What else can happen?

STUDENTS: If you lose your balance when kicking, the ball won't go where you aimed it.

TEACHER: Good. Now, I want you to think for a moment about what you can do to keep your balance when you are standing in place. (Teacher allows fifteen seconds of wait time.)

STUDENTS: Mary: "You can lift your arms."

Cindy: "You can keep both feet on the floor."

Jose: "You can try to stand up straight."

TEACHER: OK. In your self-space (this is the task structure), can you show me one way to balance while standing just on one foot?

(Students "think and move.")

TEACHER: Now, can you balance on two feet at a low level?

(Students "think and move.")

TEACHER: I see a lot of creative balancers! Now, can you show me how to keep your balance while touching three different body parts to the floor?

(Students "think and move.")

Notice that the teacher used the first part of the task presentation to make sure students understood the basic concept of balancing. Without that knowledge, the students would not have been ready for the series of balancing tasks that followed. The task structure (to be described in the next section) was simple, allowing all students to "think and move" on their own once each question was asked. It was clear that the teacher had a content progression in mind, consisting of a series of small, increasingly complex problems for the students to solve.

Task Structure.   Inquiry teaching can use a wide variety of task structures, within which students "think and move." The task structure will provide students with the parameters for their engagement, including one or more of the following:

1. Space to be used
2. Equipment to use or select from
3. Grouping (individual, partner, small group, large group)
4. Safety information
5. A time limit for completing the problem

Extending the example of the second-grade balancing lesson, the teacher could begin to use some different task structures to increase the cognitive and psychomotor problems for the children:

1. Partner up with the person closest to you. Can you and your partner show me two ways to balance while making contact with each other?
2. One of the persons from each of the partner pair should go to the box in the center of the gym and take one of the shape pieces of any size you wish. (The box contains a variety of flat pieces of geometric shapes, ranging from small to large). Now, with your partner can you show me how to balance while standing on your shape, with each of you having only one foot on the shape? (Students "think and move.") Which size shape is it harder to balance on? Why?
3. Now, you and your partner find another pair to join up with, so you have a group of four. Can you try balancing all four of you on one shape? Is this easier or harder than before? Why?
4. For this last task you are going to have to really think hard and experiment in your group. Combine with another group to make a group of eight. Each group should get one shape and place it on the floor so that it is not near another group's shape (for

safety). I will give you four minutes to complete this task. Listen carefully. Try to balance all eight persons on the shape, so that no one has more than one foot touching it. You may choose any shape and size your group wishes. If you can do this with a large shape in less than four minutes, try it with a smaller shape. Go.

The task presentations are very brief, and the task structure changes several times, building on the previous structure. In task 4, the teacher is introducing students to the concept of counterbalancing, anticipating that they will not be able to fit all eight students on the shape at one time with individual balancing. They will need to learn how to use each other in ways that allow them all to be balanced on the shape.

Task structures similar to those used in the Tactical Games model (Chapter 13) can also be used in the Inquiry model. Students can be placed in lead-up or modified games for a short time, followed by questions from the teacher to teach tactics, strategy, game skills, and rules. Highly open task structures can be used to allow students to explore and be creative, such as the teaching of expressive movement and some forms of dance. The teacher might simply put on a musical piece and give students ten minutes to devise a short dance that expresses the emotions they hear in the music. Each student is then asked to do a short performance, followed by an explanation for their movement interpretation of the music. As you have recognized by now, the task structure in the Inquiry model needs only to be prompted by a question, and leads to the students "thinking and moving" in response to that question.

Teacher Expertise and Contextual Needs

Teacher Expertise

Teachers who use the Inquiry model will need to have particular expertise in several areas of the proposed knowledge base presented in Chapter 2.

Learners. Inquiry teachers will need to consider students' cognitive and psychomotor abilities to use the model effectively. Students' abilities will determine the degree to which they are able to comprehend questions used by the teacher and be engaged in the problem-solving process. Teachers should have good knowledge of the stages of cognitive development and be able to place students at the correct stage.

Learning Theories. There are many cognitive learning theories in education today. Inquiry teachers should be familiar with those that contribute to the foundation of the inquiry model: constructivism, discovery learning (Bruner, 1964), and Jean Piaget's theories on child growth and development. The key here is for the teacher to recognize which part of each theory is applied in the inquiry model. No single theory, nor the teaching strategies set forth in it, can fully encompass the scope of the Inquiry model.

Developmental Appropriateness. The strong emphasis on cognitive learning that then leads to outcomes in the psychomotor domain makes the teacher knowledge of learning domains and their interactions critical in this model. The teacher must know the cognitive level at which each question is targeted and understand how that level will manifest itself through movement—both at levels that match students' developmental stages. Determining developmental appropriateness is a bit more complicated in this model, since the teacher must know if the students are intellectually ready to take on the problem *and* are able to execute the corresponding motor answer for it. It does not benefit students if they can come up with (think of) an answer but do not have the ability to demonstrate that knowledge in the psychomotor domain.

Learning Domains and Objectives.   The Inquiry model is strongly based on Bloom's levels of cognitive learning. Therefore, teachers must know this classification system well and be able to recognize indicators of cognitive and psychomotor learning at each level. For example, if the teacher asks a simple knowledge question ("Can you show me where to make contact with the ball when you kick it?"), but the student's movement answer is at the comprehension level (the student shows and explains the difference between a pass and a shot on goal), the teacher must be able to identify the mistake and redirect the question so that the student responds at the appropriate level the next time.

Task Analysis and Content Progression.   A task analysis for inquiry teaching is based on a combination of cognitive concepts and psychomotor performance demands. Rather than list a sequence of skills to be mastered and performance criteria to be met, the teacher analyzes each part of the unit content for the kinds of cognitive knowledge students will need to acquire as they progress through the unit. This requires that the teacher is himself knowledgeable of these concepts, along with the motor performance cues included within them. For example, a typical task analysis for the tennis serve might include:

1. Stance
2. Grip
3. Toss
4. Contact point
5. Follow-through
6. Strategy

The teacher would instruct students in each component of the task, working toward performance proficiency. Contrast that with the *concepts* that players need to know for that same sport skill:

1. Stance (force, balance, weight transfer)
2. Grip (force, friction, effect of grip on contact angle and ball spin)
3. Toss (arm extension, accuracy, timing)
4. Contact point (angle of contact)
5. Follow-through (momentum, power, accuracy, preparation for return)
6. Strategy (first service, second service, singles, doubles, anticipation of return, "no man's land")

This kind of task analysis would lead the teacher to design a different kind of content progression—one based on teaching students the concepts needed for this skill, not just the movement patterns it includes. The series of learning tasks would allow students to first learn each concept by responding to questions asked by the teacher, followed by exploring the movement pattern needed to execute each concept in the tennis serve.

Assessment. Student learning in the Inquiry model can be assessed with traditional and alternative techniques. It is possible to assess lower-order learning with written tests and regular checking for understanding by the teacher during lessons. Checklists can be devised to verify that students have demonstrated verbal and movement answers to major concepts in a unit. Higher-order learning is more difficult to assess because it often requires subjective judgment and interpretation of student answers by the teacher. The key to all types of assessment in the Inquiry model is the teacher's own knowledge of appropriate and inappropriate cognitive and movement answers given by students—specifically, how those answers represent students' learning of the embedded concepts. In many ways it is a matching process: the teacher asks a question that leads to students' responses. The teacher must then determine which answers indicate the desired kind of student learning targeted by the question.

Physical Education Content. By now you should understand that the content taught with the Inquiry model is not sport, fitness, games, dance, etc. Rather, it is the concepts needed to understand each movement form that contributes to proficient performance. When the learning goal is to promote student expression and meaning, these become the focal points of the moment. Therefore, the inquiry teacher must know physical education (movement) content in a very different way to be effective in this model. This knowledge will lead a teacher to observe student movement from a different perspective. When a mistake is observed, the inquiry teacher will not simply provide the student with corrective feedback. The teacher will need to determine what knowledge the student lacks and ask key questions to get the student to think through alternative response patterns that will be transformed into an appropriate movement answer the next time.

Curriculum Models. It is possible to use the Inquiry model to instruct any movement content at any grade level. However, the origins of the model are strongly rooted in several curriculum models that rely heavily on this approach to teaching:

1. Movement education
2. Educational gymnastics
3. Skill themes
4. Educational dance
5. Group initiatives and New Games

The teacher will need to become familiar with the principles and specific content taught in these models and adopt the Inquiry model for each one.

Effective Teaching Skills Applied to Inquiry Teaching

Teachers who use the Inquiry model will apply effective teaching skills in unique ways to allow the model to facilitate the learning objectives planned in content units.

Planning.   The teacher's list of knowledge areas to be learned by students provides the starting point for unit planning in the Inquiry model. The teacher plans the progression and levels of knowledge to be covered in the unit and then plans a sequence of questions, problems to be solved, and specific learning activities for student engagement. This will look like the planning process for direct instruction in many ways, except that the content will be mostly cognitive rather than skill-oriented.

Lesson planning in the Inquiry model is less structured since it is often difficult to anticipate how long it will take students to complete each problem-solving task and the length of question-based interactions needed to help students grasp the knowledge of the moment. Because students' abilities to take on new problems given by the teacher depend so much on their previous knowledge, it is important that the teacher ensures that students have grasped the prerequisite knowledge. "Covering" concepts should not take preference over learning the concepts targeted in each lesson.

It is strongly advised that the inquiry teacher does not "wing it" through the problem-solving progression in a lesson. The lesson plan should include: how each problem will be framed, the specific problems to be solved, a list of questions to ask students before they become engaged, student movement patterns to be monitored, and follow-up questions to ask when students are engaged in learning activities. This kind of planning can prepare the inquiry teacher for many possible student answers and movement patterns, giving her time to plan some of the interactions before the class begins. While most inquiry lessons cannot be scripted before class begins, the most effective ones are those in which the teacher has correctly anticipated a good number of the students' verbal and movement answers and is ready to use those answers as "teaching moments."

Time and Class Management.   Inquiry teaching lessons are characterized by the teacher having control of the flow and pacing of planned learning activities. Time and class management may appear to be somewhat informal, but in reality the teacher maintains close control of how the lesson proceeds and is well aware of how long each activity has taken to complete. The teacher will monitor students to make sure they are properly engaged during learning activities and following all class rules. It is important that the teacher have a "firm but flexible" management plan that allows students time to develop their problem-solving abilities and also keeps the pace of the class at an even tempo.

Task Presentation and Task Structure.   Inquiry teachers must have three key pedagogical skills in these areas: the ability to frame problems for students, excellent questioning skills, and the ability to design learning tasks that simultaneously challenge students intellectually and physically.

Framing the Learning Problem.   The inquiry teacher must be able to "set the stage" for the upcoming learning problem, regardless of the size and complexity of the problem.

Set induction can be used effectively to alert students to the importance of the knowledge they will learn and the context in which they will apply it. This will also increase students' interest in the upcoming task. When teaching younger students, it is often helpful to create a story line that goes with the lesson's sequence of learning tasks, allowing the children to place themselves in the story and act out the part of a certain character. This also helps them to relate class activities to familiar stories, people, characters, and places.

Levels of Questions. The teacher's skill in using questions occurs at three times: at the end of the problem-framing when the initial question directs students to be engaged, during engagement in the problem-solving process, and during the lesson review. At all three times the most critical skill is the teacher's ability to match the level of questions with the targeted level of student learning. Questions for each level share some common *stems* that can be used to prompt student engagement regardless of the content of the moment. Figure 12.2 shows some examples of question stems that can be used in physical education.

Types of Questions. Questions at the level of knowledge, comprehension, and application typically lead to one or a few correct answers. These are referred to as *convergent questions,* as they require the learner to sort out and identify one or a limited number of potential answers. Questions at the level of analysis, synthesis, and evaluation typically lead to any number of plausible answers that solve the problem posed by the teacher. They stimulate learners to "branch out" in their thinking, so are referred to as *divergent questions.* The skilled inquiry teacher must be aware of the type of questions asked to students so that answers can be assessed appropriately.

Wait Time. The major purpose of the Inquiry model is to get students to use their intellectual abilities to solve problems verbally and/or with movement responses. It is therefore essential that students are given time to formulate answers on their own, before other students are allowed to tell or show their answers. Research has shown that waiting at least three seconds before allowing any student to answer convergent questions increases all students academic performance. A wait time of fifteen or more seconds should be used for divergent questions (Tobin, 1987).

Probes. Borich (1992) recommends that inquiry teachers use probes, or redirects, regularly. A probe is a question that follows a student's answer in order to:

1. *Elicit clarification.* Get the student to rephrase, reword, or refine the original answer.
2. *Solicit new information.* When the student has given a partially correct or nearly acceptable answer.
3. *Redirect the flow.* A gentle, positive rephrasing of the question when the student has not made a correct answer. This cues the student to "think again" without using harsh or abrupt language.

FIGURE 12.2 Some Common Question Stems for Inquiry Teaching

Level	Some Common Stems	Examples
Knowledge	"Who can show me . . .?"	"Who can show me the correct way to do the first part of the 'electric slide'?"
	"Who can tell me . . .?"	"Who can tell me where you stand when your partner is serving in tennis doubles?"
Comprehension	"Can you explain . . .?"	"Can you explain why your partner's shots keep going off-line?"
	"Why would you . . .?"	"Why would you want to play a zone defense in basketball?"
	"How do you get [something] to happen?	"How do you get your (badminton) opponent in position to make an overhead smash shot at her?"
Application	"Can you combine . . .?"	"Can you combine a slide and a gallop? If so, please show me how to do that."
	"Knowing what you know now, can you tell me . . .?"	"We just discussed offensive strategy for passing in flag football. Knowing that, and if you are on defense, how would you try to prevent the offense from succeeding?"
	"How is [something] similar to . . .?"	"Can you show me three ways that playing defense in floor hockey is similar to playing defense in team handball?"
Analysis	"How is [this] different from . . .?"	"How does the (badminton) low short serve 'set up' your opponent differently than the high, deep serve? When would you use each one?"
	"Why would you not . . .?"	"Why would you not stretch cold muscles?"
	"Analyze . . .?"	"I am making a shape with my body. Can you analyze it for the class? How stable is it? Is my balance good or bad? Why?"
Synthesis	"What will happen if . . .?"	"What do you think will happen if you use a longer implement to strike the lighter ball?"
	"Can you make a new . . .?"	"Can you and your partner make a new dance from this music?"
	"If [something] changes, how will you compensate?"	"If you change your center of gravity, what will you need to do to increase stability?"
Evaluation	"What should [someone] have done . . .?"	"When Molly had the basketball on the right wing on the fast break, what should she have done to move her defender more?"
	"Is it better to . . . or . . .?"	"Is it better to hit this putt fast or slow? Why?"
	"Why do you do . . .?"	"I see you running regularly. Why do you do that so often?"
	"Is that the right way to . . .?"	"I see you use the two-handed grip for your forehand shots. Is that the right technique?"

The questions used in inquiry teaching determine the task structure to a large degree. Some questions will require students to work alone, while other questions will direct students to work in pairs, small groups, or large groups. Some questions will require very short periods of wait time (particularly convergent ones), while other questions (higher-order, divergent) will need longer periods of wait time—perhaps as long as three to five minutes. The teacher will need to use her expertise to fashion questions, determine the best task structure to answer each one, and allocate the appropriate amount of problem-solving time to students.

Communication. As you might expect, communication skills in the inquiry model are centered in the ability to frame the problem/task and to use questions as the primary pedagogical strategy to promote intended learning outcomes. Teachers need to be clear and concise in both areas, giving students what they need to know about the problem and the parameters in place for their engagement. Students cannot be expected to be properly engaged if they do not understand the problem they need to be solving at any given moment.

Instructional Information. As you know by now, the inquiry teacher uses very few direct communications to students. The major idea is to "ask, not tell," so when the teacher wishes to have students learn it involves finding ways to ask questions that will prompt students into "thinking first, then moving" to explore, solve problems, and develop multiple plausible answers. Periodically the teacher might need to give students clues, or even direct answers, to help students get "unstuck" on their way to more complex answers. This should be limited, however.

Other types of instructional information come in the form of comments made to students while they are engaged, and feedback once answers are given or shown. Comments during engagement should be supportive of effort—small hints that students are "on the right track"—or directed toward the process of students' problem solving. Feedback should be directed toward process and outcomes demonstrated through students' answers. It is also possible for the teacher to use other students as the providers of feedback, helping those students to develop analytic and evaluative knowledge.

Review and Closure. The lesson review should be consistent with the level of questions asked by the teacher during class. If the teacher has targeted the level/s of student learning intended, the review questions can serve as an informal assessment period, as well as a way to "tie it all together" and alert students to the next lesson's content. The teacher must be careful not to overextend the level of questions in the review, making them more difficult than the students' ability to answer them. It is important to focus on what students have *learned,* not what they do not yet know in the unit. The closure should follow the overall design of the Inquiry model, with the teacher asking students what needs to be done to finish the lesson, such as where equipment should go, how much time they have until their next class, and what needs to be remembered for next time.

Student Developmental Requirements

Students' developmental needs must be considered in the cognitive and psychomotor domains, separately and together. Students must be able to first understand the problem as the teacher frames it, be able to comprehend the problem-solving task or question, and have a reasonable chance of working through an answer at the targeted cognitive level. The teacher must know his students' abilities in these areas and prepare learning tasks that match students' developmental stages at that point in time. But it is not enough that students can arrive at answers only in the cognitive domain. They must have a level of psychomotor development that will allow them to move in ways that manifest their cognitive answers. They must know their answer/s in both domains to achieve the primary goal of the inquiry model—to "think and then move." Once students have learned answers in a sort of linear fashion—first thinking, then moving—at some point they must be able to learn interactively in those domains. That means they will be able to combine their thinking with their moving in ways that make the question of "Are they thinking or moving right now?" a moot point because they are doing both and each domain facilitates the other to make a unique learning experience. Therefore the teacher must know the developmental requirements for each task/problem given to students and be sure that students are ready for that level of challenge.

Contextual Needs for the Inquiry Model

The Inquiry model has few contextual demands, so it can be used in almost any physical education setting. The task structure will determine the need for activity space. It can range from every student needing only enough room to move safely in personal space to large spaces needed for group explorations and problem solving. It is important that all students (or groups of students) have enough equipment to prevent waiting for turns. The discovery process will be ineffective if one student has to wait and watch another student—who then solves the problem. For the second student, the learning process will then be imitation, not creative problem solving. The last contextual need is to give students an adequate amount of time to be engaged in the problem-solving process. Some students will take longer than others, but all students should be provided ample time to "think and then move" for themselves. Again, if the class progresses at a pace that is too fast for some students, those students will learn by imitating their peers' answers or not learn at all.

Teacher and Student Roles and Responsibilities in the Inquiry Model

Each instructional model will have certain operations that need to be completed to make the model function according to its design. Some of these operations are carried out by the teacher; others are carried out by one or more students. The following table shows the major operations within the Inquiry Teaching model, and indicates who is responsible for completing them during each lesson.

Operation or Responsibility	Who Does It in the Inquiry Model?
Starting class	The **teacher** begins class with a set induction.
Bringing equipment to class	The **teacher** brings the equipment or delegates that task to students.
Content listing	The **teacher** determines the list of cognitive and movement problems to be presented in the unit.
Task presentation	The **teacher** makes task presentations by framing each learning task or problem for students.
Task structure	The **teacher** typically decides the task structure for each task/problem, but can allow students to make their own groups when such a structure is used.
Content progression	The **teacher** decides when the class will move on to new learning tasks/problems.
Assessment	Two options: 1. The **teacher** provides students with comments and feedback on the quality of their cognitive and movement answers. 2. **Students** can be asked to view and critique other students' answers.

Teaching and Learning Benchmarks for the Inquiry Model

Teachers who use the Inquiry model can learn the benchmarks for their own and student behavior patterns. The following teacher and student benchmarks verify that the Inquiry model has been designed and implemented with an acceptable degree of faithfulness, increasing the likelihood that the stated student learning outcomes will be achieved.

Teacher Benchmarks

Benchmark	How to Verify
Unit content is based on a list of cognitive and movement knowledge areas to be learned by students	Examine the teacher's unit plan.
The teacher frames each task/problem for students	The teacher should write out each task/problem to be given to students on a lesson plan.
The teacher makes content progressions based on taxonomic levels	The teacher should classify each task/problem according to Bloom's hierarchy and show a developmentally appropriate progression throughout the unit.
The teacher plans questions for each task/problem	The teacher should write out a list of potential questions to be used in each task/problem.

(continued)

Teacher Benchmarks   Continued

Benchmark	How to Verify
The teacher monitors student engagement during tasks/problems	Record the pattern of teacher movement during tasks/problems.
The teacher uses questions to facilitate student learning (rather than direct statements)	Record and monitor the teacher's verbal interactions with students.
The teacher provides students with adequate time to complete tasks/problems	Observe and record the number of students who have completed a task/problem when the teacher moves to the next task/problem.
The teacher assesses student learning in the targeted domain/s and level/s	The teacher uses a checklist to indicate students' successful completion of tasks/problems given to them.

Student Benchmarks

Benchmark	How to Verify
Students understand the problem as it is framed by the teacher	Observe students right after the teacher indicates students should begin to "think and move." Students should quickly show evidence of thinking through the problem, and should begin to explore movement answers soon after that.
Students understand the task structure as it is explained to them by the teacher	Once engaged in the task/problem, students should show evidence of working toward answers that correspond to the structure as described by the teacher.
Students have the appropriate level of cognitive and movement knowledge demanded by the task/problem	1. Students' engagement is purposeful. 2. Students ask few clarification questions. 3. Students do not alter the task/problem as described by the teacher. 4. Students find the task/problem challenging, but can complete it in a reasonable amount of time.
Students have learned to "think and move"	1. Use questions to check student understanding. 2. Students can provide more than one answer to divergent questions. 3. Students can explain the processes used to complete tasks and solve problems.
Students achieve higher-order learning (when that is targeted)	1. Students move creatively and purposefully. 2. Students' cognitive and movement answers match. 3. Students can critique others' answers. 4. Students need little direction to take on complex and longer tasks/problems.

Assessing Learning in the Inquiry Model

Assessment in the Inquiry model takes on several forms, due to the multiple levels of knowledge to be assessed and the need to assess both cognitive and psychomotor learning—sometimes separately and sometimes simultaneously. No one assessment technique will be adequate for all of the possible kinds of learning that can be intended in this model. Teachers will need to develop their own assessment techniques that focus on each targeted learning outcome, using a variety of informal, formal, traditional, and alternative approaches.

Informal Assessment.   When the teacher has planned a series of short, fast-paced learning tasks or problems, it is likely that informal assessment will be the most practical way to go. Most of this assessment will be based on the teacher's observation of students as they "think and move" to develop answers to questions from the teacher. The teacher should begin the assessment process during the time of lesson planning, when questions are framed and developed. For each question, the teacher should ask herself, "What will my students say and/or do to indicate that they have answered this question?" Convergent questions will lead to one or a few correct answers. Divergent questions will lead to several answers that the teacher will consider as indicators of student learning. The teacher observes and counts the number of students who have formulated correct/acceptable answers to each question, allowing the teacher to determine if student learning has occurred.

A teacher can also use *checking for understanding* at the class level as an informal assessment strategy by asking the class to respond to the same question at one time, and noting how many students provide a correct or acceptable answer. This is done frequently and quickly in class, with simple question stems like:

"Who knows . . .?"
"Who can tell me . . .?"
"How many of you were able to . . .?"

It is important to use sufficient *wait time* so each student can formulate his/her own answer, giving the teacher a better picture of student learning.

Formal and Traditional Assessment.   It is appropriate for a teacher to use traditional, formal assessment techniques to assess some lower-order learning outcomes in the Inquiry model. Short quizzes, computer-based tests, the completion of worksheets, and simple skills tests can provide the teacher with assessment information when learning is targeted at the levels of knowledge, comprehension, and application. These techniques have less validity and are often impractical in the assessment of higher-order outcomes.

Alternative Assessment.   Alternative assessment techniques can be used for all levels of learning in the Inquiry model, especially for the higher-order outcomes. When questions are framed creatively to reflect "real-world" learning, their assessment will become highly authentic as well. The inquiry teacher can use several ways to assess learning in this model:

1. Student-peer observation with a checklist
2. Student-peer critiques of other student's answers
3. Student self-assessment with a checklist
4. Student journals that explain how they arrived at answers
5. Using the GPAI (Griffin, Mitchell, & Oslin, 1996) for game and other application-level outcomes
6. Student-generated movement and media presentations
7. Checksheets based on the levels of knowledge

Figure 12.3 shows an example of this last assessment technique—one that could be used by the teacher in a single unit of instruction or be kept even two or three years—to document student progression through knowledge levels in one area. The top of the check-sheet indicates that the area being assessed is balance. It is divided into the two major domains of learning to be assessed: the cognitive (through students' verbalization of answers) and psychomotor (through students' ability to move). Each level of knowledge lists one indicator of student learning that must be observed (heard and seen) by the teacher. It is important to note that these indicators will need to be determined by the teacher, to satisfy herself that the student has learned about balance at each level and in both domains.

Selecting and Modifying the Inquiry Model for Physical Education

As you learned in the beginning of this chapter, the Inquiry model as presented here is a merging of strategies from several physical education curriculum models, such as movement education and skill theme learning, and used mainly in elementary school programs. "Teaching by questioning" is used regularly in these models, but can be applied across many other physical education content areas and grade levels. I would recommend the Inquiry model as an effective teaching model for the following physical education content areas:

1. Movement education/movement concepts
2. Educational gymnastics
3. Educational games
4. Dance
5. Group initiatives and New Games
6. Personal fitness concepts
7. Sport and activity concepts
8. Skill themes

FIGURE 12.3   Student Checksheet for Balance Knowledge

Movement Concept: Balance		
Level Assessed	**Cognitive Indicator**	**Movement Indicator**
Knowledge	Can provide his/her own definition of "balance" when asked Achieved _____	Can follow along with the teacher on several examples of static balancing Achieved _____
Comprehension	Can identify when a person is "in balance" or "off balance" Achieved _____	Can show the teacher two examples of being "in balance" and two examples of when he/she is "off balance" Achieved _____
Application	Can identify three games or sports in which balance is important Achieved _____	Can demonstrate the different kinds of balancing movements used in those three games or sports Achieved _____
Analysis	Can correctly predict what will happen to a person's balance (increase or decrease) when changing from one position to another Achieved _____	On the teacher's cue, can demonstrate how to increase or decrease his/her balance from a given starting position Achieved _____
Synthesis	Can explain the importance of center of gravity in keeping one's balance Achieved _____	Can show three ways to change his/her own center of gravity in a static balance position Achieved _____
Evaluation	With a scoresheet, can observe another student's gymnastics routine and correctly score that student's performance (re: balance) Achieved _____	After making the observation, can demonstrate the correct balancing movements for any part of the other student's performance that was scored low Achieved _____

The key thing to remember is that the model emphasizes the process of "thinking, then moving" so it can be used with nearly any content area, not those just listed. If the teacher wishes to promote students' cognitive knowledge, exclusively or in a way that leads to enhanced movement performance, then the inquiry model will be an appropriate choice.

Grade-Level Adaptations.   The inquiry model can be effective at all grades if the levels of cognitive and psychomotor problems given to students match their developmental readiness. That condition will apply to all of the grade level selections and adaptations shown in Figure 12.4.

FIGURE 12.4 Grade-Level Adaptations for the Inquiry Model in Physical Education

Grade Level	Select Inquiry Model?	Possible Adaptations
Preschool	Yes	1. Limit to knowledge level. 2. Focus on student attention and listening skills.
Elementary	Yes	1. Frame the task/problem clearly. 2. Check for understanding before and during. 3. Use shorter tasks/problems.
Middle school/junior high	Yes	No adaptations needed. The full Inquiry model can be implemented.
High school	Yes	1. Focus on higher-order learning. 2. Use fewer, longer tasks/problems. 3. Promote answers that require media and technology.
College/adult	Yes	1. Focus on higher-order learning. 2. Use fewer, longer tasks/problems. 3. Promote cognitive answers that require the use of media and technology.

Summary

The Inquiry model as presented in this chapter is designed on the basis of instructional strategies used in several physical education curriculum models, such as movement education and skill theme development. These and many other approaches use questioning as the primary instructional interaction pattern that prompts learners to "think, then move." There is enough commonality in these approaches to merge them into the Inquiry model as a way of helping teachers to formally design and implement question-based instruction for many content areas and grades in physical education.

All physical education teachers use questions in their instruction, and good questioning skills are necessary in nearly every model presented in this book. However, the Inquiry model is different because the use of questions is not unplanned or sporadic. Asking questions and the framing of learning tasks in the form of problems are the most essential pedagogical operations in this model. There are some new conceptualizations of teaching that will likely make the use of inquiry-based teaching even more prominent in physical education. Constructivist teaching strategies are becoming more and more commonplace in all subjects and share many of the same attributes as inquiry teaching, particularly getting students to formulate new knowledge from existing knowledge, prompting students to learn by exploring and placing the teacher in the role of facilitator of student learning.

It is clear that question-based teaching has been used in physical education for over four decades, emerging as the primary strategy for movement education and movement-based programs. With the recent emergence of other student-centered strategies and instructional models, along with the promotion of cognitive learning outcomes in physical education (NASPE, 1995), a formal Inquiry model as presented here can be an effective way to teach a wide variety of program content at all grade levels in physical education.

Sample Unit Plan for Inquiry Teaching

Content unit:	Locomotor skill themes
Grade level:	Second
Students:	32, about the same number of boys and girls
Length of unit:	10 classes
Length of classes:	About 30 minutes of activity time
Facilities:	Gym or other larger open space with no obstructions
Equipment:	CD player with remote control
	Children's music CDs
	Posters with illustrations of skill themes, levels, pathways, and directions

Content Listing and Schedule

Lessons	Skill Theme	Learning Activities
1–2	1. Space concepts 2. Levels 3. Pathways 4. Directions 5. Locomotor: Walking	1. Explain self-, general, and scatter space 2. Walking in scatter space 3. Walking levels 4. Walking pathways 5. Walking directions 6. Games that feature walking
3–4	Locomotor: Running	1. Running in a circle pattern 2. Running in scatter space 3. Running levels 4. Running pathways 5. Running directions 6. Games that feature running
5	Locomotor: Fleeing and dodging	1. Walking tag games 2. Running tag games 3. Fleeing and dodging tactics
6–7	Locomotor: Skipping	1. Elements of the skip 2. Skipping in scatter space 3. Skipping levels 4. Skipping pathways 5. Skipping directions 6. Games that feature skipping

(continued)

Content Listing and Schedule   Continued

Lessons	Skill Theme	Learning Activities
8–9	Locomotor: Galloping	1. Elements of the gallop 2. Galloping in scatter space 3. Galloping levels 4. Galloping pathways 5. Galloping directions 6. Games that feature galloping
10	Review of skill themes	1. Stations to practice each locomotor skill ■ Poster at each station with a picture of a locomotor movement and various levels, pathways, and directions 2. Teacher introduces each station and tells students to "do that movement just like the picture shows" 3. Freeze tag using the various locomotor movements covered in the unit

Lesson 8: Introduction to Galloping

Lesson Segment	Learning Activity	Questions for Students
Set induction		1. What is a 'locomotor skill'? 2. What locomotor skills have you learned so far? 3. (To the whole class) can you show me how a horse moves? (Students show several versions of a gallop.) 4. Does anyone know what we call the horse's movement? (After 3 seconds of wait time the teacher calls on a student who says "Gallop!") 5. Right. Can people gallop? 6. Today and next class we are going to learn how to gallop—just like a horse!
Elements of the gallop	Pinpointing. The teacher asks one student who used a correct gallop to show the rest of the class how she did it just a minute ago.	As the student gallops, the teacher asks: 1. Look at her feet. What is she doing with her feet when she gallops? 2. Look at her head. Which way is she facing when she gallops? 3. Does she move high off the floor when she gallops? Why not? 4. Can you hear the beat of her gallop? Can you make that beat with your hands?

Lesson 8: Introduction to Galloping   Continued

Lesson Segment	Learning Activity	Questions for Students
Galloping in scatter space	On the teacher's cue, students gallop in scatter space while music plays in the background	Before they gallop: Who can tell me what scatter space means? Why is it important to watch for others when moving in scatter space? What will you do when the music stops each time? (Students were instructed to "freeze" in previous lessons.) As students gallop (to individual students): Are you going too fast? Are you keeping your head to the front? Can you gallop to the beat of the music? During planned pauses in the music: What happens if I gallop really slow? What other locomotor movement is like the gallop? Is galloping easy or hard to do?
Galloping levels	On the teacher's cue, students gallop in scatter space while music plays in the background. As they gallop, the teacher asks them to try it at different levels: low, medium, and high.	Before they gallop: What is a 'level'? How many levels are there? During planned pauses in the music: Which level did you gallop the best in? Which level was the hardest for you? Why was one level harder than the others?
Galloping pathways	On the teacher's cue, students gallop in scatter space while music plays in the background. As they gallop, the teacher asks them to use various pathways: zig-zag, curved, straight, and corners.	Before they gallop: Who remembers what a pathway is? How many pathways can you think of? Are pathways only on the floor, or can they be in the air, too? During planned pauses in the music: Which pathway causes you to make the fastest turns? What do your feet do when you make turns?
Galloping directions	On the teacher's cue, students gallop in scatter space while music plays in the background. As they gallop, the teacher asks them to change direction from forward to backward a few times.	Before they gallop: How many directions can you gallop in? This is a hard one—Why can't you gallop sideways? During planned pauses in the music: Is it hard to gallop backwards? What makes it so hard? How can you make it easier?

(continued)

Lesson 8: Introduction to Galloping   Continued

Lesson Segment	Learning Activity	Questions for Students
Games that feature galloping	"High five" tag while galloping. Nonelimination game—students can get 'untagged' by standing still in the area and getting a "high five" from another student. Teacher explains the rules that students must gallop as they try to avoid being tagged and try to tag others. If they do not gallop, the teacher will count them as being tagged.	Before the game begins: How can you remember to keep galloping? During pauses in the game: What do you have to do to keep from getting tagged? (Gallop fast, change pathways, keep head up to watch the taggers.) How can I gallop faster? Which pathways are easier when I gallop fast? Tameeka, what did you do to watch the taggers, but not run into your classmates?
Review and closure		What skills did we learn today? Can you think of times when you would use those skills in games other than tag? Who can tell me the difference between a gallop and the skip we learned last week?

SUGGESTED READINGS

Dillon, J. T. (1988). *Questioning and teaching.* New York: Teachers College Press.

Gallahue, D. (1996). *Developmental movement experiences for children.* New York: John Wiley and Sons. (Inquiry model for skill themes)

Graham, G., Holt/Hale, S., & Parker, M. (1998). *Children moving* (4th ed.). Mountain View, CA: Mayfield. (Inquiry model for skill theme teaching)

Mosston, M., & Ashworth, S. (1994). *Teaching physical education* (3rd ed.). Columbus, OH: Merrill. (Chapter on Guided Discovery style)

Stanley, S. (1977). *Physical education: A movement orientation* (2nd ed.). New York: McGraw Hill.

CHAPTER

13

The Tactical Games Model

Teaching Games for Understanding

The largest single content area in most physical education programs is the teaching and learning of sport-related games. While other movement forms are always being introduced into physical education, it is safe to say that the traditional games content still remains the biggest part of most schools' curriculums—particularly in the middle school grades through college. Except for a few innovative curriculum and instructional models, like Sport Education (Chapter 10), little has changed in the way teachers plan and implement games units: students get a brief time to practice isolated skills, followed by an introduction to game rules, with an extended time to play the game for the rest of the unit. It is unlikely that students who do not enter the unit with existing game skills and knowledge will improve any as the unit goes on. This approach favors those students who come to the unit with previous experience and abilities in the game being taught. It is also likely that this approach will focus mainly on the development of skills and, to a lesser extent, the strategies needed to play the game well. There is rarely an attempt to teach students things like the game's structure, its traditions, its rituals, and the various human roles needed to carry out competitions.

But the teacher is not entirely at fault in this scenario. Students like to play games; they like to practice games skills in repetitive drills much less, and will often show great resistance when directed to work on discrete skills that they perceive as having little to do with game performance. Once a teacher tells a class that they are starting a games unit (e.g., soccer) there is one predictable question that students will ask: "When do we get to play?" That question will be asked early and often in the unit, until the games segment actually begins. Experienced teachers also know that a "faux pas" of physical education is to start the games segment of a unit and then direct students into drills later on. Student resistance can become almost a rebellion at that point.

The most difficult part in this scenario is that physical education students are rarely ready for the complexities of game play when that segment of a unit begins. They possess neither the skills nor tactical knowledge to carry on even a semblance of the game, so the game becomes an exercise in futility and frustration defined by poor play. The irony of this is that many students think the best way to learn a game is to play the full version of the game, so they would rather keep the game structure than revert back to skill development through drills, lead-up games, or modified games.

The Tactical Games model cleverly uses student interest in the game structure to promote skill development and tactical knowledge needed for competent game performance. In most game units, the teacher plans a progression that goes from basic drills to more complex skills, followed by explanations of rules and the playing of the game's full version. In the Tactical Games model, the teacher plans a sequence of learning tasks in game-like contexts to develop students' skills and tactics, leading to modified or full versions of the game. These game-like tasks and modified games are called *game forms*. The emphasis is on the development of tactical knowledge that facilitates skill applications in smaller versions of the game so that students can apply that learning in the full version when the time comes. In a sense, students are always "playing the game," but are working on essential skills and tactics in a developmentally appropriate sequence.

As the name indicates, the organizing center of the Tactical Games model is *tactics*, the combination of strategy and skill needed to perform in games and game-like situations. For instance, in a softball unit the goal would not be for students to "learn how to field ground balls." Rather, the goal would be for students to learn situational applications for fielding ground balls—positioning, decision-making, and understanding that leads to the correct execution of fielding skills according to the demands of the game situation. Tactics and skills are developed in the sequence of games forms, each of which contains a stated *tactical problem* that defines the learning objective for the current task (Griffin, Mitchell, & Oslin, 1997). It is critical that students can solve the tactical problem by knowing the correct position, options, and plays in the given situation. Performance follows from that understanding.

The Tactical Games instructional model evolved from a British conceptualization of games teaching called *teaching for understanding* (Bunker & Thorpe, 1982). Dissatisfied with the ways games content was typically taught (such as that mentioned at the start of this chapter), Bunker and Thorpe argued that physical education programs should attempt to teach the underlying principles of games so that students really understand each game's structure and tactics, as well as the necessary performance skills. This approach also emphasized the use of developmentally appropriate versions of games at all grade levels. In fact, it would be rare for students to play full, adult versions of games. Bunker and Thorpe (1982) promoted the notion of *games classification* to help students understand the underlying structure of each game by identifying common attributes among games that could carry across similarly classified games. Almond (1986) suggested that nearly all games taught in a physical education program can be classified into one of four types: invasion, net/wall, fielding/run scoring, and target. Examples of each type are shown in Figure 13.1.

FIGURE 13.1   Games Classifications and Examples

Game Type	Examples
Invasion	Basketball
	Hockey (ice, field, floor)
	Football
	Lacrosse
	Netball
	Soccer
	Ultimate Frisbee
Net/wall	Net:
	Badminton
	Pickleball
	Table tennis
	Volleyball
	Wall:
	Handball
	Racketball
	Squash
Fielding/run-scoring	Baseball
	Cricket
	Kickball
	Softball
Target	Croquet
	Billiards
	Bowling
	Golf

Games in the same classification share many common features that students can be taught to recognize and carry over to other games in that category. Basic concepts like positioning, off-the-ball movements, with-ball skills, playing offense, playing defense, and tactics become the building blocks within each category, with direct attempts made to teach students how to generalize these concepts across similar games. For instance, the concept of defensive positioning is quite similar for soccer, basketball, and hockey. Students will be taught the concept of defensive positioning in ways that will allow them to generalize across these three games, building on their tactical awareness and skills from one game to the next.

Bunker and Thorpe's (1986) *Teaching Games for Understanding* model was based on six components, using the selected game as the organizing center in the instructional unit (see Figure 13.2).

Step 1 is an introduction to the game, including its classification and an overview of how it is played. Step 2 serves to promote student interest in the game by teaching students its history and traditions. Step 3 develops students' tactical awareness by presenting the major tactical problems within the game. Step 4 uses game-like learning activities that teach students to recognize when and how to apply tactical knowledge. Step 5 begins to combine tactical knowledge with skill execution, again in game-like activities. In step 6 students develop proficient performance ability, based on this combination of tactical and skill knowledge. As you can see, the learning of motor skills does not come until step 5—which is the *first* step in many traditional approaches to teaching games in physical education.

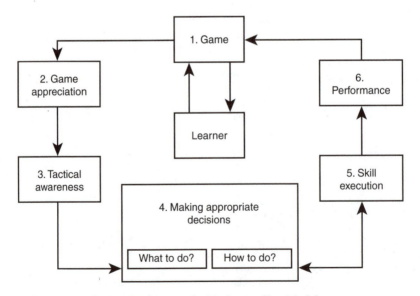

FIGURE 13.2   The Teaching Games for Understanding Model

From Thorpe, R., Bunker, D., & Almond, L. (1986). *Rethinking Games Teaching*. (Permission given by R. Thorpe, Sr. Editor)

Several U.S. physical educators have collaborated with the British developers of the teaching for understanding model in the last fifteen years. While still based on the work of Rod Thorp, David Bunker, and Len Almond, the American version has evolved into a more formal instructional model, called the Tactical Games model (Griffin, Mitchell, & Oslin, 1997). The tactical games approach has begun to be used by more and more physical education teachers at all grade levels, representing an interesting and effective way to teach the traditional games content in an nontraditional way. The model as presented by Griffin, Mitchell, and Oslin (1997) will be the one presented in this chapter; however, it must be noted that their model owes a huge debt to the work of Thorpe, Bunker, and Almond.

Overview

The Tactical Games model is based on a sequence of developmentally appropriate game and game-like learning activities (called game forms) that focus on *tactical problems* for students to solve—first cognitively and then through the execution of skilled motor performance. The teacher begins by determining the most essential tactics needed to play the game. This becomes the content listing for each unit of instruction. For example, the most essential tactics for a middle-school basketball unit might involve:

1. Moving the ball on offense
2. Shot selection
3. Off-the-ball movements
4. Defensive guarding (zone and player-to-player)
5. Positioning for rebounding
6. Fast breaks
7. Out-of-bounds plays and defense

The teacher would then design a series of learning activities within each tactical area. The first learning activity in each area would involve simulations of game situations, progressing from simple to more complicated simulations. During each simulation activity, the teacher analyzes students' tactical knowledge and abilities, identifying skills that need to be worked on. The teacher can then decide whether to have students remain in the simulation or have students practice skills in drill structures. To use the model as it is designed, it is recommended that the simulation structure be used as much as possible to keep the focus on tactical applications of skills. Repetitive, static drills should be used only to develop the most basic skills needed to participate in the simulation activities.

According to Griffin, Mitchell, and Oslin (1997), the simulation activities (or game forms) should be *representative* of the full game and use *exaggerated* situations to focus on tactical skill development. To be representative means that a game form contains realistic situations that students will face later in the full game. To exaggerate means that the game form is set up in a way that forces students to focus on the tactical problem of the moment and no others. For example, if teaching students the offensive and defensive tactics of the "run-down" play in baseball, the teacher should stage the learning activity so that it looks like a real run down; the distances between bases are regulation, all players start in the correct fielding positions, and base-running rules are in effect. That makes it representative. By isolating that single play and practicing it many times, students remain focused on that tactical problem for an extended period, rather than the few times it might occur in the flow of a game. Within these repetitions, each student would have the opportunity to participate in all of the positions involved in the run down—something not likely to happen in a real game. In combination, the repetition and the varied participation formulates the exaggeration feature of the game form.

Doolittle and Girard (1991) discuss the role of the *tactical problem* in the model and how the teacher can prompt students to solve it with targeted questions. The tactical problem is the key concept that students must understand in order to execute the situated skill proficiently from each involved position. Think back to the previous example of the rundown play in baseball or softball. If you are the runner, what might be the most important tactical problem to solve once you are in that situation? How would you improve your chances of getting to a base safely? The teacher would ask students to consider some tactics for that scenario before the simulation begins, as well as during it. Once students tell the teacher a viable solution, the students then try to execute that solution in the simulation. It starts first with solving the tactical problem cognitively.

Foundations of the Tactical Games Model for Physical Education

Theory and Rationale

The Teaching Games for Understanding model and the Tactical Games model presented in this chapter both recognize the central role of games in nearly all physical education programs. But, both models were developed in direct contrast to ways we typically teach games in an attempt to improve student interest and learning in this large program content area. It is the developers' way of not "throwing the baby out with the bathwater." Game content is still the largest area in physical education, so it is essential that we explore alternative ways to teach it.

The basic theory is not explicitly stated for the Tactical Games model, but it is possible to suggest the theory by analyzing the key features in the model's design. It contains many of the attributes of constructivism, a cognitive learning theory that allows learners to make new learning from previous knowledge in an attempt to foster understanding—not just the simple recall of memorized facts or the execution of static skills. The use of the tactical problem in situated game forms and the emphasis on cognitive learning before motor performance are strongly based on constructivist learning theories.

Griffin, Mitchell, and Oslin (1997) provide three major rationales behind the Tactical Games model. First, students' *interest and excitement* in games and game forms is used as a positive motivator and the predominant task structure in the model. In some sense, students are always playing the game or some version of it, keeping interest and excitement high. Because students are almost always applying tactics and skills in game-like situations, they are more likely to see the need for knowledge development more clearly and immediately, further increasing interest in learning activities. Second, *knowledge is empowering*, allowing students to be better players from their increased understanding of the game, and less reliant on the teacher for their participation and decision making. Third, students can *transfer their understanding and performance* across games when applicable. Since games in the same classification contain many similar tactical problems, it is possible to teach games concepts in ways that students can transfer to other like games, reducing the time needed to become proficient in new games.

Assumptions about Teaching and Learning

Assumptions about Teaching

1. The teacher is able to identify the major tactical problems in a game and organize each learning task to focus on the development of solutions to the inherent problem.
2. The teacher is able to use games and modified game forms to design learning tasks that develop tactical awareness and the motor skills needed to perform in the game.
3. The teacher is the primary source of games expertise, but provides the students with indirect learning experiences to be engaged with tactical problems.
4. All games and game forms must be developmentally appropriate versions for students at the grade level being taught. There is no expectation that students need to learn full-scale, adult versions of games.

Assumptions about Learning

1. Most students find games participation to be more interesting, motivating, and authentic than skill-development drills that have little applicability to game play.
2. Students can develop tactical awareness and decision-making abilities when these become the primary objectives of instruction.
3. Tactical awareness is prerequisite to performance ability, but at some point in time students must have both types of knowledge to perform well in games.
4. Tactical awareness and decision making should be developed from a constructivist approach, using a planned progression of learning activities based on tactical problems.
5. Tactical awareness and other types of student learning will transfer across games in similar classification categories.

Major Theme of the Tactical Games Model: Teaching Games for Understanding

As you can see, the major theme for the Tactical Games model is the label used for its predecessor, developed by Bunker and Thorpe (1982). This theme summarizes the single most important learning outcome in the Tactical Games model—to facilitate a deep level of understanding that can be applied in game and game-like situations and that can be transferred to other similar games. This theme also denotes the primary emphasis on students' tactical awareness and decision-making abilities.

Learning Domain Priorities and Interactions

The most basic assumption in the model is that motor-skill performance will be more proficient if it follows cognitive learning. While it is important that students know *what* to do and *how* to do it in game settings, the "what" comes first in the Tactical Games model (Griffin, Mitchell, & Oslin, 1997). This provides a clear statement of the *domain priorities* in the Tactical Games model:

First priority: Cognitive domain
Second priority: Psychomotor domain
Third priority: Affective domain

The *domain interaction* in the Tactical Games model is also quite clear. Students solve a given tactical problem first in the cognitive domain, which in turn facilitates game-situation performance in the psychomotor domain. At some point it is necessary for students to execute tactical decisions to test how well they have solved the situated problem, but again the skill development components follow from the cognitive problem solving activities.

The affective domain is addressed when students learn to combine their tactical awareness with motor performance to produce authentic learning outcomes, improving their appreciation of the game and their own self-esteem. As in many other models, learning in the affective domain occurs mostly through indirect interactions with learning in the other domains.

Student Learning Preferences

The Tactical Games model uses mostly direct teaching. Indirect strategies are used to solve tactical problems, but by and large the teacher controls much of the learning environment, so the student learning preference profile will be closely similar to that of direct instruction and appeal to students who are classified as avoidant, competitive, and dependent on the Reichmann and Grasha profile (1974). As mentioned in Chapter 6, these labels should not be given a negative interpretation. They are simply used to describe how some students would prefer the instructional environment to be designed.

Validation

Research Validation.   The Tactical Games model is new to physical education instruction. To date, there has been little research completed on the model, so it is difficult to know if and when it can be used most effectively. Griffin, Oslin, and Mitchell (1995) compared the tactical games approach with skill-based techniques (direct instruction) in middle-school net games classes. It was reported that students had more interest and motivation in the tactical games classes, but did not differ on the amount of skill knowledge acquired with either technique. Using the Games Performance Analysis Instrument as an authentic measure of student learning in game settings, it was found that students who received the tactical games instruction had better performance in two important areas: court position and decision making.

Some early studies of the Tactical Games model showed mixed results on its effectiveness. Turner and Martinek (1992, 1995) used the Tactical Games model and a skill-based model in two middle-school field hockey units of two different lengths. There were few significant differences in the shorter, six-week unit; however, the tactical students showed more improvement in two of the game performance variables. In the longer, nine-class unit, the tactical students showed more improvement in procedural knowledge and game decision making. McPherson and French (1991) studied college tennis classes to test for differences between a tactical approach and a skill-based approach. The tactical groups were not given skill instruction initially, which resulted in significantly lower skill scores for that group. However, once given skills instruction as part of the model, their scores quickly improved. No differences were reported for knowledge gains or games performance.

Turner (1996) compared the Tactical Games model (using the Teaching Games for Understanding [TGFU] label) with a skills-technique approach in a seventh-grade field hockey unit. Her results indicated that the TGFU students improved significantly on skill development, declarative knowledge, and game performance. By using student interviews, she also reported that the TGFU students enjoyed the game-like structure, giving those students more satisfaction than their counterparts with technique-based instruction.

A 1996 monograph of the *Journal of Teaching in Physical Education* (Rink, 1996 b) featured two research reports of studies conducted on the Tactical Games model, as compared to other approaches to teaching skills and tactics to ninth-grade students. In their summary of these studies, Rink, French, and Graham (1996) surmised that the tactical approach was no more effective than a skill-based approach in promoting student achievement, decision making, or positive affect. They cautioned that the tactical model might tend to develop tactics too far ahead of skill, so that students understand *what* to do but are no more able to execute the needed skills in game play than students who learn skills first, then tactics.

Oslin and Mitchell (1998) studied the degree to which a small sample of ninth-grade students were able to transfer tactical knowledge across two net games units. While supportive of the Tactical Games model, these results are still very preliminary and cannot provide a research-based validation for the Tactical Games model at this time, as noted by Chandler (1996) and Rink, French, and Graham (1996). That does not mean the Tactical Games model is ineffective, since many of the findings show that tactically taught students improved at least as much as skill-taught students on skills, knowledge, decision making, and game performance. The completed research would suggest that the tactical model is one of several *viable* ways to teach games to students, even if it is not demonstrably superior in some respects.

Craft Knowledge Validation. With the newness of the Tactical Games model, it is not yet clear how many physical education teachers use it. Most of what we know about implementing the model has come from general descriptions of the model, with implications being drawn for its role in physical education teaching. However, at least one teacher's experience with the Tactical Games model has been made public. Rebecca Berkowitz (1996), writing in the *Journal of Physical Education, Recreation & Dance,* outlined her philosophical shift from "teaching skill" to "teaching tactics" (p. 45):

> Changing the way I teach games has been an enlightening and challenging endeavor. For me and my students, the tactical approach appears to have been beneficial. It has made me rethink my philosophical view of teaching for skill proficiency. Even though skill proficiency was my major focus, it was never an outcome in my classroom. Now [with the tactical approach] improvement can be seen in my students' game play performance and their

understanding of the game. I think I am now accomplishing more now, and I see my students truly succeeding and enjoying physical education.

Only time will tell if more physical education teachers will use the Tactical Games model and come to view it in this same way.

Intuitive Validation.   Some would argue that the Tactical Games model goes against some of the traditional foundations for teaching games to students. Chandler (1996) suggests that the lead-up games used in the model do not adequately represent full-game situations and can give students a false sense of accomplishment because the game forms do not have the immediacy and reality of the game situations they simulate. By citing their research and that of others, Rink, French, and Graham (1996) suggest that the practice of teaching tactics before skills is not the correct sequence for learning. They argue that students need to have mastered at least the rudiments of skill before they are introduced to situated tactics. Acknowledging the power of these arguments, there is still much about the Tactical Games model that makes good sense for its use in physical education. First, we know that students of all ages like to play games, so using games and game simulations as the major task structure is appealing and will hold students' interest. Second, most physical education teachers know games content well, providing a strong base of expertise. Admittedly, the tactical games approach requires a shift from "teaching skills" to "teaching tactics" (Berkowitz, 1996), but many teachers' personal histories in sport will allow that to be a relatively simple shift. Third, the game structures provide ongoing authentic learning tasks for students. They need to learn in "real time" so that they can use the tactical and skill knowledge immediately—not at some unknown time in the future. Finally, the tactical games approach takes a developmental perspective—it does not place students in full-scale adult versions of games right away or perhaps for the entire unit. It recognizes that students need to learn tactical awareness, decision making, and performance skills through progressively complex tactical problems and structures. All of this adds up to an innovative and defensible way to teach the most popular curricular content area in many physical education programs.

Teaching and Learning Features

Directness

The directness profile for the Tactical Games model is shown in Figure 13.3. As you can see, it is similar to the Direct Instruction model, with the exception of instructional interactions.

1. *Content selection.* Content in the Tactical Games model is represented by the sequence of tactical problems that students solve throughout the unit. After selecting the game to be learned in the unit, the teacher makes a list of tactical problems and plans the game and game-like situations that students will use to develop tactical awareness and decision making. This function is carried out entirely by the teacher.

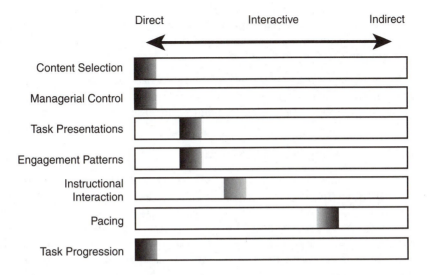

FIGURE 13.3   Directness Profile for the Tactical Games Model

2. *Managerial control.* The teacher determines the managerial plan, class policies, and specific procedures in the Tactical Games model. This is done to improve efficiency as students progress through the series of tactical simulations and drills. This model can require increased amounts of managerial time to set up each learning activity and get students engaged for practice, so it is often best that the teacher takes direct control of these procedures.

3. *Task presentations.* Since the teacher is viewed as the main resource for games knowledge, he will be the one who plans and implements learning tasks that develop tactical awareness and decision making. The tactical problem is posed in the task presentation by the teacher, who uses deductive questions to get students to solve the problem before engaging in the simulation to combine tactics and skills. Therefore, this part of the profile is strongly teacher-centered, with some interaction with students as they respond to questions.

4. *Engagement patterns.* The teacher determines all of the learning tasks and their structure, gets students to solve the tactical problem, and then directs students to practice the simulation or drill. To that point, the engagement patterns are teacher-centered. After that, students can practice on their own and are allowed to make several decisions that affect their engagement patterns.

5. *Instructional interaction.* The teacher initiates most of the instructional interactions, first by using deductive questions to solve the tactical problem and then by providing students with cues, guides, and feedback during the game simulations and drills. The profile indicates that the model is somewhat interactive on this dimension, because the teacher should continue to use deductive questions even after the tactical problem is solved in order to further develop students' understanding.

6. *Pacing.* Once engaged in game simulations, students are able to make their own decisions about when to begin and end practice trials, giving the model a strongly student-centered approach on this dimension.

7. *Task progression.* The teacher determines when each learning activity is over and when students will move on to the next tactical problem and its learning task/s. Therefore, the model is strongly teacher-centered on this dimension.

Predominant Engagement Patterns

The major task structures in the Tactical Games model lead to three different engagement patterns for students. In skill drills, students will likely practice the same task individually. Each student would have her own practice space and needed equipment. The engagement pattern in game-like simulations and modified games will be small groups, with each group having enough students to make the simulation or modified game work to focus on the tactical problem at hand. The last type of engagement pattern, regulation game play, may or may not be used by the teacher, depending on the students' readiness. Of course, the engagement pattern will be determined by the game being played: individual, dual, small team (e.g., basketball), or large team (e.g., football).

Inclusiveness

Teachers who use the Tactical Games model can plan to make it inclusive for all students, if considerations are made for differing levels of cognitive and skill-performance abilities. The model is not inherently inclusive when all students are expected to progress through the tactical problems and learning tasks at the same rate. More experienced and higher-skilled students can come to understand things faster and better, leaving other students still figuring out current tactical solutions when the class moves to new problems. Since learning in the model is built on previous understandings and performance skills, students' needs are not served if the class moves on before everyone is ready. The answer lies in the teacher identifying groups of students who are at the same level of understanding and ability, and allowing groups to move through the series of tactical problems—rather than all students in class at once. Groups that move through the sequence faster can advance to modified and full games when their tactical awareness and skills predict proficient performance. Slower groups will spend more time on simulations and modified games, providing them with the appropriate level of complexity to develop their awareness and skills. In this way, the model can be inclusive in the sense that all students are working at their own level, even if they are not progressing at the same rate. The model is also inclusive in that all students are engaged in the small-sided, modified, or full games. There should be little waiting time in this model, because every student is working on some aspect of game skills and tactics in every game form learning task.

Task Presentation and Task Structure

There are four primary kinds of learning tasks used in the Tactical Games model: skill development drills, game-like drills, game forms, and full games. Each type of task will have its own task presentation and task structure, but all of them will be centered on the solution of tactical problems by students. The sequence of tasks just mentioned does not represent the task progression used in the model. According to Griffin, Mitchell, & Oslin (1997), the teacher presents a tactical problem that will carry through a full sequence of tasks. That sequence begins with a *game form,* which is a modified version of the full game that is used to assess students' tactical and skill knowledge in a targeted area of a game. The following are some examples of initial game forms and areas that can be assessed.

Game	Game Form	Used to Assess
Basketball	3 on 3 half court	1. Defensive positioning 2. Off-the-ball movement 3. Rebounding positioning 4. Freeing up the shooter 5. Defensive communication
Volleyball	2 vs. 2	1. Defensive positioning against attacks 2. Offensive passing 3. Team communication 4. Serving tactics
Golf	Putt-putt	1. Stance and aiming line 2. Judgment of ball speed 3. Judgment of "break"
Lacrosse	Half-field scrimmage (one team stays on offense, one team stays on defense)	1. Establishing a defensive position 2. Marking 3. Off-the-ball movement 4. Finding gaps in the defense 5. Team communication

Once the game form has been played, the teacher identifies students' needs related to tactics and skills and then designs one or more drills that target those areas of needed development. Following the drills students can return to the initial game form and then progress to modified games. A modified game uses many aspects of the full game, but with some planned changes in rules, scoring, field/court size, and length of the game. These modifications should reflect students' developmental readiness and should allow certain aspects of the game to come into play more often so that students get more in-game repetitions on key tactics and skills. The following table shows some examples of games modifications and what each change is designed to do.

Game	Modification	To Focus On
Floor hockey	Teams cannot shoot on goal until all players have touched the puck	1. Passing 2. Teamwork 3. Communication
Soccer (elementary grades)	Reduce the width and length of the field by half and reduce the size of the goal	1. Increased opportunity to touch the ball and to play defense 2. Off-the-ball movement 3. Shooting accuracy
Ultimate Frisbee	Increase the allowed possession time after catches	1. Off-the-disk movement 2. Passing decisions 3. Communication
Badminton	No overhead smashes allowed	1. Offensive accuracy and touch shots 2. Longer rallies

The final type of learning task is the full version of the game. The full version does not have to be the adult version of the game—it can be any developmentally appropriate version that includes all or nearly all aspects of the game in ways that allow students to practice tactics and skills with maximum participation. At times it will be difficult to tell the difference between modified games and developmentally appropriate full versions, but that is OK. The important thing here is that the students will be participating in the fullest version of the game *for them.* It is also not necessary to include the formalities that go with many full-game versions, as the Sport Education model would do. The idea is to get students in the game quickly and to give them many opportunities to learn tactics and skills in game situations.

Task Presentation.   The task presentation is used to frame the tactical problem and to explain the importance of the situated learning task. The key is to present enough information to students about the tactical situation without giving them the solution; that part is for them to think about and explore. Once they have constructed one or more solutions, they begin to practice the task in order to develop the proper decision-making and performance skills needed in that situation.

Task Presentation for the Initial Game Form.   The teacher should explain how the game form relates to the full version of the game and why it is important from a tactical perspective. The teacher gives students only the information needed to visualize and understand the game form or the situation (applicable rules, how the situation occurs, which players are involved). After that the teacher uses deductive questions to get students to arrive at one or more feasible solutions. Once there, the teacher then explains the task structure and gets students actively engaged in decision making and skill practice in the learning task and observes students to assess their level of awareness and proficiency in that situation. This stage ends with the teacher and students identifying areas of tactical awareness and skills that must be developed in more isolated and repetitive learning tasks—most often drills.

Task Presentation for Skill Drills. Once students' needs for tactical awareness and skill development are identified, the teacher ends the game form task and plans a progression of skill learning tasks. By starting with the game form, the teacher can identify more authentic learning needs and get students to understand the importance of those needs for playing the game well. Skill drills are presented to students in much the same way as in direct instruction, with the teacher explaining and modeling the movement patterns to be learned and providing verbal cues to students. An extra dimension is included to help students become aware of the tactical importance of the skill and how the skill is used to solve the tactical problem of the preceding game form task. Therefore it is important that the teacher explain not only how to perform the skill, but also why and how it should be used when students return to the game form or go on to modified games or full games.

Task Presentation for Modified Games. Modified games are designed to reduce the tactical and performance complexity of full games, allowing students to focus on certain aspects with multiple attempts. The task presentation for modified games should include an explanation of how it relates to the full game (differences and similarities), why and how rules have been changed, and the tactical objectives of the modified version. By stating the tactical objectives, the teacher can lead into one or more tactical problems presented in the modified game. As mentioned, it is important for the teacher to provide students with an explanation of the situated game, before allowing students to deduce the answers to the tactical problems.

Task Presentation for Full Games. At this point the task presentation looks much like the one for modified games. The teacher sets that stage for the game, explains the tactical objectives, and poses the tactical problems that students must solve before the game begins. Once the teacher is confident that students have good tactical awareness and the prerequisite skills, the full game becomes an appropriate learning environment.

Task Structure. The task structure is determined by the type of task the teacher plans at each stage of the model: game form, skill drill, modified game, and full game. Because all tasks are situated, much of the task structure will be revealed to students during the task presentation and the solving of the tactical problem. Students cannot deduce the answer to the tactical problem without knowing much about the way each task will be set up. After the tactical problem is solved and the basic task structure is explained, the teacher needs only to give students information about allocated time, safety, and the exact place for each learning station.

Task Structure for Game Forms. In a sense, game forms are simulations of common situations that can occur in modified- and full-game contexts: a run down in softball, a goal-line defense in flag football, a breakaway in hockey, or an opponent coming to the net in tennis. The teacher constructs a learning task that gives students a reasonable representation of that situation in order to practice and assess tactical awareness, decision making, and the needed skills. The teacher must know the situation well enough to identify which players are involved, how the situation occurs in the flow of the game, and how to provide students with a challenging, authentic game form. Remember, by this time the students will have already solved the tactical problem in the cognitive domain—the objective for task structure is to give them many repetitions to make and carry out the needed tactical decisions.

Task Structure for Skill Drills.   Many different drills can be designed to help students develop the necessary skills for executing tactical decisions. Also, many different task structures can be used: individual practice, paired practice, small groups, and large groups. The instruction for skill drills will look like the Direct Instruction model with one important difference: the teacher posing the tactical problem to students before the drill begins. In direct instruction the teacher will show and tell students how to perform the movement proficiently and then ask students to imitate that example. In the Tactical Games model the teacher attempts to get students to understand what the skill is and how it needs to be carried out to meet the tactical demands of the drill being practiced. The teacher also goes to great lengths to help students understand the need for the skill in game applications. Once that level of understanding is reached (that is, the tactical problem has been solved), the teacher should engage students in a drill that is designed to promote both tactical and skill knowledge at the same time. Therefore, the task structure should allow students many opportunities to make and carry out tactical decisions, rather than simply performing a number of automatic repetitions.

Task Structure for Modified Games.   The task structure for modified games must be both representative and exaggerated (Griffin, Mitchell, & Oslin, 1997). To be representative means that the modified game closely resembles the full version of the game so that students are practicing in a realistic environment and making authentic tactical decisions. While it is possible to modify game rules, boundaries, the size of the goal, and more, the teacher must be careful to retain the most essential features of the game in its modified version. The task structure is also used to exaggerate certain aspects of the game, giving students more opportunities to practice isolated tactical decisions and skills. The exaggeration helps students to focus on these certain events by eliminating or reducing the possibility of other events that occur in the typically unpredictable flow of a game. For instance, if a teacher engages students in a half-court game of basketball, both teams will have many opportunities to practice and execute tactical decisions about offensive patterns, set defense, and rebounding. By eliminating fast breaks, this structure reduces the complexities of the full-court game, and provides many more "teaching moments" for the tactical and skill knowledge being learned.

The modified games task structure is key in the Tactical Games model because it provides a direct bridge between skill tasks and full games. It allows students to develop game-based decision-making abilities and to apply skills in highly authentic situations that will occur often when the full game is played later. Teachers should bear in mind that the modified game structure will be the culminating structure for many units, particularly when students are at the novice stage of tactical and skill development.

Task Structure for Full Games.   Only when students have demonstrated sustained competence in modified games should they be placed in full versions of a game. The teacher can make informal and formal assessments of students' knowledge in modified games, which then informs the teacher's decision to progress to full versions of the game. Again, it must be emphasized that the full version is not automatically played in every unit—students must be ready for that task structure.

The task structure for full games will tend to look much like a practice scrimmage used in the coaching of many sports. The teacher should watch for "teaching moments" that occur in the game and interject when it is appropriate to focus on tactical awareness, tactical decisions, and game skills. However, each teaching moment should contain a tactical problem posed to students when play is stopped momentarily.

Metzler (1990) suggested some ways teachers can structure and interject in game tasks that would be quite useful in the Tactical Games model:

1. *Instant replay.* The teacher stops the game and resets the last play, so that players can have the chance to review and change their tactical decisions. Only the results of the original play count in the scoring.
2. *Player-coach.* The teacher enters the game for a strategic purpose and to manipulate certain parts of the game to promote student's tactical and skill practice. For instance, the teacher is the pitcher for both teams in a softball game and deliberately pitches in ways that force certain situations to occur (hitting ground balls, hitting to the opposite field); the teacher enters a basketball game as the point guard on one team and uses that position to control the pace of the game.
3. *Situations.* During the course of the game, the teacher stops play to ask a question to check tactical awareness and decision making before it happens in the game. For instance, in a doubles tennis match, the teacher would ask one partner, "What will you do if your partner has to come to the net when that's your territory?" With runners on first and second and one out in a softball game, the teacher would ask the right fielder, "What do you do if you catch a deep fly ball?"
4. *TV analyst.* After the teacher notices a pattern emerging during a game, he stops the game to ask, "What's going on, and how do you change it?" For instance, if one team in a soccer match has had several breakaway shots on goal, the teacher would ask the defensive team, "Why is that happening?" and "What does your team need to do to stop that?"

The important feature of the full-game structure in the Tactical Games model is that the focus remains on tactical awareness, tactical decisions, and skill execution, so the teacher must use interactive teaching that gets students to think about and solve the large number of tactical problems that occur in most games. Only then can the full-game structure differ from simply "playing games" in class.

Teacher Expertise and Contextual Needs

Teacher Expertise

Teachers who use the Tactical Games model will need to have particular expertise in several areas of the proposed knowledge base presented in Chapter 2.

Implementing Developmentally Appropriate Instruction.   Games, and even modified games, can make for complex instructional settings that require a relatively high level of cognitive and psychomotor readiness on the part of students. It is very important that the complexity of the tactical problem of the moment and the skill needed to execute tactical decisions matches students' ability levels. Teachers must be able to analyze the concepts and skills in each tactical situation and then design an appropriate game form, drill, or modified game to help students acquire that knowledge. Perhaps the two most important decisions occur as students go from modified games to the full-game version—and when they must go back to modified games when the full game is shown to be too complex or demanding for them.

Learning Domains and Objectives.   The Tactical Games model is based on an interaction between the cognitive and psychomotor domains; the teacher gets students to solve the tactical problem through a series of deductive questions, and then directs students to execute tactical decisions within the various kinds of task structures. Teachers will need to keep that interaction in balance so that students can actually execute the skills called for by the tactical solution. It is not desirable to have students come up with complex tactical solutions that are well beyond their physical abilities to carry out.

Teachers who use the Tactical Games model will need to know how to identify and state tactical problems to students. The solutions to these problems become some of the main instructional objectives within this model and form the basis of tactical learning progressions (Doolittle & Girard, 1991). Therefore, teachers will need to transfer tactical problems into learning tasks that facilitate these objectives.

Task Analysis and Content Progression.   Task analysis in the Tactical Games model is centered on the tactical knowledge and skills needed to play a game proficiently. Therefore the process begins with an analysis of the tactical requirements of each game, along with consideration of students' developmental stages. The resulting list of tactical areas becomes the content listing for the unit and is presented to students as tactical problems. From there, the teacher plans the series of learning tasks for the unit that help students solve and execute the tactical problems.

It is critical that the teacher can correctly assess students' readiness for each of the four main task structures: game forms, skill drills, modified games, and full games. These structures form a plan, or stages, for task progression to occur within the model. Remember that a tactical games unit will begin with a game form that is used to assess students' tactical awareness, decision making, and skills. While students are in the game form the teacher must make an assessment of which tactical knowledge and skills are needed most— and then plan a sequence to promote that knowledge. All of that must be considered with students' developmental readiness, and adjustments made for the complexity and physical demands of each learning task.

Physical Education Content.   Teachers must have strong expertise in games taught with the Tactical Games model. Teachers must know each game well enough to be able to identify the tactical demands, formulate tactical problems, and design developmentally appropriate game forms and modified games. This goes well beyond being familiar with game rules and basic strategies. The teacher must know all players' positions and the most typical tactical situations that can occur in the flow of a game so that authentic game forms and modified games can be designed.

Assessment. Tactical knowledge is demonstrated in two learning domains in this model—the cognitive (knowing what to do) and the psychomotor (knowing how to do it proficiently). Furthermore, that knowledge must be demonstrated in game and game-like situations. Therefore, assessment in the Tactical Games model should rely mainly on authentic techniques, taken while students are actively engaged. Some assessment can be made of students' declarative knowledge by asking them to think about and verbally solve tactical problems, but the major focus should be the assessment of tactical knowledge in action.

Griffin, Mitchell, and Oslin (1997) developed the Game Performance Assessment Instrument (GPAI) specifically for use with the Tactical Games model. It is essentially a checklist system that a teacher can use to observe and assess various components of game performance to determine if students are making and executing tactical decisions during game play. Teachers who will use the tactical games model should become proficient with the GPAI or be able to design their own games assessment checklists.

Effective Teaching Skills Applied to the Tactical Games Model

Many of the effective teaching skills for the Tactical Games model are similar to those used in direct instruction, along with some questioning skills used to help students solve the tactical problem within each learning task.

Planning. Unit planning for the Tactical Games model will require some planning prior to the start of the unit, but most of the planning will occur once the teacher has assessed the students' initial tactical knowledge and skills. The teacher can plan ahead for the first game form used to determine students' tactical knowledge and skill. What the teacher observes in that game form will determine what comes next: either a modified game (if students are ready) or a series of skill drills. From there, the teacher should have a good grasp of what students need and which learning tasks can help students learn best. The tactical problem is the starting point for every learning task after the initial game form. The teacher will need to formulate the tactical problem ahead of time and prepare a series of deductive questions that will lead students toward its solution.

Time and Class Management. Since learning tasks should be designed to simulate game situations, the teacher will need to pay particular attention to details in the planning of each skill drill, game form, and modified game. Good planning will facilitate higher rates of engagement and more opportunities for students to practice their situated game skills. Learning tasks should be planned so that all students are actively engaged and transitions between tasks are efficient. This will reduce the likelihood that transitions will lead to the loss of momentum in a lesson.

Task Presentation and Task Structure.   Task presentations in the Tactical Games model are similar to those used in direct instruction, with the added dimension of using deductive questions to solve the tactical problem before each task begins. Task presentations should include an explanation of the tactical importance of the skill or situation to be practiced and the key tactical decisions to be made. The teacher should stop short of telling students the one or more correct tactical decisions to make so that students can solve the tactical problem themselves. Teachers should review the guidelines for effective questioning techniques presented in Chapter 4. It will be especially important to use the *wait time* technique with the deductive questions so that all students have the opportunity to formulate their own solutions before one is made publicly.

Communication.   Communication skills are important in the Tactical Games model because of the many situated learning tasks given to students. These tasks will require a full and clear explanation of the situation to be practiced and the major tactical decisions that need to be made. If students do not understand the explanation or the tactical problem, they will be less able to come up with an acceptable solution.

Instructional Information.   Most of the instructional information comes from the teacher in the form of task presentations and verbal interactions while students practice. The key skill for teachers is to recognize when to "ask, not tell" students solutions to the tactical problem. The model relies on students being able to work out solutions on their own, increasing their understanding and learning.

As students practice the situated learning tasks, the teacher should give high rates of verbal guides and feedback. Guides are learning cues given to students while they are actively engaged. During game forms, modified games, and full games the teacher should be observing the flow of the action and alert students to upcoming situations—cueing them to make tactical decisions (without giving students the answers) in the course of game events. Augmented feedback from the teacher is important because many practice situations will be quite complex; students will realize when a mistake has been made, but they will need feedback on why it occurred to prevent it from happening the next time.

Review and Closure.   The tactical problems presented to students in a lesson should be the focal point of the lesson review. The teacher can restate the problems and have students respond with the correct solutions as one last check for understanding. The review can also be used to preview tactical problems and learning tasks planned for the next lesson. The teacher could even choose to give students the next tactical problem and ask them to think about solutions before the next lesson, providing a nice way to start class the next time. The closure should allow enough time for equipment to be returned to its proper place, followed by an orderly dismissal.

Student Developmental Requirements

The Tactical Games model relies on the students being able to comprehend game- and game-like learning tasks and their embedded tactical problems. Therefore, students will need to have a sufficient level of listening skills and intellectual ability in order to benefit from the tactical games approach. Of course, the instruction and all learning tasks can be adjusted to meet students' levels, but if students do not have the ability to make tactical decisions at any level the model should not be used.

Contextual Needs for the Tactical Games Model

The Tactical Games model can be used in nearly all physical education contexts. The major requirements are to have sufficient equipment and teaching space to allow all students to be engaged with no waiting turns. When there is not enough equipment or space for all students to be in the same situated learning task, it is recommended that the teacher plan multiple tasks that need different equipment and space size. The Tactical Games model can support a high degree of flexibility, giving it few contextual limitations in physical education units.

Teacher and Student Roles and Responsibilities in the Tactical Games Model

Each instructional model will have certain operations that need to be completed to make the model function according to its design. Some of these operations are carried out by the teacher; others are carried out by one or more students. The following table shows the major operations within the Tactical Games model, and indicates who is responsible for completing them during each lesson.

Operation or Responsibility	Who Does It in the Tactical Games Model?
Starting class	The **teacher** usually begins class as a whole for the first task presentation and tactical problem.
Task presentation	The **teacher** will make the task presentation. It is also possible to use instructional media to show students a tactical situation.
Stating the tactical problem	The **teacher** sets the stage for each situated learning task and then gives the tactical problem to students.
Solving the tactical problem	**Students** can think on their own or work in small groups to solve the tactical problem.
Dispersing and returning equipment	Since most learning tasks will use a small-group structure, each **group of students** can get and return its needed equipment.
Task structure	**Students** set up each task (learning station) from the teacher's directions.
Assessment	The **teacher** should design the assessment technique for each task. Once designed, it can be used by either students or the teacher.

Teaching and Learning Benchmarks
for the Tactical Games Model

Teachers who use the Tactical Games model can learn the benchmarks for their own and student behavior patterns. The following teacher and student benchmarks verify that the model has been designed and implemented with an acceptable degree of faithfulness, increasing the likelihood that the stated student learning outcomes will be achieved.

Teacher Benchmarks

Benchmark	How to Verify
Teacher uses tactical problems as the organizing center for each learning task	Check content listing, with tactical problems written out.
Teacher begins each unit segment with a game form to assess student knowledge	Check unit plan.
Teacher identifies needed tactical and skill areas from game form	Teacher can make a list of tactical areas in each unit segment and makes a written assessment of students' knowledge in each area after observing each game form.
Teacher uses deductive questions to get students to solve the tactical problem	1. Check teacher's lesson plan. 2. Make a list of all questions asked and students' responses.
Teacher uses clear communications for situated learning tasks	Observe students as they organize each task. Students should quickly set up and be engaged in the task according to the teacher's directions.
Teacher uses high rates of guides and feedback during situated learning tasks	Record the content and frequency of the teacher's instructional interactions.
Teacher provides a review that includes the tactical problems of the lesson	1. Check the teacher's lesson plan. 2. Record the number of times the teacher checks for understanding at the end of each lesson.
Assessment	1. Check the teacher's unit and lesson plans. 2. Review the teacher's checklists for tactical decision making and skill execution (e.g., use the Game Performance Assessment Instrument).

Student Benchmarks

Benchmark	How to Verify
Students are given time to think about deductive questions about the tactical problem	1. Observe the teacher's use of wait time. 2. Make a record of how many times each student is called on to answer.
Students understand how to set up situated learning tasks	Observe students as they organize each task. Students should quickly set up and be engaged in the task according to the teacher's directions.
Students are making situated tactical decisions	1. Record correct and incorrect answers given by students to teacher's questions during learning tasks. 2. Observe students' tactical decision making and skills during learning tasks.
Game modifications are developmentally appropriate	Observe students as they are engaged. Does the modification make the game too simple or too complex for them?
Students are able to progress on tactical knowledge as they move along in the task progression	Monitor game forms, modified games, and full games with the Games Performance Assessment Instrument. Note which game performance components are not demonstrated as the complexity of learning tasks increases. Some drop-off will occur each time the complexity increases, but the drop should be only temporary.
Students have learned tactical awareness, decision making, and situated skills	Monitor students with the Game Performance Assessment Instrument or another authentic assessment technique.

Assessing Learning in the Tactical Games Model

The major learning objective in the Tactical Games model is to get students to make and carry out tactical decisions in games and game-like learning activities. It is a combination of knowing what to do and how to correctly execute it in a game context. That well-defined objective helps teachers to devise valid and authentic assessment techniques when using this model, since the assessment question is clear and direct: "To what degree can students make correct tactical decisions and carry them out in the flow of game play?"

Assessment in the Tactical Games model should focus on students' abilities to make and execute tactical decisions while playing a game. The game can be a full game, modified game, or a game form that represents a game situation. In addition, assessment should be authentic, based on observations made during game play. With that in mind, there are two primary ways to make assessments in the Tactical Games model: objective game statistics and evaluations of students' decision-making and performance abilities.

Assessment with Game Statistics.   If you were coaching a team (e.g., floor hockey) and someone asked you, "How did your team play in its last game?", how would you answer? Most likely you would use the game score as the major indicator of their play. While winning or losing can tell you if the primary goal was accomplished, it does not always indicate how well the team played. To better assess your team's play, you would likely look to the statistical summary for that game. Such a summary might show things like the number of shots on goal each team took, where these shots were taken from, which players took the shots, time of possession, turnovers, other errors, and total penalty time for both teams. With a complete set of game statistics you would be able to assess many aspects of each player's performance based on his/her position. Each student could be given a summary report that would include the statistics relevant to that position, with a written assessment of the performance.

Assessment of Tactical Decision Making and Skill Execution.   Assessing student performance with game statistics can be useful, but that information will not tell the teacher how well students made and carried out tactical decisions during the game. For instance, the summary statistics for goal keeping in floor hockey will show how many shots were taken on goal and the percentage of saves, but it will not show how often the goalkeeper made situationally-correct decisions and actions—one good measure of tactical knowledge. Griffin, Mitchell, and Oslin (1997) have devised an authentic system for assessing tactical knowledge in a wide variety of games typically taught in physical education. The Game Performance Assessment Instrument (GPAI) is a generic template that can be adapted to many types of games to assess students' tactical knowledge. The GPAI includes seven common components of game performance, shown in Figure 13.4.

FIGURE 13.4   Game Performance Assessment Instrument Components (GPAI)

Component	Criterion for Assessing Performance
Base	Appropriate return of the performer to a home or recovery position between skill attempts
Adjust	Movement of performer, either offensively of defensively, as required by the flow of the game
Decision making	Making appropriate choices about what to do with the ball (or projectile) during a game
Skill execution	Efficient performance of selected skills
Support	Off-the-ball movement to a position to receive a pass when player's team has possession
Cover	Providing defensive help for player making a play on the ball or moving to the ball (or projectile)
Guard or mark	Defending against an opponent who may or may not have the ball (or projectile)

Reprinted by permission from Linda L. Griffin, Stephen A. Mitchell, and Judith L. Oslin, 1997, *Teaching Sport Concepts and Skills.* (Champaign, IL: Human Kinetics), 221.

When using the GPAI for a specific game the teacher identifies which of the seven components apply to that game and determines one or more criteria on each component that indicates good tactical decisions and performance. The GPAI focuses on three aspects of performance on each component: decisions made (appropriate or inappropriate), skill execution (efficient or inefficient), and support (appropriate or inappropriate). The teacher then observes each student in the course of the game and records appropriate/inappropriate and efficient/inefficient instances of tactical knowledge and performance on each selected component.

Using a soccer example from Griffin, Mitchell, and Oslin (1997), Figure 13.5 shows how the GPAI can be used to assess students' tactical knowledge in soccer (component to be assessed: restarts [including throw-ins, goal kicks, corner kicks]).

FIGURE 13.5 An Example of Using The GPAI for Soccer

Aspect	Criteria
Decision making	1. Player attempts to pass to an open teammate.
	2. Player attempts to shoot when appropriate.
Skill execution	Reception: Control of pass and setup of the ball
	Passing: Ball reaches target
	Shooting: Ball stays below head height and is on target
Support	The player appeared to support the ball carrier by being in or moving to an appropriate position to receive the pass.

This is the record of the teacher's observations during the soccer match. Each x indicates an instance in which a student was viewed making a tactical performance.

Name	Decision Made		Skill Execution		Support	
	A	IA	E	IE	A	IA
Matthew	xxxxxx	x	xxxxxx	x	xxxxxxx	xxxx
Bryan					xxx	xxx
Katie	xxxxx	x	xxxxx	x	xxxx	x
Kelly	xx	x	xxx	x	xxxxx	xx
Peter	xxx	xx	xx	xxx	xx	x
Alison	x	xx	x	xx	xxxxxxx	x

Key	A = appropriate	IA = inappropriate
	E = efficient	IE = inefficient

From the teacher's record it is possible to·calculate several measures of tactical game performance for each student (Matthew in this example).

Index	How to Calculate
Game involvement	Number of appropriate decisions + Number of inappropriate decisions + Number of efficient skill executions + Number of inefficient skill executions + Number of appropriate supporting movements
Decision-making index (DMI)	Number of appropriate decisions made ÷ Number of inappropriate decisions made
Skill-execution index (SEI)	Number of efficient skill executions ÷ Number of inefficient skill executions
Support index (SI)	Number of appropriate supporting movements ÷ Number of inappropriate supporting movements
Game performance	[DMI + SEI + SI] ÷ 3 (Number of indexes used)

Matthew's GPAI assessment:
Game performance = 6 + 1 + 6 + 1 + 7 = 21
Decision making = 6 ÷ 1 = 6
Skill execution = 6 ÷ 1 = 6
Support = 7 ÷ 4 = 1.75
Game performance = (6 + 6 + 1.75) ÷ 3 = 4.58

As Griffin, Mitchell, and Oslin (1997) are quick to point out, a student's game performance score is a ratio, not a percentage or an absolute number. That means it reflects a balance between appropriate/inappropriate and efficient/inefficient instances, so that students with more positive occurrences in a game will not necessarily score higher than students with fewer positive instances. The highest GPAI scores occur when students have more positive instances relative to the number of negative instances. This scoring encourages students to make good tactical decisions and fewer negative ones, so that a higher number of good plays is not necessarily better. What counts is making fewer tactical mistakes per each positive tactical execution.

Selecting and Modifying the Tactical Games Model for Physical Education

The Tactical Games model is obviously designed for use in teaching students how to make and execute tactical decisions in the context of games. These games can be the more formal versions of sport or any game form that requires a degree of tactical knowledge to play it well. I would recommend using this model with the following types of physical education content:

1. Low-organizational games (tag games, group games)
2. New Games and other creative games
3. Cooperative games
4. Individual and dual sports
5. Team sports

Grade-Level Modifications.   The Tactical Games model can be used to instruct students across a wide range of developmental stages if the teacher carefully matches students' abilities with the tactical complexity and skill requirements needed to play the game proficiently. Figure 13.6 shows some possible grade level adaptations teachers can devise for the Tactical Games model in physical education.

FIGURE 13.6   Grade-Level Adaptations for the Tactical Games Model in Physical Education

Grade Levels	Select the Tactical Games Model?	Possible Adaptations
Preschool	No	
Lower elementary	No	
Upper elementary	Yes	1. Choose tactically simple games. 2. Focus on skill development first. 3. Use more game forms as learning tasks. 4. Do not use full versions of team sport games.
Middle school/junior high	Yes	1. Use mostly modified games. 2. Use full games rarely and cautiously. 3. Focus on skill development along with tactics.
High school	Yes	1. Use more modified games than full games. 2. Use full games only when students have demonstrated they are ready.
College/adult	Yes	None needed. Can use the full model when students have demonstrated their readiness for increasing tactical complexity and skill applications.

Summary

As mentioned at the beginning of this chapter, the Tactical Games model is new to physical education instruction. While games instruction has been used by physical education teachers for over one hundred years in U.S. schools, this model offers a fresh and innovative way to approach that key part of school curriculums. Teachers who choose to use this model should be aware that it is not a matter of teaching games content with a slightly new twist. The Tactical Games model begins the process of teaching games content to students from a different perspective, with different objectives and teaching strategies. The Tactical Games model can be a refreshing and creative way for veteran teachers to instruct content they have taught many times. For new teachers, the Tactical Games model can could become "their way" to teach games content to students of all ages.

Sample Unit for the Tactical Games Model

Content area:	Team handball (novice level)
Grade level:	Tenth
Students:	28, nearly equal numbers of boys and girls No students have previous experience
Length of unit:	12 class periods
Length of classes:	About 50 minutes for instruction
Facilities:	3 marked team handball courts with goals
Equipment:	Handballs Cones Pinnies
Media:	Instructional video from U.S. Team Handball Association

Content Listing and Schedule

Lesson	Tactical Problem/s	Learning Activities

1	**1.** Identification of the game classification
	2. Major tactics and skills
		1. View the U.S. Team Handball (TH) instructional video
		  a. What other games are similar to TH?
		  b. What are the similarities?
		  c. What game class does TH belong in? Why?
		  d. What are the characteristics of those games?
		2. Students are placed into small groups. Each group makes up a list of what they think are the major tactics and skills needed for TH. Groups share their lists and the teacher writes each tactic and skill on the board.

2	Throwing and catching while moving	Game form: Modified fast break situation, no goalie Skill drill: Partners pass and catch while moving in a circular pattern. Return to game form.

Content Listing and Schedule   Continued

Lesson	Tactical Problem/s	Learning Activities
3	Goalie defending against a fast break	Game form: Modified fast break situation, with goalie Skill drill: One-on-one shooting with goalie defending Return to game form.
4	Goalie defending against a set offense	Game form: Three vs. three, half court, with goalie Skill drill: Offensive players stand on 6-meter line and shoot at goal, one at a time, in random order. Some make high shots, some make low shots. Return to game form.
5–6	Shooting on goal	Game form: Three vs. three, half court, no goalie. Offense must shoot within 10 seconds. Skill drills: Practice set shots and jump shots to a goal/target. No defenders and no goalie Alternate between game form and skill drills.
7	Defensive positioning	Game form: Three vs. three, half court "keep-away." No shots. Defensive players move to position as the ball is passed around. Skill drills: "Mirror" drill to develop footwork Stance and slide practice Return to game form.

8	Offensive attack tactics: set offense	Game form:
		Three vs. three, half court, with goalie
		
		Skills drills:
		Demonstration and slow motion practice of:
		   ■ Give and go
		   ■ Pick and roll
		   ■ Screens
		
		(Teacher relates these to similar tactics in basketball—ones that many students know.)
		
		Return to game form. The offensive team "huddles" on each possession to devise a set play. No "playground ball" allowed!

(continued)

Content Listing and Schedule   Continued

Lesson	Tactical Problem/s	Learning Activities
9	Offensive tactics: fast break	Game form: Three vs. three, full court. No transitions. The offensive team takes the ball from its own goal and must shoot within 8 seconds. Decision development: Teacher videotapes the game form, and uses each possession as a "teaching moment" to explain tactics for fast breaks. Return to game form.
10	Off-the-ball movement (set offense and fast breaks)	Game form 1: Three vs. three, half court. Teacher uses verbal guides to get off-the-ball players to move into correct positions in the course of action. Play is stopped at "teaching moments" that focus on off-the-ball positioning. Game form 2: Three vs. three, full court. Teacher uses verbal guides to get off-the-ball players to move into correct positions in the course of action. Play is stopped at "teaching moments" that focus on off-the-ball positioning.
11–12	Full-game play	Students play full court with full teams. The teacher monitors with the team handball version of the Game Performance Assessment Instrument (Griffin, Mitchell, & Oslin, 1997).

Lesson 7

Tactical Problem:	Defensive positioning for team handball
Tactical concepts:	Defensive stance Positioning relative to ball and offensive player being guarded
Equipment:	Handballs Pinnies
Facilities:	3 handball courts, divided in halves (6 playing areas)

Lesson Segment	Time	Description
Game form	10 minutes	Keep-away: Students are placed in teams of three—no goalies. Two teams on each court with different colored pinnies. The defensive players position themselves just inside the 6-meter line to start. The offensive players are dispersed outside the 6-meter line, about equal distances apart as circle runner, left wing, and right wing. The object of the game is for the offensive players to make as many passes as they can in 30 seconds without dropping the ball or allowing the defense to intercept it. The defense attempts to limit the number of passes made in 30 seconds and tries to intercept all passes.
Teaching for understanding	10 minutes	Teacher stops the keep-away game and asks questions. To the offense: Were you more successful with short, crisp passes or with lobs? Did you have to move around to get open? If so, how did you do that? To the defense: How were you positioning yourselves? What happened when you got overly aggressive? The teacher then explains the principles of defensive positioning for TH, including stance, sliding, anticipation, and timing.
Drills for skill development	20 minutes	Drill 1: Stance and slide Teacher explains and demonstrates the proper defensive stance to the class. The teacher explains that the first step out of the stance is critical—it must be quick and decisive. Students assume their stances while the teacher moves around to provide feedback. On the teacher's signal, the students practice making the correct first step quickly—in all directions. Drill 2: Mirror drill Students all face the teacher and assume the correct defensive stance. The teacher points in a direction, and the students slide-step quickly in that direction. The teacher changes directions quickly and often.
Return to game form	8 minutes	Students play "keep-away" again
Review and closure	2 minutes	Teacher reviews the key concepts included in defensive positioning for TH.

SUGGESTED READINGS

Griffin, L. L., Mitchell, S. A., & Oslin, J. L. (1997). *Teaching sport concepts and skills: A tactical games approach.* Champaign, IL: Human Kinetics.

Rink, J. (Ed.) (1996). Tactical and skill approaches to teaching sport and games. *The Journal of Teaching in Physical Education, Monograph, 15*(4).

Thorpe, R., Bunker, D., & Almond, L. (1986). *Rethinking games teaching.* Loughborough, England: Department of Physical Education and Sport Science, University of Technology.

REFERENCES

Alberto, P. A., & Troutman, A. C. (1999). *Applied behavior analysis for teachers: Influencing student performance* (5th ed.). Columbus, OH: Merrill.

Alexander, K., Taggart, A., & Luckman, J. (1998). Pilgrims progress: The sport education crusade down under. *Journal of Physical Education, Recreation & Dance, 69*(5), 21–23.

Alexander, K., Taggart, A., & Thorpe, S. (1995, November). Teacher renewal through curriculum innovation: Australian teachers tell their stories. Paper presented at the Australian Association for Research in Education.

Almond, L. (1986). Reflecting on themes: A games classification system. In R. Thorpe, D. Bunker, & L. Almond, eds. *Rethinking games teaching* (pp. 71–72). Loughborough, England: Authors.

American Alliance for Health, Physical Education, Recreation and Dance. (1989). *AAHPERD tennis skills test manual.* Reston, VA: AAHPERD.

Anderson, W. (1980). *Analysis of teaching physical education.* St. Louis: C. V. Mosby.

Annarino, A. (1979). Individualized instructional materials. In *Personalized learning in physical education* (pp. 64–76). Washington, DC: AAHPERD.

Ausubel, D. P. (1968). *Educational psychology: A cognitive view.* New York: Holt, Rinehart & Winston.

Bandura, A. (1977). *Social learning theory.* Englewood Cliffs, NJ: Prentice-Hall.

Barrett, K. R. (1970). Exploration—A method for teaching movement: Discussion and summary. In R. T. Sweeney, ed. *Selected readings in movement education* (pp. 141–146). Reading, MA: Addison-Wesley.

Baumann, J. F. (1988). Direct instruction reconsidered. *Journal of Reading Behavior, 31,* 714.

Bennett, R. G., & Hastie, P. A. (1997). The implementation of the sport education curriculum model into a collegiate physical activity course. *Journal of Physical Education, Recreation & Dance, 68*(3), 62–73.

Berkowitz, R. J. (1996). A practitioner's journey from skill to tactics. *Journal of Physical Education, Recreation & Dance, 67*(4), 44–45.

Blitzer, L. (1995). "It's a gym class . . . What's there to think about?" *Journal of Physical Education, Recreation & Dance, 66*(6), 44–48.

Bloom, B., Englehart, M., Furst, E., Hill, W., & Krathwohl, D. (1956). *Taxonomy of educational objectives: The classification of education goals. Handbook I. Cognitive domain.* New York: McKay.

Borich, G. D. (1992). *Effective teaching methods* (2nd ed.). New York: Merrill.

Bredekamp, S. (Ed.) (1987). *Developmentally appropriate practice in early childhood programs serving children from birth through age 8.* Washington, DC: National Association for the Education of Young Children.

Bredekamp, S., & Copple, C. (Eds.) (1996–97). *Developmentally appropriate practice in early childhood programs* (rev. ed.). Washington, DC: National Association for the Education of Young Children.

Brophy, J. E. (1987). Synthesis of research on strategies for motivating students to learn. *Educational Leadership, 45*(2), 40–48.

Bruner, J. S. (1961). The act of discovery. *Harvard Educational Review, 31,* 21–32.

Bunker, D., & Thorpe, R. (1982). A model for teaching games in secondary schools. *Bulletin of Physical Education, 18,* 5–8.

Canter, L., & Canter, M. (1976). *Assertive discipline.* Santa Monica, CA: Canter and Associates.

Carr, N. (1987). *Basic stuff: Series II.* Reston, VA: AAHPERD.

Carlson, T. B., & Hastie, P. A. (1997). The student social system within sport education. *Journal of Teaching in Physical Education, 16,* 176–195.

Chandler, T. (1996). Teaching games for understanding: Reflections and further questions. *Journal of Physical Education, Recreation & Dance, 67*(4), 49–51.

Cheffers, J., Mancini, V., & Martinek, T. (Eds.) (1980). *Interaction analysis: An application to nonverbal activity* (2nd ed.). Association for Productive Teaching.

Christensen, D. (1996). The professional knowledge research base for teacher education. In J. Sikula, T. Buttery, & E. Guyton, eds. *Handbook of research on teacher education* (2nd ed., pp. 38–52). New York: Macmillan.

Clark, C. (1983). Research on teacher planning: An inventory of the knowledge base. In D. C. Smith, ed. *Essential knowledge for beginning educators* (pp. 5–15). Washington, DC: American Association of Colleges for Teacher Education.

Cleland, F., & Pearse, C. (1995). Critical thinking in elementary physical education: Reflections on a yearlong study. *Journal of Physical Education, Recreation & Dance, 66*(6), 30–38.

Coker, C. (1996). Accommodating students' learning styles in physical education. *Journal of Physical Education, Recreation & Dance, 67*(9), 66–68.

Coker, C. (1998). Observation strategies for skill analysis. *Strategies, 11*(4), 17–19.

Cooper Institute for Aerobic Fitness. (1994). *FITNESSGRAM.* Dallas: Author.

Cregger, R. (1994). *Effects of three presentation formats in a PSI college level bowling course.* Unpublished doctoral dissertation, Virginia Polytechnic Institute and State University, Blacksburg.

Cuseo, J. (1992). Cooperative learning vs. small-group discussions and group projects: The critical differences. *Cooperative Learning and College Teaching, 2*(3), 5–10.

Deutsch, M. (1949). A theory of cooperation and competition. *Human Relations, 2,* 129–152.

Doolittle, S., & Girard, K. (1991). A dynamic approach to teaching games in elementary PE. *Journal of Physical Education, Recreation & Dance, 62*(4), 57–62.

Dugas, D. (1994). Sport education in the secondary curriculum. In D. Siedentop, ed. *Sport Education: Quality PE through positive sport experiences* (pp. 105–112). Champaign, IL: Human Kinetics.

Dunn, R. (1996). *How to implement and supervise a learning styles program.* Alexandria, VA: Association for Supervision and Curriculum Development.

Dunn, R., & Dunn, K. (1993). *Teaching secondary students through their individual learning styles.* Boston: Allyn and Bacon.

Dunn, R., Dunn, K., & Price, G. (1989). *Learning styles inventory.* Lawrence, KS: Price Systems.

Ellis, S., & Rogoff, B. (1986). Problem solving in children's management of instruction. In E. C. Mueller and G. R. Cooper, eds. *Process and Outcome in Peer Relationships* (pp. 60–69). New York: Academic Press.

Ennis, C. (1991). Discrete thinking skills in two teachers' physical education classes. *Elementary School Journal, 91,* 473–487.

Fink, J., & Siedentop, D. (1989). The development of routines, rules, and expectations at the start of the school year. *Journal of Teaching in Physical Education, 8,* 198–212.

Foot, H. C., Morgan, M. J., & Shute, R. H. (Eds.) (1990). *Children helping children.* Chichester, England: John Wiley & Sons.

Frieberg, H. J., & Driscoll, A. (1996). *Universal teaching strategies* (2nd ed.). Boston: Allyn and Bacon.

Gallahue, D. L. (1996). *Developmental physical education for today's children* (3rd ed.). Madison, WI: Brown & Benchmark.

Good, T. L., & Brophy, J. E. (1990). *Educational psychology: A realistic approach* (4th ed.). New York: Longman.

Goodrich, H. (1996–97). Understanding rubrics. *Educational Leadership, 54*(4), 14–17.

Graham, G. (1992). *Teaching children physical education.* Champaign, IL: Human Kinetics.

Graham, G., Holt/Hale, S., & Parker, M. (1998). *Children moving* (4th ed.). Mountain View, CA: Mayfield.

Graham, G., Hopple, C., Manross, M., & Sitzman, T. (1993). Novice and experienced children's physical education teachers: Insights into their situational decision making. *Journal of Teaching in Physical Education, 12,* 197–214.

Graham, K. (1988). A qualitative analysis of an effective teacher's movement task presentations during a unit of instruction. *The Physical Educator, 11,* 187–195.

Grant, B. (1992). Integrating sport into the physical education curriculum in New Zealand secondary schools. *Quest, 44,* 304–316.

Grant, B. (1994). High school touch rugby and tennis. In D. Siedentop, ed. *Sport education: Quality PE through positive sport experiences* (pp. 83–92). Champaign, IL: Human Kinetics.

Greenockle, K., & Purvis, G. (1995). Redesigning a secondary school wellness unit using the critical thinking model. *Journal of Physical Education, Recreation & Dance, 66*(6), 49–52.

Greenwood, C. R., Carta, J. J., & Kamps, D. (1990). Teacher-mediated versus peer-mediated instruction: A review of educational advantages and disadvantages. In H. C. Foot, M. J. Morgan, & R. H. Shute, eds. *Children helping children* (pp. 177–206). Chichester, England: John Wiley & Sons.

Gregorc, A. F. (1982). *Gregorc style delineator.* Maynard, MA: Gabriel Systems, Inc.

Griffin, L., Dodds, P., & Rovegno, I. (1996). Pedagogical content knowledge for teachers: Integrate everything you know to help students learn. *Journal of Physical Education, Recreation & Dance, 67*(9), 58–60.

Griffin, L., Mitchell, S., & Oslin, J. (1997). *Teaching sport concepts and skills: A tactical games approach.* Champaign, IL: Human Kinetics.

Griffin, L., Oslin, J., & Mitchell, S. (1985). An analysis of two instructional approaches to teaching net games. *Research Quarterly for Exercise and Sport, 66*(Suppl), A-64.

Grineski, S. (1996). *Cooperative learning in physical education.* Champaign, IL: Human Kinetics.

Gusthart, J. L., Kelly, I. M., & Rink, J. E. (1997). The validity of the Qualitative Measures of Teaching Performance Scale as a measure of teacher effectiveness. *Journal of Teaching in Physical Education, 16,* 196–210.

Harageones, M. (1993). If we're going to get out of the sandtrap, we've got to get on the ball: Fitness education is our responsibility. In J. Rink, ed. *Critical crossroads: Middle and secondary school physical education* (pp. 33–36). Reston, VA: National Association for Sport and Physical Education.

Harlow, A. (1972). *Taxonomy of the psychomotor domain.* New York: McKay.

Harrison, J., Blakemore, C., Buck. M., & Pellett, T. (1996). *Instructional strategies for secondary school physical education* (4th ed.). Dubuque, IA: Brown & Benchmark.

Hastie, P. A. (1998). Benefits of the sport education model from an applied perspective. *Journal of Physical Education, Recreation & Dance, 69*(4), 24–26.

Hellison, D. (1995). *Teaching responsibility through physical activity.* Champaign, IL: Human Kinetics.

Hensley, J. E., East, W. B., & Stillwell, J. L. (1979). A racquetball skills test. *Research Quarterly, 50,* 114–118.

Hensley, L. (1997). Alternative assessment for physical education. *Journal of Physical Education, Recreation & Dance, 68*(7), 19–24.

Hetherington, C. (1910). Fundamental education. *The Physical Education Review, 15,* 629–635.

Hicks, D. (1998). *A fourth grade Ultimate Frisbee Sport Education season.* Unpublished masters' collaborative action research project, Georgia State University, Atlanta.

Hilke, E. V. (1990). *Cooperative Learning.* Bloomington, IN: Phi Delta Kappa Educational Foundation.

Hopple, C. (1995). *Teaching for outcomes in elementary physical education: A guide for curriculum and assessment.* Champaign, IL: Human Kinetics.

Housner, L., & Griffey, D. (1985). Teacher cognition: Differences in planning and interactive decision making between experienced and inexperienced teachers. *Research Quarterly for Exercise and Sport, 56,* 45–53.

Houston-Wilson, C. (1997). Peer tutoring: A plan for instructing students of all abilities. *Journal of Physical Education, Recreation, and Dance, 68*(6), 39–44.

Johnson, D. W., Johnson, R. T., & Holubec, E. J. (1994). *The new circles of learning: Cooperation in the classroom and school.* Alexandria, VA: Association for Supervision and Curriculum Development.

Jonassen, D. H., & Grabowski, B. L. (1993). *Handbook of individual differences, learning, and instruction.* Hillsdale, NJ: Lawrence Erlbaum.

Jones, D. (1992). Analysis of task systems in elementary physical education classes. *Journal of Teaching in Physical Education, 11,* 411–425.

Jones, D., & Ward, P. (1998). Changing the face of secondary physical education through sport education. *Journal of Physical Education, Recreation & Dance, 69*(5), 40–45.

Joyce, B., & Weil, M. (1972). *Models of teaching.* Englewood Cliffs, NJ: Prentice-Hall.

Joyce, B., & Weil, M. (1980). *Models of teaching* (2nd ed.). Englewood Cliffs, NJ: Prentice-Hall.

Joyce, B., & Weil, M. (1996). *Models of teaching* (5th ed.). Englewood Cliffs, NJ: Prentice-Hall.

Kauchak, D. P., & Eggen, P. D. (1998). *Learning and teaching: Research-based methods.* Boston: Allyn and Bacon.

Keller, F. (1968). Goodbye, teacher! *Journal of Applied Behavior Analysis, 1,* 79–88.

Keller, F. S., & Sherman, J. G. (Eds.) (1974). *The Keller Plan handbook.* Menlo Park, CA: W. A. Benjamin.

Keller, F. S., & Sherman, J. G. (1982). *The PSI handbook: Essays on Personalized Instruction.* Lawrence, KS: TRI Publications.

Keller, J. (1983). Motivational design of instruction. In C. Reigeluth, ed. *Instructional-design theories and models: An overview of their current status* (pp. 383–434). Hillsdale, NJ: Erlbaum.

King, A. (1992). From sage on the stage to guide on the side. *College Teaching, 41*(1), 30–35.

Kneer, M. (1981). *Basic stuff.* Reston, VA: AAHPERD.

Knop, N., & Pope, C. (1998). Design, redesign, and dissemination of sport education. *Journal of Physical Education, Recreation & Dance, 69*(5), 46–48.

Kolb, D. A. (1981). Learning styles and disciplinary differences. In A. W. Chickering, ed. *The modern college* (pp. 232–255). San Francisco: Jossey-Bass.

Kounin, J. (1970). *Discipline and group management in classrooms.* New York: Holt, Rinehart and Winston.

Krathwohl, D., Bloom, B., & Masia, B. (1964). *Taxonomy of educational objectives: The classification of education goals. Handbook II. Affective domain.* New York: McKay.

Kraus, H., & Hirschland, R. (1954). Minimum muscular fitness tests in school children. *Research Quarterly, 25,* 178–185.

Kruger, H., & Kruger, J. (1982). *Movement education in physical education.* Dubuque, IA: Wm. C. Brown.

Locke, L. F. (1970). The movement movement. In R. T. Sweeney, ed. *Selected readings in movement education* (pp. 208–212). Reading, MA: Addison-Wesley.

Lowry, W. H., & Thornburg, M. S. (1988). A working bibliography on the Keller Plan (P.S.I.) Unpublished bibliography.

Mager, R. F. (1984). *Preparing instructional objectives* (rev. ed.). Belmont, CA: Fearon.

Manross, D., & Templeton, C. (1997). Expertise in teaching physical education. *Journal of Physical Education, Recreation & Dance, 68*(3), 29–35.

Maslow, A. H. (1970). *Motivation and personality* (2nd ed.). New York: Harper and Row.

McBride, R. (1992). Critical thinking: An overview with implications for physical education. *Journal of Teaching in Physical Education, 11,* 112–125.

McBride, R., & Bonnette, R. (1995). Teacher and at-risk students' cognitions during open-ended activities: Structuring the learning environment for critical thinking. *Teaching & Teacher Education, 11,* 373–388.

McCaslin, M. M., & Good, T. L. (1996). *Listening in classrooms.* New York: HarperCollins College Publications.

McPherson, S., & French, K. (1991). Changes in cognitive strategy and motor skill in tennis. *Journal of Sport & Exercise Psychology, 13,* 26–41.

McTighe, J. (1996–97). What happens between assessments? *Educational Leadership, 54*(4), 6–12.

Mercier, R. (1993). Student-centered physical education: Strategies for teaching social skills. *Journal of Physical Education, Recreation & Dance, 64*(5), 60–65.

Metzler, M. (1979). *The measurement of Academic Learning Time in physical education.* Doctoral dissertation, The Ohio State University, Ann Arbor, MI: University Microfilms, No. 8009314.

Metzler, M. (1984). Analysis of a Mastery Learning/Personalized System of Instruction for teaching tennis. In M. Pieron & G. Graham, eds. *The 1984 Olympic scientific congress proceedings, Volume 6: Sport pedagogy* (pp. 63–70). Champaign, IL: Human Kinetics.

Metzler, M. (1986, April). *Teaching tennis by the Keller Method: A comparison between "traditional" and PSI-based instruction.* Paper presented at the Annual Meeting of the American Educational Research Association, San Francisco.

Metzler, M. (1989). A review of research on time in sport pedagogy. *Journal of Teaching in Physical Education, 8,* 87–103.

Metzler, M. (1990). Teaching during competitive games: Not just playin' around. *Journal of Physical Education, Recreation & Dance, 61*(8), 57–61.

Metzler, M., Eddleman, K., Treanor, L., & Cregger, R. (1989, February). *Using a Personalized System of Instruction for teaching tennis.* Paper presented at the Eastern Educational Research Association Annual Meeting, Savannah, GA.

Metzler, M., & Sebolt, D. (1994). *Instructor's manual for the Personalized Sport Instruction Series.* Dubuque, IA: Kendall Hunt.

Morine-Dershimer, G. (1985). *Talking, listening, and learning in the elementary classroom.* New York: Longman.

Mosston, M. (1966). *Teaching physical education.* Columbus, OH: Merrill.

Mosston, M., & Ashworth, S. (1994). *Teaching physical education* (4th ed.). New York: Macmillan.

Napper-Owen, G. (1994). . . . And justice for all: Equity in the elementary gymnasium. *Strategies, 8*(3), 23–26.

National Association for Sport and Physical Education. (1992a). *Outcomes of quality physical education programs.* Reston, VA: Author.

National Association for Sport and Physical Education. (1992b). *Developmentally appropriate physical education practices for children.* Reston, VA: NASPE Council on Physical Education for Children.

National Association for Sport and Physical Education. (1995). *Moving into the future: National standards for physical education.* St. Louis: Mosby.

National Association for Sport and Physical Education. *Looking at physical education from a developmental perspective: A guide to teaching.* Reston, VA: NASPE Motor Development Task Force.

Oberteuffer, D., & Ulrich, C. (1962). *Physical education: A textbook of principles for professional students* (3rd ed.). New York: Harper & Row.

Orlick, T. (1982). *The second cooperative sports and games book.* New York: Pantheon.

Oslin, J., & Mitchell, S. (1998, April). *An investigation of tactical transfer in new games.* Paper presented at the AAHPERD National Convention, Reno, NV.

Oslin, J., Mitchell, S., & Griffin, L. (1998). The game performance assessment instrument (GPAI): Development and preliminary validation. *Journal of Teaching in Physical Education, 17,* 231–243.

Phillips, D. C., & Soltis, J. F. (1991). *Perspectives on learning* (2nd ed.). New York: Teachers College.

Poole, J., Sebolt, D., & Metzler, M. (1996). *PSIS student workbook for volleyball.* Dubuque, IA: Kendall-Hunt.

President's Council on Physical Fitness and Sports. (1985). *The Presidential Physical Fitness Award Program.* Washington, DC: Author.

Rauschenbach, J., & Vanoer, S. (1998). Instant activities: Active learning tasks that start a lesson out right. *Journal of Physical Education, Recreation & Dance, 69*(2), 7–8.

Reichmann, S. W., & Grasha, A. F. (1974). A rational approach to developing and assessing the validity of a student learning styles instrument. *Journal of Psychology, 87,* 213–223.

Rink, J. (1996a). Effective instruction in physical education. In S. Silverman & C. Ennis, eds. *Student learning in physical education: Applying research to enhance instruction* (pp. 171–198). Champaign, IL: Human Kinetics.

Rink, J. (Ed.) (1996b). Tactical and skill approaches to teaching sport and games. *Journal of Teaching in Physical Education, 15*(4).

Rink, J. (1997). Teacher education programs: The role of context in learning how to teach. *Journal of Physical Education, Recreation & Dance, 68*(1), 17–24.

Rink, J. (1998). *Teaching physical education for learning* (3rd ed). Boston: McGraw-Hill.

Rink, J., French, K., & Graham, K. (1996). Implications for practice and research. In J. Rink, ed. Tactical and skill approaches to teaching sport and games (pp. 490–502). Monograph, *Journal of Teaching in Physical Education, 15*(4).

Rink, J., & Werner, P. (1989). Qualitative measures of teaching performance scale (QMTPS). In P. Darst, D. Zakrajsek, & V. Mancini, eds. *Analyzing physical education and sport instruction* (2nd ed.). Champaign, IL: Human Kinetics.

Rosenshine, B. (1979). Content, time, and direct instruction. In H. J. Walberg & P. L. Peterson, eds. *Research on teaching: Concepts, findings, and implications* (pp. 28–56). Berkeley, CA: McCutchan.

Rosenshine, B. (1983). Teaching functions in instructional programs. *Elementary School Journal, 83,* 335–350.

Ross, J., & Gilbert, G. (1985). A summary of findings. *Journal of Physical Education, Recreation & Dance, 56*(1), 45–50.

Rowe, M. (1986). Wait time: Slowing down may be a way of speeding up! *Journal of Teacher Education, 37,* 43–50.

Safrit, M. J. (1995). *Complete guide to youth fitness testing.* Champaign, IL: Human Kinetics.

Schempp, P. (1982). Enhancing creativity through children making decisions. In M. Pieron & J. Cheffers, eds. *Studying the teaching in physical education* (pp. 161–166). Leige, Belgium: International Association for Physical Education in Higher Education.

Schempp, P. (1997). Developing expertise in teaching and coaching. *Journal of Physical Education, Recreation & Dance, 68*(2), 29.

Schunk, D. H. (1996) *Learning theories: An educational perspective* (3rd ed.). Englewood Cliffs, NJ: Merrill.

Sherman, J. G. (Ed.) (1974). *Personalized system of instruction: 41 germinal papers.* Menlo Park, CA: W. A. Benjamin.

Sherman, J. G. (1974). PSI: Some notable failures. In J. G. Sherman, ed. *Personalized system of instruction: 41 germinal papers* (pp. 120–124). Menlo Park, CA: W. A. Benjamin.

Shuell, T. J. (1986). Cognitive conceptions of learning. *Review of Educational Research, 56,* 411–436.

Shulman, L. (1987). Knowledge and teaching: Foundations of the new reform. *Harvard Educational Review, 15*(2), 4–14.

Siedentop, D. (1991). *Developing teaching skills in physical education* (3rd ed.). Mountain View, CA: Mayfield.

Siedentop, D. (Ed.) (1994). *Sport education: Quality PE through positive sport experiences.* Champaign, IL: Human Kinetics.

Siedentop, D. (1998). *Introduction to physical education, fitness, and sport* (3rd ed.) Mountain View, CA: Mayfield.

Siedentop, D. (1998). What is sport education and how does it work? *Journal of Physical Education, Recreation & Dance, 69*(4), 18–20.

Siedentop, D., Mand, C., & Taggart, A. (1986). *Physical education: Teaching and curriculum strategies for grades 5–12.* Palo Alto, CA: Mayfield.

Silverman, S., & Ennis, C. (Eds.) (1996). *Student learning in physical education: Applying research to enhance instruction.* Champaign, IL: Human Kinetics.

Silverman, S., Tyson, L., & Krampitz, J. (1993). Teacher feedback and achievement: Mediating effects of initial skill and sex. *Journal of Human Movement Studies, 24,* 97–118.

Slavin, R. E. (1977). Classroom reward structure: An analytic and practical review. *Review of Educational Research, 47,* 633–650.

Slavin, R. E. (1980). Cooperative learning. *Review of Educational Research, 50,* 315–342.

Slavin, R. E. (1983). *Cooperative learning.* New York: Longman.

Slavin, R. E. (1988). Student team learning: An overview and practical guide (2nd ed.). Washington, DC: National Education Association.

Slavin, R. E. (1990). *Cooperative learning: Theory, research, and practice.* Boston: Allyn and Bacon.

Slavin, R. E. (1995). *Cooperative learning: Theory, research, and practice* (2nd ed.). Boston: Allyn and Bacon.

Snow, R., Corno, L., & Jackson III, D. (1996). Individual differences in affective and conative functions. In D. C. Berliner & R. C. Calfee, eds. *Handbook of educational psychology* (pp. 243–310). New York: Macmillan.

Stevens, R. J., & Slavin, R. E. (1995). The cooperative elementary school: Effects on students' achievement, attitudes, and social relations. *American Educational Research Journal, 32,* 321–351.

Strand, B. N., & Wilson, R. (1993). *Assessing sport skills.* Champaign, IL: Human Kinetics.

Stroot, S., & Morton, P. (1989). Blueprints for learning. *Journal of Teaching in Physical Education, 8,* 213–222.

Tannehill, D. (Ed.) (1998). Sport education. Two-part feature presented in the *Journal of Physical Education, Recreation & Dance,* May (Vol. 69, No. 4) and June (Vol. 69, No. 5).

Thorpe, R., & Bunker, D. (1986). The curriculum model. In R. Thorpe, D. Bunker, & L. Almond, eds. *Rethinking games teaching* (pp. 7–10). Loughborough, England: Authors.

Thorpe, R., Bunker, D., & Almond, L. (1986). *Rethinking games teaching.* Loughborough, England: Authors.

Tillotson, J. (1970). Problem-solving. In R. T. Sweeney, ed. *Selected readings in movement education* (pp. 130–135). Reading, MA: Addison-Wesley.

Tishman, S., & Perkins, D. (1995). Critical thinking and physical education. *Journal of Physical Education, Recreation & Dance, 66*(6), 24–30.

Tobin, K. (1987). The role of wait time in higher cognitive level learning. *Review of Educational Research, 57,* 69–95.

Turner, A. (1996). Teaching games for understanding: Myth or reality? *Journal of Physical Education, Recreation & Dance, 67*(4), 46–48, 55.

Turner, A., & Martinek, T. (1992). A comparative analysis of two models for teaching games. *International Journal of Physical Education, 24*(4), 15–31.

Turner, A., & Martinek, T. (1995). Teaching for understanding: A model for improving decision making during game play. *Quest, 47,* 44–63.

Van Dalen, D., & Bennett, B. (1971) *A world history of physical education: Cultural, philosophical, comparative* (2nd ed.) Englewood Cliffs, NJ: Prentice Hall.

Wagner, S. (1990). Social and historical perspectives on peer teaching in education. In H. C. Foot, M. J. Morgan, & R. H. Shute, eds. *Children helping children* (pp. 21–42). Chichester, England: John Wiley & Sons.

Watts, R. (1998). *A middle school pickleball sport education unit.* Unpublished masters' collaborative action research project, Georgia State University, Atlanta.

Webster, G. E. (1987). Influence of peer tutors upon Academic Learning Time—Physical education of mentally handicapped students. *Journal of Teaching in Physical Education, 6,* 393–403.

Werner, P., & Almond, L. (1990). Models of games education. *Journal of Physical Education, Recreation & Dance, 61*(7), 23–27.

Wood, T. M. (1996). Evaluation and testing: The road less traveled. In S. J. Silverman & C. D. Ennis, eds. *Student learning in physical education: Applying research to enhance instruction* (pp. 199–220). Champaign, IL: Human Kinetics.

Woods, A., & Book, C. (1995). Critical thinking in middle school physical education. *Journal of Physical Education, Recreation & Dance, 66*(6), 39–43.

Yoder, L. (1993). Cooperative learning and dance education. *Journal of Physical Education, Recreation & Dance, 64*(5), 47–51, 56.

INDEX